ROVERS REVOLUTION

BLACKBURN'S RISE FROM NOWHERE TO PREMIER LEAGUE CHAMPIONS

JOHN DUERDEN

ROVERS
REVOLUTION

BLACKBURN'S RISE FROM NOWHERE TO PREMIER LEAGUE CHAMPIONS

JOHN DUERDEN

deCoubertin
B O O K S

First published as a hardback by deCoubertin Books Ltd in 2019.

First Edition

deCoubertin Books, 46b Jamaica Street, Baltic Triangle, Liverpool, L1 0AF.
www.decoubertin.co.uk

ISBN: 978-1-909-245-587

Cover design and Typeset by Thomas Regan | Milkyone Creative.

Printed and bound by Jellyfish.

This book is dedicated to the people of Blackburn and fans of the club everywhere, especially those in my family: my granddads Harry Duerden and James Blackwell, my dad Colin Duerden and brothers Anthony, Mark and Ben and nieces and nephews Rebecca, Jack, Emma, James and Daniel. And, of course, the biggest fan of them all – 'Uncle' Jack Walker.

CONTENTS

PROLOGUE

'We took it away from the big city boys and they didn't like it.
There was some jealousy. We had money and that brought us
success. People say that we bought the league but we didn't spend
as much as the big boys. We were always going to get stick for
that as a small town club but that just made it sweeter.'

KEVIN GALLACHER

AS I LEFT FOR UNIVERSITY IN LONDON IN THE SUMMER
of 1991, Blackburn Rovers were stuck in the bottom half of the Second
Division. It was a league they had, over the previous decade or so, threatened
to escape on a few occasions – usually upwards, occasionally down – without
ever finding the exit. Ewood Park had not changed that much since it became
the club's permanent home in 1890. It was homely but had seen better days.
When David Pleat had been fired by Tottenham Hotspur in 1987 and then
took the Leicester City job, he said that it was only when the team bus arrived
at Ewood that the fact that he was no longer a top tier manager finally sunk in.

At least Pleat had been there. For the Rovers, the prospects of playing a season in the First Division for the first time since 1966 were looking as murky as a January afternoon over the nearby moors. What only a few people knew at the time, however, was that just four months before I left for the capital, Jack Walker had been there, entering the dressing room at Millwall's Old Den to tell a team that had just lost and barely avoided the drop to the third tier that everything was different now. The local boyhood fan made good steel and then good deals, leaving him with plenty of money to spend. He informed the players that promotion, a tantalising dream for much of the eighties, was finally going to be achieved. In short, funds would be available and Rovers would be going up.

He was true to his word. By the time I finished my studies, everything was different. The manager was the legendary Kenny Dalglish, the old ground had been transformed into a soon-to-be-completed 30,000 spanking new stadium that now towered over the surrounding streets and the Blues, runners-up the year before, were about to embark on a title-winning season never to be forgotten. Walker had been true to his word. 'Jack Walker was a very clever and very tough businessman but he was a winner and one I respected hugely,' Alan Shearer told me almost three decades later, finding the exact sentiments of the town of Blackburn just as accurately as he used to find the back of the Ewood net.

I grew up in Blackburn, born and raised on 'the tops' (the coldest part of a cold town, where the wind whistled through on its way from the Atlantic to the Pennines) not that far from where Walker had built his massive Walkersteel factory in which workers cycled from one part to the next. Look down into the valley and you see rows and rows of terraced houses of the type that still surround Ewood Park, with the cobbled streets that gave television producers up and down the country the kind of archetypal northern backdrop that could never be resisted. There weren't many cameras around in the late seventies, at least I don't think there were, as I was too young to make the ten-minute walk down the hill to Ewood. It was easy to hear what was going on though, all you had to do was open a window.

After leaving for university, the one year I spent back in the town was the one that ended with the title. It was timing as fortuitous as Walker's sale of his company to British Steel just before Kenny Dalglish was to become available. English football would never be the same again.

That is because there is a little more to this tale than Blackburn winning the championship for the first time in 81 years. When captain Tim Sherwood lifted the gleaming English Premiership (as it was still called) trophy on 14 May 1995, in the bright sunshine of Anfield, it ended much more than eight decades in the – as newspapers loved to put it – wilderness: it brought down the curtain on a momentous campaign in English football. Tony Evans, former sports editor of *The Times* and author of a number of books on Liverpool, remembers it well. 'It was a pivotal, watershed season, the season when you can look back and say that English football was really changing. That was the time.'

It was. Looking back, that season was the bridge between the old and the new, the dividing line between the old Division One and the new dawn and the soon-to-be unleashed global juggernaut.

Sherwood, without the mid-length mid-nineties style hair he would sport in Liverpool that day in May had been beamed into a nation's living rooms almost three years earlier in the summer of 1992 ahead of the big and special kick-off. He was Blackburn's representative in the Sky Sports commercial that tried to convince fans that the new era really was going to be different from the old football league and, for the first time, would be worth shelling out for. With 'Alive and Kicking' by Simple Minds blaring out, the footage shows a host of players from the-then 22-team competition. There was Vinnie Jones in the shower, Gordon Strachan getting a massage, Paul Stewart breezing in with a shell suit, perm and sunglasses combo and Andy Ritchie talking into a mobile phone almost as big as the gleaming new league trophy.

Despite all that glitz and glamour, it wasn't the 1992/93 season with The Shamen at half-time at Highbury and cheerleaders – whose Premier League careers didn't last much longer than Ali Dia at Southampton – that represented a 'whole new ball game', but 1994/95. That August, when Rovers kicked off at The Dell, the top tier still felt largely like the old First Division. By May, the Premiership juggernaut was starting to move up through the gears. In the past there had been plenty of Irish and a smattering of Scandinavians, with Eric Cantona thrown in as an outlier. That started to change. As English fans watched the 1994 World Cup without a team to support, they would at least see some of the talent that was on display in the United States. The biggest and the best was Jürgen Klinsmann from Germany. Following the conclusion of the tournament he joined Spurs, as did Romania's Ilie Dumitrescu. Bryan

Roy of the Netherlands joined Nottingham Forest, Dan Petrescu went to Sheffield Wednesday, Stefan Schwarz of Sweden moved to Arsenal and Daniel Amokachi was at Everton. Rumours of foreign additions were more common than dodgy-looking mid-nineties away shirts. Everton, who had just avoided relegation on the final day of the previous campaign, had an injection of cash to play with and saw their name in newspapers alongside such names as Oliver Bierhoff, Paulo Sousa and Anthony Yeboah.

There were concerns back in the summer of 1994 about what this foreign invasion would mean for English football. Gordon Taylor, the chairman of the Professional Footballers' Association, warned in a press conference against the decline of the national team and the danger of smaller clubs going bust. Klinsmann was not a problem, but those who were not at the level of the 1990 World Cup winner potentially were. '... The vast majority have not made the grade and have been no better than our home-grown players,' Taylor said. 'Millions of pounds have been lost into thin foreign air and if it continues it may cause our natural full-time breeding clubs, those such as Crewe Alexandra, to collapse.'

Taylor went on. 'We are going to have to decide if we want to be a cosmopolitan domestic league, albeit successful in its own back garden, while remaining a wallflower at the world dance.' While poetic, there was a whiff of hypocrisy from a player who had moved to the United States in 1977 during his own playing career. This was denied, however. 'I went because I was better than their own indigenous players. I do not mind any players coming in if they are better than what is available domestically, not because they are cheaper. This is a false economy, particularly for our international football, for which we paid the price this summer and may pay a stiffer price in the future.'

It may have been a new topic at the time, but the arguments have not changed that much. The trickle that started in the 1994/95 season widened and the following season Ruud Gullit, Dennis Bergkamp and many more arrived. The Premier League went on to become the most international of any major domestic tournament, a development boosted in 1995 as the quota on foreign players that was imposed on clubs participating in UEFA club competitions was lifted, leading to more doom-laden predictions from Taylor, who called for a ban on non-European players.

Look back at the newspapers from the time and football is just starting to push other sports off the back pages, even during the close-season. *FourFourTwo*, a quality and weighty magazine, was launched in August 1994. The fanzine craze was still going strong (though I remember one away fan at Ewood that season reacting with shock when seeing Blackburn's fanzine named *4,000 Holes*. 'What have you got to moan about?' was the understandable question, even if fanzines were about more than getting gripes off chests). And then there was the internet. It was just starting to become a thing and the number of users in the UK hit the one million mark not long after Rovers went top of the table on 26 November 1994 as Alan Shearer sealed a 4-0 win against Queens Park Rangers with a 30-yard rocket.

New rules were introduced that season which had major changes on how the game was played, to make it more attractive and protect the artists. Ahead of the 1994 World Cup – in response to what was seen as an overly defensive 1990 tournament – FIFA told referees to clamp down on tackles from behind, an action that was outlawed completely in 1998. Referees in England were told to follow suit ahead of the new season. After a referee briefing, there were concerns expressed of a red and yellow storm in the coming season. Taylor, again in the news, predicted a rush of games being reduced not to ten-vs-ten but to 'nine against eleven'. QPR boss Gerry Francis was also worried. 'The World Cup was a success but there was a real increase in red and yellow cards there. I hope that doesn't happen here. The rules from the tackle from behind have always been there. We must not put the referees under too much pressure to book players just for tackling.'

The Championship, still known as the First Division, kicked off a week earlier than the Premier League, giving an early taste of the new regime. After the Fulham and Walsall clash saw seven yellows and one red, Ian Branfoot let rip. 'It is absolutely bloody ludicrous,' said the Fulham boss. 'We are being dictated to by duffers in UEFA and FIFA who haven't a clue about our business. In England people want to see blood and thunder. The way we are going we'll be down to five-a-side by December.' He didn't blame Andy D'Urso, officiating his first league game and the target of abuse from Walsall fans after sending off one of their players. 'I feel sorry for the refs. The crowds will be after them more. They'll need police protection in a few weeks if it carries on like this. Referees should make a stand but if they do they get sacked.' Dundee United's Ivan Golac threatened to resign if the new system continued after seeing Alec Cleland sent off. 'Cleland was booked for his first tackle and sent off for his second. It's ridiculous.'

If that wasn't enough to deal with, being in an offside position was no longer an automatic offence. The issue of interfering with play or seeking to gain an advantage now came into the equation. As the rules were changing to encourage more open play, there were more women around to see all the action unfold. A report released just days ahead of the 1994/95 season said that 3,000 of the average attendance of 23,000 from the previous season had been female fans. Supporters were getting richer too. 30 percent earned more than £20,000 a year and 10 percent more earned over £30,000.

Complaints about facilities at stadiums were becoming rarer because there was less to complain about. There had been talk of a roof being put on the men's toilets in the Blackburn End for years, and it was only when Walker's cash rebuilt Ewood that male fans could pee without getting wet. The implementation of the Taylor Report that followed the inquiry into the causes of the Hillsborough disaster in 1989 led to the removal of standing areas in famous old stadiums such as Anfield, Highbury and Old Trafford.

With capacities reduced, ticket prices were going up. Television revenue was starting to make up for any shortfall. The original Sky deal that was said to herald a new dawn was first signed in 1992 and was up for renegotiation in 1996, though talks behind the scenes started much earlier. All knew that there was going to be a lot more television money coming into the game when the new deal started in 1997. This was despite the fact that there were going to be fewer games. 1994/95 was the last 22-team top tier as fans of Crystal Palace, the team who took that fourth relegation spot despite having 45 points to their name, will remember all too well.

And, of course, there was the spending. There was an increasing amount of money sloshing around the game. Walker did play a part in that, though it should be remembered that Alan Shearer only cost a few hundred thousand more than the £2.9 million Liverpool paid to Derby County a year earlier for Dean Saunders. Some of Walker's contemporaries were wary when he and Rovers arrived in the top flight in the summer of 1992 and wasted no time in breaking the British transfer record for Shearer, but some welcomed him with open arms. 'He is certainly driving up prices for the rest of us,' said Manchester United chairman Martin Edwards, while the Leeds United chairman Leslie Sliver saw things in a slightly more positive light: 'Great, there is now some real money coming into the game. It's about time.' There is no denying that the transfer market stepped up a gear ahead of that 1994/95 season which soon saw Crystal Palace slap a £6 million price tag on Chris Armstrong amid interest from Everton and Newcastle United sell Andy Cole to Manchester United for one million more midway through. The summer after, Liverpool paid £8.5 million for Stan Collymore while the one after that saw Shearer leave Blackburn for Newcastle, though it took a world record fee of £15 million.

Cole, a future Rover and a popular one at that, was to play a part in the title win to spark massive celebrations in a town that had been on tenterhooks for weeks, months. Nobody in that corner of Lancashire would claim the club were the biggest, far from it, but for a time Blackburn Rovers were one of the most-talked about in Europe. It is almost impossible to remember the feeling of seeing the club discussed in such detail for the first time up and down the country – all of a sudden everyone had an opinion. For the previous three decades, an appearance on *Match of the Day* was enough to cause the entire town to stay home on a Saturday night. Now Rovers were everywhere at a time when football was only starting to move towards the comprehensive coverage in the national press that it gets today. It was a novel experience.

The online world was still very much a fledgling one back then, and perhaps that was for the best. I am not sure I could have handled the internet's take on the club's rise. Daily reports from the *Lancashire Evening Telegraph* had to suffice and this was surely a golden period for that paper too. It would have been impossible to get anything done with the enticing prospect of online trawling through the forums of rival clubs, reading every opinion piece or checking out videos of possible transfer targets. Sometimes less is more, but that doesn't mean it is not time for a look at how Blackburn Rovers became the champions of England for the third time. It is 25 years since it happened, almost 29 since Dalglish arrived and more than 30 since Walker started to show interest in the club he loved, but there is a little more to the story of Blackburn Rovers than that.

1
KENDALL AND DALGLISH

'We had no money at Blackburn, but you got used to it and worked with it. What happened a few years after I left was quite a surprise to be honest.'

HOWARD KENDALL

IN MAY 1986, LIVERPOOL AND EVERTON WERE THE BEST two teams in England and the nation watched as they met in the all-Merseyside FA Cup final, which was won 3-1 by the Reds. The rivals were led by two of the greatest managers in modern football history and certainly the most successful of the eighties. Howard Kendall, who had left Blackburn five years earlier, was in charge of Everton, and their appearance at the 1986 final was sandwiched by title wins in 1985 and 1987. Kenny Dalglish was in his first season as player-manager of Liverpool and just about to deliver the double. Who would have thought that not much more than five years later, Dalglish would be on his way to Ewood Park to join the Everton goalkeeper of that day,

Bobby Mimms, just a few weeks after Blackburn had a big-money bid turned down for Gary Lineker, the Everton goalscorer at Wembley who would soon win the World Cup golden boot and sign for Barcelona?

June 1991 was when the world first started to realise that the Rovers were no longer the cash-strapped but homely Second Division club that all knew, and many were fond of, but were newly rich and seriously ambitious. The club wanted Lineker, the man who was scoring in the World Cup semi-final just a year earlier. Chairman Bill Fox confirmed that the money was in place. 'Obviously, we wouldn't have made the bid if we were not confident we could meet the players' terms,' said Fox, a man who was as accustomed to spending time in the national press talking about signing international stars as he was to having money to spend.

Spurs seemed shocked. 'This is complete news to us,' said spokesman John Fennelly. 'Any such offer would be rejected out of hand.'

'It's true,' Lineker told *FourFourTwo* in 2015. '... My agent actually phoned me and said: "I think this is some kind of publicity stunt."' My own father remembers being in a pub in London at the time and overhearing comments that Lineker should sue Blackburn for using him to get some headlines. Attempts to explain that Jack Walker had the finances to buy Tottenham never mind their striker were met with scepticism. It was still a little time before the world was to take the new Rovers seriously.

'Obviously, it turned out that Jack Walker actually did have a few bob and was ready to spend it,' said Lineker. 'But I was ready to do something different at that stage.' The striker went to Japan instead to join Nagoya Grampus Eight, a club in an industrial city looking to spend big in order to win the league.

Don Mackay was manager at the time and is still shaking his head almost three decades later. 'We tried to sign Lineker and we were deadly serious. We made an approach to Spurs as he was on the fringes then and we saw our chance. Our chairman Bill Fox went to their chairman, Irving Scholar, and he demanded one million. We went back to Jack Walker and told him, and he said, "Offer them £900,000." So we went back to Spurs and the chairman said no. It had to be £1 million. So we went back to Jack and he said okay, and we thought then that the deal would be done. It was exciting. But when we went back and offered a million, they said no again. They later sold him to Japan for

£500,000 or something like that. Spurs didn't want me to talk to Lineker so there is not much you can do about that. Bill Fox was old school. He wanted to do it chairman to chairman and do it by the book. He was very scrupulous like that. We never got him but that is the way it goes in football.'

It is understandable that a player of Lineker's stature was not going to entertain a move north. Rovers were one of a number of those old Lancashire clubs that had fallen from the top table – though not as far as others, such as Preston, Burnley, Bolton and Blackpool. The old stadium, the cobbled streets and – usually – four figure crowds were not going to tempt the former Barcelona star. Even though Blackburn fans knew of Walker, most were still getting used to the idea that Rovers had the money.

All doubt was removed as Dalglish went to Blackburn in October 1991 just over ten years after Kendall had left Ewood for Everton. Both were to spend just one season in the Second Division with the Rovers (in Dalglish's case, a little less), and both oversaw promotion challenges that really put fans through the wringer. Kendall was to finish higher in the league but Dalglish had the play-offs to fall back on as well as financial backing to buy first-class talent that his predecessor, told to use second-class stamps, could only have dreamed of.

The place still looked similar, the only major difference being the replacement of the old Riverside stand with the new one, built with the help of WalkerSteel in 1988, while the training ground remained exactly the same. But this was a very different club now. Blackburn now had money, and things were about to change.

The prospect of Dalglish coming to Blackburn started to materialise in the summer of 1991. The Rovers had started the year by hosting Dalglish's Liverpool in the third round of the FA Cup in what was simply a fantastic cup tie. Don Mackay's side were battling against relegation to the Third Division and were 7/1 against to defeat the champions of England. At a packed Ewood on a murky January afternoon, Blackburn took an early second half lead, both teams had a man sent off and Mark Atkins scored an own goal in the last minute. There were more headlines to come as on *Match of the Day*, Jimmy Hill blamed a home ball girl for throwing the ball back too quickly to the Liverpool players to take a desperate throw-in in the final seconds.

Hill subsequently apologised to the distraught Gillian Maynard (who actually went to the same school as me) and quite right too according to Rovers chairman Bill Fox. 'She was doing her job properly and should be complimented on her behaviour not criticised,' he said. Barbara Magee looked after the ball boys and girls. 'She rang me, worrying that she might not be able to do it anymore. But she certainly will. She's one of the best we've got.' It was not the last time that year that the club would be making national headlines.

IN SEPTEMBER 1991, THE MAN WHO FOLLOWED THE MAN
who followed Kendall was fired. Don Mackay had been at the club since 1987 but after four memorable years he was on his way out. A few months earlier Jack Walker had publicly taken over the club. A much bigger bank account meant much bigger expectations. Mackay failed to land Lineker, Teddy Sheringham and Mike Newell, but did spend over a million on David Speedie from Liverpool and Steve Agnew from Barnsley. Agnew, a cultured midfielder, quickly picked up a serious injury and after one point from the first three games of the season, the Scot was shown the door to end a period that Rovers fans can look back on with fondness.

'Don probably felt that he didn't get the benefit of what he had put in, but he did at least put the club in a situation where it looked attractive to Jack Walker,' said Bobby Mimms. The goalkeeper had played in that 1986 FA Cup final for Everton, and his £250,000 move from Spurs to Blackburn in December 1990 provided the first evidence to those who were watching that something was starting to happen at Ewood. 'Mackay was a great manager for Blackburn but was unlucky in that Kenny was available and wanted to get back into football.'

Dalglish had left Liverpool in February 1991. Being the manager during and after the Hillsborough disaster that took 96 lives in May 1989 took its toll, with the Scot attending all the funerals and impressing everyone with the dignified way he handled himself, representing the club and the city in what must have been a terrible situation.

Liverpool were still top of the table as he left, as they had been pretty much ever since I could remember. This winning machine seemed very remote from the world Blackburn Rovers occupied and there was little suggestion that their dominance would end. The Scot embodied that feeling: unsmiling but unstoppable. His departure, when it came, was huge news, one of those sporting events that made the front page and for football fans, one of those moments when you remember what you were doing when you first heard it. What Ferguson became in stature in later years, Dalglish was then, and he had the added cachet of being a world-class player too.

'Dalglish was probably the biggest name football manager in British football at the time,' said Scott Sellars, a silky midfielder who had joined Rovers in the late 80s. 'People may not realise it or remember now but he was a huge figure. His resignation was a big shock, but it was not something that we thought would affect us. After all, at the time we were fighting against relegation to the Third Division.'

Blackburn would retain their Second Division status, but on a Monday morning in early September 1991, Mackay was gone after an emotional meeting with Fox. The pair had enjoyed an excellent working relationship. On Thursday there was another board meeting, with the rumours strong from the off that Dalglish was right at the top of the shortlist. Names such as Neil Warnock, Don Howe and Steve Coppell were also mentioned, names that now seem as unthinkable as Kurt Russell getting the Han Solo part he auditioned for or Tom Selleck becoming Indiana Jones, but at the time they were probably quite exciting. Fox even hinted that Franz Beckenbauer was a possibility after the West German World Cup winning captain and then coach had just left his job with Marseille, and fuelled speculation with his comments about working in England. 'I don't know if I will return as a manager,' Der Kaiser said in early October 1991. 'If I did, England would interest me, of course. I am a great admirer of your game and the competitive way it is played. It would be a challenge.'

The national media was saying by this time that Rovers had missed the deadline and the boat when it came to Dalglish. The local press had a different take and insisted throughout September that the Scot was still very much the main target. The *Lancashire Evening Telegraph* noted that there had been no denials from the club in response to the regular Dalglish stories. In fact, said the paper, the tight-lipped approach from the club was reminiscent of the great man himself.

By the end of the first week of October, all were singing from the same back pages – Dalglish was on his way. As dream-like as this all seemed to every Rovers fan, it wasn't music to the ears of Tony Parkes.

As caretaker, Parkes had done a fine job since taking the reins from Mackay, taking 17 points from eight games to move Rovers safely into eighth, a solid base camp from which to strike for the summit. The man himself was not feeling too happy about all the speculation, obviously feeling that if Dalglish did come then so would his coaching staff. Just five days before the Scot actually arrived at Ewood for the first time, Parkes was finally open about his worries.

'I think I have done my little bit to keep the club stable and help put us in a position where we can make a promotion push,' Parkes told local television. 'If a new man had come in and had a similar record, the red carpet would have been rolled out for him. People would have been jumping through hoops. As for the manager's job, I think they are working on bringing someone in. I will feel a little hard done by.'

Parkes did not feel any better as early October rolled by and there was a first mention in the media that Ray Harford could join Dalglish as a number two. 'Nothing has changed as far as I am concerned. I don't know anything until someone tells me what is happening. I have read all the speculation for the past month but no one has said anything to me. It doesn't surprise me because I have always known deep down that this was likely to happen. It's still only speculation but the longer things have gone on, it has confirmed that the club is likely to bring someone in. The speculation that more than one man could be coming in seems to put me in an even more precarious position, but I just don't know anything.'

For a while nobody did, but the wheels had been in motion for a few weeks. Dalglish had been in Monaco, and had come close to getting the Marseille job, when he received a call from Fox. 'Bill wanted to know whether I would be interested in the Blackburn job,' Dalglish said in his autobiography. 'The papers had already been speculating about it but I hadn't heard anything. I never took any notice of such talk until it became official. Now it was.' Travelling from Monaco to Blackburn may not have been the most exciting journey but the Rovers wanted a taste of the high life themselves. Getting Dalglish, still the biggest name manager in British football, was a quick and effective way to do it.

And there it was. On 12 October fans read national headlines such as 'Rovers Kop Kenny' before heading to Ewood to watch the mid-table team take on Plymouth Argyle. The anticipation was building and all the talk was whether the man himself would make an appearance. He did, along with new assistant Ray Harford, taking seats in the old Nuttall Street Stand to a general round of applause and flashing lights. 'When I left Anfield, it was well-versed that I had had enough,' Dalglish said in that day's press conference sat alongside Bill Fox. 'I had to get away and recharge the batteries. Now I think they have been recharged fully and I am looking forward to getting back to work. I think the ambition that was stressed to me by Blackburn, the ambition for the future and the stability of the club was the most important thing in my discussions with them. There is pressure everywhere in whatever you are doing. But it's not so much pressure as pride. If you are a proud person you want to be successful.'

It was obvious from the start that appointing Ray Harford as assistant was inspired, perhaps even more than that. Harford had been mentioned in the Rovers boardroom as a possible candidate for the main job so there was some satisfaction when Dalglish talked of bringing the Londoner in as the number two. Harford was highly regarded as a manager in his own right, leading Luton Town to League Cup glory in 1988 (the club's first ever major trophy) and the final of the same competition the year after. A spell in charge of the England Under-21 team meant he also had worked with, and impressed with his coaching abilities, some of the brightest young talent in the country, something that was going to come in useful when attracting players to the club. 'I think Kenny bringing in Ray Harford was one of the best signings he ever made,' said Kendall when I talked to him ahead of his sad passing in 2015. 'Everyone in the game respected Ray for his coaching abilities and football knowledge. It gave Kenny the time and space to manage.'

Parkes had played under Kendall at Ewood years earlier and soon learnt that he was still very much part of the plans at the club; handed a better contract at the request of Dalglish. The former midfielder was probably the happiest person in Blackburn on a day when there was plenty of competition. His reaction was understandably quite a bit different in tone than his earlier comments. 'I have been here for 21 years, but these past eight games have been the best of the lot. But the biggest thing is that I am staying at the club and I am going to be working with the first team. We can now do together what we set out to do, to put the club into a position where we can make a promotion push. Kenny will put Blackburn on the map.'

The town's mayor hoped it would do that and more. To mark the 40th anniversary of the queen's accession to the throne in 1952, there was a prize of a town being granted city status. Blackburn was in the running, though a 14-1 outsider. George Bramley-Haworth believed that the arrival of Dalglish would give the town's hopes a boost. 'There's no doubt about it, this has really put Blackburn on the map. Nothing would give me greater pleasure than to see them promoted and win the cup in my year of office.' He got the first but not the second. In the end Sunderland won the race to city status, but few in Blackburn would have swapped that for what ended up happening.

There was certainly lots of talk in the national media as Dalglish arrived. It was helped by the fact there were no top-flight games that weekend, though the dark satanic mills trope could never be resisted. The *Sunday Express* went with a club that was, 'Steeped in tradition and cobwebs with optimism as high as a mill chimney.' *The Sun* shot with 'Hovisland with kindly folk of that old town.' The *Guardian* was a little more poetic. 'Ewood Park may be a rusting edifice but… Blackburn could be enjoying a status they have not held since the first Battle of Ypres.'

If Blackburn fans were amazed, Liverpool supporters also had questions. 'The first thing most of us felt was disappointment,' said Tony Evans. 'It was clear that after Hillsborough and all the pressure that he had been under, he was an emotional wreck. The first thing we asked was "Why didn't Liverpool give him a break?" That would have been the logical thing; give him some time off and then welcome him back. But he was one of the great heroes, we wished him well. To be honest we didn't think he would be building a title-winning side. It was more like "Aah, Kenny has got another job, hope he is going to do okay."'

Despite the appointment, Rovers and Liverpool were mixing in very different circles, but that was about to change. 'It [Kenny's appointment] coincided with our decline and Souness coming,' added Evans. 'At the time we thought the success would continue but suddenly it became apparent this was not the case. It was a bit of a shock but at the time we didn't really see Blackburn as a future competitor.'

It was a move that shocked plenty of others such as John Brewin, a Manchester United fan and later a writer for the *Guardian* and many other publications. 'When Kenny went to Blackburn, it seemed a strange move and if anything, it seemed as if he had gone for the money,' Brewin said. 'I remember Dalglish leaving Liverpool and I was on holiday and heard it on world service radio. It felt like the end of Liverpool and funnily enough, it was. Finally, the spell had been broken. Until he went to Newcastle, you felt he had Fergie's measure even if Fergie was not at his peak then.'

'It was obvious that Blackburn had money. Clubs didn't have money in that way at the time. Derby did it and you had Jack Hayward at Wolves, but this idea of millionaires ploughing money into a club was an alien one then. United and Liverpool made their money by being famous clubs with big gates and a reasonable amount of sponsorship but nothing major. It was always going to be interesting to see how Blackburn and Kenny would do together, though I am not sure anyone thought they would be champions.'

2

1981 & 1992: TWO PROMOTION CAMPAIGNS

'We had promotion challenges before, but this
was all different. Kenny was here.'

SCOTT SELLARS

THE BIG BOYS COULD WAIT. THE FOCUS FOR THE ROVERS
at first was on just getting into the same league. On Saturday, Dalglish arrived.
On Monday, William Hill had the club 5/4 to win promotion. Ladbrokes were
offering odds on how many points would be collected over the next five games
and it ranged from 200/1 for zero and 25/1 for all 15. There was more talk
about who would follow Dalglish to Ewood. The first raft of names included
Ian Rush, Jan Mølby, Bruce Grobbelaar, David James, Don Goodman, Colin
Hendry, John Fashanu, John Scales, Derek Mountfield and Mike Stowell.

On Monday, the new boss arrived for work at Ewood and struggled to get
into the stadium, while 200 fans also turned up to the local park to watch the

team train. Dalglish, though, wasn't present. After taking care of some business at Ewood he had prior business to attend to, a testimonial in Edinburgh.

North of the border he received a standing ovation when he came on the pitch for Hibernian against Aston Villa. This was a different kind of manager for the Rovers, a club unaccustomed to having their boss in such demand around the country. At home, the ticket office was open and doing good business. 'It's incredible,' said club secretary John Howarth to local television reporters. 'We have been selling season tickets all morning. They have always been a bit cautious with their brass around here but now it seems they believe we are ready to take off. I have never known anything quite like it before. The whole town is talking about the team. We have had more publicity this weekend than for any match I can recall.'

Rovers fans needed a little time to get used to all this, as did the players. All knew that things were different under Walker but just how different was as much of a surprise to them as to everyone else.

'I didn't know anything about Jack Walker when I first went there,' said Sellars. 'Some people said that he was trying to get involved and he was very wealthy. All of a sudden, there was a takeover. Even so, I thought that Kenny coming was not possible. I thought that he would not leave Liverpool and I never thought he would join Blackburn. I didn't believe it until he came into the dressing room and introduced himself.'

It was clear then that this was a new era and a new regime. 'There had already been a change in the players who were coming in such as David Speedie,' said Sellars. 'Don was still there but you could sense that he was under more pressure. When the club has money then you know you have to perform as a player or manager because if you don't they will bring in someone else.'

That was the case for Mackay but Sellars was delighted to work with the new boss. 'He was a massive figure and from my point of view it was massive. I enjoyed playing for him. He knew what he wanted. He had an excellent coach in Ray Harford. He would join in games in training and was still a good player – a very, very good player. He had a great personality and was very much for the players and players responded to that. He wanted to change things and he knew he would be successful. That was the difference I think.

He had a confidence and that spread throughout the club. We had never had that before.'

Mimms's recollections from that period are similar, and just like the average fan he would read the paper, wondering who was going to take charge.

'We saw the headlines, but we never really believed it. In the end though, it was pretty low key,' said Mimms. 'It was rumoured for a day or two and then he walked through the door with Ray. He said a few words and that was it. You could say we were surprised. We were all left looking at each other when he walked back out, as you can expect. There had been the pressure of managing Liverpool. He loved the club but it had got intense there. He wanted to get back into football. Money talks and Kenny doesn't come if Blackburn didn't have the power to go and start recruiting better players. It was attractive to Kenny as he could create his own club. It may have been an eye opener for me, but then there was Kenny and he is training at Pleasington [part of the larger Witton Park in the town, a public park where the players trained] and washing his own kit and everything that goes with it, but he just got down and started work.'

A week later and it all started at Swindon. The Scot's introduction to the second tier was on a bitterly cold Saturday afternoon in October with a full house in the County Ground waiting to see two modern legends of the game. Glenn Hoddle was the Swindon boss and welcomed the fact that Dalglish was a rival once again.

'It's certainly going to be an interesting game,' Hoddle told local media. 'Rovers have had a good series of results under Tony Parkes, but Kenny's arrival might just put a bit of extra pressure on them. It's always good to be in the spotlight and I certainly hope my players respond well. I am sure Kenny's arrival would have given the club an even bigger lift if they had been going through a bad patch. As it is, everyone will expect them to get a result on Saturday and that can only be good for us.'

The former Spurs star said it was ridiculous that the Lancashire team had suddenly been made the frontrunners for promotion and warned Dalglish that the Second Division was far from easy. 'I can't see why everyone is making them favourites for promotion. There is still a long way to go. Kenny will find there is a different type of pressure in the Second Division. After this week, he will be out of the media eye much more than he was at Liverpool. But while he won't have the same high profile, there will still be plenty of demands.'

The only demands in that game were from the Rovers fans shouting for a wave. Apart from the surprisingly cold temperatures, I remember the sound of 'Kenny Dalgliiiiiiisssssh, real good!' to the tune of 'Everybody's Free (To Feel Good)' by Rozalla, a hit at the time. It didn't really catch on but 'King Kenny's Blue and White Army' did. The *clap, clap, clap-clap-clap, clap-clap-clap-clap* 'Dalglish', was also heard, as it had been so many times at Anfield. Rovers fans have never been afraid to steal chants or songs off others, though perhaps the classic, 'Who ate all the pies?' line of inquiry originated at Ewood.

There was speculation whether he would stand by the dugout, as he often had at Liverpool, but for the first game he was in the director's box. While Rovers lost 2-1 thanks to a last-minute goal, the mood was still upbeat among fans. There was a sense that good times were just around the corner. A lot of the media were not that interested in whether Swindon or Blackburn won this Division Two clash, but whether the Scot carried the same demeanour as his last days at Liverpool, when the pressures and stress from the Hillsborough disaster eventually proved to be too much.

The early signs were good. David Speedie, who arrived at Anfield late in Dalglish's time there, believed that the boss had changed. 'I get the feeling Kenny is more relaxed this time,' he told reporters. 'There are lots of smiles and jokes, although he did joke at Liverpool too. I just hope I don't get him the sack because he's the eighth manager I've had in less than 12 months. There was John Sillett and Terry Butcher at Coventry, followed by Kenny, Ronnie Moran and Graeme Souness at Liverpool and then Don Mackay, Tony Parkes and Kenny again at Blackburn!'

As well as Kenny's attitude, there was, of course, a focus on who he would bring in. All knew the money was there and all knew that Dalglish had been tasked with bringing back the good times. That meant new players. Rumours identified former strike partner Ian Rush as the first signing while Andy Hinchcliffe, out of favour at Everton, was seen as the kind of defender who would bring plenty to the team. Everyone was waiting.

In the end, the first addition was neither big in name or stature. Alan Wright, or Little Alan Wright as he was usually known, was signed later that week from Blackpool, a cash-strapped club unable to resist the £500,000 on offer, the most ever paid to a club in the Fourth Division. 'It's an honour to be wanted by Kenny Dalglish,' Wright said, the first of many times such a sentence was to be uttered in the coming weeks, months and years. The left-back came straight into the team for his debut at home to Grimsby, Dalglish's first game in charge at Ewood, a 2-1 win. A first away victory soon followed, but first there was a 3-0 bonfire night loss at high-flying Southend as Brett Angell, later linked with the Rovers, scored twice.

Rovers stayed down south and four days later won 2-0 win against Charlton Athletic at Upton Park. It was a game notable for a classy Sellars strike and a return to the Blue and White for Colin Hendry, signed for £700,000 from Manchester City. Hendry had originally joined Rovers in 1987, signing from Dundee as a striker, but Mackay had successfully converted him into a central defender. After two successful seasons he left to join Manchester City in 1989. His second signing for the club was to be one of Dalglish's best buys, though Mackay had already lined up his return.

'When Don Mackay was sacked I thought I was never going back – that Mr Dalglish would want his own players,' said Hendry. 'My heart is at the club irrespective of the money. I'm at a very, very big club no matter what the financial position is. I didn't sign for the sake of Kenny Dalglish, although it adds an extra dimension. When I was at the club before we were in the play-offs three times. I live in Blackburn. I would not have left the First Division if I thought I wasn't going back. Blackburn is as ambitious as most First Division clubs.'

Hendry had done well at City and was voted the Player of the Year in the 1989/90 season by fans, even though he had missed almost half of the season. He continued to impress the next year as City finished the 1990/91 campaign in fifth, but that summer Peter Reid paid £2.5 million for Keith Curle, a huge amount of money at the time for a central defender. That was the beginning of the end. 'I didn't do anything wrong at City. There were third from bottom when I joined. We escaped relegation and the next season finished fifth and I won a Scotland B cap. But this year I was not given a look in. During my career I've never taken a step back and I don't look on this as one.'

Rovers were climbing the table. Barnsley were next and for the third time in almost as many weeks there was an expensive signing set to start, and it marked the first seven figure sum that the club had ever paid. Don Mackay had tried to sign Mike Newell from Everton in the summer, but the striker stayed at Goodison. Howard Kendall had turned down a £1 million bid from Dalglish in early November. 'It was certainly a turnaround and it is fair to say that I was not expecting to be fighting off big-money bids from Blackburn,' Kendall said. 'We didn't have two pennies to rub together when I was there and now Blackburn had Kenny and were making million-pound bids. To say I was surprised at how things had turned out would be an understatement.'

The Scot returned with £100,000 more. Kendall said yes and so did Newell. 'When Kenny came calling it was hard to say no,' remembered the striker. 'There was obviously something happening at Blackburn and the chance to be part of that was an exciting one. I was sure that I would not be out of the First Division for long.' The deal was done just in time for the former Luton star to make his debut against Barnsley. He scored and impressed in a 3-0 win that sent Rovers fifth.

A goalless draw at Newcastle was followed by three successive wins as Rovers eased into top gear. For the first of those, Gordon Cowans, former England midfielder and winner of the 1982 European Cup with Aston Villa, arrived for £200,000. His debut came against promotion rivals Middlesbrough in a 2-1 win that was more comfortable than the scoreline suggested, though Stuart Ripley helped to earn his move to Ewood the following summer with a fine display.

Rovers players who had been at the club for a number of years could have been forgiven for worrying about their own places in the team. 'It goes both ways,' Sellars said. 'Some players want to protect themselves. There is pressure but I was looking forward to playing with better players – Newell, Speedie, Price came back and there was Gordon Cowans. My thinking was that these players are going to help me become successful. You can lose your place but you have to get your head down and work hard. If you have confidence in your ability and you are prepared to work hard then you should welcome the arrival of good players who have won and achieved things in the game.'

Sellars was a very talented player but Mark Atkins, who had signed in 1988 as a right-back from Scunthorpe for £45,000, knew that he was going to have to fight hard for his place. 'It was a step up for me. It was the summer of 1988 and I was out of contract. I was all set for Barnsley. Alan Clarke signed me for Scunthorpe at 14 and he offered me a deal. A day after Blackburn phoned and asked me to come. I signed the same day. It was that good and I was impressed with the set up. Chris Price was a good right-back and he had gone to Villa. It was a big step up for me as Blackburn were often in the play-offs and didn't look that far away from the First Division.'

Three years later and Dalglish was following in the same footsteps. 'We had heard rumours, but nobody really believed that it was going to happen. The first I knew about it was when Kenny walked into the changing room before the Plymouth game and that was that. It was amazing to see him there.'

Dalglish had an aura about him that few others could match and just to have him at the club gave Rovers instant credibility along with the money. 'Don couldn't attract the players and Kenny could,' said Atkins. 'That was a big problem. It is no good having the money if you can't attract the players.'

They were attracted and the squad was growing in size and quality. Chris Price, the player Atkins replaced, returned and there was always the potential of more to come. 'I was definitely concerned when the first set of players came in,' said Atkins. 'They were paying a lot of money, but Kenny was good that way. You know, it was a step up for me to join a team that could reach the play-offs in the Second Division from the Fourth Division. I had adapted to that I think, but then the arrival of Kenny meant that that I had to improve again as the club were aiming much higher. The good thing was with Kenny was that you were never guaranteed a first team place just because you cost a lot of money. If you played well then you kept your place. I admired that. He was never pressured to pick the big players. I always felt part of the team even when I was not playing. I always felt that I was doing a job for him and he knew that, and he was great with me. I knew I had to be 100 percent every game. In training too, perhaps the bigger-name players could relax sometimes, but I never could. I had to fight for my place all the time, but it made me a better player.'

❉

ALL THIS WAS QUITE A CHANGE AND IT ALL HAPPENED

so fast. Rovers had not been talked about for quite some time. From 1888 to
1966, the club had spent just 13 years outside the top tier, but by the seventies
and eighties the best days had long gone. Things got worse in 1972 as the
Blues dropped down to the third tier for the first time ever. They returned to
the Second Division for the 1975/76 season with Jim Smith at the helm, but
his departure in 1978 meant that a fifth place finish in the 1977/78 campaign
became 22nd the season after. The drop was confirmed with four games still to
play, and the fact that the team without a manager won the last three games in
the style, according to one newspaper, of a 'rudderless chariot wreaking havoc',
did not make anyone feel much better.

The relegation resulted in the appointment of Howard Kendall ahead
of the 1979/80 season, and the start of fun and frustration in equal measure
over the next decade. The former Preston North End and Everton star became
Blackburn's first-ever player-manager and it was Kendall's first managerial
position after a spell as player-coach at Stoke City. 'It seemed a natural move
for me to make at the time,' Kendall told me. 'I was ready for the challenge.
Blackburn had some decent players and I knew about their history.'

He remains one of the most successful bosses that the club has ever had. 'It
was a real coup to get him,' said Simon Garner, Blackburn's record goalscorer,
in his autobiography. 'He was a breath of fresh air at the club.' Garner, who
was loved by fans as much for his liking of beer and ciggies as much as his
goals, also liked that the new boss liked a drink.

Rovers needed freshening up. 'The club had just been relegated and there
was something of a gloomy atmosphere about the place,' said Kendall. 'It took
time to try to lift that but it was difficult at first. From the beginning though,
I felt it was the right place for me. I was involved in everything. Later when
I went to Spain and Bilbao, I was the head coach. I just coached the players
and told them who I wanted. I didn't have to get involved with the contracts
or travelling around the country looking at players. I just did the training
and that was great, I liked that. But my time at Blackburn gave me a great
experience in running a football club and it was the perfect place for me to

start out.'

The job seemed even more difficult when two of the team's stars, both dynamic full-backs who liked to get forward, departed. John Bailey was just 22 in 1979 when Everton, a club that has taken its fair share of talent from East Lancashire over the years, came calling. He would soon become one of the first players whose fee was to be decided by a tribunal: Rovers wanted £500,000, but in the end the clubs settled on £200,000, with Blackburn to receive another £100,000 if Bailey made over 50 appearances in an Everton shirt. The Liverpudlian had lodged in a house that backed on to ours during his stay in Blackburn, and my eldest brother talks of swapping headers over the hedges. By 1984 Bailey was an FA Cup winner. In the same year, right-back Kevin Hird headed to Leeds United for £357,000. At the time he was the most expensive full-back in British history, a lot of money for a talented but inconsistent player.

Yet these sales gave Kendall the opportunity to build a less cavalier but much more solid defensive unit. Out went Bailey and Hird, in came Jim Branagan at right-back, who rarely crossed the halfway line, and Mick Rathbone at left-back. They were to make over 600 combined appearances for Blackburn. With Glenn Keeley and Derek Fazackerley in the middle, Kendall had the back four that was to serve the club so well for so long.

Another important signing was Jim Arnold as goalkeeper for £20,000. The new number one, who had played for England's semi-professional team, came from Stafford Rangers and impressed from the start behind a solid back four. The goals started to be stopped. Kendall turned a side that had been relegated so dismally the season before into something much more compact and organised. On the way to relegation Blackburn had conceded 72 goals in 42 games; on the way back up under Kendall they conceded just 36 in 46. One wonders whether a young George Graham was an interested observer. There were certainly plenty of 1-0 wins that season: eleven in total.

It wasn't all dour defending. Further up the pitch there was Noel Brotherston, a Northern Ireland international winger who played at the 1982 World Cup, a man with a distinctive haircut and the ability to beat any defender when his mood was right. Somehow, he never got the big move to the top league. And then there was someone on the way down from the top.

Duncan McKenzie, the former Leeds and Everton star who was also famous for apparently being able to jump over a Mini from a standing position and throw a golf ball the length of the Elland Road pitch without bouncing, joined in March 1979 from Chelsea in a surprise move that nobody could really explain. The £80,000 was not only a club record but a desperate attempt to avoid the drop and while the hugely talented striker was not always influential, he had his moments. 'It was a great little love affair. The club was as tight as you can possibly imagine, the board used to count every shilling, in fact every penny, but it made for great camaraderie,' McKenzie recalled in 2001. 'The skipper Jim Branagan would go round the dressing room once a week collecting a pound from every player so we could pay for our end of season trip to Majorca. It was just incredible when you consider the money in the game now, but the likes of Simon Garner, who was an absolutely brilliant little goal scorer despite the 40 cigarettes a day and the pints he would down, was probably on no more than £70 a week.'

£50,000 was spent on Andy Crawford from Derby County. Unpopular with teammates but single-minded in attack, the striker would eventually score the goals that the team needed.

In the early days though, Kendall was required to show just how good a player he still was, as one win in the opening ten league games of the season suggested that he was needed on the pitch as much as in the dugout. 'I had an idea of the way I wanted to play,' Kendall said. 'I had a good set of players and I had the system that really suited them. It just took a little time to get it all organised, but once we settled down, there was no stopping us and when you start to get the results then, of course, everything becomes much easier. The confidence returns, players are full of energy and want to play, they listen and take on board what you say more quickly. Soon we were flying.'

As the eighties dawned, Rovers were still in 14th, not exactly suggesting that a quick return to the second tier was on the cards. But soon after, they were to go on quite a run. It started at Grimsby in January – the team that was to go on and win the title – with two goals from McKenzie, and it never stopped. On the way Kendall's men eliminated Coventry City from the fourth round of the FA Cup just a week after the Sky Blues had beaten the mighty Liverpool in the league.

Rovers continued to pick up points in the league, and crowds were also starting to rise well into the five figures. 30,000 came out for Aston Villa in the fifth round of the FA Cup, a team that would win the English title a year later and become European champions the year after that. A last-minute own goal from Allan Evans gave Rovers a 1-1 draw. There was a large Rovers contingent that left the town to Villa Park for the midweek replay as the Birmingham team squeezed through. Blackburn's imperious league form, built on the foundations of a strong defence, continued, and on 22 March the team finally made it into the promotion places with a 1-0 win at Chesterfield, where there were more Rovers fans than home supporters in a crowd of 14,000. I distinctly remember my dad going and it seemed clear that promotion was a formality. Three 1-0 wins over four days over the Easter Weekend (Good Friday, Saturday and Monday) went along way to securing it, and it also meant that Rovers had picked up 29 points from a possible 30, or 43 from 45 in modern money.

Promotion back to the Second Division was achieved at Bury on a Tuesday night on the final game of the season, a match that has passed into Blackburn folklore. It is no exaggeration to say that all but around 2,000 fans in the 12,000 capacity at Gigg Lane were Rovers fans. I have such a clear memory of that evening, of the whole ground shaking, of being separated from my dad when the all-important goal was scored, being swept to the front and knocked over where I was helped onto the pitch by a policeman. It was almost disappointing when my dad came to claim his number three son. On the sidelines, as a seven-year old, I could finally see.

'That was an unforgettable night,' said Kendall. 'I don't think I ever saw a game where the home fans were so outnumbered in their own stadium. With Everton, we won league titles and European trophies and those were unforgettable nights, but I also have special memories of that night in Bury. We worked so hard that season.' Even after promotion, the purse strings were tight. 'The stories are true. We had to send letters second class and all that. We had to be very careful and keep an eye on outgoings. That made the good times sweeter.'

Fresh after promotion from the Third Division in his first season as manager, Howard Kendall was preparing in the summer of 1980 to try and repeat the feat and get into the top tier. His signings did not include former England or Scotland internationals, European Cup winners and players from

Liverpool and Everton. The only summer additions were left-back Roger De Vries, who came from Hull City for £25,000 and made little impact before drifting off to Scunthorpe, and Mickey Speight. The former England B international, who had apparently turned down Bobby Robson and Ipswich two years previously, was signed for £40,000.

'We looked at players who we felt could improve the team,' said Kendall. 'There weren't many around for the money we had. We had a good core of players but if we had been able to strengthen the squad a little more then it may all have turned out a little differently. It was a case of talking to contacts, watching players and counting the coppers to see what we could afford. We couldn't afford much but we had a solid team and a great bunch of lads.'

Life in Division Two started out very well, with seven wins and two draws from the opening nine league games. With Andy Crawford – never popular with his teammates – wanting away and training alone at times, Simon Garner got more involved and scored five in that opening streak, with young Kevin Stonehouse also starting well. The goals were later to dry up.

IN 1991 ROVERS CONTINUED TO MAKE HEADLINES, BUT

the next rush of column inches came as chairman Bill Fox died after a short illness. He had been at the centre of two of the biggest football stories of 1991. As the president of the Football League, he had been a vocal and strident critic of the new breakaway Super League that was due to kick off the following season. Then, as chairman of Blackburn Rovers, he was involved in hiring Kenny Dalglish to help a desperate club gain entry into that very league. 'I always think that Jack Walker is the one that people talk about, but Bill Fox was Blackburn Rovers Football Club,' said Don Mackay. 'He lived, breathed and died Blackburn Rovers. He was also a reluctant chairman of the Football League. I still regret that Bill never saw the whole value of what he did for the club. I get a wee bit annoyed sometimes as Jack Walker gets the whole credit. He deserves plenty as he put the money in, but what Bill Fox did for the club should never be forgotten or underestimated.'

Fox missed his beloved team go top of the league on 14 December with a confident 3-0 win over Bristol Rovers. In two months and eleven games, Rovers had picked up 25 points. Bristol boss Dennis Rofe was complimentary after the game. 'I told my players how Blackburn would play, which players to watch but it was just as if I was talking to myself for all the notice they took. I can't repeat the things I said at half-time, but I told them they were letting down themselves, the fans and the club. Blackburn passed the ball superbly and Kenny has brought some of his Liverpool habits to the club.'

Mark Atkins, who had been given a new midfield role by the new boss, was the star of the show. 'I think that the first difference was that Kenny gave us confidence. We had good seasons in the past, but I am not really sure that we really believed we were going to go up before. Kenny had won everything and expected to win. And then we had better players coming to join the club too, and so there was a feeling that promotion would finally happen. Certainly I believed after Kenny's arrival that we would go up.'

Rovers had become 11-10 favourites with the bookmakers to get promoted and Atkins's comments now are an echo of what was said at the time. Normally such confident talk of promotion would never have come from a Rovers player and even if it had, it would have left fans, scarred by repeated and painful near-misses, aghast. However, the presence of Dalglish, the new players and the belief around the club had changed all that.

Being top was a pleasant development, though the boss was quick to remind everyone that there was a long way to go. It seemed that by mid-February the hard work had been done when Newcastle United, with Kevin Keegan newly installed as manager, came to East Lancashire. The Geordies scored first but that just seemed to make the Rovers mad, especially David Speedie. The player's wife had been in the papers in the days before the game and the 5,000 travelling fans were happy to remind him of the fact. His revenge must have felt sweet and the way he celebrated his hat-trick goal in front of the away fans was particularly brave. One Newcastle fanzine summed it up with an end of season fan poll. 'Most hated opponent? David Speedie. Opposing player you would most like to see at Newcastle? David Speedie.'

Amid the general euphoria as Rovers went seven clear of second was a feeling that promotion was in the bag. The club may have been in similar positions before but none quite as good, none with such a good group of players, none with the most famous British manager around at the helm and none when the club had the financial clout to strengthen the squad and the team. The broken leg suffered by Mike Newell against Newcastle was a blow, but surely not enough of one to stop the relentless push for promotion.

Dalglish seemed to agree and started to buy players with an eye on the following season in the top tier. In came the talented American forward Roy Wegerle from QPR for £1.2 million, scorer of the 1990/91 goal of the season, a dreamy dribbled effort against Leeds United. 'We have bought someone who is First Division,' said Ray Harford and there was no doubt that Wegerle, capable of sublime skills when conditions were right, was not a traditional Second Division player. Tim Sherwood arrived from Watford for £500,000 and also looked out of place, though in his case there was less to suggest that he had that top tier talent. 'He didn't impress early on,' Simon Garner remembered. 'He was an unknown quantity to everyone... and in his first season when he barely got a game, it didn't look like the best buy in the world.' I remember seeing him trot out on the pitch as a substitute against Brighton with an upturned collar. At the time, that was about all he stood out for.

3

PANIC STATIONS

'Even Kenny didn't know what to do.'

BOBBY MIMMS

AFTER THE NEWCASTLE WIN, THERE WERE THREE draws and two defeats from the next five games. Rovers, who had looked like galloping out of sight, were reined in. A 3-0 win at Brighton in March did suggest that the slump had just been a hiccup, with Roy Wegerle impressing down on the south coast. Following that result Danny Baker told the nation to forget about catching Blackburn on Radio Five's *606*, as they had started to win again. Yet it was that win that turned out to be the blip as a run of uncertain form became something much worse. Six straight defeats followed, with the nadir a 2-0 loss to a struggling Port Vale. That was followed by a 2-1 defeat at Watford as Rovers slipped down into fourth. Wegerle scored at

Vicarage Road but admitted that he was worried he had become something of a jinx.

The American international, who went on to become a golf professional, had been called the new Rodney Marsh when playing for Queens Park Rangers and was worried that he was following in Marsh's footsteps. The blond bombshell was famously blamed for costing Manchester City the 1972 title – many thought he destroyed the rhythm of the team that had been on course for the championship. After his fifth defeat for the Rovers since joining in early March, Wegerle voiced his fears. 'I can't help feeling I'm Blackburn's unlucky omen. I haven't had a good season. When I left QPR they put a good run together. When I came here, everyone was confident we were going up. Everyone thought we were the best team in the division. It is a scramble now. I can't put my finger on why it's gone wrong. Kenny Dalglish and Ray Harford are scratching their heads too. We've got to get it right and quickly.'

Rivals such as Derby County were investing. Owner Lionel Pickering, who made his money in free local newspapers, started to spend. Despite insisting that he wasn't going to 'do a Jack Walker', he shelled out £1 million on Marco Gabbiadini, £500,000 on Paul Simpson and £300,000 on goalkeeper Steve Sutton. In March, manager Arthur Cox then paid the considerable sum of £1.3 million on striker Paul Kitson. 'I've come to Derby because they are ambitious,' said Kitson, then explaining why he chose the Rams over East Midlands rivals Leicester. 'I feel Derby have a better chance of promotion... there is money.'

Blackburn's football had become predictable and one-dimensional. The fluid play of earlier in the season was rarely seen, with long balls up to the strikers an increasingly favoured tactic. Defensive slips did not help and the confidence had well and truly gone. Fans were starting to think promotion was never going to happen. If they couldn't do it now, when could they?

Mimms had a theory that the focus had switched too much to the following season in the new Super League. 'I think we were doing that well that we had started to build for the next season in the Premier League before we had even got promotion,' he said. 'We were buying players that were not suited for the Second Division but would show what they could do in the next season.'

It was true that Rovers were the big scalp that everyone wanted and this made things a little tougher. Any wobble, to be expected over a long season, was seized upon by the media with the question as to whether King Kenny had lost his midas touch. Norman Fox of the *Independent* wrote later that year that there were plenty in football who found the sudden struggles pleasant, as those in football are wont to do.

'[Liverpool] more than anyone enjoyed watching Blackburn squirm towards the end of last season.' He called Walker the most unpopular man in English football, outside a certain corner of East Lancashire of course.

Another major reason for Blackburn's poor form was surely the fact that Mike Newell had broken his leg against promotion rivals Newcastle. Speedie had got most of the goals, but the former Everton man was the one making things tick. 'The injury to Newell was big,' said Sellars. 'He was such an intelligent and skilful player who made everyone else play better. He was key. Off the back of that, we lost confidence. Mike was a big loss to us and we lost belief. We just couldn't seem to get a win. We just didn't know what was happening.'

In March, Dalglish turned to a player for the here and now. He went to Swindon and signed Duncan Shearer, one of the leading scorers of the division. For Shearer, a Scot, the chance to train with Dalglish was something else, a feeling that was shared by players that followed.

Shearer Mark I had little impact at the club but while his stay was short, the signing was an interesting one. Many in Blackburn and Swindon felt that the striker had been bought to deprive a promotion rival of their best player. Swindon were not in the hunt for an automatic promotion spot, but they were within reach of the play-offs. Speedie was perhaps the best in the division but his fellow Scot was not far behind. In his autobiography, Shearer quotes Gordon Cowans as saying something along those lines not long after he joined. 'You know what they say about cowboys and Indians. If they wanted to get the better of the Indians then they had to take out the chief.'

According to Shearer, that was the motivation for Blackburn's interest, as much as there was a need for cover for Newell. At the end of March, Rovers were still in the hunt for automatic promotion, but the play-offs were looming large. Shearer claimed that Rovers were worried about meeting the Robins again, with Ray Harford confiding that they didn't know how to handle Swindon.

That sounds strange. After all, Rovers had beaten Swindon just the previous month and only lost at the County Ground earlier in the season due to a last-minute goal without the likes of Newell, Cowans, Hendry, Wright and Price, hardly a sign that Swindon posed a major problem. The Wiltshire club were struggling a little too and upon selling their star striker, had lost seven of their previous 13 games. When Shearer arrived he joined the league leaders, who were 11 points better off with just nine games to go. Blackburn hardly needed to be scared of Swindon down in ninth.

Swindon were already looking like missing the play-offs even before the sale, and their form actually improved without their star striker, losing just one of their last nine games in the league. Shearer may have made a difference in turning one or two of the five draws into wins, but it was still unlikely that the Wiltshire club would have taken that final play-off spot from the Rovers. The Lancastrians could afford, after signing the striker, to collect just eight points from the next nine games – relegation form – and still finish five clear of the Robins.

The simplest explanation is probably the most likely one. Rovers, a club that had missed out on promotion in the past through being unable to strengthen in the final stages, were desperate for more firepower in attack. Shearer was a proven Championship goalscorer and if he was the difference between getting to the promised land of the Premier League or not, then £700,000 would be very well spent indeed. Any weakening of rivals was a surely a bonus at best.

Shearer admits in his autobiography that as a Scot, it was difficult for him to turn Dalglish down. 'He hadn't long finished playing and was still as fit as a fiddle and had all the touches. He was also a real nark if things didn't go his way – a stray pass or a bad touch and he was on you like a ton of bricks, even in training games.' He still found David Speedie hard to handle and one wonders what Dalglish felt after leaving the player behind at Anfield only to be greeted with him at Ewood. 'The two of them fought like cat and dog,' recalled Shearer. Shearer was put up in a local hotel along with other mid-season signings Tim Sherwood and Roy Wegerle. Then Speedie would arrive in midweek from London and 'wreak havoc'. Shearer's sole contribution to Blackburn that season was a fine goal on his debut at Barnsley. Rovers still lost and were in freefall.

❊

SIGNING STAR STRIKERS WAS NOT SOMETHING THAT

Kendall had to deal with in 1981. All was looking good for a return to the top tier for the first time since 1966, but injuries had an effect. Tony Parkes broke his leg and more damaging was the injury to Noel Brotherston, clattered by Mel Sterland of Sheffield Wednesday, which weakened the team at a crucial time of the season. 'We lost Brotherston with about ten games to go I think and it came just a day or two after the transfer deadline and so we could not do anything about it.' said Kendall. 'It really hurt us as he could make things happen.'

After the Wednesday win Rovers lost just once in the last nine games of the season (crucially against Swansea), but the problem was they scored in just three.

On the final weekend at Bristol Rovers, Blackburn needed to win and hope that Swansea City didn't at Preston. Bristol was not like Bury from a year before. My abiding memory is the Rovers fans crammed into Eastville pretending that Preston had scored during the second half to inspire the boys. It worked and the points were secured, but Swansea actually won to take third on goal difference, giving Wales a first top-flight team for 19 years.

'That was tough to take and I felt sorry for the fans,' said Kendall. 'We should have won promotion that year but injuries did not help and our squad was not the biggest to begin with. If we had Brotherston then I am sure that one of those 0-0 draws would have ended in a win but that's football.'

It was not just Brotherston. Garner and Stonehouse had started the season well in the goalscoring stakes. In the first 13 games of the campaign, they had six each. In the following 29, they produced just five more. Garner was to find his consistent goalscoring groove from the following season. Kendall brought in Viv Busby from Stoke via Tulsa Roughnecks. The striker had made a name for himself during Fulham's run to the final of the 1975 FA Cup, but he wasn't the answer. With McKenzie going the other way in a swap deal, it meant that with the subsequent injury to Brotherston, there was zero creativity going forward and no reliable goalscorer.

Dalglish signed Wegerle, Newell and Duncan Shearer to add to David

Speedie – over £3 million of striking talent – and that was only just enough to get over the finish line, though Rovers finished sixth. Despite having almost nothing to play with Kendall took Rovers into fourth, missing out only on goal difference (three teams were promoted automatically at this time).

Swansea seemed to be the neutral's choice, and much was made of them going from Football League re-election to the First Division in the space of six years and to be fair, they scored 64 goals to Blackburn's 42. They were a little more romantic off the pitch too as manager John Toshack had published a book of poetry in 1976 (*Gosh, it's Tosh* was the title, honestly) and, given Swansea's strong performance in the top flight, he was soon tipped as the next Liverpool boss once Bob Paisley stepped down.

Still, it was all very disappointing. I remember for years to come walking past a little ditty written in black marker pen on top of someone's front wall on the way to school. 'It was that famous Saturday, the second day of May, we met some Swansea City fans on the motorway, we said we'd win promotion, we said we'd win the cup [getting a bit carried away here] but on that famous Saturday, Preston fucked it up.' The last line wasn't really accurate, but then putting it down to Blackburn's lack of firepower at the pointy end of the season and an away record that produced just four wins and 14 goals in 21 games would not have made for the catchiest climax.

It was a long drive back home from Bristol to Blackburn. 'It was heartbreaking,' said Kendall. 'We came so close and thought we were going to get there. In the end though, we just didn't quite have the squad. Another player or two and I am sure we would have made it, but to say we had been in Division Three just the season before we had done so well, but it was not easy to feel that at the time given the disappointment.'

As McKenzie pointed out, a young manager of Kendall's talents was not going to be at Ewood for long and he wasn't. Gordon Lee, another promising tactician who had left for brighter lights in 1975, was in trouble at Everton where a poor season and crowds dipping below 16,000 meant that the Toffees were seeking a replacement. Kendall, who had already turned down an advance from Crystal Palace, was on the shortlist and as he was an Everton legend as a player, it was always likely that the call would come. When it did, it was never going to be turned down. 'To manage Everton was a dream for me. It was a wrench to leave Blackburn as we had been through a lot together, but the chance to go to Everton was one I could not say no to.'

There had been rumours in the media that there would be a kind of swap deal, with Lee returning to Ewood and Kendall going the other way. That did not happen. Lee was dismissed by Everton on 6 May and Rovers gave Everton chairman Philip Carter permission to chat to Kendall. Six days after the heartbreak in Bristol Kendall was appointed Everton manager.

After a tough start back on Merseyside, Kendall delivered two league championships, an FA Cup and Cup Winners' Cup by the time he left for Athletic Bilbao in 1987. He went to Spain the most highly-rated manager in England. That is another story and it may never have happened had Rovers got an extra point that season – though it probably would have eventually – and while Kendall's departure was a blow to Blackburn, few fans could begrudge his well-deserved chance at the big time. At least Kendall left a stable and settled team, though he quickly came back to sign Jim Arnold, continuing an Evertonian tradition of taking talent from Ewood, and thoughts turned to his replacement.

IN APRIL 1992, IT WAS GETTING WORSE. ROVERS ACTUALLY played quite well for a while against Wolverhampton Wanderers but lost 2-1, with an error from stand-in goalkeeper Matt Dickins proving costly. It was the only game he would play for the club in a three-year spell. Mimms was back for the following game against promotion rivals Leicester at Easter. The heavily-strapped number one did the best he could to halt Blackburn's decline, but when Leicester's substitute Kevin Russell broke free beyond the defence, the goalkeeper could only direct his clearance straight at the striker, who then ran toward the unguarded net and scored the only goal of the game with 15 minutes remaining.

Rovers fell to seventh with four games to go. They were now out of the play-off spots, something that was almost unthinkable just a few weeks earlier, just like the idea of Dalglish being manager of Blackburn had been. The Rovers fans fell silent as the gleeful away supporters pointed en masse to the impassive

Dalglish, chanting, 'Quit in the morning, he's going to quit in the morning.' Leaving Ewood after the final whistle, it really looked like that was it. For the fourth time in five years promotion was going to be blown again, this time with a host of star players signed on big money and a world-famous manager.

Despite all the differences, the sinking feeling was the same. There was little sympathy from elsewhere, as Garner recounted. 'In just a few months we'd turned from a club who were seen as a quaint, loveable outfit, a club that the press and fans from outside the area had a real soft-spot for because of how friendly it was and how close we'd come to having success, to one people wanted to see fail.'

Jack Walker still spoke of the belief that the players had that promotion through the play-offs was possible. The fans were not quite singing from the same hymn sheet, but Walker was positive about promotion and nonplussed about the reasons for recent form in equal measure. 'We're still going for promotion,' he said. 'I thought we were robbed today and with that sort of spirit, I'm not too worried really. Nothing's lost yet and we're still in for qualifying from the play-offs. We haven't given up on this season. I've just sat for half an hour with those lads and I, like them, don't know how we lost. Leicester had two shots on target. We had a hell of a sight more.'

With six straight losses, this new-look Rovers were just a game away from equalling their worst ever run of defeats, a run that dated back to the disastrous year of 1966. 'It'll take some beating,' admitted Dalglish. 'They are liable to go and win four in a row now. The lads certainly have the ability and they just need confidence, a bit more belief and a little bit more good fortune.'

Going up automatically was now out of the question. Newell's return, earlier than expected, on Easter Monday at home to Tranmere Rovers was welcome, as was the point in a 2-2 draw. Seven points from the next three games – with Speedie grabbing a hat-trick in the last match, a 3-1 victory at Plymouth – was enough to squeeze into the play-offs.

Future Rover Nicky Marker was playing for Plymouth that day. 'We had to win to stay up and Blackburn had to win to make the play-offs,' he recalled. 'It was the start of money coming into the club and to football. As far as we were concerned, they were one of the big boys in the league but we were not having the best of seasons and were just focused on ourselves. We scored first but were disappointed to lose and Speedie was almost unplayable. We were relegated and Blackburn went on to get promoted. I didn't know at the time how that would affect my life.'

Rovers had made it into the play-offs. That would have been seen as disastrous about ten weeks earlier but had suddenly become a reason for celebration. Given the club's history however, there was plenty of trepidation among the fans. Had Dalglish come in midway through the season and led the team up into sixth, his sheen of invincibility would have been completely intact and while there was still plenty of belief in the boss, the final third of the campaign had been traumatic and, in truth, he had seemed pretty clueless as to how to arrest the slide.

Mimms had not been tarred with the club's play-off past however. 'I was pretty confident that we were good enough,' he said. 'I always thought that if we could get into the play-offs that we had the quality players that would be able to push forward and finish the job off. Then 15 minutes into the play-off semi-final first leg (against Derby County) we were 2-0 down and we were left thinking "Oh God".'

Oh God indeed. 'We started appallingly,' recalled Dalglish in his autobiography.

Derby at home, a first leg that will never be forgotten by those who were packed into the old ground. The Rams had been splashing a fair amount of cash themselves at the time and their chairman Lionel Pickering was compared to Walker. He didn't have the same amount of cash but had sold his company to Thomson Regional Newspapers for £25 million in 1989. Part of that helped him become the successor to Robert Maxwell as Derby's major shareholder. Tommy Johnson and Marco Gabbiadini, two of the players signed with Pickering's money, scored on that sunny Sunday afternoon before the Rovers had settled.

All Rovers fans will have heard tales of counterparts ripping up tickets for the away leg after 15 minutes – and we all nod along with understanding, even though this always struck me as a strange thing to do. The feeling was one of despondency but there was still 75 minutes left to get a goal or two and make the second game at least an interesting one. It is certainly true, however, that there was a feeling of 'Here we go again'. Three play-off failures in the previous five years had many all too ready to believe that it was not going to happen.

'Scott Sellars had lost three times in a row in the play-offs and there were others who had all gone through it,' Mimms said. 'I don't know what they were thinking but I think we were all shell-shocked.' Clubs were no longer scared of a team that had lost eight of their last 15 games and won just one of the last seven at home. There was little sense, at least among the fans, that Rovers would bounce back. After all, they hadn't done that for some time. Confidence was low.

'We started off and we're 2-0 down,' Sellars recalled. 'You are thinking, "Here we go, a play-off nightmare again". We just kept at it. Perhaps Derby weren't sure what to do next with a two-goal lead so early in the game. Do you sit back or go for another? But we knew we had to score.'

Sellars got the all-important first goal back ten minutes before the break. It was direct from a free-kick, not the kind of shot that curls into the top corner but a low effort that bobbled into the net. It didn't matter. The situation was still looking grim but there was hope. And just before the break, something special happened. Newell picked up the ball out wide, but there still didn't seem to be much danger when he cut inside still some distance from goal. The man some called Inspector Gadget then stuck out a long leg and bent home a beauty and suddenly Ewood Park was rocking. Sellars gave hope, Newell provided belief and the fans gave it all they had. Rare indeed has the stadium rocked all the way through half-time, but the fans were singing for the full 15 minutes while the players tried to take a rest.

'We could hear them from the dressing room,' said Sellars. 'It was fantastic, and it gave us confidence. We just felt that we were going to do it.' There was something else too. 'We had the confidence of having Kenny there and all the players. We just thought "We can do this, just keep going". We ran right over the top of them in the second half. They couldn't cope, and it was just great to be part of a game like that. It was unforgettable.'

And relentless. Speedie and Newell, ably supported by Sellars, Cowans and Atkins, attacked in waves. Speedie scored twice and Newell had one perfectly good goal ruled out for offside. It was 4-2, should have been 5-2 and should have been more. The crowd was delirious. From 2-0 down, the team had shown character, determination and incisive attacking play and the woes of

March and April had been forgotten. It would be easy to say that this was the moment everyone really felt that the club was finally going up, that this was different, but there was still the second leg.

A two-goal cushion had not been enough at Selhurst Park just three years earlier when Rovers won the first leg at home 3-1 to Crystal Palace only to lose 3-0 in South London. Nobody was taking anything for granted. 'Oh, the second leg was tough,' said Sellars. 'The Baseball Ground was tight and the crowd was right up for it. The noise was constant. You could feel the pressure and the tension in the air. It was one of those games that you just have to get through.'

Even Dalglish felt it. A man who had won leagues and European Cups was having his first taste of an away game in the play-offs. 'The second leg was really nerve-racking. I thought I was okay, until just before kick-off, in the dugout. There was something on my shirt and as I went to rub it off, I felt my heart pounding away. I had only been in the job from October to May and I was determined not to get myself into the state that had forced me out of Liverpool.' It all went to show what was at stake.

Derby pounded away with their fans in full voice. They got a first half goal and one more would have taken them through to the final. I listened on the radio. It was horrible, with the constant noise suggesting non-stop County attacks. My dad went to Ewood to watch on a big screen, describing it as the most torment he ever suffered watching football, initially leaving before the end only to turn back around and see it through. Temporary respite came in the second half as Kevin Moran bundled the ball over the line to make it 1-1 on the night and 5-3 on aggregate to send the travelling thousands behind the goal wild. Yet Derby soon scored again and were in the position of needing just one more. 'It was a battle,' said Atkins, still relishing his role as midfielder. 'We had that atmosphere in Blackburn for the first leg which was wonderful but that was pushing us on. At Derby it was crackling, and we knew that we would have to fight. This was not going to be a flowing game of open and attacking football.'

The only thing flowing was the sweat and probably beer for those who couldn't make it to the ground. The last ten minutes were painful, especially when Ted McMinn hit the post, but the Rovers hung on. 'We didn't want to celebrate too much as we knew there was another game,' said Atkins. 'But we knew that we had taken a massive step.'

There were twelve long May days before the final with another East Midlands club. Leicester had done the double over the Rovers and were last seen gleefully pointing at Dalglish and predicting that he would resign in the morning. On a hot May bank holiday afternoon, 30,000 fans headed south, hoping that this would not be play-off heartbreak number four in just five years. Playing at Wembley made it feel different.

Rovers were in yellow and the first half was a scrappy affair. Right at the end of it, Speedie turned Leicester defender Steve Walsh in the area and went down.

Was this one a penalty? Nobody in the Blackburn end really cared. It is of the 'Seen them given but wouldn't be happy if it was given against us' type of decisions. 'He took a dive,' said Walsh. 'It was nothing more than obstruction and I'm obviously very disappointed.' The *Guardian* agreed, calling it a moment of 'pure craftmanship', though also noted that Walsh had used rugby methods to tackle the striker.

In the end, referee George Courtney pointed to the spot, the first of two penalty kicks he gave to the Rovers that day. He was detested, *properly detested*, for giving a penalty that never was against the Blues in the second leg of a play-off final against Crystal Palace three years earlier, but perhaps his appointment was a blessing. Having Courtney in charge did not go down well with most Rovers fans but he did go some way towards redeeming himself.

Former boss Don Mackay had been in more play-offs than most and was commentating on television. A few days prior to the game, having noticed that Courtney was taking charge, he called Leicester boss Brian Little. 'I was reasonably friendly with the Leicester manager and before the play-off final I called him and told him that the referee was going to be under pressure because of what happened three years before at Selhurst Park. I don't mean that he was not honest, but that he was going to be under pressure. I told him that he should complain to the Football League. He didn't want to be childish and complain; I told him that he should be childish. I did the commentary for TV that day. Blackburn got two penalty kicks. I am not saying that they weren't penalties, they probably were, but the referee was under pressure that day.'

Leicester had spent much of the second half putting Rovers under pressure without creating much in the way of clear chances. There were lots of long balls, plenty of headers and a few scrambles. It was all very tense and so the relief when Atkins was brought down in the box five minutes from time – and there was no debate for this one – was massive. Newell's kick was tired and saved by Carl Muggleton and the torture continued. Leicester continued to pour forward but the whistle finally blew and the celebrations – as well as the ubiquitous 'Rovers Return' headlines – could begin.

'We got a bit of payback in 1992, Blackburn fans never forget,' Atkins said of Courtney before he added with a laugh. 'Only he will know if he wanted to help us. The first, I thought it was probably a pen. The second definitely was as it was on me. That was a great day. The season had been up and down, and it became all about promotion. It was a relief at the end of it all.'

It was noted that Bill Fox, the Rovers chairman until his death just after Dalglish had arrived earlier in the season, had fought against the formation of the Premier League as president of the Football League. What he would have made of it all is anyone's guess, but whatever irony there may have been, the 30,000 or so Rovers fans at Wembley cared little.

Jack Walker was immediately focused on the next step. Survival in the top tier was not on his mind, Europe was. 'It's been worth every penny,' he said. 'It's taken us 26 years to get back here. That's a lifetime, but now we are looking at Europe. There's more money where that came from if Kenny wants it. How can I be satisfied now? We'll sort it out.'

For Sellars, who had just played his last game for the club – though he didn't know it at the time – it was a welcome change from past heartbreaks. 'It was a big game and with every emotion, I was looking forward to it. There were nerves and we had had play-off disappointment before. It was unbelievable at the end. For a few of the lads who had been there a long time it was an emotional day and for me too. More than that, I was buzzing to get to the Premier League.'

4

A GLORIOUS PAST

'London witnessed an incursion of Northern Barbarians on Saturday
– hot-blooded Lancastrians, sharp of tongue, rough and ready, of
uncouth garb and speech. A tribe of Soudanese Arabs let loose in
the Strand would not excite more amusement and curiosity.'

PALL MALL GAZETTE, 1884

THE LAST SIGNIFICANT TROPHY TO BE DECORATED
with the blue and white ribbons of Blackburn had come in 1928 with the FA
Cup. The last league title in 1914. Had Archduke Franz Ferdinand never been
assassinated in Sarajevo in that summer then maybe Jack Walker would never
have seen the need to get involved as Rovers could have established themselves
as a power for decades to come. Gavrilo Princip's actions in killing the heir to
the throne of the Habsburg Empire sparked off a chain of events that resulted
in World War One and thereby ended what could have been a Blackburn
Rovers period of domination in English football.

Champions for the second time in three years when the Serbian fired his fateful shots, Rovers had already started to strengthen for the following season and it would surely have not been long before title number three was heading to Ewood Park, especially with the great Bob Crompton, England captain, still in the side and the champions ready to spend in the transfer market. Rovers finished the 1914/15 season third, just three points behind champions Everton before war intervened and league football was cancelled. The Blues were never quite the same force again – until the nineties.

Every fan in the town can cite Martin Tyler's remark, commentating live on Sky Sports, when Sherwood became the first Blackburn captain to lift the English title for 81 years. 'Blackburn Rovers. For so long a club with a glorious past, now with a glittering future.' The first part of that statement is more accurate than the second. The history of one of the oldest clubs in the world, founded in 1875 and not far off its 150th birthday, is as glorious as it is important.

This is a club that was one of the founder members of the sport's first ever professional league in 1888. It was the FA Cup, however, that gave Rovers its first taste of silverware. In 1882, Blackburn became the first club from outside the south east to reach the FA Cup final, losing 1-0 to Old Etonians. It was disappointing for the estimated 900 or so fans who had made the journey south. Two special trains left the town in the early hours with one heading off the previous day. Rovers, a team that preferred to play on the ground, struggled with the direct tactics and the long-ball game of their southern opponents and were unable to recover from conceding a goal after eight minutes. It also didn't help that Old Etonians played in a similar top to Blackburn, who had been forced to change colours and found it difficult, at times, to stop passing to the opposition.

That disappointment spurred the club on and they were soon winning three consecutive cups at a time when many of the current giants at home and on the continent did not even exist. The first came on 29 March 1884 with a 2-1 win over Scottish outfit Queen's Park – the first from north of the border to reach the final, which was held at Kennington Oval in south London. The Scots had defeated Blackburn Olympic in the semi-final, depriving the country of an all-Blackburn final.

Olympic, the working-class team from the town as opposed to the ex-public schoolboys that had started Rovers, were the holders, becoming the first northern team to lift the trophy in 1883 with a 2-1 win over Old Etonians. They had also beaten Ruabon Druids, the top team in Wales, along the way – it was a fine run to the final. They may not have had the size of the players that the southern teams had but possessed speed and fitness and were perhaps the first English team to adopt the Scottish passing game. This was propelled by a diet of raw eggs, oysters, mutton and port but no beer. Blackburn was the prime mover in the English game becoming more northern and professional and there was some disquiet in the south when Olympic prepared for the 1883 final by heading to a Blackpool training camp. This was just not football and the Old Etonians complained as such after the final defeat. It is estimated that 8,000 turned out at the Oval, many wearing top hats and almost all supporting the Old Etonians, who were the holders. Olympic's time in the sun didn't last – they started to lose their best players to the Rovers, who were ready to dominate the competition – but they burned brightly and did much to end the early public school domination and ensure that professional football became a working man's game.

In 1884 there was pressure on the Rovers to replicate Olympic's win and there was pressure from elsewhere too. While the 1995 title may have been reasonably popular given the team that was being challenged – though more of that later – the 1884 FA Cup win was anything but. The whole debate about professionalism in football was in full swing. Rovers had Scottish players in their team and while it was hard to prove that payments were being made, the media was not happy. Neither were Notts County, who filed a complaint after John Inglis, a Scottish international, appeared in the Blackburn line-up in their 1-0 semi-final win over The Magpies.

The 1884 triumph was not only notable for the win over Queen's Park but the travelling fans. The *Pall Mall Gazette* reported ahead of the final that 'London witnessed an incursion of Northern Barbarians on Saturday – hot-blooded Lancastrians, sharp of tongue, rough and ready, of uncouth garb and speech. A tribe of Soudanese Arabs let loose in the Strand would not excite more amusement and curiosity. It was a sight not to be forgotten… strange oaths fell upon southern ears, and curious words, curious but expressive, filled the air.'

The Times focused more on the football. 'With such keenness had the contest been anticipated,' wrote the newspaper, 'that it attracted one of the largest gatherings ever seen at a football match in the south of England, it being estimated that there were between 10,000 and 12,000 spectators present.' The spring weather was perfect for a fast-paced game of football and the newspaper noted that the game kicked off at exactly 3.30pm. At four o'clock, Jimmy Douglas had put Rovers ahead. Jimmy Forrest (the first professional player to represent England) added a second not long after but Queen's Park came back into it with a goal from Robert Christie.

'After this double reverse, the Scotchmen played with increased vigour and a corner kick fell to them. This was well made and some pertinacious attacks in front of the posts ended in Christie's sending the ball under the crossbar.'

Rovers held out until half-time and started to get back on top in the second half, yet as the minutes passed by, Queen's Park threatened to equalise. 'The Rovers, who had for some time been content with playing an almost purely defensive game,' were hanging on until 'Time' was called. The 2-1 win was greeted with enthusiasm by the press as was some of the play. 'A noticeable feature of the game to southern players was the way in which both sides butted the ball,' *The Times* reported. 'This too, in no haphazard manner, as many times, it passed from the head of one player to another, and then on to a third.'

The same two teams met again in the following final when Blackburn ran out 2-0 winners. In 1886 (by this time professionalism had been legalised, with Rovers among the first to start paying players a total of £615 during the 1885/86 season) the Blues defeated West Bromwich Albion in a replay after the first game in Kennington ended goalless. The second game was played in Derby, where 12,000 turned up to see the holders win 2-0.

Just as a striker who grabs a hat-trick gets to keep the ball and a team that wins a trophy three times gets to keep it, there was thought to be a special benefit handed to Blackburn for being the only club to win the oldest cup competition in the world three times in a row. Many Rovers fans believed that the FA had allowed the club the unique honour of putting club crests on their corner flags as a reward for such an achievement. Some fans complained in 2009 when a televised game at Manchester United showed a cheeky red devil on the flags at Old Trafford. However, a spokesman at Ewood admitted that there didn't seem to be any evidence of any special right earned from the 19th century. The club did receive a specially made silver shield from the FA.

Rovers returned to the Oval in 1890 – the year they moved to Ewood Park – thrashing Sheffield Wednesday 6-1 in front of 20,000, with *The Times* noting just how good Rovers were (in particular William Townley, who became the first man to score a hat-trick in an FA Cup final) and how the game had become as important as an international fixture. There were 23,000 there the following year as Notts County were dispatched 3-1, with Townley on the scoresheet again. That was FA Cup win number five.

Founder members of the Football League in 1888, Rovers started to struggle a little as the new century approached and were saved from the drop in 1898 only because the division was expanded from 16 to 18 teams, thanks to a proposal from local rivals Burnley. Fortunes started to improve as a Blackburn-born businessman started to get involved with the club, much in the same way as they did decades later when Jack Walker took charge. The team became league champions in 1912 for the first time, helped by a solid defence.

Lawrence Cotton became chairman in 1905 and started to spend money on improving the stadium and, once that was looking exactly how he wanted, more funds went into the playing staff. In 1911 he spent £1,800, a British transfer record, on Jock Simpson, a winger from Falkirk and just one of many Scots that played a big part in the early success of the club.

In 1913, he broke the British transfer record again, paying £2,000 to West Ham United for Danny Shea. In February 1914, that record was broken once more as Percy Dawson headed south from Hearts for £2,500. At the time, the title was almost in the bag – Dawson was a signing for a future that never came. Once war broke out, the directors felt that the right thing to do was shut down and not try to encourage people to come and watch football. In 1917 Cotton also became the mayor of the town. He died four years later, two years after resigning as Rovers chairman.

There was one more trophy, a sixth FA Cup win in 1928 over the then-mighty Huddersfield. To say the Lancashire team were the underdog would be an understatement, as they kicked off on the back of six successive league losses, a run that included a loss to Huddersfield who were to finish second, ten places higher. However, a first trip to Wembley ended in a 3-1 win.

Relegation in 1948 spelled ten years of fighting to get back into the top tier and they were eventually successful in their endeavour in 1958. 'My first memory is the 1952 cup run, probably the last two games, West Brom and Burnley, fifth and sixth round at home,' said Colin Duerden, also my dad. 'Apparently I had been before but I have no memory and I probably remember those games because of the big crowds, 50,000 plus. I remember running on the pitch as Rovers scored, I think it was the third against Burnley, from the little benches that kids sat on around the pitch. Against West Brom, there was some dispute about the penalty and Bill Eckersley ended up telling the goalkeeper where he was going to send the penalty. He did but he still scored. I don't know if he did it every time, but he could really kick a ball.'

'I didn't go with my dad, he went with his mates, I went with my mum, grandad and uncle. After we would go back to my Grandma's for tea. She used to wait before cooking, so I was told, to find out how Rovers went on as we ate less if we lost. We got good crowds in cup matches, it was the big thing in football then, more than the league. Nobody ever remembered, well, not nobody, but kids like me knew all the cup winners for years but not the league champions. I think it was because the final was at Wembley and it was the only live game you ever saw if you didn't actually go to a game.

'I remember the players from then, 1952, better than those who came later. Reg Elvy was the goalkeeper, right-back was Ron Suart, who managed Chelsea later on. Ronnie Clayton must have been in the army, but I think he played in those games I watched. Then Will Kelly was centre-half, Jackie Campbell or Eric Bell would be left-half. Forwards would be Eddie Crossan and centre-forward, Bill Holmes, my favourite and an amateur. He scored important goals in that cup run. League games would be 20-odd thousand in the Second Division, not bad, as there wouldn't be many away fans.

'But the 50,000 fans for the cup games were packed in. I remember the Liverpool game later, in 1958 in the quarter-final, and I was sat in the Riverside with my mates by then. We used to get there early and have a kickabout and our shoes would be red from the cinder track around the pitch. We could see them swaying in the Blackburn End.' Promotion was finally achieved in 1958 with a nail-biting 4-3 win at Charlton.

'There were more than 50,000 at Charlton. My dad drove down with my mum too. We were behind the goal and Charlton scored first. They just needed a draw to go up, but we needed to win. Then Rovers scored four. [Peter] Dobing got two, [Bryan] Douglas and [Roy] Vernon [the others]. We were winning 4-1 until late on and then Charlton suddenly scored two. With about ten minutes left, we were hanging on and goalkeeper Harry Leyland made some good saves. There were no whistles for the referee to blow his whistle then, the game just finished. We had a good team, Douglas and Clayton went to the World Cup with England that year and Vernon went with Wales and they got to the quarter-final and lost to Brazil. Eckersley was still there. He used to have a sweet shop near Ewood and we would go about half past one to get some for the game and he was still serving then. Ninety minutes later and he was playing.'

The next sniff at major silverware came in 1960. The run to the final had been thrilling. Tottenham Hotspur, who finished third in the league, were defeated in the fifth round and then came a mighty tussle with eventual champions Burnley. Three goals down at Turf Moor, Blackburn equalised with the last kick of the game and won the replay in front of 53,839 – the last time there was a 50,000 crowd at Ewood. Sheffield Wednesday, who were to finish fifth, were downed in the semis thanks to a brace from Derek Dougan.

Wolves waited in the final, the team that had just been pipped to the title by Burnley. It was Blackburn's turn to try and ensure the Wanderers won nothing. It could be the reverse of the 1913/14 season when the league went to Ewood and the cup to the Clarets. The *Manchester Guardian* was looking forward to more Lancashire success. '… Thousands of partisans from Darwen to Dunnockshaw, and from Rishton to Rawtenstall will look to Blackburn Rovers to complete an East Lancashire double over the Midlands' club… If nothing else, there should be an interesting contrast in style – Wolverhampton's forthright, uncompromising methods against Blackburn's more delicate and more technically precise approach. The artisan opposed to the artist as it were…'

It was a disaster. Star striker Derek Dougan handed in a transfer request on the morning of the game and future Wigan Athletic chairman Dave Whelan broke his leg just before the break at a time when there were no substitutes. This came after Mick McGrath had scored an own goal. It ended 3-0 to

Wolves.

It took place 'in one of the quietest, most apathetic FA Cup finals Wembley has known', wrote Eric Todd in the *Guardian*. 'Wolverhampton Wanderers beat ten-man Blackburn Rovers 3-0 with a pitiless efficiency on Saturday.'

While the paper noted that Blackburn had fought well, and Douglas was clever and persevering, Dougan was 'anonymous in the clammy heat. Just once was Dougan recognisable as the character he is at Ewood Park. Bimpson was tackled in the penalty area and performed a most spectacular somersault. Whereupon Dougan glowered at him as much as to say "You're stealing my act."'

On Monday, FA secretary Sir Stanley Rous said in a radio interview that it was possible that substitutes would be allowed in the cup the following season. That was no consolation for the fans who had gone back to school and work.

The game was played in unusual heat. The media called it 'The white shirt final' as fans, who still dressed up for the occasion, removed their jackets. 'It was scorching and Rovers came out in tracksuits and nobody could believe it,' my dad said. 'I remember the disappointment and it was basically a non-event. I remember thinking "I wished I had stayed at home and watched it on the telly". They started coverage at nine in the morning on the BBC and it was a good day. I remember before my dad got his ticket, I told him he could have mine and that I would watch on telly. He said "No, you might never see it again". He was right.'

The FA Cup final was a low point. Worse than defeat, in the long run at least, was that many fans were very upset with how the club's allocation of just 15,000 was allocated. Instead of having supporters queue outside the ground for their tickets, usually how it was done then, they did it via a lottery system. The accusations that Blackburn's players had been taking advantage of the scarcity and had been making a killing by selling their own tickets did not improve their moods. This caused a rift between some supporters and the club and even 20 years later there were plenty in the town who said they had never again been to a game after events of 1960. It is impossible to know how many used it as an excuse as the years passed but numbers certainly dipped after: from an average attendance of 27,299 in 1960 with a 17th place finish to 19,344 the following year despite taking eighth spot. Blackburn folk sometimes may forgive but never forget.

'If you went through Woolworths, Rovers had a stall, just for the cup final,' dad said. 'Players were selling stuff but I don't know if they were selling tickets, but we were only allowed 15,000 tickets. Those were sold in a raffle; you applied for a ticket. Most games, you had to queue. I got one, my mum got one but my dad didn't. He got one from somewhere eventually. There was a lot of talk about the players selling tickets. I don't know if they did, but my dad stopped going after the cup final, never went again.'

That was as good as it got for some time. The start of the 1965/66 season was as bad as it could get. A polio epidemic in the town meant that the Rovers couldn't play home or away and were bottom of the table before they had even kicked a ball. 'I was working in Preston then and couldn't go but the company had an office in Blackburn that I went to,' my dad recalled. 'Other teams had played three or four games before Rovers started. But Douglas was injured most of the season and that was the real problem.'

They never really looked like staying up and relegation was confirmed long before the end. The summer of 1966 may have been a special one for English football but in Blackburn it meant that the club was facing life outside the top tier for just the thirteenth season in history.

Things got worse in 1971 as the Blues dropped down to the third tier for the first time ever. Back in the Second Division in 1975, manager Gordon Lee was snatched by Newcastle. Jim Smith came in until leaving for Birmingham and the top flight in March 1978. A year later and Rovers were heading down again.

After the Kendall years, the next boss to arrive at Ewood Park, in the summer of 1981, was Bobby Saxton, who had been managing Plymouth Argyle. 'Nobody, and I mean nobody, had heard of Bobby Saxton,' said Garner, yet the Yorkshireman was to stay at Ewood until Christmas 1986. Perhaps best-known in the football world as the sweary second in command to Peter Reid at Sunderland, wonderfully captured by the 1997 documentary *Premier Passions*, Saxton was popular with the players and, initially at least, with the fans.

Saxton replaced Jim Arnold, who followed Howard Kendall to Goodison, with the popular and long-serving Terry Gennoe from Southampton, who played against Nottingham Forest in the 1978 League Cup final and went on to play 289 league games for Blackburn. 'There was always such a fantastic team spirit,' Gennoe told the *Lancashire Evening Telegraph* in May 2015. 'For example, at the end of my first season the then chairman Bill Fox sat us all down in the changing room and said, "Listen lads, I can't afford to give anybody a rise, so if any of you want to get up and leave this club now, then you can do it." But not one player left. That's what it was like. The team spirit was fantastic.'

Money really was tight, said the goalkeeper. 'I remember when we had to sell a player to pay the electricity bill because we couldn't put on a floodlit game. The player we sold was Kevin Stonehouse, to Huddersfield Town, for about £30,000.'

Saxton's first season went well until the wheels fell off and the club slipped down to tenth. The following season was a much more boring eleventh. The 1983/84 campaign was better, with the emerging Simon Barker a highlight in midfield, but the club finished poorly and let any chance of promotion slip, eventually finishing sixth. The following year was closer as the Blues ended in fifth, just a point off promotion. At Christmas, Rovers were clear at the top but again, without the funds to strengthen a stretched squad for the final push, the tumble down the places came. This time, however, there was still a chance of a final day miracle. All that was needed was three points against already-relegated Wolves and for Manchester City and Portsmouth to lose. According to Garner, Wolves boss Tommy Docherty offered Blackburn's players some encouragement in the build-up, informing them that his team was 'crap' as he sat in on their pre-match team talk. Rovers did their bit, securing a 3-0 win, but City and Portsmouth secured equally comfortable victories.

Rovers were becoming the nearly-men. Fans in the town complained that the powers-that-be at the club didn't actually want promotion and ensured that there was enough to get the fans excited and attending, but not enough to actually go up and start having to buy expensive players and pay bigger wages. As conspiracy theories go it wasn't the most exciting, but it was to resurface again.

Whether or not there was quite enough in the squad to achieve promotion ceased to be a question in the 1985/86 campaign as Rovers finished just one place above the relegation zone, only securing safety after victory against Grimsby on the final day. The next season wasn't much better and after a poor run up to Christmas, Saxton was fired, despite the fact that every player signed a petition demanding he stay.

'...We had such respect for the manager, Bob Saxton,' said Garner. 'He did a fantastic job because he didn't have anything to work with whatsoever. He understood the players and he got really close to them. Times were different then. He'd play cards with us and have cans of beer with us on the way back from away games. Sometimes we lost and sometimes we won but it was always a positive mood. Even if we'd lost, we'd always get something out of it, and put things right the next time. So I was absolutely heartbroken for Bob when he was sacked.'

After a short spell under the guidance of Tony Parkes who was to become the 'eternal caretaker' on 3 February 1987, in came Don Mackay, former coach of Dundee and Coventry, who arrived at Blackburn from his role on the coaching staff at Glasgow Rangers under Graeme Souness. His coaching record was modest but he was brasher and more media friendly than Saxton who was shouty behind the scenes perhaps but quiet in front. 'He understood my position because he'd been a goalkeeper himself,' said Gennoe. 'You couldn't get a word in edgeways with Don. I remember one training session, when we went through the whole of the set-plays, I swear we were out there for three hours. But he was passionate, and he did take the club very close.'

One of the gifts Saxton left for Mackay was the very talented left-sided midfielder, Scott Sellars. 'I signed from Leeds and was bought by Bobby,' remembers Sellars. 'Everyone at the club respected him as a manager and a coach. As a young player I knew about Blackburn. They were always well-organised and perhaps had overachieved in many ways. I had been at Leeds and Billy Bremner came in as manager and I just didn't seem to be in the picture. My contract was up and Bobby came in for me. Blackburn had some success in Division Two and I thought it would be a good team and a good move for me. The first season was a struggle. The team was aging a bit and he was bringing in some younger players. The season did not start well and he was sacked. In came Don, who was a very different character.'

The Scot breathed new life into the club. 'My situation was that I had been manager at Coventry and I wanted to do one or two things there and wasn't allowed to,' Mackay said. 'I lost my job and went to Rangers to work with Graeme Souness. Then I had two interviews at Blackburn and they seemed to be impressed and I got the job.

'They were very down at the time; the team were erratic. Bobby Saxton had done a good job. Blackburn had always had problems and always will – until Jack Walker came in – in that you have Burnley, Preston, Bolton and Blackpool, so many teams close by. That is before you even get to the Manchester clubs and Liverpool. The finances would never be strong enough to bring in players. The only way to move forward is with youth and developing players, bringing through your own talent. I was very fortunate in that Jim Furnell was there and did a great job with the youth team and brought through players like Jason Wilcox. I believe this is still the way forward for Rovers.'

There wasn't much money to spend. 'We paid £28,000 for Colin Hendry. I had worked with him and he was a striker. He was a good striker but was never going to be European-class and so we moved him back to centre-half. He wasn't happy at first but then the whole thing changed.'

That was in the future. Mackay was helped immensely by the 1987 Full Members Cup, a short-lived competition introduced for teams in the top two divisions. By the time he arrived, Rovers were already in the last eight and he took full advantage of the opportunity. After a 3-0 win over Chelsea and then the same scoreline over Ipswich in the semi-final, the town was looking forward to a first Wembley appearance in 27 years. Out of a crowd of not much more than 40,000, Rovers took over 28,000, leaving behind a ghost town.

'The thing that shattered me was the number of people that we took there,' said Mackay. 'Charlton were a Division One side from London and they had a third of the crowd that day. So many people wanted to go to that game as it was Wembley and it was Blackburn. It amazed me and started me to think that maybe we could move things forward a little more.'

The Full Members Cup final appearance in March 1987 was a respite from the relegation battle in the league, although the national media pointed out that the game with Charlton was going to produce a smaller crowd and gate receipts than the previous and inaugural final between Manchester City and

Chelsea (it is interesting when looking back at old newspapers how often gate receipts were mentioned in the past). Both the Addicks and the Rovers were fighting relegation from their respective divisions of one and two. It was noted that Blackburn could become the first team ever to win a Wembley final and also be relegated from the Second Division.

What had started as a distraction from the relegation battle ended up being something special, though the game was anything but, with *The Times* noting that the pre-match five a side games outside the stadium were of a higher quality.

The much-maligned goalkeeper Vince O'Keefe had a blinder and new boy Colin Hendry half-volleyed home an Ian 'Windy' Miller cross with just minutes left. 'I have already achieved my ambition, to score the winning goal at a cup final at Wembley,' the then 21-year-old told local television.

With Rovers pulling away from the bottom of the Second Division, the season was deemed a success and with the addition of Hendry adding to the craft of Sellars and the attacking ambitions of right-back Chris Price, hopes were high that the next season would be better.

It was. For Rovers fans it would be perhaps the most exciting of the decade. After a 2-0 loss to Middlesbrough at the end of September, the club had just eleven points from the first ten games – though a 1-1 draw at home to Liverpool in the League Cup was a pleasant sideshow – but big things were on the horizon.

5

ARCHIBALD AND ARDILES

'Barcelona wasn't my culture – Blackburn was.'

STEVE ARCHIBALD

IN THE MID-EIGHTIES, THE RIVERSIDE, THE STAND THAT runs along the side of the pitch and which used to be, until recently, the one facing television cameras and the players' tunnel, was found to be structurally unsafe, with foundations that had seen better days and a roof that could present a danger in high winds. Walkersteel provided the materials to build a new 5,000-seater stand.

Its proprietor, Jack Walker, was soon getting a little more involved. Mackay wasn't the only one impressed and enthused by how the fans took to the Full Members' Cup. With Bill Fox whispering in the steel magnate's ear, there was soon a little more cash coming in and a lot more excitement.

On 30 September 1987, Rovers drew 1-1 at Aston Villa to go on an unbeaten run in the league that was to stretch for 23 games. Just before Christmas, the club went and signed a player from Barcelona who had been playing at the World Cup the year before.

Steve Archibald had replaced Diego Maradona at Barcelona after leaving Tottenham in 1984, but while he eventually won over fans at the Nou Camp, by the end of 1987 the Scot had not played for six months. Manchester United had been sniffing around but were caught unawares by Rovers. Instead of sitting and waiting for a call from Spain, Rovers tried a different tactic.

'What we did,' said club secretary John Haworth, 'was to get off our backsides and go.' The deal was for six months, from just before Christmas to the end of the 1987/88 season. 'If anything goes wrong at the Barcelona end and they suddenly want him back,' added Haworth, 'then he can go back with seven days' notice.' Haworth asked the fans to get behind the club. 'Blackburn have shown the public they are willing to have a go. To get him under the noses of big clubs – especially Manchester United – is tremendous. We've got some good press today and the town is buzzing.'

Archibald was quietly pleased too and obviously has happy memories of his time in the town. 'Don Mackay had called me because I had been injured,' the Scot said. 'At the time only two foreigners were allowed to play in the team [in the Spanish league] and they had bought someone else. So while I was waiting in recovery and seeing where that would lead, he was on the phone and then came over to see me and watch me train. We had a chat and he was a really good man. Since I wasn't going to play, I decided to go on loan.'

Mackay's attitude was one of 'if you don't ask, you don't get'. 'I knew Steve from a distance and I don't think he was ever happy in Spain,' he recalled. 'Of course, they were a very ambitious club and if you didn't get in the team then it could be hard. I talked to Bill Fox and he said that we should try, and John Haworth and I went over there and talked to the board and Steve. We brought Steve over and he had a look and he wanted to come and play regular football. They put a price on him, but we said they would just take over his contract..." There were some complications but it was all worked out.

Archibald was impressed with his visitors. 'I wasn't really entertaining anything else and Don was nothing if not persistent and he actually came to

Spain. He does not let go until it can't be done. He's a persistent guy. I liked what he was saying, and he told me about Jack Walker in the background at the club and the plans that were in place to make it a big club. Without that kind of ambition then I wouldn't have gone.'

You can see videos of Archibald talking to media about the move at the time. The first and most obvious question was what the hell was he thinking?

'I could have easily stayed in Barcelona, made more money and stayed in the sunshine and had an easy life,' he told local television at a wet Ewood Park in 1987 with the voiceover questioning his mental health.

Three decades on and living in Spain, he is of the same opinion. 'It wasn't strange at all and there was no culture shock. I wasn't born in Barcelona; I played for Clyde and Aberdeen. This was my culture, Blackburn was my culture and as a club it was similar to Aberdeen, friendly and homely.'

The tabloids claimed he was being paid £6,000 a week. Mackay was quick to dismiss such talk amid concerns it would upset the other players, who were after all, doing a pretty good job. 'I don't know where they get their prices from,' he told local media and then added with a smile, 'there's no way anyone gets half as much as I am getting every week! It is a gamble in terms of the other players, but it may lift the lads.' It did. 'One of the lads said after his first game against Birmingham City that "I don't care if he is on ten grand a week if he plays like that, we'll win the league."'

Sellars was also happy to see the star arrive. 'There was no bad feeling at all and no truth in that but of course, we were all shocked. He was at Barcelona. You just didn't expect a player to come on loan from Barcelona to Blackburn. When you are playing and he comes from Barca than you expect him to be getting paid more than people at Blackburn, a club without much money in the Second Division. There was no surprise or anger. I wanted him to make us a better team and he did that. He worked hard and helped us a lot.'

'Archibald had a great influence on the team and on me. He was a great player and a good goalscorer. It was really helpful to me as a young player. The difference, I felt, was his movement and his awareness, the timing of the runs and all the little details that made him a top player. When I got the ball on the left, the first thing I did was to look up for the striker and he made that job easier.'

Rovers were going well before Archibald arrived, but with him they were soon flying. The high point came on 20 February as Aston Villa came to Ewood as second hosted first. With the Riverside stand being redeveloped as an all-seater, there were just three sides open and the club got special permission to admit 17,000 on a wet and windy afternoon. Garner scored one and made one of Archibald's brace to give Rovers a thrilling 3-2 win (David Platt scored one for the visitors) to send the team top. It was a 22nd league game unbeaten and there was genuine excitement around the town.

'Blackburn fans still send me clips of that game on Twitter and I have seen it on YouTube,' said Archibald. 'That was a good game, full of pace and skill and it was all quite hectic. Winning that gave us some belief and I think I scored twice. It was a great atmosphere. It could easily have been a game in the First Division. There was a good team then at Blackburn, Don had them working well. They were lacking in a couple of areas such as scoring goals and I tried to help. Garner was a good goalscorer and we worked well together. There was a good goalkeeper and then we had a pair of good midfielders, Simon Barker and Scott Sellars.'

'Villa were a big club in the league at that time,' said Sellars. 'We had been on a run of 20-odd games unbeaten. It was probably about that time when I established myself as a player and it was an enjoyable time.'

There was a six-point cushion above Middlesbrough in third, and only the top two went up automatically due to the new play-off system. A draw at Leeds took the run to 23 games but then came defeat at Stoke. The gap above third was now only four points with ten games left and things were getting tense.

There was more stunning news to come, however. Not long after Archibald arrived, Mackay was soon telling media that he was interested in a loan deal for Ian Rush, then with Juventus. 'The standing joke in Blackburn is that Maradona is next on the list,' Mackay said. 'But that's too much – even for me.'

Yet it was another Argentinian World Cup winner who arrived on the last day of the season that teams could sign players. The same day that Julian Dicks went from Birmingham City to West Ham United, in came Ossie Ardiles from Spurs.

Rovers called Ardiles in the morning but while the midfielder was interested in the prospect, he missed a flight to Manchester and only arrived at 4.05pm, 55 minutes before the transfer deadline closed. A quick trip to use the fax machine – 'facsimile equipment' as the press at the time put it – at Old Trafford and the player was registered.

'Apparently I'm not in Spurs' future plans and when this chance came along I jumped at it, though I think it is no secret I wanted to stay at White Hart Lane,' Ardiles said as he arrived at Ewood. 'It could be good for me. I came for the opportunity.'

The heads-up and the recommendation came from Archibald, a former teammate. 'As I said, we had a good team at the time, but we were lacking in a couple of areas and we needed some creativity and we were lacking experience in the middle of the park. There was a good combination of skill and vision and there were hard workers in there too. Ossie was a perfect piece of the jigsaw. He wouldn't have come if it wasn't for me, there is no two ways about it.'

Fans were starting to believe. 'We have shown the Blackburn public that we are determined to get promotion,' Mackay said with his team second in the table with eight games remaining. 'I felt Ardiles could be the final piece in the promotion jigsaw.' One attraction was the fact that it was a loan deal and therefore cost nothing, though the feeling was at the time that Ardiles would join the club permanently at the end of the season. 'I could have gone for a lesser-known player and been faced with finding the sort of money that we just don't have,' Mackay said. 'Regardless of age, he is still a very good player who we couldn't possibly afford to buy. But if we do get promoted I can sit down and think about a transfer. Without the First Division, we couldn't finance it.'

Ardiles confessed that he had never seen the team play and he may well have been unaware of life in the lower leagues. 'Ossie Ardiles coming was surreal,' recalls Sellars. 'He had won the World Cup. He was a fantastic guy and we brought him in to help us and to calm things down a little bit. He was a great player. I think the problem was the size of the squad. We didn't have the biggest squad and often played the same team. We also weren't used to being in that situation. So it was great to see Ossie arrive but he soon got injured.'

It was his first game at Plymouth Argyle in fact and he was crocked by local hard man Nicky Marker, an apt name for a player who was later signed by Kenny Dalglish to become a squad player in the early Premier League years, on the stroke of half-time. 'To watch Ossie Ardiles hobble painfully across the Plymouth car park was possibly the saddest sight in sport this weekend,' declared one national newspaper.

Talking to Marker, 30 years after the tackle, he gives the impression that he is tired of being asked about it. 'We all knew it was a big game publicity-wise and he was coming to Home Park and everyone was excited to see him,' he said in a soft Devon burr. 'From what I remember, it just came out of the blue and we found out pretty much the day before. We all wanted to play against him. There was a buzz around the ground.'

The crowd of over 12,000 was a bumper one for the Pilgrims that season. 'I was young and I just wanted to go out and play my best and while we all knew that Ardiles was playing, once the game starts you forget all that and just want to do well.'

The challenge against the 1978 World Cup winner was a hard one but Marker, then just 22, insists that there was no malice, though admits that the two-footed tackle may have looked bad. Mackay said after the game that it was the worst tackle he had ever seen. The belief now seems to be that Ardiles suffered a broken leg, which is not true. He was back in action just two weeks later. That made his marker feel better.

'I got a lot of stick for the challenge after the game but as I pointed out to everyone, we got a throw-in out of it. The referee did not even give a free-kick never mind a yellow or red card. It wasn't a bad challenge. You don't go out to hurt someone. I must have gone in wrong but as you get older, it is harder to shake it off and maybe that is what happened to him. I didn't go out to sort him out. I loved playing in the FA Cup as you like to play against the big players in the big teams. Ardiles had been playing for one of the best teams in the world, had won the World Cup and was world-class. It was brilliant to see him and that game, he brought people to the ground and there was a different atmosphere and it made the game. It is remembered for the wrong thing, however.'

After the game, Marker's comments to the media upset many: 'It was nice to see him go off,' was his reaction. 'He was the playmaker, the man we were most worried about. Ardiles is going to be hounded for the rest of the season. In the First Division, he was just one of so many good players but he will probably get more stick as a class player in the second.

He regrets what happened now. 'I got a lot of bad press from the likes of the *Sun*. I was only a young lad. I was asked how I felt when he didn't come out for the second half. I was asked a question and I replied that it was good for us because he was such a good player and it gave us a better chance of winning, but it was quoted out of context.'

The headlines focused on how the young rough and ready English defender was happy that he had crocked one of the classiest players around. 'I didn't mean it in the way that I was happy he was injured. I was a bit naive at the time I guess. I was taken aback by the whole thing. The FA made inquiries. It wasn't nice.'

There was certainly a view that Ardiles had been nobbled and Archibald had a pretty good view of what happened. 'I was right there next to it, I saw it. It wasn't an accident.' Even three decades later there is an edge in his voice, anger creeping in. 'It was a typical idiotic challenge from an idiot who was trying to make a name for himself. He knew what he was doing. It was a terrible tackle.'

'Ossie had a fracture in a bone in his knee. He tried to play on. It was his first game and he didn't want to let anyone down but there was no way he could continue.'

The game was a disaster as Rovers fell to a 3-0 defeat at Home Park, comfortable losers of what was, according to the *Guardian*, 'a guileless, wind-affected affair that exposed the shortcomings of the team with centre-backs Hendry and David Mail as mobile as pantomime horses'. Defeat on Good Friday to Oldham Athletic and an incredibly frustrating 2-2 draw at home to Shrewsbury Town on Easter Monday meant that Rovers dropped out of the promotion places.

Such form just when the top tier was in reach revived the old theories among many fans that Rovers didn't actually want to go up. The club was happy to flirt with the First Division but didn't want the expense of having to get ready for a series of dates with the biggest and best in the land. It never really made sense, but on the way out of Ewood after more points dropped, it was a common refrain.

'We heard that,' Sellars said. 'It was said a lot. I never felt that as a football club that we didn't want to go up. We are a bunch of players and we want to play at the highest level possible. The benefits of going up were massive for the players too; we wanted to be successful. I saw the difference coming from Leeds. Everything there was in place from the Revie days, such as the training ground. It was a massive club but at Blackburn we trained in the park and there was nothing to eat after training. You just sorted yourself out, went and bought a sandwich or something. You just have to get on with it really but getting in Archibald and Ardiles in, that showed real desire. If that didn't show that the club didn't want to go up, what would?'

Still, the lack of money did have its benefits. 'Blackburn was a close-knit club, with the fans, the directors and it was very different to what I had been used to. That could be difficult at times as everyone knew everyone else but if the directors had a spare tenner in their pocket, they would give you a tenner. This never happened at other clubs. There was a real homeliness at Blackburn that I never experienced elsewhere. We all wanted to do well for ourselves, each other, everyone at the club and the fans.'

Only a final game 4-1 win at already-promoted Millwall, which included a scary pitch invasion by home fans celebrating their rise to the top, earned entry to the play-offs, only the second year these games had been in effect.

For Archibald, the injury to Ardiles was the difference between making the play-offs and going up automatically. 'If Ossie had been fit and played in all of the games then we would have gone up. I have no doubt about that. We were on the up and up. The players had a great work ethic and there was an excellent manager who could motivate players. Jack Walker was there and Don realised that there was something special there too. It would have been a dream come true for Don and everyone.

'In football you need a quality squad and a quality team. We were a couple of players short at crucial times. Ossie getting injured was deflating for everyone. You could see him in training and he was great. It gave everyone a lift and the players were really looking forward to working with him. It was a big blow when he was out. It was not just his skill and his ability to make things happen but the fact that he worked his socks off and was always helping out in defence. People didn't realise this about him. He was a dream to play with and a real example to others.

'We had quality and we were motivated and there was just a lack of experience. If you don't have winning experience or mentality because you have never won anything then it is tough. The younger players didn't know how to force it through. It is not easy. When you are going great then all is fine but then the goals stop and then the doubts start. And you have to somehow force a result but if you don't have the right kind of experience in the team, it is tough. It is not easy to win things.'

If Rovers had gone up, then it is possible that both Archibald and Ardiles could have stayed. 'You never know,' said the Scot. 'If Jack Walker had come in properly – and we had seen the plans – then it was possible. But once it didn't happen then there was never any possibility. The deal was for six months and that was it.'

'Walker was in the background. If he had come in at the beginning of the season and spent some money, then maybe it would have been different. In the end though, it is down to the players. There was disappointment of course but I loved my time at Blackburn. I especially remember the fans and they were great to me and really took me in as one of them. Coming from Barcelona to Blackburn, the culture was not a problem, but I did have to change my mindset and the fans were brilliant. Don was brilliant. Blackburn was brilliant.'

There were still the play-offs, a new innovation that had yet to scar the club. Yet the first game against Chelsea, when the third-lowest team from the top tier was involved, was depressing.

The ground was full to 16,500 capacity, with the side stand still not finished. The nationals noted that 'Freebie Hill' contained half of the town too. This grassy bank, part of the 'lost world' as we called it as kids, long overlooked much of the pitch and there were always a few people on here, even back when there was plenty of space on the terraces. The new stadium with its taller stands put paid to most of the view, though the events against Chelsea were painful to watch even for those who had not paid to do so.

Rovers were a little unlucky and should have had a penalty when Garner was fouled in the area by Colin Pates while chasing one of a number of fine passes from Sellars. The injured Archibald was missed. Chelsea were also missing players, and had won only one of the past 26, but started to play.

The *Guardian* noted that the two teams looked to be exactly what they were: Chelsea a poor First Division side and Rovers a reasonably good one from the second. However, soon enough Chelsea's top-flight quality proved telling, as Gordon Durie curled home the opener past Gennoe.

Then David Mail's mistake fed Pat Nevin, who made it 2-0, and that seemed to be that. The second leg three days later ended 4-1 to the Londoners and while Rovers, who were able to start Archibald and Ardiles, had some good moments, the 6-1 aggregate thrashing ended what had been such a promising season on a real low and revealed just how far away Rovers were.

That seemed to be the end of something. The two high-profile loan stars went their own way. Simon Barker joined QPR for £400,000, which seemed like a huge deal at the time, while popular right-back Chris Price joined Aston Villa, who may have lost the battle of Ewood but won the war of promotion, for £150,000. 'It was just one of those things,' said Archibald. 'As I said, with promotion it may have been different.'

If the replacements were not exactly at the same level, it didn't seem to matter at first. The opening game of the 1988/89 season was back at Stamford Bridge. Chelsea had lost out to Middlesbrough in the play-off final and were relegated. Blackburn went and won 2-1 and then took 16 points from the first six games to go top. Still in pole position at Christmas, surely the experience of the previous season would stand the team in good stead. Alas, it was not to be and before long, Rovers had slipped out of the top two as Chelsea went on to dominate the league, finishing with 99 points, 17 ahead of Manchester City in second.

Rovers finished fifth to earn another play-off tie, this time against Watford. The first leg at home ended goalless and I remember going down for the second the day before a GCSE exam. Garner scored in the first minute and then Rovers tried to hang on. Watford equalised but the away goal rule meant, that after 120 minutes of nerves and defending, a first play-off final awaited.

At home to Crystal Palace (play-off finals were two legs just like semi-finals at this stage), it looked as if 23 years of hurt were coming to an end. 'Blackburn on the Brink' read the headlines after a 3-1 home win. Howard Gayle, one time of Liverpool, scored twice in the first half and all seemed well. But in the second half, he missed a penalty that would surely have been enough and not long before the end, Eddie McGoldrick bundled one in for Palace. There was still time for Garner to give the Rovers a two-goal cushion ahead of the second leg.

3 June 1989 is a day that will long live in infamy for Rovers fans. My second eldest brother went and still has trouble talking about it. At Selhurst Park, the yellows missed an early chance to perhaps take control of the tie, or at least depress the home fans, but soon Ian Wright opened the scoring at a crammed stadium. Early in the second-half the Eagles scored a penalty and in extra time Wright grabbed a third to secure a 4-3 win on aggregate. Rovers had their chances but it was backs to the wall stuff for most of the game, and the fans never forgave referee George Courtney for giving that penalty for a foul that took place outside the area. What also annoyed the Rovers faithful was that before the game was over a sizeable number of Palace fans had already left their seats and climbed over the hoardings to stand on the touchline in preparation for a full-time pitch invasion. Rovers players were taking throw-ins surrounded by home fans.

'That [penalty] made it 2-0, they got the third in extra-time, and I can just remember their fans being on the pitch, stood around me in the penalty box, and the referee allowing the game to go on,' said Sellars. 'And that was the reason why, or one of the reasons why, it was decided the final would, in the future, be a one-off game at Wembley. It was very hard to swallow.'

'Glad All Over', Palace's song, rang out on the tannoy, a tune that still gives Rovers fans of a certain vintage the shudders.

'That was heartbreaking,' said Gennoe. 'We were 3-1 up from the first leg at Ewood and Ian Miller had a great chance early on in the second leg. If he would have put that away it would have been 4-1 and game over. 'The referee that night had a horrendous game. When we were losing 1-0 he gave a penalty to Palace. I still don't know how he gave it. Mark Atkins was running out of the box and a Crystal Palace player [Eddie McGoldrick] just collided with him and the referee gave a penalty even though the ball was nowhere near them. It was a horrendous decision.'

'At the home game, we played well,' said Sellars. 'We knew that Wright and Bright were a handful and we had to be right on them from the start. I watched the game back recently. Gennoe was beaten up and not given any protection. We had chances. The first game we were excellent, but they got the away goal. Selhurst Park is never easy and I never enjoyed playing there. It was hostile and they were really up for it.

Mackay was not too surprised at what happened.

'It was like a death in the family, seriously. I almost packed it in. I was so broken-hearted. It was a dangerous scoreline from the first leg and I tried to warn the lads, but we just did not play that day. You can't blame anyone. We did everything right in preparation, but it was never a penalty kick. Later I worked for Arsenal, scouting for Arsene Wenger. Ian Wright always admitted that it wasn't a penalty kick. He knew. Rovers fans knew too. The next season they never chanted "Who is the bastard in the black" at the referee but "Are you Courtney in disguise?" It was hard to take though as we were so close. If we had not conceded the goal near the end of the first leg and had we got a decision or two at Palace then things would have been very different.'

Atkins was also devastated but prefers now to look back on the positives. 'The first season I was at Blackburn we got to the play-offs and we got to the final. We were 3-1 up and missed a penalty at the end. We went down there fully expecting to get to the First Division.' The penalty decision gave Palace the edge. 'Somebody just ran in front of me. I tried to stop and he went down. It was never a penalty. With hindsight, it was the right thing to happen as we were nowhere near ready for the First Division. There was no money to buy anyone and it could have been painful.'

But Mackay was desperate. 'In hindsight, I should have left after Crystal Palace. It would have made me a better manager. But Bill Fox wasn't having it. We went and beat Burnley 3-0 in the Lancashire Cup and he offered me a three-year contract. He said he was shitting himself in case we scored a fourth and he had to offer me another year. They were loyal to me and so I was to them.'

6

WALKER IN, MACKAY OUT

'Finally we had money but spending it wasn't easy.'

DON MACKAY

THE FOLLOWING SEASON SAW ANOTHER FIFTH-PLACE finish and another play-off ordeal, though this was a season that lacked some of the excitement of previous campaigns. Unusually, Mackay's men were stronger in the second half of the season than the first. The play-off semi-final came against Swindon Town. The team coached by Ossie Ardiles won 2-1 at Ewood and then did the same at home. Swindon would go on to beat Sunderland 1-0 in the final but were later denied promotion and demoted to the Third Division after admitting 36 charges of breaching league rules, 35 of which were due to illegal payments made to players. Some felt that as Swindon were not allowed to be promoted that the final should be replayed between Rovers and Sunderland, but that was about as likely as the Blues being champions of England just five years later. The result was that once again, Rovers players had to clear the pitch as home fans celebrated a famous victory. The play-offs really were becoming a pain.

There were no such worries the following season as Rovers spent pretty much all of it battling against the drop to the Third Division. It was notable mostly for the signings that were made during the course of it, signings that suggested that after years of austerity, there was a little more cash floating around behind the scenes.

The first hints to those outside that the club had a little more money than in the past came in December 1990. Mimms had been to Ewood before, on loan from Everton when he played six games in 1987, just a few months after he had understudied for Neville Southall in the 1986 FA Cup final against Liverpool. At the age of 22 he had been the youngest player on that Wembley pitch and acquitted himself well despite ending on the losing side. 'It was a great experience. I had come from Rotherham to Everton and they had just won the league and the Cup Winners' Cup. They were a great side, dominant at the time along with Liverpool and that final was something I will never forget.'

Just after Christmas Mimms arrived to fill a hole at Ewood Park. The number one had been one of the first signings made by Terry Venables at Spurs, joining from Everton and playing 37 games that included a number of high-profile errors. Mimms had become, wrote Steve Curry at the *Express*, an albatross around El Tel's neck. At the time, Tottenham were not exactly the most defensively solid team but Mimms looked nervous from the start. Clive Tyldesley talked to Mimms just after his move to Blackburn for television show *Saint & Greavsie* ahead of the Liverpool FA Cup game on 5 January 1990.

'There was no hiding place,' Mimms said. 'Nobody around was confident enough to take some of the pressure off me. I was that busy and every little mistake was highlighted.'

'I think the television cameras made sure of that,' said Tyldesley cheerfully. 'You seemed to make your worst mistakes in front of us.'

'That's the problem,' Mimms replied. 'It was more difficult as every time I turned the telly on, it was on the news.'

Such mistakes obviously didn't help but he took the flak for others' failings as well as his own, and so when he was offered an escape at Ewood he took it.

'It was fair to say that I was having a bad time,' he recalled. 'I was the first to admit that I found it difficult down there. It started okay but then I made a couple of mistakes. In hindsight I should have been sent out of the team a lot earlier, but the manager didn't love the number two so I was left there to sink or swim and I went under a little. I got going again but when I got the chance to go somewhere full-time, I jumped at it. I wasn't having a great time and Blackburn had just missed out on the play-offs again. It was a good team I was going to, but I didn't know that Jack Walker was hanging around behind the scenes.'

Tottenham were going through a time of transition themselves with new stars such as Paul Stewart and Paul Gascoigne signing for big money. 'It was more a problem with settling in at the club. It was just a different environment to Everton. Everton was a really tight club then I went to Spurs, which was a bit cliquey. There were different groups: the older pros, the foreign pros, a number of young lads coming up through the ranks and then players that Terry Venables had brought in, like me. So the dressing room was not that tight and I always felt that the Tottenham fans wanted a bit of the players which was something I didn't enjoy.'

Rovers paid £250,000, a sizable sum. Much of the reporting was on Mimms and the end of his time at Tottenham, understandably so, as he was heading to a club struggling in the second tier. Few wondered why or how Blackburn Rovers, a club that had never had much money, were splashing out a cool quarter of a million.

'I didn't know the amount. Spurs just told me that I could go. I was on the transfer list, so I used to go and see the boss every day to see if there was any news or interest but the one day I didn't, Terry called me in. He just said that we have accepted a bid for you and asked me if I knew who it was from. Perhaps he was trying to find out if I had been tapped up, but I had no idea. So he said Blackburn. I missed the flight to Manchester and had to go to Leeds/ Bradford. Maybe it was harder for me settling at Spurs being a northerner. We really enjoyed where we lived, my second son was born there, but perhaps it is because everyone is running around trying to pay off their massive mortgages, but nobody has time for anyone. I found it difficult from that side and found the people different.

'A day or two later, I was driving across the top of Blackburn and I could see a steam train chugging on the line that runs behind the Riverside stand (the now smallest and oldest stand at Ewood but brand new at the time). I remember that I thought at the moment "I am back in the north". It was a nice feeling. I had always felt part of the club from when I was on loan to when I eventually left.'

Mimms had been signed to replace Gennoe. The old legend was not far from his 40th birthday and played his last and 334th game for the club on the opening day of the 1990/91 season. The likes of Darren Collier and Mark Grew did not seem to the be answer. Mimms was. Don Mackay, a former goalkeeper himself, was a perfect boss for the new arrival, blaming his past troubles on the media and the Tottenham fans. Blackburn's new number one was ready to show what he could do.

'As a player, you don't think too much about that the size of the fee. I was just happy to be at a club that wanted me. When I did find out about the amount, I did wonder where it had come from. It was rumoured that Jack Walker had put the money in. Just three weeks later Steve Livingstone and Tony Dobson came in for quite a lot of money and that was publicised.'

On 16 January, the *Lancashire Evening Telegraph* displayed an unlikely back page headline. 'Rovers in £¾ million double swoop.' The report continued: 'Blackburn Rovers look set to make a sensational double transfer swoop by signing striker Steve Livingstone and defender Tony Dobson from First Division Coventry city for a total outlay of about £750,000.'

Dobson didn't sound too thrilled to be making the step down divisions after new Coventry boss Terry Butcher dropped him down the pecking order. 'I don't want to leave but I am not getting my chance.' he said. 'The gaffer said quite clearly that there are many people in front of me, so I had no choice.'

On the same day that fans were reading about the new playing additions, there was something much more significant being announced. Jack Walker had taken control of the club. In the local paper, it shared front page headlines with the outbreak of the Gulf War. 'Steel Tycoon Takes Control of the Rovers' said the *Lancashire Evening Telegraph*. 'Control of Blackburn Rovers has been taken over by Jack Walker with the full approval of the board at Ewood where an unprecedented spending spree has almost reached one million. The Jersey-based Blackburnian has obtained a controlling shareholding – more than 50 percent – in the club to signal the dawn of a potentially-exciting new era at Ewood.

'Walker, despite now owning a controlling interest, will not join the board. But he was made vice-president of the club only last year and – apart from his involvement in the past – has worked increasingly closely with directors over recent months. A few years ago the board made it plain that they were open to offers should someone come forward with the capability of providing the sort of cash needed to compete at the top these days. The fact that it has come from a man who has supported the club for almost half a century and has similar feelings for Rovers to themselves seems the perfect solution.'

Walker told the fans that brighter times were ahead. 'I know some of Rovers' performances have been abysmal and I fully understand why the supporters are fed up but the situation will change. The main issues for Bill Fox and Don Mackay have been to keep the club viable but now we can look to strengthening the team which began with the signing of Bobby Mimms.'

In the past, Walker said he had been too busy with business to think about the Rovers but that had changed following the sale of WalkerSteel. 'Now I have become very much involved and I am looking forward to seeing Rovers firmly established in the Second Division this season and, hopefully, with the fans happy, we will be in the First Division next year.'

Bill Fox was happy to see the arrival of the new man. 'We are highly delighted that Mr. Walker is now the majority shareholder of Blackburn Rovers. He is a son of Blackburn, a supporter of the club from his early days in the town and now he is intimately involved in the club. It is vital that we all work together for the sake of the club and being a Blackburnian, he appreciates this. He has been a Rovers supporter for 45 years.'

There was no doubt that it increased the pressure on Don Mackay and the Scot was as honest as usual when asked how it felt to suddenly have money to spend on the likes of Livingstone and Dobson, and others in the future. 'Money has been made available and I hope I have used it wisely. I am concerned that I have done the right thing but I am also certain in my mind that I have done so. They are only young players but they have both played in the First Division.'

Despite the seismic events during the week, there was no bumper crowd for the visit of Ipswich at the weekend with just 8,256 turning up to watch the most expensive Rovers team ever assembled, slightly above the season average of 8,100. Rovers were in poor form and had lost their previous three home games.

With Jack Walker sitting in the Director's Box, this was going to be different. It wasn't. Ipswich won 1-0 to leave the hosts a point above the relegation zone. Mackay said nine wins from the remaining 19 were needed. It wasn't looking good. Livingstone had missed a glorious early chance but the new boys did not stand out, though Dobson was at least providing plenty of optimism. 'I have looked at the table. I think we are fifth from bottom, but two or three wins and we could be fifth from top. It's so close.' It wasn't really.

Rovers didn't win nine, but the seven that were managed and the five draws were just enough. 'They were exciting times and it was exciting to be part of it all,' said Mimms. 'The 1990/91 season was a battle and we only stayed up on the last day of the season at Millwall. Then we had the first proper contact with Jack as he came into the dressing room. He told us that he was going to sort the club out and get promotion and that there would be money spent on the club and on the kids, and he was true to his word on that.'

Had Rovers gone down then history would likely have been very different and that is why the money had been forthcoming earlier in the season. 'I could see them going very fast into the Third Division,' Walker told a television documentary about himself. 'To get back from the Third Division can take a long time. Money doesn't come into it as once you are down there, you can't get the players and you can't get the atmosphere. That's when I decided I had to do something and that is what I did it for.'

Mackay was not used to having money to spend. 'I knew my budget. When I bought Colin Hendry, Bill Fox said I had £30,000 and that was it, no more. He was ambitious but would not let the club suffer financially. When we had to sell Colin Hendry and put the money in the bank, Bill took me along to see the bank manager. It was the first time that Blackburn had been in the black and it was obviously an unusual feeling for him. He was so fastidious. Bill loved Blackburn. So did Jack Walker but he had more money than Bill. The thing that stood in my mind was that chairman Bill Fox wasn't really liked by Rovers fans. They felt that the club had not attained the heights they thought they should have but Bill kept the club secure and he deserves more praise than he got.'

Walker was starting to take it to the next level. Jack Walker. The chant 'There's only one Jack Walker' can still be heard at Ewood Park and around grounds all over England, despite the fact that the man himself died in August 2000. This chant is not just a response to the Venky's ownership of the club and the problems that have come with that, it was being sung when the team was winning the League Cup and qualifying for Europe through top six finishes. No Rovers fan will ever forget or underestimate what Walker did for the club.

A well-known figure in Blackburn before he started getting involved in the Rovers, there are reports of Jack and his brother Fred helping fans who had been standing on a wooden bridge that collapsed while waiting for a train home after a game in Bury in 1952. 'I was on the bridge with my brother Fred, but we didn't go down,' recalled Walker four decades later. 'We were at the other end. There were thousands of people trying to get on the bridge, then suddenly it started vibrating, rumbling and shaking, and then the middle just dropped out. It was frightening. We went down on to the railway line and Fred and me helped get people off the tracks – including the mascot.'

A witness to the collapse, which saw one die and 175 injured, said: 'One of the heroes of that day was Jack Walker. He was just another supporter from the terraces, a true Rovers supporter.'

A true supporter yes, but not destined to be just another one. After the Second World War, he went to work for his father, who had started a small car repair and sheet metal working business. Five years later, the company, which had been started with just £80, had an annual turnover of £6,000. Upon finishing his national service, he took over the business after his father died in 1951. With his brother Fred, they focused on steel and became very big indeed. The 54-acre site that opened in Guide, located on the windy 'tops' of the town, became a major place of employment and so big that employees had to cycle from one end to another.

His determination to succeed was legendary. There was a story that he was in New York in 1960 when Hurricane Donna hit the east coast, one of the worst in the city's history. All rail and air systems were down, meaning that Walker couldn't get to the opposite coast to do a major deal. He somehow persuaded a taxi driver to make the trip, the two shared the driving and Walker made it. The story also goes that he subsequently set up the driver in his own business.

Like Mackay, Walker had seen the 30,000 fans that Blackburn sent to Wembley in 1987 for the final of a little-known or rated competition, so desperate they were for some success. He had been behind the scenes with Archibald and Ardiles in 1988 and helped with the building of the new Riverside stand.

At the start of 1989, the company had over 3,000 workers in the United Kingdom. By the end of the year, the Walker brothers decided to sell to British Steel for £330 million. At the time, it was the highest price ever paid in the United Kingdom for a private company. By then, the man himself had taken his family to Jersey where he had bought an airline, originally called Jersey European and later changed to British European. In 2002, it became Flybe, a well-known budget flyer.

His first love, though, was Blackburn Rovers. The *Guardian* called him the 'Berlusconi of the Black Pudding belt', a clever phrase but not exactly accurate. He was a quiet local lad who had time and a lot of money on his hands and a local club, one that he loved, in need of help. Not one to seek the limelight or give interviews, there were no scandals attached to the man.

Former England international turned media man Jimmy Armfield went to Jersey in 1992 on the off chance of catching up with Walker and was called a 'cheeky bugger' for his actions. Walker confirmed to Armfield that he had been behind the Lineker bid, but other than that he offered nothing but a few clichés, such as money not buying success, and then sent him on his way.

Arsenal fan, writer and actor Tom Watt had plenty of time for Walker. 'When Arsenal play Chelsea, the chants are all about the "Chavs buying it all" but there wasn't resentment or bitterness with Blackburn,' said the *EastEnders* star. 'Even though there was money spent, there was a homespun feeling about it all, with British players being bought, even if it wasn't exactly homegrown.

Walker was good news. How could you knock a fellow for getting involved in the town, his club? Fair play to him. I remember going to Blackburn in the eighties and then going back a few years later and everything had changed. The whole club was unrecognisable and it was all down to one man. It all seems like a much more innocent time when you look back at it now.'

Mackay played a big part in helping Rovers move forward, showing that ambition can be rewarded on and off the pitch, yet Howard Kendall should also not be forgotten. He, rightly, is best remembered for his time as Everton boss and the twin title triumphs but it was his two seasons in charge, with one glorious promotion and one glorious near miss, that set the scene for the rest of the decade. He built a solid foundation for much of the decade, taking the team from the Third Division to the top of the second. His defence stayed at Ewood a lot longer than he did. Without Kendall, who knows where the club would have spent the eighties?

It would almost certainly have been grimmer. You never know, but perhaps a look at Blackburn's Lancastrian stablemates provides a glimpse of what could have been. Burnley almost fell out of the Football League entirely in 1986, Bolton spent much of the eighties in the bottom two tiers, falling down to the fourth, where Preston also headed.

Kendall's defence stood Rovers in good stead for a few years and ensured that while the glory days never really came back, there was always a chance they could. Archibald, Ardiles and that season showed the hunger in the town for success, as did the Full Members' triumph.

Fans had sung in hope for years about going up. 'First Division here we come, right back where we started from, open up those golden gates, First Division here we come,' went the ditty anytime Rovers got anywhere near the top six. In the past, Don Mackay had started every season as Rovers boss with the hope that promotion would finally happen. At the start of the 1991/92 season, that vague target had become set in stone. 'Jack was definite from the middle of the previous season,' Mackay said. 'He wanted this to be the last season in the Second Division.' And he wasn't talking about going down.

It wasn't just the manager who was served notice. The players were also under no illusions. As Mimms recalled, Walker had informed them of the plans and goals at the end of the previous season as Rovers survived on the last day, despite losing at Millwall.

What made things all the more pressing was the new breakaway league that was set to start the following season. Despite Bill Fox's opposition to this new competition as chairman of the Football League as well as Blackburn, Walker and the club were doing all they could to make sure they were in it.

'It is imperative that we get into the First Division and we must do it this season,' Walker said early in the new campaign. 'It is vital that we don't get left behind when the new Super League is formed. We want to be recognised. It was 1928 when we last won the FA Cup so it's about time we started doing something. When it comes to buying players we have a lot to talk about. But there is a limit. It is not a bottomless pit at all.'

Not bottomless, but the pile was substantial. Still, Blackburn were having problems spending it as nobody took the club, or rather their new ambitions and large bank account, seriously. Like Lineker, players were proving difficult to attract.

'I wanted to sign Teddy Sheringham,' said Mackay. 'I had the idea of playing him, Speedie and Lineker up front. Teddy would be playing off the front two; I didn't see him as an out and out striker. He could be in the hole, with Speedie causing all kinds of problems for defenders and then Lineker would be there to take advantage. Can you imagine what that would have done to the Second Division? Nobody would have seen anything like it. Then with Scott Sellars on the left and the energy of Nicky Reid in the middle, it would have been perfect.'

The Scot cut short his holiday to go and see the Millwall man. 'I flew from Plymouth to London. I spent two or three hours in a hotel with Sheringham and tried to persuade him to come to Blackburn, but he said no. Brian Clough already had an eye on him and wasn't too happy that we were sniffing around.'

While Lineker and Sheringham never came, Speedie did, eventually. The Scot had been Dalglish's last signing at Anfield in January 1991 and though he did pretty well on Merseyside, new boss Graeme Souness made it clear that he didn't see him as a vital part of his plans. One Friday morning before the season started, Mackay received a phone call. 'Souness had put him in the reserves at Liverpool and he called me and just said "I am coming to sign for Blackburn."'

'I didn't get on with Graeme Souness,' said Speedie on his arrival. 'My big mouth and his big mouth didn't go together, but I don't hold grudges. Signing for Liverpool was still the best thing that ever happened to me. I am here to get Blackburn into the First Division and if that means giving people a rollicking then that's their problem. I didn't have to leave Liverpool. I could have sat there on a three-year contract and made more money but that didn't matter to me because all I want to do is play football. When I sat back and thought about what Blackburn were trying to do, I wanted to be part of it.'

Liverpool's loss and all that. Speedie was a big name and a big signing but still there was an expectation that more would happen. Kevin Moran had arrived at the club in 1990 and scored the only goal on the opening day in a 1-1 draw with Portsmouth that was a bit of a damp squib. Only 11,000 or so turned up for the game, perhaps wary of being served more disappointment.

The other big signing was Steve Agnew, who arrived from Barnsley for a fee of £700,000. He picked up a serious injury and never played in the famous Blue and Whites halves again. 'That was a blow,' said Mackay. 'Agnew would have been great for us and was the missing link in the middle. We lost him and then we lost the third game of the season against Ipswich.'

That prompted Walker to call for a meeting of the club directors and the manager's fate was sealed, helped by the fact that Rovers fans made their displeasure known after the game.

It was not a surprise with a feeling that regardless of results in the short-term, Mackay just did not have the name, reputation and weight in the game to take Rovers to where they now wanted to be. 'Obviously the situation at the club had changed and there were serious ambitions. I tried to sign Mike Newell but he didn't want to come. He came for Kenny though. That was the reason and it was probably right for the club. Don Mackay and Kenny Dalglish, there was no comparison. I wasn't in the same class in terms of the name, but management? I don't know.'

The Scot had had some success at the Rovers and brought plenty of excitement. It perhaps felt that he had always been a little more ambitious than the club, but that all changed and suddenly the club's ambitions far surpassed anything he could offer. Anything less than a stellar start to the season was always going to result in a change.

Perhaps because it was half-expected, the sacking seemed very civilised and it was over very quickly. If there were any doubts as to who was making the decisions, they were removed by Bill Fox, who had a close relationship with Mackay. 'Now that we have a majority shareholder involved in the club who has a lot of money and is prepared to put the money in as is obvious with what has gone on in the last month, then the decision was made to have a change of direction at the top.'

'The influx of money had brought pressure,' said Mackay. 'I was not given the time and when it comes to football you either need time or you need money and if you have both then you can have success. But when there is a lot of money then there are expectations and that means there is not much time. We see this now in the modern game. I was sad to leave of course. It was a lovely time. I enjoyed Blackburn and the fans. The family had settled and were happy. We eventually came back to Blackburn to run a hotel but that was a disaster and another story.'

'It was probably inevitable to a degree that Don would go,' said Mimms. 'He did well with Rovers and I will be forever grateful that he took me to the club when he did. Unfortunately, you know what football is like. Jack hadn't brought Don to the club and more often than not, the new owner is always going to be looking for their own man. There was a little bit of that. Steve Agnew was the big signing but got injured very early. Don spent some money and gave it a go. It didn't quite happen, but he was a victim of circumstances.

'He probably felt that he didn't get the benefit of what he had put in, but it put the club in a situation where it looked attractive to Jack Walker. He was also unlucky in that Kenny was available and wanted to get back into football.'

7

BACK IN THE BIG TIME

'If they finished in the top half of the table, they, and Kenny
Dalglish in particular, would be quite happy but it is a
promising start and with the start they have had expectations
are quite high. I wouldn't expect too much of them.'

GARY LINEKER, AUGUST 1992

AFTER 26 YEARS OF TRYING, ROVERS WERE BACK IN THE
big time but for some, as Scott Sellars pointed out, promotion meant the end
of the road.

'It was possibly bittersweet for players, like Simon Garner,' Sellars said
of the striker who had been at the club since the late seventies and had been
involved in numerous near misses. 'He had been there a long time and he was
older than me. He was a legend for Blackburn and it didn't happen for him,
though he would have loved to play in the Premier League for the club. But
that is football, sometimes you are just surplus to requirements. When that
happens, you just have to accept it and find a new club.'

With Garner it was almost expected. While he was loved by the fans, he was the wrong side of 30. There had been debate as to whether he was good enough for the top flight when he was in his prime but, at the age of 32, he was unlikely to be needed by a club that was aiming for more than survival and a few nice days out at famous old stadiums. The old poacher knew it too, noting that when Newell had been injured at a crucial point of the previous season, the club had bought Duncan Shearer rather than coming to him.

He was not even on the bench at Wembley for the play-off final, giving him more time to have a few cigarettes from the sidelines. 'We were up,' he said. 'And so was my time at Blackburn.' The last time he was seen by the public as a member of Blackburn Rovers was on the balcony of the Town Hall and the fans chanted 'There's Only One Simon Garner'.

'Drunk on a combination of beer and emotion, I conducted it,' said Garner. 'I knew it was the last time I would hear it as an employee of Blackburn Rovers and milked it for all it was worth.'

Ossie Ardiles remembered Garner from their short time together just four years before. Now in charge of West Bromwich Albion, the Argentine was keen to sign the striker. Dalglish had already told the player not to expect much playing time in the top flight. The Baggies were willing to pay £30,000 and promised Garner the difference as a signing-on fee if Rovers agreed to sell for less. They didn't, which looked a little petty when it came to a loyal and faithful servant who had not pushed for a move. £30,000 was the deal and that was that. The Boston boy scored a club record 168 league goals and 194 all in all. Even Shearer did not break that.

It was different with Sellars. At 26, he was in his prime. He had shone in the Second Division but all in Blackburn knew that the top flight was his natural home. If there were any members of the pre-Dalglish team that Rovers fans would have wanted to see in the top tier – after the emotional pull of Garner – it was Sellars.

Sellars wasn't concerned about the prospect of more talented players coming to East Lancashire now the team were in the top tier. 'There was a feeling that Blackburn would go again and buy again after promotion. Kenny had conversations with me in terms of whether I wanted to stay. I wasn't being pushed out. I knew they would buy players, build a training ground and all the rest. I wasn't worried about playing time. I believed in my ability and I knew I had served the club well. I had got over my injury problems and was ready to kick on.'

That newly-crowned English champions Leeds United came in for him wasn't a surprise considering his talent. More worthy of a raised eyebrow was the fact that Rovers let him go for a fee that was reported to be close to being seven figures. 'I left for two reasons. One was the new contract. The club had been telling me for a while that it was all there but I was a bit disappointed to get an offer of just two years. Leeds offered four. The second was that I felt there was unfinished business at Leeds. I had been there as a kid but had not really broken through. They had just won the title and I wanted to go back and show them what I could do.'

It did not work out. Rovers may have been the new boys and Leeds the champions, but their fortunes over the next few years were somewhat different and his second spell at Elland Road did not go much better than the first. The next move seemed to be the right one. Sellars joined Newcastle for the final third of their promotion push the following season and was soon enjoying playing under Kevin Keegan, becoming a favourite in the north-east and looking completely at home in the top tier. However, a cartilage injury in early in the 1994/95 season was a blow and the Sheffield-born schemer had to sit and watch as a certain David Ginola came in. Perhaps he should have stayed at Ewood?

'I have regrets as the club went on to win the league, but I was happy to see them do so and I had a great time in my career. I think that the best football I played was when I scored 15 goals [in the 1989/90 season] when Mackay gave me freedom to stay wide. I had a big influence when we went up, especially later in the season. It didn't work out at Leeds but I had a great three years at Newcastle. Football changes and Blackburn was a fantastic, successful time in my career. The fans were fantastic and I will never forget them or the club.'

Given what was to happen in the years that followed with players coming and going, it is striking that stars of the past still have a special feeling for the club. That was even the case for those who stayed just for a season. David Speedie had arrived just the summer before but had quickly become a cult hero, a fan favourite and then a legend thanks to 26 goals, the winning of crucial penalties, a never-say-die attitude and a wonderful habit of winding up opposition fans.

Plenty were looking forward to seeing Speedie in the top tier and while he did appear in the new league, it was in the red and white of Southampton. Rovers were after Alan Shearer, but the deal was dependent on Speedie going in the opposite direction. Saints boss Ian Branfoot wanted to reunite Speedie with his former Chelsea strike partner Kerry Dixon. If this was standing in the way between Blackburn and Shearer then there was only going to be one outcome. The Scot was soon heading south.

'I was gutted,' said Speedie to the *Lancashire Evening Telegraph* in 2015. 'I didn't want to go. Kenny in the end said, "We don't want you to go, it's just business." And when he said that, I said, "Okay, pay my contract up," and that's what they did. So I went for money. Jack Walker paid my contract up and then I got a very good contract at Southampton. It set me up for life, at the end of the day. But I'd sooner have stayed at Blackburn. I'd have sacrificed all that to stay at Blackburn for two more years at least.'

That was the time remaining on his contract and Rovers had promised a new deal if promotion was achieved.

'... Obviously things changed and Southampton wanted me as part of the deal for Shearer,' said Speedie. 'So I was forced into it and I went for all the wrong reasons. As I say, it was a good move for me financially, but career-wise, it was disastrous. It's a massive regret.'

It was sad to see Sellars, Garner and Speedie go, three players who were loved by fans for different reasons. Sellars for his class that shone through even when the team was closer to the Third Division than the first. Garner for his goals and the fact that fans felt he was one of them and Speedie for the way he played and the way that opposing fans hated but rated him.

Despite all that, the summer was a magical one for Rovers fans. For years, there had just been a desperation to get back in the top tier, to play the big boys once again. The thought of going to Anfield, Old Trafford, Highbury and all the rest was a thrilling one for those who had not been able to enjoy the last time back in the late fifties and early sixties. Many would have settled for a season or two, but there was more.

Rovers were not going up just hoping to survive. The ink was barely dry on the match reports that told of the Wembley win before sportswriters were speculating on who the club would try to sign. Ian Rush was again mentioned as the legendary Liverpool striker was out of contract. For fans, there was the excitement of opening up the newspapers and seeing who the club were being linked with. Alan Shearer was obviously the main target man. There had been other names such as Mark Bright and David Hirst mentioned, but Shearer was the top of the list.

First however came Stuart Ripley, an exciting winger from Middlesbrough, Blackburn's promotion rivals from the year before. Boro had made it automatically compared to the play-offs. There was other interest however. 'Brian Little of Leicester rang me and said "If we get up into the Premier League, do you want to come?"' Ripley told Middlesbrough's *Gazette Live* in 2017. 'I said that I would be interested. When Blackburn beat Leicester, I thought that the chance had gone but it's funny, Blackburn came in. Kenny Dalglish came up and said "We'd like you to come to Blackburn." It's funny how things turn out.'

Despite helping Boro back to the big time, Ripley felt the time was right to leave. 'I had a fantastic time at the club, I had a great season that season and got back to my best. If I was going to leave the club, I wanted it to be on a good note. It was my hometown team and I always get a great reception when I go back. It was the right decision for me as I left with images of me playing well and not with images of me struggling with hamstring injuries.'

'Kenny Dalglish just doesn't turn up at Blackburn for no reason. That was my thinking. "There has to be something big going on." I spoke to people about what was going on and they told me they were going to sign Alan Shearer. It just convinced me it would be a good move and it was not too far geographically.'

Shearer had been mentioned as a Rovers target during the promotion season. All knew that the promising young striker was going to be leaving Southampton, it was just a question of where he was going to go. Once Kerry Dixon arrived at Southampton on 19 July for £575,000, the way was clear for Shearer to leave.

'We scored just 17 goals at home last season and that's not enough. We needed a proven goalscorer,' said Southampton coach Ian Branfoot. 'As far as

Shearer is concerned, he will go if there's a move right for the club and for the player.'

More than a quarter of a century later, Shearer recalls being confident in his own ability and believes that he was already a proven goalscorer. 'I scored over 20 goals in my last season at Southampton,' he said, counting three from the Full Members' Cup, as every good striker should. 'I was more experienced and my understanding of the game and position was getting better every year. I was also aware of who was already at Blackburn and how they were going to play under Kenny.'

Shearer was not the kind of character to be fazed about breaking the English transfer record as the figure ended up being £3.6 million, a sum which included Speedie heading in the opposite direction. 'It was a statement to everyone,' said Jason Wilcox. 'We knew, of course, that there was money available but it was still a strange feeling to see the club breaking the record. If you'd gone back 12 or 18 months and told people that, they wouldn't have believed it. I certainly wouldn't have.'

The English transfer record stood at the £2.9 million that Liverpool paid to Derby County for Dean Saunders in the previous summer, but there were some eyebrows raised over the fact that Shearer was going to be the most expensive player in British history. Despite the improvement, his goalscoring record was actually not all that hot. The *Independent* noted that he had scored only ten goals in the four seasons before the previous campaign but admitted that he was the leading striker of his generation, more highly regarded than David Hirst, who Alex Ferguson had initially preferred over Shearer, simply because he was three years older at 24 and had that extra experience.

But United wanted Shearer – especially after Trevor Francis, Hirst's boss at Sheffield Wednesday, had given Ferguson short shrift when asked about his striker. According to Shearer, despite an initial phone call from 'someone' at the club, a bid was never made. Ferguson claims that he had a conversation with a surly Southampton hotshot, one that the striker has never mentioned. In the end, Shearer signed for Rovers.

Dalglish's reminder that Walker's investment was staying in English football was backed to some extent by the chain of transfers Shearer's imminent move was to set off. The money Southampton were about to receive helped pay

Chelsea for Dixon and contributed to the fee the Blues paid for Norwich's Robert Fleck. Norwich then turned to Mark Robins of Manchester United. The removal of Shearer from the market meant that the next big-name striker available was going to be Brian Deane, who was valued at £3 million.

Shearer made his debut a couple of days later, one that was not exactly memorable. Rovers lost 3-0 at Hibernian. Apart from Ripley and Shearer, the team looked similar. Mimms was still between the sticks, Colin Hendry and Kevin Moran brought brawn and experience to the centre of defence. There was David May at right-back and Alan Wright on the left. Atkins and Sherwood were in the middle, as was Gordon Cowans when fit, and then there were Ripley and Wilcox on the wings feeding Shearer and Newell in attack. 'We were looking forward to the first season up,' remembers Wilcox. 'We had signed players the season before who were First Division players and then we got Shearer. We knew he was good but we soon saw just how good he was. There was always talk in the papers of more players coming, but we just focused on what we had to do.'

8

TWO THAT GOT AWAY: GEOFF THOMAS AND ROY KEANE

'It took me a while to get over not going to
Blackburn, I didn't know what to do.'

GEOFF THOMAS

SHEARER'S TRANSFER SAGA WAS BARELY THAT AND
was a good deal less interesting than the on-off deal with Crystal Palace captain
Geoff Thomas. In the summer of 1992, Arsenal had already bid £2.5 million
for the midfielder, but Rovers were ready to go a little higher. To make matters
more interesting, the Blues' opening day fixture – the first in the top flight
since 1966 – was at Selhurst Park.

Rovers were having some problems getting the players they wanted
and everyone knew the size of their wallet. 'Kenny spent wisely,' said Don
Mackay. 'But when people know you have money then things can become
more complicated.' This was especially the case with Crystal Palace and their

chairman Ron Noades.

'There's one thing you can be certain of,' said Palace boss Steve Coppell. 'Today there is a price for football and there is a price for Blackburn. Can we afford to turn down £3 million? I'm not in a position to say that. I only have an overview of the financial situation. It's Ron's money and his club. He tells me that we don't have to sell so I just go along with that. As far as I know, they have not matched any valuation that Ron thinks is realistic. We have been phoning around like every club looking at player purchases this summer. Supply is short, demand is great. You have the right to demand high prices. I have said all along Geoff Thomas is not for sale. But other clubs are actively trying to buy him. It would be a tremendous blow to lose Geoff. And the present situation is unsettling for the player.'

Even the Dalglish name didn't always work. That summer there was a struggle to sign Craig Short from just relegated Notts County, with champions Leeds and Nottingham Forest also chasing the centre-back. Despite an offer of £2.5 million, County, who were facing a hefty bill to redevelop Meadow Lane, said no. 'Craig is the best centre-half in the country,' said County boss Neil Warnock. 'He should be in the England team now.' Rovers, when they were going very well in the top tier in September, went back for Short and offered £2.7 million, but Short chose to go to Derby. 'It's his decision,' said Dalglish. 'I can't do anything about it.' Short said he had been set for Ewood. 'I had second thoughts,' he said. 'I had my bags packed for Blackburn, but I changed my mind after my wife told me to go and have a lie-down and give it a few more minutes. People may say I have lost my bottle and taken the easy way out. But I knew my heart was set on Derby.'

Thomas was different. He wanted to come and a deal was expected as the season opener approached. It didn't happen in time so there was some surprise when Palace made it clear that he was going to play against Blackburn, the team he was expected to join days later.

'This transfer speculation has been going on all summer but I'm confident I can go and play my normal game,' he said. 'It is in my interests to play well and not look like a two-bob player. But I'm happy to stay with Palace.' Thomas admitted that he was worried about the kind of reception the home fans would give him on the day of the game. 'I don't know how they'll react when I set foot on the pitch. If they give me the bird I'll be upset because the transfer is all pie in the sky at the moment.'

Palace wanted the player to officially request a move, but he was not about to do that. 'I've never asked for a transfer and I won't be doing so. I've got three and a half years of my contract left but the valuation between the two clubs are the key to my future. There have been lots of big deals this summer and I feel unsettled because mine has caused so much controversy. I am prepared for anything at this stage and I could still be staying at Selhurst Park. Whatever happens I want to help Palace give Blackburn a blank start.'

On a sunny August afternoon Thomas led his team out, but that was as good as it got. He played but played badly as the two teams produced an exciting 3-3 draw.

Thomas was being chewed up by the transfer machine. 'I thought I could handle today but I was wrong. Things were playing on my mind. I didn't really know whether I was a Blackburn or a Palace player. It's been a saga. I think I need a fresh start.'

Coppell was not too impressed. 'I hope he soon loses interest in Blackburn and discovers women or something like that.' It happened the other way around. Rovers lost interest in the unfortunate Thomas.

He still remembers the whole situation well. The midfielder had skippered Palace to the 1990 FA Cup final, but his career had not progressed as much as he wanted in South London. 'I loved my time at Palace,' he said. 'But I was having a few niggly injuries and my season wasn't going spectacularly after my England faux pas against France.'

Unfortunately for the player at the time, his reputation had been defined in part by a failed goal attempt against Les Bleus. Thomas, making his ninth appearance for his country in a game where Alan Shearer scored on his international debut, had made a run from deep and had been found with a smart pass from Gary Lineker. The midfielder advanced on the French area with just the goalkeeper to beat and from about ten yards outside the area, tried to chip Gilles Rousset. The ball instead never got more than a foot in the air and rolled harmlessly out of play, well wide of the French goal. The player got plenty of stick for that, despite it only being a friendly, and perhaps that is one reason why he had been dropped from the England team. A big-money move to

Ewood could have served as a gateway back into the national team.

'I felt a move to Blackburn could really help me get in form and perhaps get back into the England set up. They were a club that was obviously going places and to be part of it was an exciting prospect.'

'I had heard whispers in pre-season and then I was contacted from an agent. From that, the club told me that there was interest from Blackburn. That's how much I knew up to a point. It really went from there.

'Alan Shearer had just gone for £3 million and there was a lot of noise with Dalglish and Jack Walker saying they were going to go for it. They were being talked about a lot, they were always in the papers. My career with Palace was coming to a point where I felt I needed a new challenge. There were younger players coming through and I was getting to an age at 28 when I needed to have another go and refocus on something else. It was just the perfect time for me to leave. It all seemed very exciting. I would be an important part of an ambitious club that was looking to go places.'

Thomas was born in Manchester and after three years at Crewe Alexandra, he headed to Selhurst Park in 1987, but after six years in the capital he was more than open for a return north. 'Palace had bought me for £50,000. Blackburn had offered £2.8 million. I thought from a business point of view it would be good for Palace and I thought it would be good for me and I was sure that I could be good for Blackburn. I wanted to be part of something, to help build something.'

It could be hindsight talking, but Thomas did look a little awkward as he entered the Selhurst pitch that Saturday. How Shearer would perform in his first game had removed some of the attention, but there was still plenty on how Thomas would perform against his suitors. If that wasn't enough, there was then a call from Dalglish.

'I spoke to him the day before the game – things were different in those days – but it was great to speak to him.' The jist of the conversation was that Rovers were planning to sign Thomas on Monday so he should look after himself during the game. To say it was a tricky situation for a player is an understatement. 'It was surreal and my head was all over the place. I didn't really know what to do. There were Palace fans telling me not to go and there was a moment in the game when the Blackburn fans were singing my name.

That can't have happened to many players!'

Perhaps fortunately for Thomas it finished in a 3-3 draw. Everyone was happy. Palace had scored a last-minute goal to avoid defeat while Rovers fans couldn't believe the quality of the two goals scored by Shearer. On a sunny and hot mid-August afternoon in South London the blue and white halves had rarely looked more beautiful. On this day, Selhurst Park was nothing like the intimidating play-off final arena that it had been three years earlier, in fact it was all a little low-key. Palace had the better of the first half despite still adjusting to life without Ian Wright. Mark Bright, the former partner-in-crime of the new Arsenal striker, headed the Eagles into the lead eight minutes from the break. Five minutes later Ripley equalised, also with his head.

Early in the second half, Shearer fired well wide from outside the area to prompt a few cries of 'What a waste of money.' It was a chant that may not have been aimed at him ever again. Not long after a first league goal from Gareth Southgate, a half-volley over Mimms from outside the area, Blackburn's new forward decided to get involved.

A long free-kick was headed by Newell, chested down by Shearer from 25 yards out and moments later a shot that can only be described as a rocket hit the roof of the net.

Soon after, it looked as if the England striker had picked up a famous win, with a goal that was even more delicious, eight minutes from time. He picked up a clearance on the left midway inside the Palace half, cut inside and then bent a powerful shot around the defender and past the dive of Nigel Martyn. Such goals were almost enough to wipe away the painful memories of 1989, though a late equaliser took a little of the gloss off. They also helped to take a little attention away from Thomas's situation, but only for a while.

'I remember doing press after the game as Steve Coppell had told me that they wanted to talk to me and, of course, I was prepared for more questions about Blackburn. On the way to see them, Alan Shearer was coming down the stairs. He had scored two great goals, they were just stunning. He just looked at me and said, "See you Monday." That was it. My head was all over the place.'

'Looking back, it is not a surprise that I didn't play well – I didn't have a good game at all – but I don't think that was connected to the deal not going through.'

Over the weekend, there was no reason to think that the deal was anything but on. 'I went to see Ron Noades and he said that there was £2.8 million on the table but there was still the issue of £300,000 that Crewe would get as part of the deal. Blackburn didn't want to pay that as it would have taken me over the value of Shearer. They wanted Palace to pay it. Palace refused and it all become a bit of a stand-off. A couple of days later, Blackburn said the deal was off. I didn't know what was going on.'

'There was also the fact that Steve Coppell didn't want to sell after losing Ian Wright to Arsenal. Steve was seeing the side that he had built, and had done well in the league and also reached the cup final, being pulled apart. I heard that I was not leaving so I am not sure the deal would have been done anyway.'

On Monday, Jack Walker put a stop to the deal. There were rumours that he had been less than impressed with Thomas's display in the opening game of the Premier League, which would have been harsh given the player's unique situation. But as Thomas indicated, the man who had built up Walkersteel from almost scratch was not about to pay Crewe as well as Palace. Dalglish said something similar. 'I make the football decisions; Jack Walker makes the financial decisions. The decision not to proceed with the Thomas deal was a financial one.' Rovers chairman Robert Coar denied the next day that Rovers had pulled out, saying that if Palace lowered their asking price to £2.5 million, it would be very much back on. That didn't happen and so nothing happened.

Thomas was left to deal with the collapse of a move that had seemed to be the perfect one for him. 'It was something I had to get my head around. You run away with all these thoughts in your head and you start thinking about joining Blackburn and how you will play and what it will be like. It was hard to get my head around it all. It was a bit of a sliding doors moment for me,' added Thomas, referring to the Gwyneth Paltrow film that shows her character go through two separate lives that diverge when she just misses her tube train.

His performances suffered. 'If you are playing at that level then you need to be fit and focused and it felt like an opportunity had gone for me and it was difficult to deal with. My form dropped, I have to admit. I had a young family and I was 28. I felt that I had done my bit at Palace and they were getting a big profit. I felt it was a win-win situation for all, but then football doesn't always work the way you expect. Someone said that Dalglish had put it in his book that he was disappointed that nothing happened but that is football I guess. It could have been a great move for me, but it just didn't happen.'

Thomas then watched from South London as the Rovers stormed to the top of the table. 'It just wasn't my time and there were some regrets watching Blackburn, especially as they went from strength to strength and became a top team. Of course, I wondered what would have happened if I was there too but that is human nature. I saw other players go there and I felt that I could have done a good job too, so there was a little frustration and wondering what might have been and whether I could have won things and played for England again.' That feeling faded over time. 'By the time they won the league I had removed myself from that scenario of wishing. It just wasn't my time to go. I managed to play for a number of more years and then injuries played a part. It was frustrating but that is the way it goes.'

It was perhaps not only Thomas that regretted the fact that the deal never happened; Palace must have been a little rueful too. At the end of the season, just ten months later, he was on his way to Wolverhampton Wanderers, in the second tier, for a much smaller fee. 'It was recorded as £800,000 but was actually a million. There was interest from a few clubs, but Wolves were saying at the time that they wanted to be the next Blackburn and build something with the Hayward family and go on to better things. Ian Wright always wanted to win medals and that is why he went to Arsenal, but I wanted to be a part of something and to make a difference. That didn't happen at Blackburn, but I thought it still could at Wolves.'

Just over a year later, there was an abortive move for Roy Keane. With all respect to Thomas, who may have been a highly-regarded midfielder, the Irishman was a cut above and soon became a legend of English football. In the Thomas no-deal, much of the regret came from the player, who missed a chance to join a club that was going to challenge for the title. When it comes to Keane, it is a little different. It is unlikely that he regrets not heading to East Lancashire. Missing out on a player who was to become one of the best midfielders in the Premier League's history was painful for Rovers. Young Keane and peak Shearer in the same team? It would have been irresistible. No wonder that Dalglish was interested.

The Irishman had quickly become one of the top young talents in the top flight after impressing for Nottingham Forest in a breakthrough 1990/91 season that culminated in an FA Cup Final appearance. With the club relegated at the end of the 1992/93 season, it was inevitable that he would be on his way, especially as there was a clause in his contract to that effect. Keane did not even have an agent at the time when he first met Dalglish and had the PFA's Brendon Batson with him.

'I was on about £250,000 [a year] at Forest, which was a good deal. Blackburn offered me four hundred [thousand a year],' Keane wrote in his autobiography. United initially offered £300,000. 'It was important, because this is the business side of the football, and straight away I learned about Man United was that it is business, as well.' Keane didn't think the offer marked a big enough increase on his current salary. In the end, United came back with an extra £50,000.

The story about Keane's change of heart has become legendary. The midfielder had agreed to head to Ewood but initially wanted £500,000. After some bargaining, he accepted £400,000. By the time negotiations had finished, it was Friday afternoon. So when Dalglish called the club to get the contract drawn up, everyone had gone home. No problem, the two shook hands and agreed to get the legal stuff all sorted on Monday. Back home to Cork for a weekend of celebration, he was interrupted by a phone call from Ferguson. The Scot had read about Keane's transfer talks and wanted in, in fact had done so since 1990 when impressed by the teenage Irishman as Forest won at Old Trafford. United had been linked with Carlton Palmer but Keane was the one he wanted and after the hungover player had confirmed that nothing had been set in writing, invited him for a chat. That happened over snooker once Ferguson had picked Keane up at Manchester Airport. 'I liked him straight away,' Keane said. 'He was unaffected, funny and reassuringly human. He was also clearly hungry for more trophies.'

'I felt bad because I had kind of agreed to go to Blackburn,' Keane said, with a smiling Dalglish looking on, as they appeared on a television show in 2017 to mark the 25th anniversary of the Premier League. 'When you shake hands with someone, you are almost there. Then United came in a few days later. I agreed to go to United and, of course, there was no regrets. I knew I had made the right move.'

Dalglish admitted that Rovers had been in there behind the scenes. 'We were in there pitching,' Dalglish said. 'I was playing golf at Wentworth and got a phone call to say Forest had accepted a bid from us. So we met at a hotel near Stoke after their secretary had told me that a fee had been agreed. Frank Clark was the manager and he phoned me a day after I met Roy and he said "What are you doing?"

'I said: "Well, we have agreed a fee?" He said: "No we've not." I had to say I was awfully sorry as I felt we had agreed a fee and the parting shot was him telling me he was going to United. I told him he had made a bad move. The next time I saw him, he'd won about three championships, the European Cup... I said to him I told you I had made a mistake.'

He could joke about it then but at the time, he was not too happy. 'He was effing and blinding (on the phone), saying "You're a f**king disgrace,"' Keane said. 'I said, "Listen, I'm going on me holidays next week," which I was, I was going to Cyprus with a few lads... just to do some sightseeing. "I'm going to Cyprus with me mates, and when I come back I'm going to sign for Man United." He said: "I'm going to find you. I'm going to come to Ayia Napa and find you." So, every bar in Ayia Napa, I was looking over my shoulder waiting for Kenny Dalglish to walk in.'

Keane was the biggest fish that slipped through Dalglish's net at Blackburn. In the first summer, however, any regrets over the Thomas situation did not last long. There were too many other exciting things happening.

9

SHEARER WONDERLAND

'There were a lot of good strikers around at the
time but Shearer was the best, easily.'

BRIAN DEANE

THE DISAPPOINTMENT OF THE LAST-MINUTE EQUALISER

conceded at Palace was a little lost amid the buzz of Shearer's goals and the
upcoming midweek home game – against the mighty Arsenal. The talk around
the country was understandably that Blackburn would do okay, that they
would score plenty of goals but let plenty in. They would, in essence, be an
improved version of Oldham Athletic, as Des Lynam suggested on *Match of
the Day*. The next two games showed that this may not be the case.

Talking to Arsenal fans in Blackburn, they didn't really rate the side
they were about to face – why would the champions of 1989 and 1991 be
concerned about a side that had finish sixth in the tier below? – but they also

realised that being the visitors in a promoted team's first home game of the season was never going to be a comfortable fixture. And so it proved.

Rovers were impressive, especially Stuart Ripley, who hit the bar with a scorcher and gave the much-vaunted Gunners backline a torrid time. It wasn't a pretty game and a 0-0 was very much on the cards until a few minutes from time. Shearer went for a ball just inside the Arsenal half, shoulder charged Jimmy Carter back to Liverpool and then saw his shot deflect off Tony Adams, over David Seaman and into the net. Rarely has the Blackburn End jumped so high. 'I managed to nudge Jimmy Carter out of the way,' said Shearer with typical understatement. 'There was a huge space in front of me. I said to myself, "Get your head down, go for goal and shoot."'

It not only gave home fans a first look at Shearer but at the wing pairing that would drive the team's attacking engine for years to come – Wilcox and Ripley. 'People talk about wide players and I don't want to compare, but it was almost like Giggs and Beckham, the SAS, Cole and Yorke,' remembers Wilcox. 'People also naturally put people in pairs. From our point of view, we knew what we brought to the team. We couldn't have contributed to the team like we did if we didn't have the service from midfield and without those lads up front. We had to put in the right crosses. We had a game plan, Kenny and Ray set it out, and anyone wavering from that would find that he was not playing. There was a real understanding that for Alan to be as effective as he was, he needed balls into the box. We had different styles. I am good friends with Stuart now, I was then off the pitch and respect him as a guy.'

The game against Arsenal showed that the Rovers could live with the big boys. 'The atmosphere at Ewood was special,' Wilcox said, adding that Arsenal were not quite that. 'They were a good strong team with experience and were well-organised, but we matched them. Winning that game really got us going.'

Rovers fans were in dreamland. 'City, you are next. City, City, you are next,' went the chant as they left Ewood to celebrate. Blackburn beat the blue side of Manchester 1-0 thanks to a fine Mike Newell goal. Soon after a 2-0 win at Coventry put Rovers top of the pile with 11 points from five games and Shearer was making headlines for his play rather than his price.

Graham Taylor was at Highfield Road and the England boss was happy to break his rule about not talking about individual players. 'When I first took the England job, I said it would be interesting to see who developed out of three outstanding players at Southampton at that time.' Compared to Rodney Wallace and Matthew Le Tissier, Shearer was the one making strides. 'In Shearer we have someone who can handle pressure and in all the dealings I've had with him, he has come across as a confident person.' It wasn't lost on the nation that during the European Championships just a few weeks earlier, Taylor had left Shearer on the bench to bring on Alan Smith when England needed a goal against Sweden. Anyway, the boss was impressed at how Shearer was working with Newell. The two lived near to each other in Southport (as Tim Flowers was to do too, leading rise to a so-called 'Southport Mafia' in the Ewood changing room). An intelligent forward, Newell enjoyed the partnership, and it was vice very much versa.

After a 4-1 victory over Nottingham Forest, Newell was on the scoresheet again in a bruising encounter at Highbury. If the 1-0 win at Ewood was special, then fans could not believe another victory by the same scoreline in London. George Graham was not exactly gracious in defeat. 'I'm sure Kenny knows that they are nowhere near a championship side. They are tough, solid, well-organised and try to catch teams on the break as they did to us today. I don't think we deserved to lose either game against Blackburn. And I don't think anyone can say they are a better team than us.'

Graham had earlier called for his team to be more aggressive and it showed. Shearer had seven stitches and was kicked from the Clock End to the North Bank mural that covered construction work (controversial because every Arsenal fan depicted on it was white). Shearer simply told Graham to look at the table where Rovers were second and Arsenal, who Graham had declared were title favourites before the start of the season, were mid-table after losing four out of their first eight games.

'I remember the two Arsenal games,' said Mimms. 'We played really well at Highbury. Al got battered all over the place. In the home game, he had dumped Tony Adams on the gravel [that surrounded the Ewood pitch]. In return, he was kicked all over the place at Highbury. We just dug in and played well. Newelly benefitted from that and scored. We were buzzing. To beat Arsenal home and away in the first month of the season was special and even Kenny was smiling. We all were.'

While Shearer was getting the headlines, there was plenty of praise for Mimms. The number one had gone through a tough time at Tottenham but excelled on his return to the top flight. There was often speculation that he was going to be replaced but in that first season, he barely put a glove wrong, keeping a record number of clean sheets. In October, he made a wonder save as Rovers drew 0-0 at Aston Villa, in their first ever televised league game. Had Rovers won they would have gone back top, but Nigel Spink had an excellent game himself between the sticks for the hosts. It came two days after Dalglish had been spotted at Wolves and all thought he was watching goalkeeper Mike Stowell, a hot property at the time and valued at around £1 million. There had also been rumours that Rovers had bid for Vince Bartram at Bournemouth. It can't have been easy for the number one.

'There was always that in the back of your mind that you could be replaced especially when you get promoted and, of course, you read the papers like everyone else,' Mimms said, adding that it would be worse these days with social media and the internet in general. 'Who Blackburn were going to sign next always seemed to be there in the papers so it did keep you on your toes. But I thought I was playing some decent football and there were other areas where the team needed strengthening and that was on my side. I did have something like 18 or 19 clean sheets in that season which helped.' One of the best performances came near the end with a fine 2-1 win at White Hart Lane. 'There was a little bit of vindication after what had happened. It is more satisfying really, to go back to the club where I didn't show my best form. I knew I could have done better, and I knew I could have done it at Tottenham, but I don't think I got the help I needed. I went back with a club I enjoyed playing for and I think that showed in my form. I was at a club where I felt comfortable and confident.'

There was no replacement for Mimms before or during that first top-flight campaign, but the squad was added to. If Thomas missed out, Nicky Marker did not, though the transfer that was much more low-key. In September, the man who had played a part in recent Rovers history, with a tackle on Ossie Ardiles that made many more headlines than the average old Division Two game, had arrived from Plymouth for £250,000. He never made as many headlines when playing for the club but that was not the point. He went on to stay at Ewood for almost five years, when he was sold by Roy Hodgson in the summer of 1997 in order to get more first-team football. Marker, who could play in the centre of defence or in midfield, was never first choice but played over 50 times in the Premier League, doing a job whenever a job needed doing.

'I remember at Plymouth we had played Fulham away and Peter Shilton pulled me to the front of the team bus,' said Marker. 'He told me that there was a Premier League club interested and said that it should happen very soon. He told me that I would get a phone call over the weekend.'

Thanks to the football grapevine, the player already was aware of the identity of the club interested. 'Of course, I knew. Anyway, I went home but I didn't sit by the phone all weekend. Me and Shilton did not see eye to eye and I went to a testimonial do on a boat trip up the Tamar but when I got home there were no messages, nothing. I was 26 and I thought that if they want me, it will happen.'

'So, on Monday, he called me into his office and told me that it will happen. It was just about arranging the part exchange.' Rovers players Keith Hill and Craig Skinner, young players who had been regular starters in the first team when the team was a solid Second Division team but were not judged to be good enough for a potential title challenge, were being sent south. 'I knew how much the deal was for in total but I didn't know the specifics of each player. I did know my own worth though. As a player, you have to. I think it was the Tuesday when Kenny called, and he gave me terms and conditions.'

For a player who was settling down to life in the third tier and with little prospect of that changing for a while, to talk to Dalglish was quite a shock.

'Even before we talked, I was never, never not going to go but it was tremendous to talk to him. I had so much respect. His knowledge of football was second to none, but it was also the way he spoke. He spoke and you listened, but it was the way he spoke. He spoke as a player almost. That was the thing, he had all this respect and was such a big football manager but at the same time, if you didn't know who he was and just talked to him, you would have thought that he was just a player – that is how he talked. That was why he had something special.'

'And then there was Ray Harford who was a great coach. To be honest, I would have gone anyway, I wanted to play in the Premier League, it didn't matter who was the manager, but it was great to not only play against the best, but I was playing with the best. Blackburn were not the biggest club or brand in the country but in those times, they were talked about so much, it was something else and great to be a part of.'

Marker realised that there was going to be competition for places at a club doing well in a league two levels above where he had come from. 'I went up there and the season had already started and they were doing well and were up at the top of the league. Of course, I was nervous as this was my big chance and I knew I had to prove I was good enough. I knew Blackburn had a settled defence but like at Plymouth, my issue was that I was a jack of all trades and a master of none. I played mostly in midfield at Plymouth, but I was really a centre-back and it was the same at Blackburn. I didn't mind. It helped me stay involved at many levels.'

More than most who arrived at Ewood, Marker was making a step up. From playing against third tier strikers, he was now facing the most expensive British signing ever in training.

'When I first went, it was hard, it was really hard and even though I knew it would be like that, it was still a shock. You go into training and it moves up a level and more. I had gone from Exeter to Plymouth, which was a different level in itself but then, of course, you are not just going to the Premier League, but you are going to a team that wants to win the Premier League. It was something else. I was playing against Shearer in training. He was world class and there were others too. Rovers were on the up and everyone wanted to play and be part of it and that showed in training. Perhaps there was always the worry for some that they could be replaced, so it could be intense.'

If the growing number of stars was not enough to deal with for the new boy, there was also Kenny. 'He was still fit and loved to play. He was something special. In the first month after training I went home... I was just knackered, it was unbelievable. Everyone is faster, stronger and just better. You have to step up or you don't play. Once you are there, it becomes the norm. I became a better player. I had to. I think we all did.'

Marker had to sit, watch and admire perhaps the highlight of the entire season as Rovers went back to the top. It came on 3 October 1992. Norwich were the surprise leaders and came to Ewood in good form. They were thrashed

7-1. Shearer got two, made two and was involved in everything.

The press had been in two minds about Shearer. The talent was undoubtedly there, but the price tag was a little high. However, his blistering start to the season meant that any narrative that he wasn't worth the money never developed. His performance against Norwich, top of the league, removed any doubts.

'To go to the top of the Premier League is one thing; to do so by beating the leaders by the biggest score the league has seen seems to be stretching the storyline,' wrote the *Independent*.

'But with Alan Shearer in his present form there is nothing incredible about the rise and rise of the Rovers. Norwich were poor enough to make a mockery of their own early-season success, but few sides could have lived with Blackburn yesterday.'

Shearer was sublime as he moved on to 12 league goals in the first 11 games of the season, but there was so much more to his game than that. He created the first, outpacing Ian Butterworth down the right to set up Roy Wegerle just feet from goal. The American had time to slip to his knees, 'perhaps in thanks for his good fortune in coming into a side to partner a player throbbing with Shearer's confidence', said the *Independent*. Then for the third, he knocked over Butterworth and set up Wegerle with another chance he could not miss.

Norwich pulled one back but that just served to inspire Shearer to get his first and the team's fourth and surely one of the best the old stadium ever saw. He picked up the ball in the middle, advanced towards the Norwich area and then, at full speed, chipped Bryan Gunn with a casualness and confidence that was as breathtaking as its beauty. That it came in a top of the table clash was all the more impressive and as Shearer celebrated, Sherwood summed it up with a repeated gesture towards the scorer than can only be described as an exhortation for everyone to hail the British transfer record signing, who was demonstrating that he was the best striker in the country and, after all the talk, a real bargain. Three more followed in the second-half: Chris Sutton brought down his future strike partner outside the area, allowing Gordon Cowans to make it 5-1 from a free-kick, before Ripley added another. Fittingly, a Shearer header rounded off proceedings.

'I was on the bench that day,' Marker, who had made his debut the week before, said. 'It was the complete striker's performance. We knew that he was a good player, but I sat there and saw him take apart the league leaders. It was not just the goals he scored but his all-round play. He was everywhere and doing everything. It was just a complete performance and one of the best I've ever seen. I had seen the standards in training that were a different level than what I was used to but that day you could see that the best players moved to the next level when it mattered, and that was during a game. I could see that Shearer was world-class and I am just happy I didn't have to face him.'

Those who still doubted Shearer were as rare as a missed shot on goal. As the venerable James Lawton wrote in the *Express*, 'The broader picture is that when Shearer destroyed Norwich with his pace and his vision he was leading something more than a smash-and-grab raid on the old establishment. He was fuelling something that looked encouragingly like a revolution in football values. Blackburn's football was touched by sunlight. It said that the resurrection of Kenny Dalglish is about a lot more than money.'

'The day belonged to Alan Shearer, as cleanly, as dramatically, as any day belonged to any football player but there was a deeper, wider triumph and it was the exclusive property of Kenny Dalglish. Dalglish knew Shearer was the greatest prize in the English transfer market. He held his nerve when Manchester United's wavered. The Old Trafford club must worry that with one bout of spending Dalglish may achieve what they have been pursuing desperately for 25 years. In football, it is painfully easy to spend money. Desperately difficult to make it work.'

United fans, still coming to terms with losing the title to Leeds the previous season, were worried. 'There was a real doldrums period in that winter when United couldn't score a goal,' remembers John Brewin. 'At that point, Shearer was tearing everything up and United fans were fuming.'

It was only when Cantona came and then got going that everyone started to forget about Shearer – for a while at least. 'There was some bad feeling about Shearer. I remember him as a 17 or 18-year-old when he scored a hat-trick,' said Brewin. 'He didn't actually score that many until he joined Blackburn but he did look like the real deal. I saw him play for Southampton at Old Trafford in the league. My memories were that there were a lot of elbows, but he wasn't afraid of Steve Bruce or Gary Pallister and they were the main men at the time. United would probably sing "There's only one greedy bastard" if they saw him on the street today. He says the reason that he went there was to work with Kenny Dalglish and you could see that would be attractive. Dalglish had that cachet as a manager. Even at the price, Shearer didn't look like a risk. I remember the start of that 1992/93 season and he was fantastic until he got that injury. That opening day when we lost to Sheffield United, it was the first *Match of the Day* to show all the goals in every game and we saw his against Crystal Palace and thought, "Wow, these look good". At that point, they looked like they could challenge for the title.'

'I never thought that I would see a player who was worth £3million. I have now,' wrote Alan Hansen after watching Shearer play.

Not long before, the prevailing view was that Shearer wasn't worth the money, but now he was the new darling of English football. Well, kind of. There was soon a backlash of sorts. John Giles refused to have anything to do with the bandwagon. 'It is premature to hail him as a new Lineker or Greaves,' he wrote in the *Daily Express*. The former Leeds star compared the new sensation with Leeds striker Lee Chapman. 'In almost every aspect of the striker's art, you have to give Shearer the edge... but Chapman scores goals that would elude Shearer because he, like Lineker and Greaves, is on the mystery of timing, the bounce of the ball, the subtle, often erratic flow of a game.'

Such an analysis almost defies belief and Giles can't have watched the player enough or he would have seen what was obvious to Rovers fans watching him play every week: that their new number nine was something truly special. He just did not have a weakness. In those early years, before the injuries, he had surprising acceleration and pace and what remained was the intelligence, an eye for a pass and a cross, bravery, determination and incredible strength. His low, almost non-existent backlift, was responsible for balls being put in the back of the net before the goalkeepers even realised a shot was imminent.

Wilcox's job was to supply the number one number nine with the ammunition to do what he did best. 'We knew what we had to do. As soon as our midfielders got the ball we started running and we wanted to get the ball into the area. On the other side there was Stuart Ripley and we worked hard on both wings.'

Later Kevin Gallacher was to star up front for the Rovers. The Scot would play alongside Shearer or out wide. 'Shearer was alright!' he said. 'We knew we had to work hard all through the team and we were built around what Alan was about. He was a great goalscorer and he wasn't only that. He could go wide and always put the ball into the box, passed well and had a good football brain.' Yet Shearer could usually be found in the penalty area or haring down on it, in the expectation that the ball would be forthcoming. 'If you were wide and didn't cross the ball into the box then you would get stick – you were always under that pressure to make sure that the delivery was good and when you have a player like Alan then that is what you have to do.'

Ripley soon realised that Shearer was the real deal and was also relieved that the mantle of Blackburn's record signing had been passed on rather quickly. 'We had the jewel in the crown in Alan Shearer, who was absolutely incredible,' he said. 'People forget he had a terrible knee injury and was out for quite a long time. When he came back from the cruciate injury, he was a different type of player. When he first signed, he was incredible, all over the place. He was knocking people over, holding the ball up, scoring goals, chasing people down, just phenomenal. Then he had his injury, but he was clever enough to modify his game slightly to become a finisher. He wasn't chasing down the wings all the time, but he was just an amazing player.'

Shearer himself denies that he changed the way he played when I put it to him. 'I didn't adapt my game until later in my career,' he said. 'My goals and stats improved after my injury, as did results!'

Brian Deane scored the first ever Premier League goal on the opening day of the 1992/93 season for Sheffield United against Manchester United and was in no doubt that Shearer was the top striker in the English Premier League. 'I was never linked to Blackburn. I signed a new contract at Sheffield United in the same year Shearer moved,' Deane said. 'Blackburn were never interested in me and I can see why. Shearer was fantastic. It is hard to describe how good he was when he was at his peak. He was the best around... he was at least eight out of ten in every aspect and better than that in most – he was good in the air, strong, quick, a good passer, hard-working and very intelligent, and just had no weaknesses. There were some good English strikers around at the time but Shearer was the best.'

As the goals continued to flow and the performances continued to be top-class, Rovers fans such as Ian Herbert just could not believe what they were watching. 'When we signed Shearer, the impact he had! He didn't hit the ground running but sprinting. He sets a benchmark for the rest of the team. There were people being sniffy about Chris Sutton [who signed in 1994 from Norwich] for a while as he wasn't Alan Shearer, but I always felt that side was a team. But it was a team with a focal point, there's no denying that. We weren't a one-man team as everyone had a job to do and if serving Shearer to help him get 30-odd goals a season was the job, then that is what you did. He was categorically the best player I ever saw at Blackburn – there is clear blue sky before you get down to anyone else. We've seen some decent players at Rovers over the years, but Shearer is head and shoulders and something else above the best that I've seen. I have never seen a player in a blue and white shirt who could create something out of nothing. His athleticism, power and strength of shot. Anyone who watched him play in the nineties and doesn't say he was the best player in the country by a country mile was not watching the same player I was.'

Then the injury came, sustained against Leeds United on Boxing Day in a challenge with Chris Fairclough. That was the one downside in a fine 3-1 win over the champions, notable for a virtuoso performance from Jason Wilcox, perhaps the game when he really demonstrated that he could perform at the highest level.

The seriousness of Shearer's injury was not apparent for a few days. He managed to trick a fitness test to play in the League Cup quarter-final against Cambridge United in early January, though he didn't last long before leaving the pitch. Without Shearer, Rovers won just two of the next eleven in the league and slipped out of the title race that was always likely to be too much too soon anyway. The signings of Kevin Gallacher and Graeme Le Saux just before the transfer deadline day at the end of March made a difference. Henning Berg came in February, though didn't really get in the team until the following season. There was more expectation on the incoming Patrik Andersson, who signed for £800,000 from Malmö, but the future Bayern Munich and Barcelona star didn't really settle in England.

Gallacher and Le Saux, who arrived from Coventry and Chelsea respectively, made their debuts against Liverpool in a fine 4-1 win. 'It always helps when you start well,' Gallacher said. 'I had played Liverpool a few months earlier for Coventry and we won 5-1. It was unbelievable to do it again with a new club in my first game. Le Saux crossed it in and I scored – two new boys making their debut.'

It had been a busy few days for Gallacher, who signed for the Rovers for either £1.5 million or £2.5million, depending on how you view it. 'Blackburn were the last to contact me. Bobby Gould was the manager coming in to Coventry and another new beginning. He pulled me into his office and told me, "We have no money so I am selling you." He then asked me where I wanted to go and I told him that I had no idea. He said that nine clubs were interested and Blackburn weren't one of them. Manchester City were one I think but they had just spent a lot of money on Terry Phelan. Then I got asked to stay by the phone as Kenny was going to phone me. I couldn't believe it. It was just one of those moments. Of course, there were no mobile phones then so I had to stay home and wait. That afternoon, Kenny called and said, "I want you to come to Blackburn." I thought fair enough, the club had agreed a deal and I said I would go to speak to them. I remember that there was a mad rush.' After finding dogsitters and talking to his wife, Gallacher drove up north to meet Dalglish, his wife Marina and Ray Harford.

Like many others, the chance to play for Dalglish was irresistible. 'For me Kenny was a big deal and it was great just to meet him. To play under Kenny was phenomenal. It was Kenny first and Blackburn second at that time. I had to look at the map to see where Blackburn was and I had to read up on a few things.' He may not have known much about the town but the club was making waves.

'They were big news. They got promoted and I had kept a close eye anyway because I followed Kenny. The £3.3 million for Shearer had opened the world's eyes and at Coventry we thought "wow". We had already sold two players to Blackburn in Tony Dobson and Steve Livingstone and so I had an inkling about the club, not much more than that, but we just knew that they meant business.

'Kenny was huge. It showed the club's ambition that they went to get Kenny. You hear about Jack Walker who owned the club, but from the outside it was another club spending money and they came and beat us at Highfield

Road and started the season really well.'

The size of the fee was not an issue. 'There was no pressure at all. There was Shearer there and then Coventry went and bought Roy Wegerle for one million which made it look like I cost £1.5 million instead of £2.5, so there was no pressure at all.'

With the new signings, Rovers finished the season with eight wins from the final ten games. There were some excellent performances. A 2-1 win at Tottenham was full of slick, fast passing football, with Gallacher working well with Newell. There was also that 4-1 win over Liverpool in front of a disbelieving Ewood that came just over two years after that FA Cup tie in early 1991 which they were 7-1 to win. Rovers then also downed Aston Villa 3-0 to virtually end the title hopes of the Birmingham outfit, effectively handing the trophy to Manchester United.

Rovers finished fourth, just a point behind Norwich, meaning they missed out on a first ever appearance in Europe by just one point. 'That was the only disappointment, not qualifying for Europe,' said Mimms. 'We just missed out and I never got the chance to play in Europe, and that is a regret.' Had Shearer been around for the second half of the season, then Rovers would surely have finished higher than fourth and booked a spot in the UEFA Cup. I asked the striker if he felt that Rovers would have challenged for the title had he stayed fit. 'Most definitely yes! It was a big blow to me and the club.'

This was also the club's best season in the cups for some time. Perhaps the one disappointment of the those early to mid-nineties was that Rovers never did anything in the knockout competitions, apart from that first season back in the top flight. The semi-final of the 1993 League Cup was an exciting prospect until, in front of a watching nation on ITV, Sheffield Wednesday won the first leg 4-2 at Ewood with Paul Warhurst running riot. That was pretty much that. Wednesday would have been the semi-final opposition in the FA Cup had Sheffield United been vanquished. Instead, after a dull 0-0 draw at home and an exciting 2-2 draw at Bramall Lane, the Blades won on penalties.

The following season saw a fourth-round FA Cup exit at home to Charlton Athletic, in a week when second tier teams were dumping out Premier League sides. Luton saw off Newcastle, Oxford won at Leeds and Bolton knocked out

Arsenal at Highbury. The League Cup ended with a loss at Tottenham. In the title year, Rovers were a little unfortunate to face top opposition early on. Ian Rush scored a hat-trick as Liverpool won in the League Cup at Ewood while Newcastle did the same in the third round of the FA Cup.

That was in the future. In the shorter-term, Rovers were looking forward to the return of Shearer.

10

FROM DOGSHIT TO THE DOG'S BOLLOCKS – A CLUB TRANSFORMED

'We were starting to see the vision we were sold.'

KEVIN GALLACHER

I REMEMBER SOMETIME FAIRLY EARLY IN THE FIRST season in the Premier League, October or November, we had a family lunch in the restaurant at the old Ewood.

In those days there was such excitement just to be near the ground but to be inside and eating your meal with the pitch below was as special a treat as the Chicken Kievs. The venue was long and thin, as you would expect being inside a smallish football stand, but there was a pleasant atmosphere and you could have a few drinks if you wanted and I think it was here where players came for a drink after a game.

This is also where they came for lunch after training and this is where they shared the space with the public: us being at the top end near the bar and their reserved tables further away. You could sit and eat and watch Dalglish and the coaching staff watch a game on television from the day before. 'At lunch time we used to sit upstairs in the John Lewis restaurant in the old stand, which some of the punters also used for lunches,' wrote Dalglish in his autobiography. 'They would pass by and say, "Keep it going." When we noticed more and more of them passing by, we knew Blackburn were on the up.'

What stands out in the memory was Alan Shearer working behind the bar, perhaps as some forfeit for a challenge lost or punishment for poor training. I seem to remember many orders of blackcurrant and lemonade from his teammates and the look of shock on the faces of members of the general public out for lunch.

Bobby Mimms was there too. He remembers those days well. 'You can see how things were as people like Alan Shearer are serving themselves and the other players. There was a real feeling of team spirit, we were all in it together. It made a difference.'

The new regime meant that things improved quickly on the pitch but off it, more time was needed. 'The standard of the training went up straight away,' Mimms added. 'Ray was fantastic, the best I had ever seen before or since. Ray did all the training and Kenny came to life on matchdays. It was very different to Don. Don knew his stuff but he did not have the full respect because you could get away with things, but not Kenny. Everything changed. There were better players coming in and the mindset was all different.'

The contrast between the team and the club was made in David Batty's autobiography in a chapter called 'Pub Team Millionaires.' Players didn't usually train at Ewood. That took place at Pleasington, part of the large Witton Park, the biggest green space in the town and also home to a large cemetery and crematorium. 'We changed at Plessy,' Atkins remembers. 'We used to stop for funerals. We used to get a call telling us that there was a Blackburn fan coming and then we stood on the side of the road. It was a family club and stayed that way.'

It was a public park and among the living fans that used to go there to actually watch the team train, there were also plenty of people just walking their dogs, and those just walking. I remember Tim Sherwood apologising to a couple of young girls who had heard him swear at a poor pass from Andy Morrison.

'We used to send the apprentices there ahead of training to clean the pitches of what had been left by dogs and whatever else was there,' said Mackay. 'The players used to work hard because there wasn't much else they could do but you saw that Jack Walker quickly wanted to sort out the training situation and you could understand why.'

After coming from Tottenham and Everton, but having already been on loan at Ewood, Mimms already knew the score when it came to training. 'It was a bleak place to train and stopping as people passed to go to the funerals. You pay all this money for players like Alan Shearer and they would turn out at Plessy, training in the local park. It must have been a nightmare from an insurance point of view with all these players that were bought for big money.'

It wasn't just the fact that the playing surface was obviously not the best – there were genuine issues as the predecessor of Mimms could attest. 'Terry Gennoe ripped his knee and that finished his career. He ended his career with a tin can. From that side of things, it was not good at all, but it was good for the team in some ways. You would get in your car pissed wet through and get back to Ewood, which was not exactly state of the art, but everyone was in it together. Players did not want to drive their own cars to training as they would have four wet and muddy footballers all sitting in your car. That became the objective, not to drive but to be driven.'

Dalglish relished it. 'The training ground was dreadful, covered in dog mess,' he wrote. 'It was next to a crematorium and we had to move the goals because the balls kept going into corteges. On Friday mornings, a few hundred people would come and watch us train, even though the conditions could be really icy. One morning Ray Harford slid in to hook the ball back and knocked an old man up in the air. The crowds thinned a bit after that incident.'

Sometimes the Scot was on the receiving end, with a tackle from Atkins standing out. 'It was the season before we won the league,' said Atkins, who had been turned into a midfielder by the boss. 'I wasn't playing much at the time because Batty had come in. I was sub a lot and I think I was frustrated at not playing. There was a tackle in the middle and I went straight through him and caught him on the shin. There was some blood and he was not happy.

There was a bit of a kerfuffle, which is the best way to put it. It was one of these things in football. On the Saturday I played. He knew that I wanted to be in the team. He didn't say that of course, as I guess he didn't want all the players who were not being picked kicking him all over the pitch. He always said that he knew what he was going to get from me. He knew what I would do and I knew what he wanted. I knew I had to be 100 percent every game. In training too, perhaps the bigger-name players could relax sometimes but I never could.'

Everything was basic. 'We all cleaned our own training kit which was a surprise,' said Shearer. 'It kept us a close-knit group though, and undoubtedly helped us with our team spirit.' Even Batty acknowledged that, although his book suggests he was not that happy about it all.

It may have been a bonding experience at the time, but Walker had made it clear that he wanted the best for the club and construction had already started on a new state-of-the-art training complex a few miles away in the beautiful Ribble Valley. 'Oh, it was fantastic,' said Mimms. 'You couldn't imagine a better place to train and you could not imagine a bigger contrast. Looking back, we have fond memories of Plessy but at the time, it was great to move and have everything you needed and also not have all the other stuff you get with training in a public park.'

It wasn't just the training pitch that was on the basic side. 'Press conferences took place in an old terraced house over the road,' said Dalglish. 'There were snide comments in the press about the facilities which really irritated me. That's why Jack was spending millions to develop Ewood… The facilities were poor, but no one complained.' The club shop was basically a living room, not the brightly lit and roomy 'Roverstore' that was soon to open.

The second season was when things changed. Blackburn Rovers had a fantastic return to the top flight and were a little disappointed to finish fourth, and more was expected. The team were starting to be seen as one of the big boys, not a massive club but one of the top sides.

In the first season back, there had been a feeling of disbelief. After those near-misses of the eighties, my dad used to say 'Just one season would be enough.' I think many would have agreed. It would have been great to get to the First Division to visit the famous old grounds at least once. Promotion eventually came, in the most dramatic of fashions, then there was a great first season where the team was not only visiting famous old grounds but taking the points back home. These were heady times and there was genuine excitement in the town on the day that Arsenal were beaten at Highbury. Fans, of course, were loving it but the people in general, even those not into football, were proud. Arsenal had won the title just over 15 months earlier, losing just one game in a season that ended with the Rovers avoiding the drop to the Third Division only on the final day.

As well as the training situation, there were other physical changes. One of English football's most historic grounds was changing. The second half of the previous season had seen the Darwen End knocked down. The bottom half of the replacement stand was ready for the start of the 1993/94 campaign. It could not have been more different. It was beginning to feel like a modern stadium; the concourses now had bars and food kiosks, and toilets with walls and a roof.

The club was still friendly and down-to-earth, but just a little bit less so. It was starting to move in different circles. Fans were excited to be part of it – indeed people used to go and watch the new stadium being built and understood all the reasons behind it – yet perhaps there were a few pangs for the old place. As the club became bigger, it seemed to move a little further away. With the new training ground, there was no chance of seeing a Rover down the local park or at the local restaurant. Now the stadium was all-seated, and so the old atmosphere of the Blackburn End with the red railings, the fans who stood with piles of beer cans at their feet and the dog-leg shaped Enclosure stand that was designed by Archibald Leitch, were all gone.

'It changed,' admitted Gallacher. 'When I went there, at the old Ewood Park, it was falling apart, but there was something there. We knew the ticket girls and guys, all the staff who worked there, and it was a lovely atmosphere. It took me back in time. It was very homely and family-oriented as a football club. I could see it grow very quickly and it moved away from all that – it was moving to be something like a superstar club. Then you see things start to change, you are away from the fans and the staff and spending more time out of the town. It was a change from being in Plessy, cleaning dog mess, putting the nets up, stopping for funerals. You could write a book on what we had to do but I think that gave us the spirit. There were no big stars, everyone pitched in and that went on to the football pitch. The training was an eye-opener. We had no facilities at Blackburn. It took me back to the Dundee United days when we had to wait for the manager to find out where we training. I even had to wash my own kit. I had to take a massive step backwards to go forwards. I bought into everything though and I was ready. I think we all did. While it changed with the new facilities and stadium, we now had a new environment, a new training pitch and stadium being built. We started to see the vision of what we had been sold when we joined the club.'

Such is the price of progress. While the stadium was quietly being transformed, Rovers spent much of the summer being linked with any high-profile player that moved. There were reports of Sampdoria being upset at a 'measly' £2.5 million being offered for David Platt, but the international midfielder that did seem to be heading to East Lancashire was Roy Keane.

Despite all the rumours, the links and the near misses, there were no new faces that summer. There were no big-name signings wheeled out to greet the fans. Gallacher and Le Saux had come fairly late the season before and felt like new players. And then there was the fact that Shearer was returning to fitness. There were pictures of him training at the new-look Ewood in the summer with headlines such as 'This is what Rovers fans have been waiting to see for months.'

This was good news, as there had been reports that Shearer would be out of action until Christmas. Two goals in a pre-season friendly at Ireland's Drogheda United made headlines as they came a week before the start of the season. It was proving tough to restrain the striker, who had been working hard to earn a place on the tour to Ireland. Dalglish agreed to put him on the bench but warned Shearer not to bend his ear about when he was getting on. The boss also had to calm down others too. 'It was a surprise when Shearer played here and it will be a surprise if I play him in the Premier League next Saturday. People shouldn't jump the gun.' The man himself said that he would be ready just a week or so into the new season and did not rule himself out of the vital 1994 World Cup qualifier against Poland on 8 September. Rovers continued to take it slowly. 'I didn't appreciate it at the time,' Shearer now says. 'I was frustrated and wanted to get back sooner but Kenny knew what he was doing, and it benefited me in future years.'

The striker did not make the squad for the opening game, a 2-1 win at Chelsea, but did appear as a second half substitute in the game on the following Wednesday as Norwich got revenge for the 7-1 thrashing of the previous season with a 3-2 win at Ewood Park, Chris Sutton getting a brace. Shearer came off the bench with 17 minutes remaining to a predictably massive standing ovation, though was unable to turn things around. He was soon exchanging niceties with defender Rob Newman after being tripped and spent his short time on the field upsetting the City defenders. Eventually he upset referee Robert Hart too, who gave him a telling off.

Shearer continued to come off the bench in the following weeks, but Rovers were doing okay without their star man. The defeat to Norwich was followed by wins at home to Oldham and then at Manchester City, the latter of which resulted in Peter Reid getting the sack. Shearer soon made his mark, however. Newcastle were the new boys in the division and were doing what the Rovers had done the season before, making big signings under a big-name coach in Kevin Keegan. Just like Rovers the year before, they had started well. Shearer was on the bench for the journey to his native north-east at the end of August but came off it to run onto Tim Sherwood's perfect through pass and finish with the same old certainly of the past. It cancelled out the earlier strike from Andy Cole, the new goalscoring sensation of the Premier League, and earned a 1-1 draw for the Lancashire side.

'As a manager you look for somebody to blame for the goal,' Keegan said, 'but you couldn't this time. You just have to admire the quality of the finish. It is what he does best, he is just a great striker. Hands on heart, Blackburn deserved the draw. We had to hang on. In the last 20 minutes they came on very strong and they nearly nicked it.'

The talk once again turned to the England squad that was going to be named the next day, as qualification for the 1994 World Cup was moving to its climax. 'If I was Graham Taylor I would have him in the squad,' Keegan added. 'Even at 75 percent fit, he's faster than some of my players.' Dalglish was understandably a little more reticent and not just because of his nationality. 'It's up to Graham Taylor if he wants to take Alan into the England squad,' said the Scot. 'If he thinks he's ready then that is up to him. But we would rather than he stayed and trained, if he is not going to play.' As the *Guardian* put it, 'The question is whether half a Shearer some of the time is better than no Shearer at all.'

In the end, Taylor decided that the promise of Shearer was enough and the striker was named on the standby list. He wasn't needed as England defeated Poland 3-0 at Wembley with Les Ferdinand, Paul Gascoigne and Stuart Pearce on the scoresheet.

The bigger news of the international week for Rovers fans was not, however, about Shearer. For the first time since March, the club had made a new signing. Paul Warhurst arrived from Sheffield Wednesday for £2.75 million.

Rovers had been in for the player in July but Wednesday boss Trevor Francis blocked the move, which was close to going through, as he was foiled in an attempt to get Brian Deane in from Sheffield United as a replacement. As the season started, Warhurst and David Hirst, seen early in his career as a Shearer equal, didn't really hit it off as a partnership. The 23-year-old, who had, signed a new four-year deal at Hillsborough, was reluctant to move back to the backline as boss Trevor Francis wanted and was transfer-listed. Once Ray Harford got in touch early in September, the move was on.

The defender turned striker was best remembered for his two goals at Ewood from February as Wednesday had won the first leg of the League Cup semi-final 4-2. Overall, he scored 18 goals the previous season and then scored a crazy dozen in eight pre-season friendlies. 'I know Rovers have three top quality strikers in Alan Shearer, Mike Newell and Kevin Gallacher,' said Warhurst upon his arrival, 'but I'm prepared to play in any position the manager might ask me. I know that the club is going places, and this is an exciting time to be here. It would be rather nice if the manager put me in for their next game at Liverpool a week on Sunday.'

'I always wanted to be a defender. I wanted to be cool and in control. I used to love watching Alan Hansen.' Then came his cameo in attack for Sheffield Wednesday to cover an injury crisis and all those goals. 'He was doing things I never thought him capable of: laying off the ball and spinning away from defenders,' said Earl Barrett, who played with Warhurst at Oldham.

Dalglish did put Warhurst in against Liverpool and it was rather nice as he eased his way into an attacking midfield role behind Newell and Gallacher

– still no Shearer – with the minimum of effort. Newell scored a fine winner, stretching to fire home a half-volley at the far post high into the net with just eight minutes remaining. It produced a satisfying 1-0 win at Liverpool – a first in 30 years at Anfield. Some Liverpool supporting friends of mine, usually very generous in their praise of the opposition if warranted, said they didn't like the way Rovers played and four of the five yellows went to the away team. This was harsh though. Neil Ruddock should have been sent off and Jan Mølby was unusually robust. It must have been pleasing for the manager. 'While Dalglish refused to gloat over his first win on his old ground,' wrote David Lacey in the *Guardian*, 'as manager of the opposition he was clearly satisfied with a measured, disciplined performance from his team which left Liverpool looking desperate and immature… This, in short, was not the Liverpool once graced by Dalglish the player.' It was a mediocre Liverpool team and six days later, they lost 2-0 at Everton and the fans singing 'Souness must stay' were not wearing red shirts.

The Liverpool win took Rovers third and it was expected that they would go top on 18 September with a home game against the lowly West Ham United. Instead it was a shock 2-0 home defeat at the hands of the team fourth from bottom who had not won away from home all season. 'This was a home banker if ever there was one,' said Jimmy Armfield on BBC Radio. 'Blackburn are a good team, but our passing game was terrific. We outclassed them,' said Hammers boss Billy Bonds. Dalglish was more succinct when asked about any injuries. 'Just our pride.'

Rovers dropped two more points at home the following Saturday with a 1-1 draw against Sheffield Wednesday. It was notable for being Shearer's first start of the campaign, and the striker delivered with a well-taken equaliser, but it didn't stop Blackburn from dropping to eighth in the table. After nine games, they were already seven points behind leaders Manchester United.

Then came a trip to Swindon. Though the likes of Hendry, May, Wilcox, Atkins and Mimms were still around, the team had changed significantly since the defeat at the County Ground just two Octobers before, Dalglish's first game in charge. It seemed like a lifetime ago. Rovers won 3-1 in a game notable for a Shearer brace and Warhurst breaking his leg. The challenge seemed innocuous, but it was a real blow for the club and player. At Sheffield

Wednesday, Warhurst had gone from being a central defender to a striker and being able to play both positions with equal ability. Technically excellent, he was quick and fine with both feet. At Rovers he was starting to look like becoming a very good all-round midfielder, box-to-box with an eye for goal and obvious defensive intelligence too. The broken leg meant that what could have been a fine Ewood career never really got going. 'Warhurst settled in really well but was unlucky to get that injury,' said Wilcox. 'You see it happen in football and you can only wonder what might have been.'

11

PUSHED ASIDE BY BATTY AND FLOWERS

'One minute you are the hero of the fans and then you are forgotten.'

KEVIN GALLACHER

DAVID BATTY WAS SOMETHING OF A REVELATION.
When Leeds United had come to Ewood on Boxing Day 1992, Rovers fans
had chanted 'If Batty can play for England, so can I.' It may not have been
original but it reflected what most thought about the midfielder: hard-working and typically tigerish, but not much more.

In October 1993, Rovers went to Elland Road and let a 3-1 lead slip,
eventually drawing 3-3. As Batty, who had been injured, came on to the field
as a substitute in the second half, Tim Sherwood said, 'You'll be at Blackburn
next week.'

'I hope so,' responded Batty, who had become disillusioned with life under

Blackburn entered the 1980s in the third tier of English football, but a strong second half of the season in the 1979/80 campaign under Howard Kendall secured promotion. 30,000 also turned out at Ewood to watch the fifth round FA cup tie against Aston Villa in February, with a late Allan Evans own goal securing a replay for the Rovers. Evans made amends at Villa Park, scoring the only goal of the game. [Getty]

It was Howard Kendall who led Blackburn back to the second tier, and he so nearly lead them back to the top at the first time of asking, but Blackburn finished in fourth, one place outside the promotion places. Swansea, who finished in third and on the same points, 50, were promoted. The latter's 2-0 win over the former at Vetch Field in April 1981 was the key result for both side's fortunes. Kendall played that day but could not prevent Robbie James from scoring a crucial goal. [Getty]

Noel Brotherston (shown taking on Gordon Strachan and John Gidman in a cup tie against Manchester United in 1985), was a key player for Kendall in 1981, and his leg break at a crucial stage in the season significantly hindered the side. While his manager would move on to Everton soon enough, the Northern Irish international stayed at Ewood until 1987. Tragically he would die of a heart attack at the age of just 38 in 1995, just a week before Blackburn clinched the title. [Getty]

Though Don Mackay was overshadowed by the man who replaced him, he served Blackburn excellently and is fondly remembered for guiding the team to the 1987 Full Members' Cup title, even if promotion ultimately eluded him. [Colorsport]

The Full Members' Cup triumph was secured with a 1-0 victory over Charlton at Wembley. Blackburn had beaten Huddersfield Town, Sheffield United, Oxford United, Chelsea and Ipswich Town to get there. [Getty]

'I could have easily stayed in Barcelona, made more money and stayed in the sunshine and had an easy life.' Midway through the 1987/88 season, Steve Archibald joined Blackburn on loan from Barcelona. He wasn't able to help Rovers to the promise land in his six months, but the club's willingness to take him to Ewood was one of the first signs of their new intent. [Offside]

The legendary Ossie Ardiles followed Archibald to Blackburn soon after. Here he skips away from Nicky Marker in his first game at Plymouth. He wouldn't be so lucky minutes later as he was injured in a challenge by the same player, who Dalglish would later take to Ewood. [PA]

Before Walker and Dalglish, the club's all-time leading goalscorer Simon Garner was the one to lead Blackburn's many promotion charges, and he eventually got there in 1992. Here he celebrates with Simon Barker in March 1987. [Getty]

The fact that Blackburn had suffered so much play-off heartbreak in the recent past made the 1-0 victory over Leicester City at Wembley in 1992 even sweeter, and with Walker now involved greater things lay ahead. [Getty]

Mike Newell, the man who secured Blackburn's place in the top flight with a penalty, celebrates at full-time. [Getty]

Scott Sellars, a classy wide midfielder who had been at the club since 1986, also started that day, but that proved to be his last much for the club as he joined Leeds United that summer. In six years for the club he played over 200 league games. [Getty]

Liverpool manager Graeme Souness and Kenny Dalglish watch on from the sidelines during a 1-0 win for Blackburn in 1993. Souness had replaced Dalglish in the Anfield dugout and would also take on the Blackburn job at the turn of the century. [Colorsport]

After joining from Tottenham in 1990, Bobby Mimms quickly became a fans' favourite due to his consistent performances between the sticks. However, that meant little when Tim Flowers joined in November of 1993. Dalglish had paid £2.4 million for his services, and put him straight in the team at the expense of an unlucky Mimms, showing how ruthless he could be. [Getty]

Shearer heads home at Ewood against Manchester United in April 1994. Though Blackburn would win 2-0 that day, they did not have quite enough in the tank to snatch the league title away. The not yet completed development of Ewood offers a glimpse into the streets that surround the ground. [Offside]

In the summer Shearer gained a new strike partner in Chris Sutton, who joined the club in July 1994 from Norwich. The £5 million paid by Blackburn was a British transfer record. [Alamy]

Jack Walker and Alex Ferguson lead Blackburn and Manchester United out at Wembley for the 1994 Charity Shield. Though United would win that day Blackburn would be on top at the end of the season. [Colorsport]

Kenny Dalglish, Tony Parkes and Ray Harford look on as Blackburn struggle against unfancied Swedish opposition Trelleborgs in the UEFA Cup. Though Rovers would win the league after getting knocked out of Europe, the nationally televised two-legged affair did little to combat the narrative that their football was one-dimensional and predictable when compared to Manchester United. [Getty]

Shearer trudges off the field in Trelleborgs as a 2-2 draw sends the Swedish outfit through to the next round at Blackburn's expense. [PA]

Jason Wilcox, a homegrown player who made the first team amongst a host of new signings, had to deal with plenty of unfair criticism early in his career from the Rovers faithful, especially those sat in the Riverside End, but he soon won them over and was impressive down the left hand side with Graeme Le Saux during the title campaign. [PA]

Rovers stalwart Mark Atkins challenges Eric Cantona at Ewood in October 1994, a game that Blackburn would lose controversially. A few months later, the Frenchman influenced the title race in a way nobody could have imagined. [Alamy]

New strike partnership Shearer and Sutton celebrate being the joint recipients of the November 1994 Carling Premier League Player of the Month award with their manager Kenny Dalglish, named manager of the month. [Mirrorpix]

In his eight years at Ewood Park Kevin Gallacher was a regular, appearing in over ten league games in five of those seasons, but in the Premier League-winning campaign he was cruelly limited to just one appearance due to injury. That came against Crystal Palace in April, and he fittingly scored a crucial winner. Minutes later, he had broken his leg for a second time, keeping him out of the run-in. [Alamy]

Dalglish had only ended his playing career in 1990, and despite the stresses of management he still found time to don the Rovers kit in 1995 in a friendly. [Getty]

Blackburn and Newcastle observe a two-minute silence ahead of their crucial Premier League clash on 8 May 1995. A win for Blackburn would mean they had the title in their own hands on the final day of the season. [Alamy]

Shearer would later become a hero in his native Newcastle, but his goal in the 1-0 win over the Magpies was the one that effectively sealed the title and earned him immortal status at Ewood. [Getty]

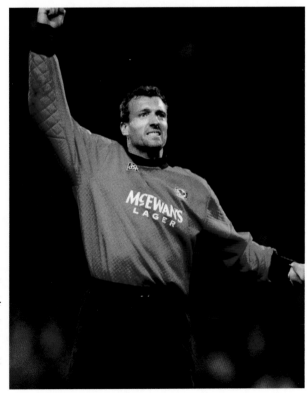

Tim Flowers was perhaps the main reason why the three points were secured though, pulling off a series of world-class saves to deny the visitors. Here he celebrates in front of a raucous Ewood crowd before giving a legendary post-match interview to Sky. [Alamy]

Shearer is presented with his PFA Player of the Year award. Six Blackburn players were named in the team of the year in total: Flowers Le Saux, Hendry, Sherwood, Sutton and Shearer. [PA]

After all his hard work, money and impetus, Jack Walker finally gets to celebrate with the trophy of his dreams at Anfield on the final day of the 1994/95 season. [Getty]

Blackburn captain Tim Sherwood rests his hands on the Premier League trophy as his teammates celebrate at Anfield. Rarely has a team looked so ecstatic directly following a loss. [Getty]

Sutton (15) and Shearer (34) scored 49 league goals between them over the course of the campaign, over half of Blackburn's 80. The SAS moniker was more than appropriate. [Getty]

Parkes, Dalglish and Harford celebrate with the trophy back in the dressing room. Harford would soon be replacing Kenny in the manager's seat, while Parkes would only leave Ewood in 2004, after 34 years of service. [Getty]

Ray Harford was a popular figure among the Rovers players and a superb coach, but he didn't find things as easy as a manager, demonstrated by his expression here after a 3-0 defeat to Spartak Moscow in November 1995. [PA]

Howard Wilkinson. The comments excited him. 'I think I decided there and then that the time for change was upon me.'

The next night he was in bed when one of his teammates called to say he had been talking to Kenny Dalglish and would Batty be interested in heading west over the Pennines. Moments later, Dalglish called to say that Leeds had agreed to sell, depending on price.

There had been no rumours or links, no build-up. It just was announced. Leeds fans were none too happy that one of their own was leaving the club. Local radio stations were inundated with angry callers. A poll ran by the *Yorkshire Evening Post* had 114 in favour of selling against 1,952 who were not. Even Batty's parents, on holiday at the time in Scarborough, only found out when watching regional news programme *Calendar*. It came as a shock, especially for Batty's dad, who had played a big part in his son's career.

His first game was against Tottenham, Blackburn's next league game after the draw at Elland Road. A 1-0 win that was not a reflection of the home team's dominance. Another tier had been added on to the Darwen End and the extra 3,000 tickets were sold out well before kick-off to give a biggest crowd of the season so far at 17,462.

Batty's ability to thread a ball through a mass of players was unknown to Rovers fans. He was always available for a pass and always looking for space and was a great deal more intelligent than he had been given credit for. He helped his new team have more and better possession. Once he arrived, the team really started motoring and moved into fourth.

Not all were thrilled with this new signing. Mark Atkins had established himself in the team and was the one to make way for the big-money signing. 'It was a disappointing as I was playing every game and playing well I think. He came in and it was a big deal. He was an England international,' Atkins said.

Despite the disappointment, he was impressed. 'I will tell you something, he was one of the best three players I ever played with, far better than his reputation.

'He wasn't a kicker – unless he got angry – he was a great passer of the ball and had a great range. He was just a great player. I had no argument with the signing as the boss was trying to make the squad better.'

Mimms could sympathise with Atkins. Mimms had been number one at Ewood since the start of the decade and – at the very least – restored a reputation tarnished at Tottenham. He had been between the sticks for promotion and then in the first season in the top tier, but there had been talk of a new goalkeeper coming as soon as Dalglish arrived. One of his first signings was going to be Bruce Grobbelaar. Early in the 1993/94 season though, it finally looked as if there was a new number one heading to Ewood.

There had been rumours linking Tim Flowers to Blackburn for weeks. Liverpool were also very much in the chase, especially as the Southampton man had refused to sign a new contract. Iain Dowie, then a striker with the Saints, told Sky Sports the story in 2017.

'He rings me, because we were roommates, and tells me they've agreed a fee. He thinks it's £3 million – either Blackburn or Liverpool. At the time, and it's no disrespect to Blackburn, I said: "Well, where are you going?" He said he wasn't sure. I was like: "What do you mean you're not sure? Liverpool or Blackburn... what are you thinking about?" Sure enough, the first one to ring him was Kenny Dalglish – so up he goes to Kenny's own house.

'He's in there, he's on his own, he finishes negotiations and says, "I'll go home overnight and think about it." Kenny said "No, no, no, stay here." Tim said "No, no, it's alright," and Kenny said "No, no, it's fine." He ended up staying overnight and in the morning he ends up signing for Blackburn. Tim said the next day: "Why did you make me stay overnight?"

'Kenny goes, "I had Roy Keane in here two weeks ago, he went home for the night and ended up signing for Manchester United. I wasn't letting you go anywhere!" It's a fantastic story – and what a keeper he was.'

There was less threat from Liverpool than Manchester United. Liverpool were in a mess and manager Graeme Souness had been complaining about the state of the team he had been left by his former teammate. This obviously riled Dalglish. 'It gave me no satisfaction to see Liverpool being slaughtered from every quarter. Graeme was harshly criticised,' Dalglish wrote in his autobiography, before doing a little criticising himself. 'Graeme said he had inherited an aging team from me, a suggestion that I cannot allow to stand unanswered. Their ages were there for everyone to see, but there was a still a great deal of life left in them as footballers.'

On 19 October, Rovers upped their offer from £2 million to £2.2 million.

Southampton admitted that they were considering the bid. By the end of the week, Liverpool had pulled out. 'Of course Flowers is an outstanding player but it will be too much money for us,' said Souness. But Liverpool did not give up, offering David James and Don Hutchinson as well as part exchange plus cash. James initially did not want to go but, according to reports, the goalkeeper changed his mind. It was Hutchinson who was less keen to head to the south coast.

Southampton then seemed to agree to take the £1 million-rated James and then pocket the rest. 'Last night [Tuesday, 26 October 1993], I agreed a deal with Ian Branfoot, the Southampton manager, for the transfer of Flowers,' said Souness. 'I was given permission to speak to Flowers then, which I did, and I arranged to meet him 2pm today at Anfield. At 10am, I spoke to Tim again and he agreed to speak with us this afternoon. An hour later I got another call from the agent [Jerome Anderson, who was to later have a close association with Rovers and the Venky's and is about as popular with Rovers fans now and he was probably was with Souness then] telling me that the meeting was off again.'

The deal was done with the Rovers for £2.4 million. It took Dalglish's transfer spend to past the £20 million mark in the two years he had been at Ewood Park, and it almost doubled the British transfer for a goalkeeper, which was the £1.3 million that Arsenal paid Queens Park Rangers for David Seaman in 1990.

'I don't think a £2 million tag will bother me,' Flowers said. 'It's not a big thing as it seems to be the going rate for a lot of transfers these days. Blackburn have bought a tremendous amount of talented players, they've got a good record so far and I believe they have a great future.'

Rovers fans were excited to see Flowers in action. A bunch of flowers had been left in his goal before his debut at QPR where the travelling fans gave him an excellent reception. A few thoughts should have been spared for Mimms, however. 'It is a consolation that it took a world transfer record but at the time I was more than disappointed to be honest. I was a victim of circumstances as Liverpool were after him and we had the money to bring him to our place. I thought we didn't need him. We had kept a lot of clean sheets the season before.'

'The biggest problem was not that we signed him, that was fine and we had the money to do it, but I had been playing well. I had eight or nine clean sheets already that season.'

Mimms, who had been a firm favourite with the Rovers fans (shouts of 'Bobby, Bobby, Bobby' had rung out in many famous old stadiums) and won respect around the country, felt that he was never given a chance to fight for his place. 'Tim came in and went straight into the team. If he had come in behind me and put me under pressure and then if I messed up and he is in, I would have held my hand up. But then when you pay that kind of money – a world record fee – then you know he is not going to sit on the bench.

'At the time I felt I was the best. They had the cash to pay for Tim and that is not his fault. Unfortunately, it is the way it is. Players wanted to play then, perhaps more than now. I felt I had grown with the club but they didn't owe me anything, but I felt I was in the right place. The feeling with the team didn't change. Kenny spoke to me and told me he still wanted me. I was still happy to be there and I didn't ask to go on the list. It was a case of hanging on in there. There are days you sit there and pick the money up. I was contracted at the time. I stayed and played in the League Cup and wasn't in a rush to leave. I never got close as Tim played well. We got on well, which helps. Otherwise it can be difficult and make going to work a long day.'

Fans talk about loyalty in football and how players show little of it when there is a better offer elsewhere, but it can work both ways. For all that Mimms had done for the club and for all his popularity, there was excitement that Flowers had joined and on the day of his first appearance at QPR. I remember it well in that packed away end. Flowers was first choice now and Mimms was not given a second thought.

Rovers may not have spent anything in the summer but had now splashed out over £7 million on three players in the space of two months. Dalglish was quick to head off any thought that the club was inflating the market. 'We will only pay what we feel is the right price,' said the boss. 'We will not be held to ransom. The cartel up there have had it to themselves long enough and it seems to bother them that Blackburn Rovers are now involved. We know where we are going, we just want to get there quickly. People don't appreciate that all the money coming into the game through Blackburn is fresh money. It has come out of Jack Walker's pocket. How can you say it is bad for the game when £20 million has been generated when it was not there before? The only ones probably who are complaining are the ones we haven't bought anybody from.'

It didn't stop the 1-0 defeat at QPR being framed as a victory for good old fashioned hard-work against big-spending pretenders. It also didn't stop Rovers being linked with a move for QPR striker and matchwinner Les Ferdinand as soon as the game was over and then Paul Gascoigne a few days later.

For Rovers fans, it was weird to be supporting a team that most neutrals wanted to see lose. This was a club that had been quite popular in the past. A good old-fashioned homely team that was welcoming, friendly, full of tradition, as well as being quite poor. Now it was different. Being able to outbid the likes of Liverpool was obviously a novel situation. It was another example of the change in the club. No longer was this 'good old Blackburn' but an aggressive force to be reckoned with.

The criticism comes with the territory when you start winning and that is what Rovers started to do. The team had been inconsistent in those first 14 games of the season. Defeats against West Ham, Norwich and now QPR had them down in eighth, a full 14 points behind Manchester United. But then they really started to get into gear, winning 18 of the next 23.

12

DOWN (AND UP) BY THE RIVERSIDE – JASON WILCOX AND GRAEME LE SAUX

'The stick I got from the Rovers fans made me a better player in the end.'

JASON WILCOX

IN THAT SECOND SEASON, THE LEFT-SIDE WAS ON FIRE.
There was Jason Wilcox developing into one of the best wingers in the league with Graeme Le Saux, soon to make his England debut, behind him. The Riverside was that single-tiered stand facing the tunnel and it was notorious for hosting, shall we say, the more critical of the Rovers faithful – as Wilcox found out as a young player.

Despite all the big-money signings, there were stars emerging elsewhere in the team and none more so than this Lancashire lad. Wilcox joined the Rovers on schoolboy terms in 1986. After a trial with Manchester City did not go as well as he hoped, his dad stepped in. 'My dad wrote about 30 letters to all the local clubs across all the leagues,' Wilcox said. 'And I got a reply from Blackburn shortly after and went down on a Sunday morning. I scored about six goals and signed the following Monday and played in the Lancashire Youth Cup final against Blackpool the following Monday. It was an unbeliev- able week. I was there as an apprentice – what are called 'scholars' now and it was a traditional scheme. After 12 months I got offered a pro contract for the following year.'

A debut came as an 18-year-old in a 2-1 win over Glenn Hoddle's Swindon in April 1990. In the following season, he started to appear more on his favoured left side, showing that he had a bright future. Throughout the Dalglish years, he was the one regular first-team player who had come up through the ranks. The sight of big-name internationals suddenly heading to Ewood didn't bother him.

'I didn't think about the new players coming in. At the time, I knew some big clubs were watching me on a weekly basis and I had confidence in my ability, but you never know what is going to happen. I was at the age that I didn't think about it. Kenny was my idol and when he was manager I knew I had to work hard, and I wanted to impress him and be the best I could. I was obsessed with being as good as I could be, and he certainly got the best out of me.'

The *Guardian* interviewed youth development manager Jim Furnell, who remembered Wilcox as a 15-year-old apprentice. 'He was so dedicated. He had pace and the ability to cross. He has had a lot of stick from the crowd but he's learned to live with it. I think he's beginning to win them over.' It took time. Simon Garner admitted that of the two wingers who emerged in the late eighties, Wilcox and Craig Skinner, he felt the latter would be the one to make it and was surprised when he was allowed to go to Plymouth in part exchange for Nicky Marker.

Wilcox quickly established himself as a Premier League class winger. There he was, athletic and pacey on the left, with the more old-fashioned dribbler in Stuart Ripley on the right. In the first season up, Wilcox showed plenty of flashes. In a Boxing Day win over Leeds at home, he was excellent. When he was given the man of the match award, the away fans (of which I was one as I couldn't get a ticket for the home end, but had some Leeds supporting friends who helped out in return to plenty of my mum's pre-match bacon butties) chanted, 'Jason, who are ya?'

'That particular game was certainly a real turning point for me personally,' Wilcox recalled. 'It is not that I improved as I always had the level, but I was starting to play better more often.'

Wilcox had his detractors at Ewood, with plenty of fans giving him plenty of stick at the earliest opportunity.

'It is no secret that the crowd started getting on my back,' he remembers. 'To have all Ewood Park booing your name as it is read out, that is not something that many kids have to cope with. I was doing it at 19. I was playing against senior professionals in midweek for the reserves and doing well and then come Saturday, with the pressure, something was not quite right. I made a decision to almost treat it as a bit of a war. I was trying to win a battle against everyone.'

Looking back now at the work he did, the goals he scored and set up, it is mind-boggling that a local lad who came up through the ranks to shine at the top level of English football got so much stick.

'I don't know the reason. My style didn't help and neither did my physique. I used to get lots of comments as I came out of grounds that I was lazy. Because of my gangly style, it didn't look like I was quick until I was running past someone. When I was 19, of course I dwelt on it and it did become a situation. I knew that I had to address the situation if I was going to achieve what I wanted to achieve. I made it like I was at war with everyone, and it was like shoving two fingers up to everyone. Other players tried to help me but you have to find your own solutions, no matter what everyone says at the time. They don't know what you are going through, they have no idea. I had to find it myself.

'Of course, Kenny was always telling me what a great player I was. He was brilliant. He kept playing me throughout it all and I think he was also shoving two fingers up just by playing me every week. I am very thankful for the support of him and Ray Harford.'

Wilcox, who was to sign for Leeds in December 1999 for £4 million after 12 years at the club, had the sympathy of teammates. 'When I played at right-back, before I was moved to midfield, I got stick from the fans and especially from the Riverside,' Atkins remembers. 'Jason got more.' The long stand along one side of the ground was notorious for its complainers but there were more, as Wilcox acknowledges.

'It wasn't just one area. Unfortunately at any football club, the intelligent ones who know the game are quiet. You only hear the vocal ones, as they express their frustration as they have every right to. They paid money to watch and I bear no grudge to the fans. It wasn't all of them, but I look back with fondness.'

Wilcox more than held his own among the expensive names and fans started to respond to that.

'I think it improved. There was an acceptance… it is not something I think about too much. I think about the time we had together, the period we had – what we were going through was incredible. I feel privileged to have been a part of that. To sit in a dressing room with 16 or 17 fellas that I believed in as people, never mind as players. The spirit we had was special. It is a shame if you have never experienced that in life. I was lucky to play for Leeds and Blackburn with two great dressing rooms.'

'If you ask any of my teammates they would say I was one of the fittest and ran the most.'

Atkins did say just that. 'Jason was a great player. He came up through the youth ranks. He has a fantastic story. I don't think he got the recognition he deserved. People didn't realise what he did for the team. They thought he just ran forward and then crossed into the box. His defensive work was outstanding and he was a great lad. He did get more stick than most, maybe because he had been there all his career. Nowadays, it is the opposite with players like Harry Kane. If Wilcox was coming through now, he would be the most popular player at the club.'

It certainly is strange that Wilcox did become a target. The team was doing well, these were exciting times with big stars everywhere, and to top it off there was also a local lad doing good.

There is a theory, and it sounds plausible, that in those heady days when big stars were coming to Ewood and big names were being linked, that a player who comes up through the ranks can be seen as, well, a little boring. Rovers fans, or perhaps fans in general, can be an unusual breed sometimes.

'He's a local lad and I think there's a bit of jealousy,' said Furnell in 1994. 'There is the feeling that he didn't cost any money so he's no good. If he left the club now, he would cost at least £1 million. The fact is that whatever some of the supporters think, the lad has pleased the manager. And he can still improve. I'm sure he can outstrip most full-backs, but at times he will take the easy option and play the simple pass rather than try to beat somebody. But he doesn't want to make mistakes and lose his place in the side and he lacks a bit of confidence. The public tend not to notice just how much work he and Ripley do defending. And when you are running 50 yards up and down the line all the time, it takes a lot of energy.'

Ian Herbert remembers it well. 'The Riverside's treatment of Blackburn's wingers extends way beyond Jason Wilcox. There is a long history of fans criticising wingers for not getting past a man or beating the first defender. And it could have been a case of "We have Ripley on the right so why are we persevering with this kid on the left-hand side?" He was effective and so many managers picked him, and he was unfairly maligned. Like Mark Atkins, his contributions didn't always catch the eye but if you took them out, you would notice.'

'One of the wingers was bought, the finished article, and if I think about Jason Wilcox… I remember going to watch him pre-season at Bolton and he used to get dreadful stick in the 4,000 Holes fanzine, who called him Balsa Boy – "This guy's never going to make it, look at him, he gets knocked off the ball." He took some fearful stick depending on which half it was with the Nuttall Street Stand or the Riverside. He came back and came back and developed and got better and better. His delivery from the left side was unerringly accurate and there was a hotspot from the edge of the six-yard box to the penalty spot and you thought, if he curls something in there then Shearer or Sutton will get on the end of it.'

With Wilcox and Ripley flying, Batty and Sherwood forming a partnership in the middle and Flowers in between the sticks, Rovers were looking very good indeed, especially with Shearer being Shearer. From his first full start after injury against Sheffield Wednesday on 25 September to a 2-0 win at Tottenham Hotspur on 12 February, Rovers scored 31 league goals. All but seven were Shearer's. It was a phenomenal run of 23 goals in 19 games. People used to bet £10 on him to score the first goal in every game and while the odds plummeted to as low as three or two to one, they still made money. 'Three to one?' asked Andy Gray after another Shearer opener. 'He'll be odds-on soon.'

It all added up to a growing feeling that the team was going somewhere special. 'The year we came second was the best football I had ever been involved with, even better than the championship winning year,' Ripley said. 'I remember just lining up in tunnels before the game and looking around me and just knowing that we were going to win. We had that unbelievable confidence in ourselves and teammates and the club and everything. It was incredible really.'

Still United were seen as nailed-on for the title. Going into Christmas, they were 12 points clear at the top ahead of Leeds United and 14 ahead of the Rovers, even with the Blues having won five of the previous six. 'The Premiership cannot be all over by Christmas, but by early New Year it is likely to appear all over bar the counting,' the *Guardian* recorded on Christmas Eve.

On Boxing Day, Rovers went to Old Trafford and were disappointed, more than that, to draw 1-1 thanks to a last-minute equaliser from Paul Ince. I still remember the headlines of 'Dane Crazy' after United goalkeeper Peter Schmeichel come up for a corner kick. Shearer did not score but hit the woodwork, while Blackburn's goal came courtesy of a fine first half effort from Kevin Gallacher. It was a fine performance that deserved a win. Still, Rovers were not seen as the likeliest challengers with one newspaper writing that Leeds players would be close to putting boots through their television screens at the late equaliser.

That was to change in the new year. Rovers ended the old one being linked with Portsmouth centre-back Kit Symons for £2 million. On 1 January 1993, Rovers won 1-0 at Aston Villa, runners-up from the year before. 8,000 fans made the journey to Birmingham to cut United's lead to just ten points. 'United need to be pushed, yet who is to do the pushing?' asked David Lacey in the *Guardian*. After counting out Arsenal and Leeds, he decided that Blackburn Rovers were the ones. He went on to compare the team to Liverpool – not to Dalglish's Liverpool, but a version from the early years of Bill Shankly. 'The tight, disciplined team formations, the determination with which the ball is won back after possession has been lost, the way opponents are forced to play square and ineffectual passes across the face of a retreating defence…'

Still, praise was sometimes grudging with Lacey pointing out that that almost £20 million had been used to build a team that was competent but hardly captivating, suggesting that Batty, Warhurst and Gallacher had cost too much. 'The sums paid for such players… are more a reflection of the funds available to Dalglish more than the class of his purchases.' Shearer, though, almost looked to be a bargain, though how anyone could qualify the obvious with 'almost' is surprising. The striker had established himself as clearly the best in a league that was not short of striking talent.

Rovers were happy to win ugly, though that was not always their fault. A 2-1 victory at Sheffield United was a scrappy affair. Shearer got both but angered the hosts by jumping out of the way of a wild tackle from Carl Bradshaw. For United boss Dave Bassett that jump helped the player get a second yellow, subsequently reducing the Blades to nine men.

'He deserved to be sent off and deserves to be banned,' said Shearer. 'If I'd not jumped out of the way I'd be on the way to hospital now.' Words were exchanged with Bassett. 'What he was saying was that I should have stood there and let him take the bottom of my leg away from the top.' For a man who had not long returned from a nine-month injury lay-off, it was an understandable reaction.

The points continued to come rolling into Ewood Park. The game against Leeds at home on 23 January was in danger of being overshadowed by the behaviour of the visiting fans before kick-off during the minute's silence for the recently deceased Matt Busby. As the players gathered around the centre-circle some of the United fans could be heard chanting 'There is only one Don Revie', in reference to their own legendary manager who, many Leeds supporters felt, had not been given the respect and send-off he had deserved by English football when he had passed away in 1989. It did not go down well. Leeds skipper Gordon Strachan could be seen shaking his head and along with some of his teammates gestured to the fans to try and shut them up. As soon as the referee sounded his whistle to end the silence, Rovers fans booed. The Leeds manager Howard Wilkinson put the fact that his team should have been out of the game by half-time, such was the hosts' dominance, down to the behaviour of the away contingent. 'To say I am disappointed is an understatement. I can't understand it. It is another world to me. A quarter of an hour went by and you could see they were as shocked and numbed as me. Adjectives can't describe how the players and I abhor such conduct and were affected by it. Four or five of my players tried to do something about it and were promptly told by those people where to go.' Leeds chairman Leslie Silver apologised to Manchester United. 'I feel sick to the stomach. This disgusting incident has set the club's image back ten years. I'd love to ban them.' Don Revie's widow Elsie also expressed her disappointment. 'Don would have been saddened, he was such great buddies with Matt. When he got the Leeds job, Matt was the first person Don turned to for advice.'

After Shearer's early opener, from a perfect Wilcox cross, Leeds somehow kept in the game to make it 1-1 with a late special from Gary Speed. It looked as if that would be enough to earn them a point until the final seconds, when Le Saux crossed from the left and a towering header from Shearer thundered into the bottom corner. The goal against was a delight and on Sky TV Andy Gray was left shaking his head – he would later select it as his goal of the season. 'What can you say about this man? Quite magnificent.' Martin Tyler agreed as the camera zoomed in on Shearer at full-time as he walked off the pitch, back slapped by delighted teammates. 'He is in the sort of form that will be marked down in the record books for years to come. It is not just the number of goals, but the timing.' Leeds boss Howard Wilkinson put it succinctly. 'They had the first half, we had the second and they had Shearer.'

Even that Lee Chapman fan John Giles had come around. 'In an impressive crop of English strikers, I believe he is the number one. He has a far more impressive temperament than Ian Wright... he has more consistency than Les Ferdinand. The QPR striker is also superbly equipped but his overall effect on a game is rarely as overwhelming as Shearer's. Andy Cole's 30 goals speak eloquently of his finishing touch but outside the penalty area he is a passenger. Teddy Sheringham has skill and leads Spurs' line but in terms of force and commitment he too fails to compete at Shearer's level. His growth since he joined Rovers has been phenomenal.'

Le Saux had made the second. The left-back had arrived at Ewood in March 1993 as a Chelsea cast-off for around £400,000 in cash plus forgotten striker Steve Livingstone. His story from Chelsea reserve to Blackburn and then England regular shows that Jack Walker's cash did not just go on the expensive forwards or midfielders, but that Kenny Dalglish and Ray Harford were happy to resurrect careers that had gone off the rails.

'I had got to the stage at Chelsea where I was on my way,' Le Saux told the *Guardian* in 1994. 'For the final couple of weeks at Chelsea, I had been training with the kids and you know when you are training with the kids on Friday you are not going to be involved in the first team on Saturday. It becomes impossible.'

His father, an accountant who wanted to be a footballer, said that under Chelsea boss Ian Porterfield, Le Saux had become frightened to kick a ball, but then Dalglish came calling. There had been a game on New Year's Day when Le Saux famously threw his shirt at the manager after being substituted off. 'I can stand up for myself. I would never lie down and let anyone walk over me but at the end of the day, a player has to be submissive to a manager because what a manager says goes. I would be the first to admit in hindsight that it was a silly thing to do. If that is being hot-headed then so be it. I think it was an emotional response to the situation. I'm a winner and a fighter and if obstacles are put in my way as I felt they were at Chelsea, I get frustrated. It was about feeling scapegoated and when you try to stand up for yourself, sometimes you do end up rocking the boat. All I can remember is having a half-decent game against Southampton and being taken off. I went into the dressing room and burst into tears. I was very upset...'

I asked Ian Porterfield about it a few years later in a hotel overlooking the beautiful Haeundae Beach in Busan, South Korea, where he worked for a while. He said it was one of those things that happens and that he was pleased to see that Le Saux had gone on to achieve success. At the time, the player was fined two weeks' wages, with a source at the club telling the press that the bad blood between player and manager had been building for some time. Le Saux, who was booed by Chelsea fans, said, 'I hurled my shirt because I was so angry, I felt cheated. I could not believe he wanted to take me off. I thought I had done enough to stay on the pitch. This is about personal differences that I have at the moment with Ian Porterfield.'

Over a year later, he could afford to be a little more philosophical about the situation. 'When you get frustrated, you try to fight the system, but you can't beat the system. Luckily, I managed to find a new one. He [Dalglish] must have seen something he liked. I didn't have a clue where Blackburn was.

I had to have a quick look at the map. The deal took about a month of juggling figures and so on and I was nervous and on edge the whole time. Every time the phone rang, I was up. Obviously to be wanted by Kenny Dalglish tells you something.'

'I didn't know much about the gaffer as a manager until I signed but I've discovered there is a lot more to him than he lets on to the public. He's not a strict disciplinarian. He's very easy going but he puts the responsibility on the players. He hasn't won everything in the game just by riding his luck for the past 10 years. He pushes me into going forward and tries to influence me with his worldly knowledge on how to get past people. I have to prove to everybody that I can defend as well as go forward. That's what I am aiming to prove to people who say I can get forward because I was a midfielder but are asking "Can he defend?"

'He's a lot more open than he's given credit for. Behind the image there is a much warmer person. He takes a joke very, very well and can give one back too. He loves the banter. But that's imagery for you. You don't know people until you live with them. In our dressing room, Stuart Ripley is the one whose head is forever in a book. There's a lot more to David Batty than perhaps people would think. I am enjoying my football. I do feel relaxed and confident. The quality of the other players in the side rubs off on you. Alan Shearer's finishing ability is great for my crossing. A ball crossed into the box is only an exceptional ball if somebody meets it. There is an honesty about everyone on the pitch and that is the difference between a successful team and an average team.'

After the Leeds game, while Shearer got the plaudits, the talk of Rovers, still 13 points behind, was how they were on course to qualify for Europe for the first time ever.

'It is difficult to say we can't catch Manchester United because you don't want to let the supporters down,' Le Saux said, 'but they are an exceptional side and I think the English league is such a fair reflection of form they will win, and deservedly... but we still hope the buggers slip up.'

Rovers turned him into a proper left-back after he had been moved around a little at Chelsea. Just under a year after his move up north his form earned him an England call-up under Terry Venables.

13

THE THRILL OF THE CHASE

'Blackburn deserve credit. They have also played some good football and pushed us harder than seemed possible at one stage of the season.'

ALEX FERGUSON, MAY 1994

IN EARLY FEBRUARY 1994, ROVERS DEFEATED WIMBLEDON 3-0. It saw the debut of defender Andy Morrison. Some of the fairly low-key signings didn't get the same playing time but still talk fondly of their time at the club. Morrison came in from Plymouth to provide cover at centre-back. '[The Plymouth manager] Peter Shilton just pulled me into his office and said that Blackburn had been on and wanted to sign me,' Morrison said. 'I didn't have a choice, I had to go, but to be honest, I was over the moon. Nicky Marker was a friend of mine and had gone a few months before and Nicky spoke highly of the club. It was a great opportunity for a young player then. I didn't know that much about Blackburn but I knew Kenny Dalglish.'

Back in those days, clubs at the top of the top tier still signed players from the lower leagues, though even that practice was starting to die out. Rovers, however, did it more than most, with Morrison coming up two divisions. It was unlikely that the barrel-chested centre-back was going to get many minutes on the pitch, for a while at least.

'I don't think the conversation about playing time ever took place when I was talking to Kenny Dalglish though in hindsight, perhaps it should have. When you have David May, Colin Hendry, Patrick Andersson and Henning Berg ahead of you, then it is always going to be difficult. I had Wolves, Leeds and Reading interested but Blackburn were the first to make a move. You are part of the squad and when your chance comes, you take it. It was not about player development then as it is now for 22 and 23-year-olds, you just go and try and do your best. I realised very quickly that the standard of the players was so great and then you have so many players in front of you that it was not going to be easy.' As Nicky Marker had already found out, moving from Plymouth to Blackburn was quite a step up.

A knock kept Morrison out of action for the first few weeks of the season after his signing. 'I was always made welcome. Tim Sherwood was the captain and a massive influence in the dressing room and always made an effort to speak and make sure you were settled. This is football. I picked up a knee injury very early in Ireland. It held me back for three months and it wasn't until February that I made my debut. It came against Wimbledon and I came on for Kevin Moran after just five minutes. We won 3-0 and I was named man of the match. Then we lost to Charlton in midweek in the cup and then David May came back from suspension. Kenny went back to the team he knew, and I could accept that. I played fleeting games after that. It just didn't work out, but it was a great experience and a chance to play with some top players even if I did come up short.'

'Dalglish was great. The person he was… he had an aura about him and it was remarkable.' Still, unlike Atkins, Morrison felt that his compatriot was not perfect. 'I can't really say he was a great squad manager. He was focused on those that were playing and winning games. If you were injured then he wasn't one to speak to you and see how you were going as he was focused elsewhere. That is what I felt at the time. I don't know if he was a great communicator with those who were injured and not in the picture. It was black and white, and some would say rightly so.'

In December of the title-winning season, Morrison was given an opportunity to try and progress his career elsewhere. 'Kenny pulled me in. I was in the reserves and he said "You are never a problem but the squad is strong and there are a few ahead of you." Swindon had been interested and Steve McMahon was there. They wanted me on loan and I was on my way down to Swindon, but I turned around as Blackpool had made a concrete offer. I met Sam Allardyce and they sold the club to me, but it was easy as I wanted to play football and start games.'

Just five months later, he watched as Rovers took the title. 'I was delighted – so many things had been put in place. I could feel that Rovers were going places. Jack Walker had obviously invested heavily and with Dalglish there, it was geared up for success. The history that was created for the town was remarkable, it would be a hard thing to recreate again to come from where they were and get so high, given the power of the top six.'

Morrison was out of the team for the 12 February trip to Tottenham as the challengers revealed the strength of depth in their squad. Without Sherwood, Batty, Hendry and Newell – half the team – Rovers won 2-0. The midfield was made up of Atkins and Marker, two unsung heroes from the lower leagues. I remember standing at the back of the away end at White Hart Lane and being unable to see all of Shearer's looping header but remember well a smart pass from Atkins to release Gallacher to score the second. It was a sixth straight win and cut United's lead to ten. Soon after ten became seven as victory over Newcastle was secured while United were busy in the cup. Was this the beginning of a true title race?

Then came a midweek clash at Norwich. It was obviously billed as the clash between Sutton, the young gun who had emerged that season, and Shearer. In the weeks leading up, City chairman Robert Chase was often in the media, telling all and sundry that the striker was going nowhere. For now. Rovers had put a bid in for £3.25 million in February, but Arsenal and Liverpool were also sniffing around. Sutton scored twice and missed a great chance to make it 3-2 in the final moments. Rovers had to settle for a point, with two goals from Gallacher. That left United six clear with a game in hand. Once again, the obituaries for the title race were written.

More so after a 1-0 loss at Arsenal four days later in what was a dreadful game, remembered – at least by Blackburn fans – for a Kevin Gallacher broken leg. The brace at Norwich a few days earlier was an example of how well the Scot was playing. 'I was playing well but that broken leg was just an accident. I was looking to half-volley it, but then Steve Bould put his knee up and my leg went across his knee and that was it.' There were over 2,000 letters from well-wishers and not just from Blackburn, a reminder of how popular Gallacher was and what a nice player he was to watch, but even he didn't realise at the time how that injury nearly ended his career altogether. 'The surgeon told me after I retired that the break should really have finished my career. That's not what he told me at the time. I was lucky. I would have missed lots of great moments in my career that followed that.'

Rovers looked like they may be out of the title race. The Scot certainly was.

'I felt part of the team and not. Players – being players – don't help with your bags. Sometimes Kenny would take us away on matchdays and I am there with crutches, and nobody helps. That motivated him to get back to action but it was a hard slog. 'I think during the week was the hardest. You are in the gym and don't see the players so much. Kenny involved you in matchdays, but it was lonely until David Batty was injured.'

What was impressive about this team was that when defeat came, it was followed by six wins from the next seven. The first three put the Blues in touching distance. Had they won at Wimbledon then, incredibly, United's lead – not long ago seen as insurmountable – would have disappeared entirely. With the Red Devils the next visitors to Ewood, then this really was a big game.

Big, but not good. Rovers lost 4-1. I remember it well, the sight of all those Rovers fans at Victoria Station, the early lead taken courtesy of a nice Jason Wilcox goal, the Vinny Jones long throws that went on to cause havoc and the tannoy announcer at Selhurst Park gleefully announcing near the end that the man of the match was Wimbledon manager Joe Kinnear. There were three goals in seven late second-half minutes. 'Rovers suffer from vertigo' was one headline, suggesting that when the pressure was finally on the team cracked, though the *Guardian* did correctly say that, 'It was Blackburn's misfortune to meet Wimbledon in their most magnificently irreverent mood last night. The party wreckers par excellence can seldom have been more destructive than in an astonishing seven minutes that may shape the title outcome.'

It always seems like a long way back to London on the train from Thornton Heath. With United winning 1-0 at home to Liverpool on the following evening, the gap was back to six.

The visit of United on Easter Saturday 1994 was a huge one. Six points behind, Rovers certainly could not afford to lose and, realistically, had to win. The visitors would be content with a draw. 'Without taking anything away from Blackburn Rovers, we have allowed them back into the race through our own carelessness,' said Alex Ferguson. 'Now we've got a cushion of six points and that is vital with eight games to go. At this stage last season, we started to show ourselves. The experience we have got in the big games will help us.'

It didn't on the day. It was cold and even snowed a little. Shearer headed the opener early in the second half, a fine finish from a fine Sherwood cross. For his second he outpaced and outmuscled Gary Pallister to get to a long ball from Ripley first, then smashed a shot past Schmeichel. 'There's the inevitable outcome,' said Martin Tyler. I can still see Sky Sports pundits George Best and Phil Thompson at the back of the Darwen End sitting next to the Premier League trophy. Fans were shouting and pointing to the trophy and saying 'that's ours'. Thompson seemed to find it funnier than his colleague. The roads surrounding Ewood rang out to 'Walking in a Shearer Wonderland' on that snowy Easter Saturday. The striker provided belief that it could happen.

There followed two more wins – a 3-0 victory at Everton two days later and then a tense 1-0 victory over Aston Villa a week after that. That saw the two teams level on points, though Rovers had played a game more. That was as good as it got, with just one win coming from the last five games. There was a slightly unlucky 3-1 loss at Southampton, which was followed by a frustrating 1-1 draw at home to Queens Park Rangers. A win at West Ham gave hope but with the leaders winning impressively at Leeds United, the gap was two points with United having three games left as opposed to two for the pursuers. That last-minute Ince equaliser at Old Trafford was making a difference.

The last away game of the season brought a loss at Coventry. It was all over. Rovers, without six of their players due to injury, had exhausted themselves so much in catching United that by the time they almost drew level, there was nothing left in the tank. 'We just ran out of steam,' said Atkins. 'It was a good effort from us, but we had just too much to do.'

A service had been provided, however. A title race that had looked like a forgone conclusion for most of the season ending up going to the penultimate round. United skipper Steve Bruce pointed to the FA Cup semi-final as the turning point. Losing 1-0 to Oldham, the team were heading out until a late spectacular volley from Mark Hughes. 'That put us right back on course and lifted the whole club.'

United fan John Brewin agrees. 'On that Easter Saturday, Ewood Park was a shell as it was being rebuilt, with the players looking like they just wandered from the street onto the pitch. Shearer was devastating that day and United were tired too. If I recall, things started to go awry and that Hughes goal against Oldham in the FA Cup semi-final was the turning point and then Oldham were beaten 4-1 in the replay. That settled everything down and we got going again. Blackburn did well to close the gap but there is no margin for error when you are chasing the leaders. You have to keep picking up points, as we saw in the season after.

'It was a deserved title though. Certain fans will say that team is the best United one and now I have to list the eleven: Schmeichel, Parker, Bruce, Pallister, Irwin, Kanchelskis, Ince, Keane, Giggs, Cantona and Hughes. That team won every game it ever played and was perhaps the highest-grade United team we'd seen. The season after it came apart.'

Rovers fans were looking forward to the next campaign. Batty won the player of the season award, defeating the magnificent Shearer by just seven votes to show how impressive he had been. There was a happy atmosphere at Ewood Park for the final day draw with Ipswich. 'We have improved by 13 points from last season,' said Dalglish. 'If we improve by another 13 next then we should stand one hell of a chance.'

That was the legacy of the second season. Finishing as runners-up and pushing a very good Manchester United side showed everyone that it could be done. Rovers, despite a mediocre start and finish, ended up seven points clear of Newcastle in third and 13 ahead of Arsenal in fourth. Liverpool were 24 points behind.

'There was such confidence that we got from that season,' said Mark Atkins. 'The first season we were high from getting promoted. Alan Shearer came in and nobody knew how good he was going to be, at least until we saw him and then we were like "wow". To finish fourth in the first season, we couldn't believe it. And then we pushed again.

'There were extra players who came in like Batts and we felt we could catch United, and especially after we beat them. We just ran out of steam, but it was good for us confidence-wise as we knew that we could beat any team in the league and we knew that we could win the league. That was a big difference between having a good season and thinking you can win the league. It was a big learning curve for us and that season prepared us for the next. It meant that we knew we could take the next step. Now we were serious about winning the league.'

14

SAS

'After I broke my leg at Arsenal, I turned into a supporter of Blackburn. I watched them and analysed them every game and watched the SAS. I wanted to get fit and break that partnership. That was my carrot, my inspiration.'

KEVIN GALLACHER

SPENDING THE SUMMER OF 1994 IN THE UNITED STATES was an experience. Enjoying a beer in the Upper West Side and watching Romania defeat Colombia 3-1 in an entertaining game alongside curious locals in Manhattan was surreal and exciting. I arrived in a humid New York just an hour or so after Ray Houghton scored the only goal of the game against Italy in the Giants Stadium to give Ireland a famous 1-0 win. It made for a strange Saturday night, with the city's Irish bars as packed as their Italian equivalents were empty.

I remember the occasional thrill of watching on television too. Henning Berg was involved, in action for Norway, and after one particularly tasty tackle the commentator said that the defender belonged to Blackburn Rovers, one of the top clubs in England and 'boy do they like their football rough over there'. There were a few Rovers references during the tournament and it was all very exciting. In 1982 Noel Brotherston appeared at the World Cup for Northern Ireland, coming on a substitute for Norman Whiteside midway through the second half of a 1-1 draw with Honduras. The same swap happened at virtually the same stage of the second-round 2-2 draw with Austria. Brotherston, besieged by injuries, was not called up four years later. Rovers striker Jimmy Quinn did make Mexico but not pitch or bench for Northern Ireland.

Seeing Blackburn players in international action at all was still unusual. That started to change in the nineties but despite the money spent, only David Batty arrived at Ewood with any kind of international career under his belt, making his debut for England in 1991. In the summer of 1992, Shearer was just breaking into the England team, though the field had just become clearer with the international retirement of Gary Lineker. There were a number of strikers in the running to become England's number nine, with Shearer among them. That was not the case by the time June 1994 came along – by that stage the former Southampton striker was the main man. Graeme Le Saux earned his international debut in March 1994. Tim Flowers played his first game in June 1993, just four months before arriving in Blackburn, but he never became a regular for his country, playing just 11 games until 1998 and never once in a competitive clash. Stuart Ripley's debut came in that San Marino game in 1993 when England won 7-1 but were still the butt of national jokes after conceding a goal after 10 seconds. The winger was in better form when selected to play against Moldova in 1997 under Glenn Hoddle but then pulled a hamstring. Wilcox made his debut against Hungary in May 1996 and hit the bar with a rocket in the opening minutes. The winger made the preliminary squad for Euro 96 but not the final one. Tim Sherwood also missed out. The title-winning skipper was expected to make his debut in March 1995 against Ireland in Dublin. On the bench, he never got on the pitch as English fans caused the game to be abandoned. By the time 1998 rolled along, Flowers made the England squad but never played. Shearer and Le Saux had left, though Hendry and Gallacher were mainstays of the Scotland squad.

Following English football from America back in 1994 was tricky. While there may have been better ways that old hands knew about, for me, keeping up to date with results consisted of buying – okay, reading at the station – *USA Today*, an American daily newspaper, a day or two after the game and just checking the listings. That was it. Just the result and nothing more. It was not ideal. Phone calls home were better but expensive. Anyway, I only missed the first few games of the season before heading back home to where Chris Sutton was already scoring goals.

As had become the case for the past couple of years, Rovers had been linked with all kinds of players over the summer. The injury to Gallacher meant that there was even more need to strengthen, though the Scot believes that he could have done the job had he been fit. 'I was in good form and I will say now that we wouldn't have bought Chris Sutton if I had not broken my leg. I had some bad luck that made Kenny go and spend on another player and take a gamble. That helped us take the title. I would have loved not to have broken the leg and then we could have seen not the SAS but us GAS the opposition.'

But Sutton was not really a gamble, he was a red-hot property of the kind that you don't get so much these days, with almost half of the top tier teams on the trail of a British player. As soon as the previous season ended, there were rumours of a £4.25 million Blackburn bid for Les Ferdinand, who was ready to leave QPR, but Sutton was the big one. In February, Arsenal offered £4 million. Sutton was interested. 'Like anything in my walk of life, you'd be silly to turn down something more successful than you've already got,' he said. 'I am very ambitious, but I am enjoying my football at Norwich at the moment. But you never know what is around the corner. Arsenal are a very successful team, they have very high standards and their record speaks for itself. Whatever move I make would have to be the right one for me. There's also been speculation from a number of other teams.'

Just after coming under fire for selling winger Ruel Fox to Newcastle, Norwich chairman Robert Chase was not about to let his other young star go so soon, especially as manager Mike Walker had also joined Everton. Walker said that the Canaries had received a bid of £1 million in 1993 from the Rovers for Sutton and Fox together. Chase was interested but Walker claimed that he convinced the chairman to turn it down. If that is true, he was right to do so and Dalglish was right to bid as soon after they would have cost seven times more.

At the time, Chase was talking the talk at least. He came out and said that the striker was going nowhere that summer and that if Sutton went he would go too, but with pretty much all the top teams in England chasing the defender-turned-striker, it was always going to be hard to keep him in Norfolk. Manchester United, Liverpool, Leeds United, Tottenham, Arsenal, Chelsea, Sheffield Wednesday and Blackburn were all linked at one point. There were plenty of talks but only two met Norwich's valuation of £5 million: Rovers and Arsenal. United were ready to pay £4 million and no more. Ferguson suggested that the player spend another season at Carrow Road. Sutton alleged in his autobiography that in an attempt to find out about his off the pitch character, United hired former SAS men to follow him around.

Chase had sent a deadline for all the interested clubs to meet the £5 million fee. Then it would be down to Sutton to choose. The date was Friday 14 July and with England not in the ongoing World Cup in the United States, the newspapers loved the headline speculation.

Then United offered £4.2 million. 'We know we might not get the chance to speak to the boy as Norwich may only accept of offers of £5 million which Blackburn will probably make,' Ferguson said. 'They could be the only ones but in the end it could turn out he would rather play for United and not Blackburn. He may want to go to play in front of 15,000 people or go to Old Trafford and play in front of 45,000. I know if I was the boy I would think of all the choices, where I'd be better off, before making a decision. We have made a substantial offer for him and we will do all can to sign him. It could be far from over. He has a great future ahead of him and it goes without saying that we would want him.' United were never going to match the asking price however, at least not quickly. 'The situation asking for bids of £5 million by Friday is more or less giving Blackburn the go-ahead.'

There was still time for Arsenal to try and scupper the deal and offer £4.5 million. Ken Friar was the managing director of the Gunners and insisted that as the deadline approached, they were still in the hunt. 'We have expressed an interest at this stage and discussions are going on.' The day before the deadline was reached, Norwich confirmed that Arsenal had finally met the asking price as well and it was now down to the player.

His father Mike hinted that Sutton junior was leaning towards East Lancashire rather than North London. 'There is a distinct possibility he could end up at Ewood Park,' Sutton senior said. 'There are many considerations to be taken into account and it's a very difficult decision. His main concern is that this is a career move for him.' Arsenal eventually dropped out: George Graham was prepared to pay the fee but was not prepared to break the strict wage structure at the club and pay the £12,000 a week that was on offer at Blackburn though later that month, there were reports that the Scot was facing a revolt from his players after breaking that very structure to sign Swedish midfielder Stefan Schwarz.

So Sutton chose Blackburn. Problem was, his going away party ended up with him being chased by three police cars and then spending the night in a cell for damaging a car by jumping headfirst into a convertible that had stopped at traffic lights. Flying into Blackburn the next day, the player was concerned that the deal may be called off once the Rovers found out.

But Sutton was perhaps unaware that high jinks and Blackburn Rovers were not strangers at the time. 'Ha ha yes!' remembers Shearer, when I put it to him. 'We had a laugh on the bus to away games. All part of our team spirit that helped us win the league.'

'The away days were crazy,' Gallacher remembers. 'We had some good times away and pranks were being played left, right and centre and you had to be on your toes. You could never relax too much or you would wake up without an eyebrow. There was all sorts of clowning around in the dressing room. I'd say 90 percent was taken in good faith. Most clubs have certain jokers, and you have fights and cliques, but it is up to the management to manage it. We put everything together on Saturday and that was the important thing.'

Jason Wilcox has an example. 'We were driving down to London on the bus and Tim Sherwood started a game. There was a group of us and you had to take the emergency hammer and hit it against the window and the next person has to hit it harder. We were still in Blackburn when Tim shattered the window. He then threw the hammer to Chris Sutton who was desperately trying to put the hammer back. The driver wasn't buying the story that it was a stone that had caused the damage. We had to kick the window through.' That wasn't the end of it. 'Then we bet Mike Newell that he couldn't sit next to the empty window without his top all the way down to London. Ten pounds each and he did it. Kenny knew what was going on, but we were getting the results.'

Something silly from Sutton as he celebrated his big move was not going to throw too big a spanner into the works then. Dalglish just laughed but the £5 million fee, the reported five-year contract and £12,000 a week did raise eyebrows and questions. The *Guardian* wrote that, 'While there has never been much doubt as to what Blackburn could do for Sutton, questions remain about the striker's ability to justify such a huge fee.' The paper noted that Ray Harford, standing in for Dalglish at the press conference, only said that Sutton was 'potentially a very good player... only time will tell how good.'

Sutton said all the right things. 'As soon as the speculation about me started six months ago I thought that if there was one club I wanted to talk to it was Blackburn. I was linked to a lot of big clubs but they were always my first choice. The club are similar to Norwich in terms of the population and area and I didn't want to move to a big city. I didn't talk to anyone else. Blackburn is the place where I felt I would score most goals and where they play football in the style that suits me best. And the chance to play for Kenny Dalglish, somebody who I admire tremendously, was another major factor.'

At the end of July, the other signing of the summer arrived, another influenced by the prospect of playing under Dalglish. It was Australian winger Robbie Slater, who arrived from Lens in France for £500,000. It is fair to say that there was less fanfare regarding this signing than that of Sutton, but the squad's strength in depth increased.

'In Australia, I am asked about two football events on a daily basis I think,' said Slater, who is now back down under and working on television. 'One is about the Australia and Iran World Cup qualification play-off in 1997. We fucked that up well and truly.' Indeed, Australia had to negotiate past the West Asian team in order to book a ticket to France in the summer of 1998. The first leg in Tehran, in front of over 100,000, ended 1-1 and with the Socceroos 2-0 up at half-time in Melbourne, Aussie journalists were calling their wives to ask what they wanted brought back from Paris. One television commentator told the viewers to pack their bags for France. Then came two late Iranian goals and that was that for Slater, coach Terry Venables and a heartbroken nation. It is a game seared into the consciousness of every Socceroos fan.

The other event is the Rovers winning the Premier League. 'Oh, it was huge here and still is. The Premier League is big in Australia and I was just the second Aussie in the league along with Mark Bosnich.'

It had been a convoluted journey for the winger to get to Blackburn in the summer of 1994. 'I was born in Ormskirk, Lancashire. My parents emigrated in 1966. I have said to my dad that we must have been the only Englishmen to leave England that summer and he listened to the World Cup final on the boat. We were what was known as "ten-pound poms".' Over a million and a half left the United Kingdom for a new life in Australia and the promise of a better life, or at least, better weather. He started out playing for St George Saints and then Sydney Croatia in the now-defunct National Soccer League. In 1989, Slater was heading back in the opposite direction to join Belgian giants Anderlecht. The following year he was in Northern France and Lens, where he stayed until Dalglish came calling.

'I had been with Lens in France and I had contact with clubs in England the year before, after the World Cup qualification play-off against Argentina (which also ended in defeat) in 1993. My agent was in discussion with Souness at Liverpool.' In the summer of 1994, he seemed to be heading somewhere else. 'I was destined to go to Villa, but my agent said that Kenny Dalglish and Blackburn Rovers wanted to talk to me. This came out of nowhere. I was training with Villa but as soon as I heard Kenny's name that was it for me. I was a Liverpool fan so we drove up the road and signed that afternoon.'

'I had followed their season the year before when they challenged Manchester United and for the seasons before that. I was playing in France and while I didn't follow that especially closely on a weekly basis, I knew the results and knew about how well Shearer was doing. I followed what Kenny did there and Jack Walker. I met Kenny at Ewood and he showed me the stadium and explained a bit of what had gone on and the plans for the future.' There was never any doubt as to whether he would sign. 'He was a hero and I don't really remember too much of what he said or the terms. I just wanted to join.'

Yet Rovers had two fine wingers in Jason Wilcox and Stuart Ripley. Slater knew that he was not going to waltz into the first team. 'Playing time was not something I really thought about at the time. I knew they had a great side. It had been a dream of mine to play in the English Premier League. I spent five years in France and one in Belgium and these were great years. I could have re-signed for Lens but going to Blackburn was a big challenge. I talked to a friend of mine who worked for the *Liverpool Echo* and had an interest in French football. I discussed with him about Villa and Rovers and he said that Blackburn were on track to win something that season and told me that even if I didn't play every game, I was still going to be part of something special. You don't get many chances in your career like this. I was quite comfortable signing. Kenny talked about strengthening the squad and I thought it was better to play 20 odd games – which I did – and get a trophy at the end of it than play 30 to 40 games somewhere else and win nothing.'

He went from one industrial city in northern France to one former industrial town in northern England. 'It was similar in some ways, but England is smaller and you are closer to bigger cities. Lens was a big club in France. They got massive support. Even now, they are in the second division and they still get 25,000 at home. They wanted to challenge in the French first division at the time but that was the period of Marseille dominance, who were European champions. It was a golden time to play in France. It was before the exodus of French players due to the Bosman ruling. It was a good time to play there. At that stage, France was full of superstars such as George Weah, Chris Waddle and Jean-Pierre Papin.'

It wasn't all great. The day after he had helped Lens to a win over Paris Saint-Germain, he was walking in the city with his wife and was attacked by two PSG fans with baseball bats. They hit him across the back of the head and, had his wife not intervened, that could have been that. There was none of that in England. 'The good thing about signing that summer was that all the attention was on Sutton with his big price tag, so I could quietly go about my business behind the scenes.'

There certainly was lots of attention on Sutton. He got a taste of what it meant to be the most expensive signing in British history in pre-season friendlies.

A 2-1 loss to Norwegian amateur team Steinkjer was always going to provide the headlines like 'Stinker in Steinkjer'. Defender Petter Christian

Singsaas was not impressed with the most expensive player in British history. 'Sutton was very arrogant,' he said. 'He didn't want to pose for a picture with me, but he never played ugly. He is a difficult player to play against but there are plenty of strikers around here who I could say the same about.'

The 3,000 crowd were singing 'What a waste of money!' as Sutton struggled to make an impact. In the end, the striker got his own back by refusing to sign autographs. 'I was satisfied with Sutton – I was satisfied with everyone,' Dalglish said. It was the first game of pre-season and all quite harsh but for the media, it was plenty of fun. Sutton and Shearer were both absent from the defeat at Celtic – the latter had food poisoning. Pre-season was poor. As well as that loss, there was another a 6-1 win over fellow Norwegians Pors. That was the only victory and was followed by defeats at Brøndby, Aberdeen and Celtic.

There was another story to take some attention away, and that was the surprise departure of David May from Ewood to Old Trafford. Part of the blond partnership in the centre of defence alongside Colin Hendry, May had established himself as a fine centre-back and joined the Red Devils for £1.5 million. According to the player's agent Paul Stretford, it was down to Blackburn dragging their heels and being slow to offer a new contract. May said he wanted to move from £500 a week basic to £4,000, still less than half of Alan Shearer. 'We had eight months trying to sort something out with Blackburn and it took just two hours to get satisfaction from United,' said Stretford. 'All I ever wanted was a decent wage, but their first offer was almost an insult,' May said after moving. 'They seemed to look at me and think "This is a lad who has been here since he was a kid. He'll sign eventually." I never wanted to leave but you have to feel wanted.'

When it became apparent that May could leave, Rovers offered a package and while it may not have been little, it was quite late. He had learnt much under Blackburn's rise playing alongside Hendry and Moran and was ready to strike out on his own. 'Players like Kevin have seen it and done it when you are only just beginning to see it,' May said. 'They'll go into depth with the answer and then you can ask another question and another. They have got so much time for younger players.'

Dalglish felt that Ferguson enjoyed taking one of his players. 'David May's contract had expired and we couldn't agree terms. Fergie stepped in and signed

May, although United weren't exactly short of good centre-halves. They had Steve Bruce, Gary Pallister, Paul Parker and Gary Neville. Fergie probably thought he needed cover but I'm sure, in the back of his mind, there must have been the thought that "us buying David May weakens Blackburn a wee bit" which didn't turn out to be true.'

Ahead of the Charity Shield there was much attention on the fact that May would start against his former teammates and perhaps mark the most expensive British player ever. 'I am not the least bit bothered about Chris Sutton,' May said. 'All that's in the past now. If Sutton's on however many thousand a week like they say he is then good luck to him. My goal now is playing for Manchester United and every game I play will feel like a bonus. It will be a dream come true to play in Europe and to think I could be in the European Cup with Manchester United, who are the biggest club on the continent. I didn't win anything with Blackburn. The reason I came here was to win trophies and I want that to start with the Charity Shield.' May also told of how he received a late-night phone call when he was first linked to Old Trafford. 'It was David Batty shouting "scum, scum, scum" at me. The papers were saying United were in for me, and Batts, taking the stories a bit to heart, decided to wind me up. In the end, I had to take the phone off the hook because he wouldn't leave it alone and I couldn't get any sleep.'

It was something of a surprise for Rovers fans. Not only was this a Lancashire lad and a product of the youth system leaving, it was a valued member of the first team leaving,. May had played all but two games in the previous season. He wasn't exactly irreplaceable but had grown and progressed. The club had become accustomed to taking such players from others, perhaps forgetting what it was like to be raided themselves.

With the retirement of Moran, it left Rovers short at the back. There was a need to bring someone in. Everybody expected Dalglish to get out the old chequebook. Instead, Ray Harford took to the phones and was soon talking with 35-year-old Tony Gale, who came in on a free transfer. The entire Blackburn backline and back-ups were put together relatively cheaply. Hendry, Gale, Pearce, Le Saux, Berg and Marker cost, in the memorable words of Paul Doyle writing in the *Guardian* in 2007, 'roughly the same as Newcastle had paid for Darren Peacock a year previously, and far less than Liverpool had just forked out for Phil Babb and John Scales.'

Gale came out of the blue or rather from deepest North London. It wasn't from Spurs or Arsenal either. He was in pre-season training with Barnet when he was suddenly returning to the top tier of English football. Now a commentator, he had become best known for a decade at West Ham that concluded at the end of the 1993/94 season. There had been offers from clubs down the league ladder for the classy centre-back and even a request from Japan. He was dragging his heels.

'Ray Harford called first, then Kenny, asking if I'd join them for pre-season in Scotland, just a week before the Charity Shield,' Gale told the *Lancashire Evening Telegraph* in 2015. 'I was lucky in that respect as Kevin Moran had just retired. So I went up there and played in a friendly and they said to me, "Right, we want to sign you and you'll be playing in the Charity Shield next week against Manchester United at Wembley." The rest is history and it turned out to be my last season because the following summer, when I signed for Crystal Palace, I got injured in pre-season and only managed to play three games before I had to retire. I had a career in which I hardly got injured and then all of a sudden I got the one at the end that finished me. So Rovers I always look at as my last season – and what a season it was.' Gale had the chance to continue at the Rovers and admitted that he regretted not doing so. He could have played in the Champions League instead of injuring himself in Second Division pre-season.

Ian Pearce could play at centre-back too, but the absence of Shearer, Sutton, Newell and Gallacher for the Charity Shield meant he was in the team as a makeshift striker that day. At Wembley Rovers lost 2-0, but with the players missing it was not much of a surprise and less of a blow. There was an expectation that over the next few years the fans would return to Wembley.

'It was a dream come true for me,' said Slater. 'Joining a new club and then making your debut at Wembley against Manchester United was something else. We didn't play that well to be honest, but we were missing lots of players and I don't remember anyone being too depressed about it as we went home. We were all excited for the season ahead. We respected United and we knew that they were a very good team, but we also knew that we could beat them when we had players back from injury.'

However, they would be starting the campaign without David Batty, who was not close to a return from injury. This was a blow as the midfielder had been excellent in his first season at the club, but towards the end of it he had been playing with injections as a piece of bone had come detached in his foot. An operation followed but when the cast was removed in June, it was revealed that it had not been a success. More operations followed but despite restarting training in November, it still wasn't right and there were doubts as to whether the former Leeds man would ever play again. A final operation took place in December and when the cast was removed in January it was deemed to have to been a success. He still needed time to get fit, and it wasn't until 28 February that he made his return in a reserve fixture, a full ten months after his last action.

He was missed in the Charity Shield and a chance for a first trophy, of sorts, was lost. A day later, Jack Walker was putting a little pressure on his manager. 'I want some silverware but I'm not going to put money in on the never-never until we win some,' he said. 'I might as well buy my own casino if I wanted a guaranteed victory. I am a winner. But anyone could just keep putting money in until they took over everything. I look at things one stage at a time. I think I am owed some silverware after 60-odd years. I don't think we will win something this year. I know it. I think I'm owed something and this squad will do it. We might need one or two players and if we do, we'll get them. Money doesn't buy success in football. Look at Derby County. They have put in £20 million and they're having a hard time of it. It is a great help, but you've got to have devotion and that is what will make Blackburn Rovers a force again.'

Looking back now, it was clear that there was pressure on Rovers to win something that season, preferably the league. There were suggestions that Walker had targeted the title by the time the club had finished the fourth season back in the top flight but given the runners-up spot in 93/94 and the £5 million spent on Sutton, it wasn't just Walker who was wondering whether this was time for Dalglish and the team to deliver. 'This is a critical year,' said the *Daily Express* ahead of the big kick-off. 'Kenny Dalglish has spent a great deal and achieved amazing progress, but this season Jack Walker will seek a return on his investments.' Mark Atkins also felt it was time. 'I am not sure there was special pressure but there was pressure when you were at the top and we knew we had to keep improving. We had done well the season before and so we knew that we had a chance. We were looking forward to it. We had spent in the summer and were ready.'

Rovers were expected to be in the mix but weren't everyone's tip for the top. It could be that injuries to Batty, Gallacher, Sutton and Shearer ahead of the big kick-off meant that others were getting the nod. The *Guardian* were not that impressed with Sutton and had Rovers down in fourth and Arsenal – who were to finish in mid-table – winning. The Gunners' signing of Stefan Schwarz was seen as the missing piece. 'I've found the midfield general I've been looking for,' George Graham said of his £1.8 million Swedish international who arrived from Benfica. 'Manchester United haven't got many great creative players in midfield but they have excellent ball winners who feed their highly talented strikers.' Arsenal certainly looked good after beating Atlético Madrid and Napoli to take the pre-season Makita Trophy.

'It suits us that people are suggesting a straight fight between United and Blackburn,' Graham said, even though that was not quite the case. 'That's the way we like it so we can get on playing our football without the pressure of being favourites. If I want to stay at Highbury, I have to bring in more silverware, it's as simple as that. Just because I have achieved a lot doesn't mean I can go on forever. I could at any moment if I fail. The desire is still there.' Ferguson saw Arsenal as a threat. 'George Graham is a winner. You know that Arsenal will give nothing away and be hard to beat. You can guarantee they will be up there.'

And there was also Newcastle chairman John Hall, building a team to make the Geordie nation proud and wanting to take the Magpies into Europe's top ten. He had already invested more than £10 million. Newcastle were also going to be in the hunt according to Kevin Keegan, who proclaimed the partnership of Andy Cole and Peter Beardsley as the best in the league. He clearly believed it as well – Newcastle were one of the few big clubs not linked with Sutton. 'For me, Andy Cole is the country's most exciting player,' said Keegan. 'Last season he scored 41 goals and it was no flash in the pan. He's capable of following that up. I'm convinced that with Peter Beardsley, he is one half of the best strike force in the country. That assessment includes Shearer and Sutton because that's a might-be. We know what we've got at Newcastle. We've seen it over 40 odd games, the way they played together and shared 65 goals. I'm not saying Shearer and Sutton won't hit it off, that's going to be a fascinating aspect of the new season. But whereas we know what we've got, they are not sure. Sutton might score goals, Shearer may dry up, or the other way round. Blackburn had a good season last time and have added Sutton so will be up there.'

Keegan was ready to install his team as Manchester United's main challengers for the 1994/95 season. 'They won last season's title race by a long way and were worthy champions. What we have to do is to close the gap – and that's our target. As I tell the players, our supporters expect. They believe it's all in the brochure. What I say is, don't underestimate us. Our aim is to win the championship and we are one of the few teams who've got a chance of doing it. I see Manchester United becoming very preoccupied with Europe this time and I believe that's going to work to our advantage. I know we are in there as well but for us Europe will be an adventure, something we didn't expect. For them, it is a totally different situation. They've got an extra weight on their shoulders. If they don't win it, they are not going to be classed as a truly great side. We went up in style, proved beyond doubt that we are a Premier League side and an excellent one at that. Now we have to put some silverware in the cabinet.'

Liverpool had finished eighth the previous season, their worst league finish for three decades, and Souness had resigned in January. Roy Evans was his successor as manager, but Liverpool did not have the look of title challengers and some problems in the build-up to the season made it worse. Mark Wright and Julian Dicks were left behind in England as the Reds went to Germany to continue a pre-season that featured a 4-1 loss at Bolton days earlier. The clear out at Anfield continued with Bruce Grobbelaar and Ronnie Whelan leaving, with young players such as Robbie Fowler and Steve McManaman now firm members of the starting eleven. There were signs of progress at Anfield after the problems of previous years, but it was expected that the season would be one of transition, though an improvement on eighth.

Manchester United were still the favourites, of course, but Keegan's feeling that the club would be distracted by Europe were reinforced by Ferguson in a pre-season interview with the *Daily Express*. 'I am asking my players are you good enough to win a third title? Do you want to win the European Cup? Because if we fail in Europe this season we are still going to be considered as also-rans in the real league of football that extends beyond the English Channel, even if we win a third Premiership title. If we want to stand shoulder to shoulder with Law, Best and Charlton then that has to be the purpose and the target for the months ahead.'

As well as the expected challengers, other teams were strengthening, boosted by high-profile chairmen with money to spend. They were inevitably compared to a certain Jack Walker. Everton had invested since escaping relegation on the final day of the previous season. Boyhood Liverpool fan Peter Johnson had finally taken control of the club in July and there were reports of £10 million being available. Almost half was spent on Vinny Samways from Spurs and Nigeria's Daniel Amokachi. Tottenham chairman Alan Sugar had been splashing the cash since saving the club from administration three years earlier. He had cut short a holiday to return to North London for the announcement of the Klinsmann deal, such was the excitement at the club.

It all meant that the league was getting stronger and the challenge to win was bigger than for some time. Newly-promoted Nottingham Forest had Stan Collymore, one of the hottest properties in English football and the two-time European champions had spent almost £3 million on Dutch international winger Bryan Roy. Chelsea bought Paul Furlong from Watford for £2.3 million and chairman Ken Bates proclaimed him better than Sutton, while admitting – or claiming – that former boss Ian Porterfield had turned down the chance to sign Cantona before Leeds did. Leeds were still a strong team and finished fifth the season before. They had signed the fourth most expensive player of the summer with Carlton Palmer costing £2.6 million. Aston Villa, runners-up just 15 months before, had bought John Fashanu and taken Nii Lamptey on loan from Anderlecht.

'It was around that time that you could see the Premier League getting stronger,' said Brian Deane, who was ready to lead the forward line in Leeds United's title challenge. 'Teams were spending more money, but Blackburn were obviously going to be there or thereabouts. We knew they and Manchester United were the ones for us to catch.'

There was also the fact that this was going to be an unusual season. Four teams were going to be relegated and this raised the possibility of the fiercest relegation dogfight imaginable. With the trapdoor bigger than ever before, more teams were in danger and more teams were going to be fighting for their lives. All the above explains why there were 22 deals that summer of over £1 million. Only one went to Blackburn, but he was the biggest.

It meant that there was plenty of interest in the opening day as Rovers went down to Southampton and grabbed a 1-1 draw. It was slightly disappointing but still a better result than the previous season at the Dell and this was not a stadium that Rovers enjoyed going to. It was also notable for Shearer missing a penalty, but he still got on the scoresheet. Sutton missed three chances and was 'deeply disappointing', said one national newspaper. 'Dalglish must be hoping he can produce far better than this.' Others were quick to pan the new signing amid the headlines of the new rules on the tackle from behind and the spectacular arrival of Klinsmann.

Three days later, the PA system at Ewood announced 'Blackburn Rovers are top of the Premiership.' A 3-0 win over Leicester saw Sutton get off the mark. It was good that he did so in his second game. One can only imagine the headlines had he gone a few matches without scoring and he felt entitled to call out his critics. 'I hope this gets people off my back. I'm disappointed people have been knocking me after just one game. It was just one bad game and I'm sure I'll have a lot more. People have been criticising me for the transfer fee but it was not of my making. I don't want the spotlight. It was nice to score and hopefully this will take some of the pressure off me. Hopefully people will get off my backs a bit. I have a lot to learn and there is no better striker to learn from than Alan Shearer. I keep watching his runs because he is the best in England without a doubt.'

There was more to come at the weekend as the new man grabbed a hat-trick in a 4-0 win over Coventry. The nerves were well and truly settled with four goals in his first three appearances for his new club. The questioning headlines would disappear, at least for a while, as would the chants from opposing fans. Yet despite the attacking prowess on display, Sutton was still on the defensive. 'A lot of people have been very unfair to me. I've been disappointed with the way I've been portrayed. I've been slaughtered. They were making judgements before I kicked a ball for Blackburn. They said I didn't look like a £5 million player. What does a £5 million player look like? I don't know. These people should reserve their judgement until the end of the season. I'm 21 and much of what has been written about me is unnecessary. If I hadn't scored in Blackburn's first three games what would have been written then? But I could have had six or eight today. I never said I was worth £5 million. I expect opposition fans to shout "What a waste of money" at away grounds. Let's admit it, it could have been a nightmare. I might not have scored for a couple of months.'

Sutton was not on the scoresheet four days later – the last day of August – as he spent much of the match playing as centre-back following the dismissal of Jason Wilcox at Highbury. The 0-0 draw with Arsenal was a good result and was followed by a 3-0 dismissal of Everton at Ewood, with Shearer grabbing two. Eleven points from the first five games was a solid start as the club prepared for a first ever European experience.

15

TRELLEBORGS TROUBLE

'With the money in football these days, a small team from Sweden does not beat a big team from England. That wouldn't happen now and that was why it was great but, really, Blackburn just weren't that good.'

JONAS BRORSSON

TRELLEBORGS. WHAT A DISASTER. THE FIRST STAY IN EUROPE was short but far from sweet. When the draw was made nobody knew what would happen, though it was fair to say that all expected a win over the Swedish part-timers.

In the UK, many talked of Dalglish's first European tie since the Heysel disaster over nine years earlier and his first ever as a manager. For most of the players, it was, as Alan Shearer said, a 'step into the unknown'. Trelleborgs had finished fourth in the Swedish league the season before and had some European experience, acquitting themselves well in the 1994 Intertoto Cup. Still, they came to England happy to lose by a narrow scoreline, especially as two midfielders Anders Palmér and Mikael Rasmusson were suspended after being sent off in the previous round against Gøtu Ítróttarfelag of the Faroes Islands.

Coach Tom Prahl was wary of Rovers. 'We have watched Blackburn many times on television,' he said. 'I was struck by the pace of their football. They remind me of Liverpool a few years ago. It is vital we get a good result for here for the first leg. Supporters in south Sweden are not too enthusiastic and we need to still be alive for the second leg.'

They were very much alive. Fredrik Sandell, as every newspaper gleefully reported, was a newspaper ink worker. He also scored the only goal of the game midway through the second half, skipping past Colin Hendry to score from the edge of the area. 'It was a wonderful moment,' he said. 'The noise from the crowd was incredible.' This feels a little hard to believe given that there were only 14,000 there and few were Swedish, but it was a crazy night.

Rovers just couldn't explain what had happened. The performance was lacklustre and then some, strange for a European debut. 'Everyone was just so down and quiet in the dressing room, they were so disappointed,' said Graeme Le Saux. 'It's the first time it has been like that since I have been at the club. In the past, if we had a bad result there have been reasons we could point to. But everyone was at a loss. The longer it stayed at 0-0, the happier they got and the more frustrated we grew. They played well in defence and worked hard to contain us.'

With the match on terrestrial television, it proved not to be a great advert for the English game and for Blackburn's football, as Le Saux admitted at the time. 'I don't think we showed any imagination in trying to break them down. They came to defend and go away 0-0 and I found it difficult to see passes because there were so many people in the way. It was similar to when I played in internationals. It was like a game of chess, and when it's like that you have to be able to move your opponents around. I thought we had enough quality players to do that, but we never seemed to get on fire at the same time.'

'We would never have imagined this,' coach Prahl said. 'A 2-0 defeat would have satisfied us. It is the biggest moment of my career – the biggest of all our careers. To win 1-0 is unbelievable. It is very good for Swedish club football. People over there don't think we can play, most of our international players go abroad.'

The story was that the part-timers were earning £320 a month compared to the £12,000 a week that Sutton was on. The headlines were bad and even worse next to Newcastle's 5-0 win at Royal Antwerp which was, on paper, a much harder game. It was surely a blip and it would surely all be sorted out in Sweden.

'To be honest, we had to perform well,' recalled right-back Jonas Brorsson, who still has a clear memory of those two legs. 'We had a lot of international games that we played. We had played in the in Intertoto Cup earlier that year. We played against teams from Germany, Denmark and also Grasshoppers of Switzerland. We had done pretty well against these teams and so when we got Blackburn in the UEFA Cup draw, we were okay about that. We had not been playing very well in the league at the time, but we were a decent team with quite a lot of international experience.

'The week before we had played in the cup and lost and on the Saturday, we had a home game and lost 2-0. I don't know if we were distracted by the thought of playing Blackburn. The coach had showed us videos of Blackburn. We didn't know everything, but we knew a lot about them before we went there. One of our coaching staff had analysed the opponents. He actually helped the national team when they played Italy in the [2018] World Cup qualifying play-off. He really knew his stuff and was very good.'

Sweden was more of a power then than now and finishing fourth in the league should have made it clear that Trelleborgs were not a bad team. 'Things were good in Swedish football don't forget. We had just reached the semi-finals of the World Cup. The league we played in was a good standard.

'We also had nothing to lose. We were facing a team that had finished second in England and we knew they had been spending money and had some very good players. As soon as we arrived in England, the press was telling us how much Shearer was making and how many goals he was going to score against us. We felt excited rather than scared when we saw the lights of the stadium and we felt we could do something, at least not lose by more than a goal or two. That would have been a decent result for us.'

The poor performance from the home team only served to inspire the Swedes. 'I remember after the first 20 minutes, I turned and said to a teammate that "they are good but not that good". They were quicker than us but we felt they were predictable. They liked to play the English way, the long ball kicked quickly forward, but we were good in the air, that was our strength. We scored and they were shocked, and we were shocked when we won the first leg. We knew how well they were paid but we were amateurs.

'We were well-organised and experienced, tough and physically strong. They tried to kick us a bit and intimidate us, I guess. It didn't bother us, we could do the same back to them. We were not the best footballers, but we knew how to defend and we worked hard to score goals. I think we were more prepared for a European game then they were. I was not surprised that this was their first time to play a European game – they seemed unsure of what to do.'

Yet after the home defeat Blackburn's league form was pretty good, and they followed the embarrassment at Ewood by winning 2-1 at Stamford Bridge, with Slater firing over a perfect cross for Sutton to slide home the winner. Then there was a home game against Aston Villa. That ended in a 3-1 victory that was more comfortable than the scoreline suggested. The SAS were making a name for themselves. That victory put the runners-up from the season before into second after seven games and just two points behind Newcastle on 19. In the Premier League at least, the Rovers were starting to click.

Then it was to Sweden for the away leg and a 1-0 deficit that needed to be overturned. The Swedish press had been fairly gleeful of the win at Rovers and had poked fun at the English team. 'We have the same respect for Trelleborgs that we had before the first game started,' Dalglish told Swedish television. 'But I don't think they have the same respect for us.'

Brorsson had respect for Blackburn but felt that Shearer was not as good as had been made out. 'Shearer scored a goal from a corner in the second leg. He had something that was quite special, but I don't think he would have survived in Italy at that point. Compared to Alen Bokšić of Lazio, who we played in the next round, he wasn't as good. He was good but not very quick. I can't compare him to Italian strikers like [Beppe] Signori, as he was a different class.'

Had the Swede said something similar at the time then Rovers fans would have been up in arms – to them it was a matter of fact and faith that Shearer was one of the best in Europe and many would have said the best. While

Brorrsson had played against all three of the strikers mentioned, judging Shearer and Rovers on two of the worst performances of the season may be a little harsh. In fact, there was constant talk through the season of Shearer heading to Italy. It was felt that Serie A would be his next destination. The player was interested and even talked of taking Italian lessons.

If the home game was frustrating then the away game was something else. Sutton scored quite early, a rebound from a Shearer free-kick, and all Rovers fans settled down for the inevitable victory live on the BBC. Five minutes into the second half however, Joachim Karlsson equalised on the night with a fine strike from outside the area for the Swedes and put them ahead on aggregate. After 54 minutes, however, Brorsson was given a second yellow and sent off. Surely now Rovers would put the Swedes to the sword? That looked to be the case with six minutes left, as Shearer scored what was surely the winner with a scrambled goal. It may not have been pretty but looked decisive. Or so Blackburn thought. A minute later, Karlsson got his second from close range with the visitors looking for an offside flag that was never waved. It was 2-2 on the night, 3-2 on aggregate and that was that.

'It was unbelievable.' said Brorsson. 'I got a red card. I got a yellow after I got involved with Tim Sherwood and that made my situation dangerous, and it was a mistake because when I did a tackle in the second half… I was going to kick the ball but at the last second, it was kicked over my leg and I got another yellow and was off. It was terrible as there was still a long time to go.' It also seemed like a long way back to the dressing room. 'Of course, I was in tears because I thought that I had cost my team the game, a famous game and also a lot of money that we would have got for going through. We were amateurs and it would have made a big difference to all of us. Then I heard the cheers and saw that it was 2-2 and we had scored. I didn't know that Blackburn had scored to make it 2-1. Joachim Karlsson had scored his second of the night. I remember that soon after I took him and his wife out for dinner.'

Trelleborgs celebrated their win with a major party. 'We were very proud. We followed English football from the seventies and watched it on television. Don't forget Gothenburg beat Manchester United in the Champions League at the same time. People still remember, and we had a 20-year anniversary party. It will never happen again, that a Swedish team can beat the English champions. The big teams are getting bigger.'

It was a bitter exit. The first-ever game in Europe had ended in humiliation with both games live on national television too; Rovers had played poorly and had been embarrassed. One issue was a lack of European experience. Sutton had played for Norwich in the UEFA Cup the previous season, with Slater and Berg appearing for clubs in Belgium and Norway. Moran had retired and taken his experience with him. Shearer had played a couple of times overseas for England, but that was about it for the whole squad.

There was a general belief that Rovers had frozen in the first leg. Le Saux put it down to, in part at least, the poor attendance. He admitted that anything he said was going to sound like an excuse, 'but strangely, we began to feel uneasy about the game when we realised all the tickets had not been sold. We believed it was such a big night for the club, its first European night.' Dalglish's predecessor Don Mackay believes, though there is not much evidence for this, that it was the poor attendance that led to Jack Walker not putting his hands in his pockets the following summer when Rovers were champions.

There was excitement about being in Europe, so a half-full Ewood was something of a surprise. The excuses are that the game was not part of the season ticket package, meaning all fans had to go down to the stadium to get tickets. With it also being shown live on the BBC at a time when there were games coming thick and fast, the demand was always going to depend to some extent on the opposition. Trelleborgs were no kind of draw at all. In some ways, 14,000 is not bad when you take into account the fact there were no away fans and the game was on live on terrestrial television. When you consider that Blackburn had a population of just 100,000 and a depressed economy, staying in and saving money sounds like a reasonable decision to make. After all, some probably felt that bigger and better teams would be coming after the Swedes had been seen off. But still, for a first European game, it can't have helped.

The headlines made for painful reading. 'There is a certain glee over the manner of Blackburn's nasty tumble at the first hurdle in Europe,' wrote Cynthia Bateman in the *Guardian*. 'Walker's wallet and Kenny Dalglish's unendearing demeanour have turned Rovers into something of an Aunt Sally. Whereas Manchester United are respected and Newcastle wished well – except perhaps by those in Sunderland – Blackburn are resented as only 'new money' can be. Blackburn seemed to have little more to offer than their reputation in the Premiership, and both at home and at the tiny ground in Trelleborg they had neither the wit nor the wisdom to dismantle the Swedes. Shearer and Sutton managed a goal apiece, but they are only as good as the players behind them; Sutton rarely received the ball at his feet, where he can use it to his best advantage. Long high passes knocked forward again and again found the two strikers backing into defenders to compete for the ball, with no one in support.' The *Guardian* noted that 'only' 600 Rovers fans made the trip to Sweden but given that the stadium only held 7,000 and tickets were limited for what was a big game for the locals, it seemed to be a decent following.

Shearer was unusually forthright. 'The popular view is that we have a style of play that is not suited to Europe. While that is an unfair accusation, it is true that in both games we have not done ourselves justice. When we were chasing the game at the end of both legs we tended to run out of ideas and lump the ball forward to the strikers and hope for the best. If you do that, you risk giving the ball away and even against a team of part-timers it is very difficult to win it back when the opposition have no need to commit themselves to attack. I think this is where we missed the injured David Batty. As well as being a great little competitor, he provides us with variety as he can pass it long and short. The ideal way of playing, whatever the opposition, is to mix and match your style and I am afraid in the UEFA Cup, we failed to do that well enough.'

Anyway, Shearer mentioned how he groaned when he saw who Trelleborgs were playing next: Lazio. He wasn't the only one. At the time, Italian football was where it was at and Lazio were big news, especially in England because of Paul Gascoigne. It would have been a great test, especially as the Rome club were one of those linked with a move to Shearer.

In the end, Lazio won just 1-0 on aggregate, showing the Swedes were a decent side. 'It was 0-0 at home,' remembers Brorsson. 'In Rome, we didn't have any attacks, but they scored after 96 minutes and we were close to extra time. I told you we were hard to beat!'

By that time however, few in England cared and Shearer was left to read notes left in his house by Liverpool defender and friend Neil Ruddock asking if he wanted Swedes for Sunday lunch. It made it a little worse that Aston Villa squeezed past the mighty Inter Milan on penalties two days later in what was a thrilling victory.

It was also the first time Dalglish had been under the spotlight since returning to the top flight. 'Presumably Dalglish had briefed his players on the difference between playing Villa at home and Trelleborgs away yet there was little evidence of received wisdom and it may be that his young side must be left to learn what they can themselves,' wrote the *Guardian*.

In front of a watching nation however, it led to more criticism that Blackburn's football was workmanlike especially when compared to the swash-buckling Red Devils.

Somehow Manchester United managed to brand their stadium as 'The Theatre of Dreams' at some point. Cringeworthy it may be, but there is no doubt that the team of the mid-nineties, and later too, is remembered for some fine football. Blackburn? Not so much.

For Rovers fans, I don't think it was that much of an issue. Even if it was, it is not an easy topic to discuss objectively. The sight of Blackburn sweeping established powers aside, the wins over Arsenal, Tottenham, Liverpool, Leeds, Everton, Aston Villa and Manchester United, was thrilling for those accustomed to second tier football. The sight of Wilcox and Ripley sending crosses into the area for Shearer to shoot home was beautiful. Even some of those backs-to-the-wall performances away from home were pure nail-biting tension for fans of the club even if they may not have been the prettiest spectacles for the neutral.

While there were some compliments in the first season back with that magnificent 7-1 win over Norwich, a fine football display at Spurs, a sweeping aside of Liverpool and more besides, increasingly Rovers became labelled as pragmatic and hard-working and not much more.

'There is an element of truth in [some of the criticism] but if you are scoring three or four goals a game – and for a lot of that season when we beat teams, we properly beat them – then it is pretty exciting,' said long-time Rovers fan and podcaster Ian Herbert. 'It depends on your definition of exciting football. I love watching Manchester City and all the passing and Jürgen Klopp's football but back then, the Premiership was very much an English game and Dalglish's gameplan was pretty simple. Win the ball in midfield, get it to the wide men as quickly as you can and they will put dangerous crosses into the area. And if that doesn't work then give it to Alan and see what he can do. So many times, he would get the ball in an innocuous position, take a couple of strides, create some space and then hit it. I have never seen a player in a blue and white shirt who could create something out of nothing. His athleticism, power and strength of shot was something else. We had a significant number of penalties as well and that was because of the amount of forays we made into the box. The number of times we had overlapping full-backs and wingers and the likes of Sherwood bursting through, all putting defenders under pressure.'

They may not have been as cavalier as their title rivals that season, but they still scored as many goals as the dominant United team from the previous season and 13 more than the one that won the 1993 crown. When I asked Shearer about this, he replied that he had no memory of any criticism. 'We played open attacking football with two brilliant wingers who were a dream for me as a centre-forward. I don't remember us getting stick for the way we played. We took the big boys on and beat them.'

But the jibes were as direct as Blackburn's play was supposed to be. 'People were talked into this way of thinking by Ferguson,' said the long-term Liverpool fan Tony Evans. 'He used to do the same to Liverpool and say, "We can't do it like Liverpool, we can do it in style," and all that. I thought Blackburn played great football, compact and neat in midfield and they played the game with two wingers, swinging the ball in for Alan Shearer who was as good as he ever was. I thought it was great to watch. They weren't all about long balls, they got the ball out wide. You knew what to expect and you knew that Shearer was there. People don't realise how good they were, and they are one of those sides that get a bad rap these days, but a lot of that was the media repeating Ferguson's line.'

In the first-half of the 1994/95 season when Rovers were really in their stride and brushing teams aside, scoring goals and looking very good indeed, there was still plenty of negativity about the style of play. Indeed, Liverpool fans were not too complimentary after losing 3-2 at Ewood in October, but Brewin doesn't completely disagree with Evans. 'There is something to that. Ferguson would have had a newspaper column somewhere. Up until he started to make mega money later in the nineties, he would do bits in the press, so it is quite possible he mentioned the football Blackburn played in a negative way.'

'But there was that image at the time. I remember Shelley Webb, the wife of Neil Webb, who said something like "Blackburn play more the style of football we like in this country," which is weird as he played for Forest. I had a friend who is a Blackburn fan and he tells the story of going to Hillsborough and taking a family friend and not being able to go to the pub, so they went to the stadium early. They watched Harford on the pitch with Batty and he was playing the ball to Batty who would then play long balls to the wings very quickly.'

'I think that at the time, there were a lot of teams who you couldn't say what their style was, but Blackburn had their own style. Perhaps Harford was the key to that as Dalglish had come through the Liverpool tradition, but then Liverpool could be quite negative at times.' Overall though, the image of Blackburn's game may be a little unfair. 'There was a perception that Newcastle played this great football and Blackburn didn't, but I remember watching a game between them and I think it was a draw. It was a pretty helter-skelter game, but I wouldn't say that Newcastle's style of football was better than Blackburn's.'

The perception was made worse by terrestrial television. This was a time where fewer people watched live games on Sky Sports, and so games broadcast on terrestrial were a bigger deal. With the two games with Trelleborgs both live on BBC One, there could not have been a worse advertisement for Blackburn's brand of football. That meant that the third round of the FA Cup at Newcastle on the BBC at Sunday lunchtime in early January came at a good time. After the Trelleborgs disaster, this was a rare chance to show the nation that Rovers were not quite the footballing Roundheads to United's cavaliers that they had been painted as, especially as the Toon were in poor form. David Lacey of the *Guardian* discussed this in the lead-up to the game, saying that Newcastle were a PR man's dream – the good football and the talkative manager in Kevin Keegan – with Blackburn the opposite on the pitch and in the dugout. Lacey admitted that Rovers fans were getting paranoid about the media. 'But are not the more rational of their supporters entitled to be a little miffed?' Lacey asked. 'After all, it was not Blackburn's players who were booed off their own pitch last Monday, It is not Blackburn who have won only twice in 14 matches

– and that from a penalty – in their last five.' Even Keegan said that his team had 'gone from brilliant to ordinary since we were top of the Premiership', which had been in early November.

'Mention it not in Gallowgate, whisper it not on Blackett Street but Newcastle's football is becoming a trifle tedious,' added Lacey. 'When the movement of good passing teams begins to break down near goal, it is like watching a bad juggling act.' With Cole's goals drying up – there were rumours that he wanted to return to London – Newcastle were looking short of ideas.

'Blackburn meanwhile are tending to be judged on away performances which often tread a fine line between the pragmatic and prosaic, while the consistent high quality of their football at Ewood is overlooked. Liverpool used to suffer in this way. Most great footballing sides go through the chrysalis stage. It happened with Leeds and Liverpool. It even happened with Manchester City under Joe Mercer and Malcolm Allison. Purple Emperors Blackburn are not but it would be foolish to dismiss them as Cabbage Whites just yet.'

Such opinions were pleasing to read, but nothing like as welcome as the beautiful team goal that Sutton scored on Tyneside to put the Rovers ahead. It started with a Newcastle attack, and then came a counter-attack of, in the words of Trevor Brooking, 'magnificent quality'. A swift move out of defence, a run from Ripley, a delightful one-two between the SAS on the edge of the area and then Sutton biding his time with defenders diving in, to slot the ball home. It still didn't change the narrative that Rovers were dull to watch.

Robbie Slater, one of the few in the dressing room to have experienced another league in Europe, felt that Rovers played a similar style to most English clubs. 'England was very different to France. Blackburn, like pretty much every team in England at the time, certainly at West Ham and Southampton where I went on to play, didn't change their play too much whether at home or away to Manchester United or Arsenal or anyone else. That may have changed now with the foreign managers, but it is still a league in which everyone attacks, and it is so exciting – and the best league in the world. France was more tactical. If Lens played at PSG, Marseilles and others, we would defend more and look to counter-attack. The Premier League was in its early stage but you could tell it was coming. Foreign players were just starting to come and then there was the influx.'

Slater was not afraid of rolling his sleeves up. 'I played for Australia against Argentina and usually played in teams that worked hard. The system we played at Blackburn was very direct which was clever as you had two up front in Shearer and Sutton. The idea was just to get the ball to them as quickly as possible and that was understandable as they were the best pairing in the league. We didn't really need instructing. We used to talk about it, of course, but there was certainly a feeling that the quicker you got the ball forward the better. It was exciting I think as we always tried to attack, and I think English fans liked to see wingers running down the wings and getting the ball into the area for some of the best strikers around. Shearer was just a different class, but overall Blackburn was pure excitement for me. If you liked wingers, you liked the way Blackburn played. It was all about the wingers and Alan Shearer, of course.'

On the other side was Ripley, a trickier winger than Wilcox and Slater. Not as naturally athletic as Wilcox, a black belt in judo, the blond winger still worked very hard indeed. 'I was part – an integral part I would say – of a very good side,' Ripley said. 'Sometimes as a player, you have to sacrifice yourself a little bit. There was Jason Wilcox on the other side, who is sometimes forgotten, but he was immense that season. We had defensive duties and we were very hard to break down and were quick and fast going forward. We put a lot of effort into it. We had to do the spadework.'

I do remember certain pub conversations that talked of how the team would be let off the leash once the title had been won and then the football really would be special. It was always going to take time for the football to develop into something a little more sophisticated. Dalglish said the same. 'We couldn't play Liverpool's style of football. That took years to achieve. Liverpool had been playing that way since Bill Shankly. We built teams to win games. Blackburn have only been at it for four years. You cannot expect Rovers's playing style to be as developed as Liverpool's. I thought we played sensible soccer... some of our goals and performances were magnificent. If you have to clear your lines, clear them, don't bring the ball down and play. When you can play, play.'

Rovers may not have been the footballing side that United were, or Arsenal shortly after, but, according to David Batty at least, tried to pass it around more than Leeds United. The 1992 champions were seen as having a decent mix of guile and craft, though were more direct than Blackburn. 'Something even more significant made an impression on me in that match [his debut for Blackburn against Spurs in October 1993]: our centre-halves were actually passing the ball to me. That had never happened at Leeds; the lads weren't encouraged to do that in case you had to give it back to them, so they hit long balls. At Blackburn, though, everything was geared to getting the ball to Alan Shearer, and subsequently Chris Sutton, as quickly as possible. The idea was to get it wide to wingers Wilcox and Stuart Ripley so that they could cross for the strikers, but we didn't hoof the ball as we did at Leeds. I loved it.' Rovers fans did too but such a performance against Trelleborgs was always going to come in for criticism.

Jack Walker was his usual optimistic self after that loss even if one of the four pieces of silverware on offer in the season had already gone. 'I still say we will win a trophy this season,' said Jack Walker. 'Don't discount us winning the championship. This will make us even more determined to qualify for Europe next year.'

It was a painful defeat. 'It was just a disaster,' recalls Slater. 'I don't know what happened. We didn't play well. The first leg killed us, but we should have come back. We were pretty confident going over there and we wanted to give a much better showing. It wasn't a pretty game. We were 2-1 up and pretty comfortable and they had a man sent off, but then they scored and that was it. It was a bit embarrassing really. Kenny told us to try and put it out of our heads and we were happy to do just that. We got over it very quickly, I remember that. It drove us on. We focused on the league and it helped us in the end.'

16

BACK TO HOME FRONT

'We had beaten Liverpool before, but this felt different and I think that was when we started to think that the season was ours.'

MARK ATKINS

ROVERS WERE HEADING DOWN TO NORWICH THE NEXT day determined to get the Trelleborgs result out of the system. Sutton scored the opener on his return, but the Canaries hit back with two fairly lucky goals: one a deflection and one from a shot that wasn't. It was a first league defeat of the season after eight games but arrived just four days after the loss in Sweden. It ended a bad week. More worrying for Rovers, who had slipped into third, was the next few fixtures: leaders Newcastle away, followed by Liverpool, fifth, and Manchester United, fourth, at home. Then came second-placed Nottingham Forest away. At least there was no UEFA Cup tie with Lazio in the middle of all that: no wonder David Lacey wrote that the defeat to Trelleborgs was looking like a convenient humiliation. Shearer doesn't agree with that sentiment, even to this day. 'We wanted to win and I'm all for momentum in football and for not going out of any cup competition.'

Newcastle away was billed as Keegan vs Dalglish of course, and not for the first time. It was also a tale of two chairmen in Sir John Hall and Jack Walker who had stepped in to transform two historic clubs that were struggling in the lower leagues. There was also much made of the difference in style, with Rovers cast as the more pragmatic of the two sides – a feeling that had been confirmed with the two live Trelleborgs performances that had been beamed into the nation's living rooms – compared to the free-flowing Geordies.

It may have been too dramatic to say that this was a game that Rovers could not afford to lose, yet had they done so, it would have been another blow to confidence and an eight-point gap between the two teams. As it was it ended 1-1 and Rovers were unlucky not to take the three points. Shearer scored from the spot and there should have been another penalty late in the game. Moments later another silly goal cost them victory. Jason Wilcox cleared off the line with two minutes remaining but it hit the backside of Flowers and bounced into the net.

15 October saw Liverpool come to Ewood, with 30,000 fans in attendance. It was some game and perhaps that victory was when fans really started to believe that a title challenge was possible. Rovers had gone behind yet showed grit, character and fight to get back in and win 3-2. Sutton scored twice and Shearer was, for once, shoved out of the headlines. A deflected Robbie Fowler goal put the visitors ahead in the first half but in the second, Atkins fired home from close range after good work from Shearer, pulling the ball across goal. Soon after Shearer was doing something similar, firing a low cross over for Sutton to bundle home from even closer range. It was a short-lived lead as John Barnes equalised with a spectacular overhead kick. Then, with 18 minutes left, Sutton won it. Ripley headed on a goal-kick, Sutton beat his defender and fired home across David James from the right corner of the area. All but four of the 20 goals Blackburn had scored by this point in the season had been scored by the SAS.

'We have just seen for ourselves that Sutton and Shearer are the best two in the business,' said Jan Mølby. 'Our own pairing of Ian Rush and Robbie

Fowler are not bad, but the two Blackburn lads take some stopping. You honestly wouldn't believe Shearer is only 24 as he has such an old head on young shoulders. The frightening thing is that the two will get better as the season goes along and it is players like them who are capable of winning championships.'

Daily Express writer Steve Curry was a little more creative and said that the SAS in tandem was like climbing into a boxing ring to face Mike Tyson, but also to find a young Joe Frazier standing alongside him. 'The heavyweights in question this time were Sutton and Shearer whose clubbing blows came from their feet and who are turning Ewood Park into the Madison Square Garden of football.'

Liverpool fans after the game may have agreed with the boxing analogy and were not too impressed with what they regarded as the victors' direct style, but it was a big three points for the Rovers. Yet while Rovers were second, Newcastle were five points clear at the top, winning eight and drawing two of their opening ten games. Just as Rovers were seeing off Liverpool, Peter Beardsley scored a last-minute winner at Crystal Palace.

Curry admitted that he had been sceptical as to how the SAS partnership would work but attributed the subsequent success in part to Shearer's unselfishness. 'When you consider we have not yet played 15 games together I would say it's going all right,' said Shearer, who at the time was being outscored by Sutton 12 to eight after league game number ten. Sutton was equally as unselfish with his praise. 'Playing up there with Alan takes a great weight off your shoulders. I find I'm getting into lots of spaces where he would probably have been last season. That is because he's being so tightly marked the opposition tend to leave space.'

While Shearer may have been unselfish – after all there was plenty more to his game than just goals – that didn't mean he had to like it, or even like his new strike partner. There were always rumours in Blackburn that Shearer was not particularly enamoured of playing with the new man. Here was the next big thing and a new British transfer record signing. Shearer had been those things himself once, and he had been getting all the goals in the previous two seasons, but now he had a rival.

The gossip went that Shearer preferred playing with Newell, his best friend off the field and a more generous strike partner on it. Sutton seemed to buy into this in his autobiography. '...Throughout the season there were constant murmurings about my relationship with Alan. The murmurings continued after Alan left for Newcastle at the start of the 1996/97 season. I supposed as a renowned striking partnership people expected we'd be great mates on and off the pitch. I would like to think we both had a healthy mutual respect for each other on the pitch. Off the pitch it's difficult for me to put into words how I felt. It's hard to explain but there was always an underlying feeling from me that there wasn't any warmth towards me from Alan...'

Sutton put it down to Shearer's friendship with Mike Newell, the man who he had replaced. 'They were a strike partnership the previous season and were best mates. I was brought in by Kenny and broke up the Shearer/Newell partnership. I felt at the time there may have been a bit of resentment towards me. I may have been feeling a little insecure, I don't know. I had moved for a record British transfer fee and maybe stole the limelight away from Alan for a short period.'

Shearer was never going to admit whether he was put out a little at having a rival for goals and headlines and even now, when I ask him, he says it was a non-issue. 'I didn't have a preference. They both were good players in a good team. I didn't score more or less with either player. I was good friends with Mike Newell as I lived near him but that didn't mean I preferred him as a partner.'

It would have been natural for a player who was single-minded in his pursuit of goals and always hungry to score to believe that he was the main man, and soon enough he was again. In Shearer's season diary he barely mentions Sutton's brace in the Liverpool win, a big result, and talks more about how he was robbed of the chance of a goal when clean through thanks to an erroneous offside decision.

'I really wanted his approval,' Sutton recalled. 'I was still very young at twenty-one and it was my first move away from Norwich. I was very high profile but hardly experienced in life at dealing with situations. I was a big fish in Norwich but was now in a pond with the biggest fish in the country at Blackburn.'

Sutton felt that Shearer didn't celebrate some of his goals as enthusiastically as he could have done. '...This left me very unsure about what he thought about me. The following season I felt Alan had a strong influence on Ray Harford when it came to team selection.' Sutton struggled to get into the team the season after the title win as Harford preferred Newell for much of it. In 1998 when Sutton was to reject a call-up to England B, Shearer said that he could not understand the decision. 'It's a bigger loss to Chris than to England as we have a lot of players capable of doing a job in that position.' That Shearer had a point did not make it easier for Sutton to swallow.

'I didn't feel surprised that Alan chose to criticise me in the way that he did,' said Sutton, who admitted that he made a mistake in turning down the call-up. 'It just reaffirmed to me that when I had had my doubts about Alan's frostiness towards me at times at Blackburn that I had read the vibes correctly. As a former teammate I would have expected him to toe the party line and adhere to an unwritten rule amongst so-called teammates and say something along the lines of "It wasn't a decision I would have made by any means but Chris is his own man and Chris makes his own decisions," rather than what he did say which was, "It's Chris's loss, not England's." Alan was probably correct. But he never phoned me or tried to cajole me into changing my mind but then again, why would he?'

At the time at least, especially after the win over Liverpool, Rovers fans did not know or care. There was a feeling after that performance that perhaps there was still plenty to play for in the season. The return of Paul Warhurst to the first team helped, especially given the suspension to Sherwood. Warhurst had been playing in defence but was effective in the middle against Liverpool.

After the loss at home to United, discussed in the following chapter, Rovers bounced back to win 2-0 at a Forest team that was going well, with Sutton scoring both. Yet again the talk was about the striker paying off some of the record fee. 'We don't have to justify the fee,' Dalglish said. 'The only person we have to justify anything to is Jack Walker and I think Uncle Jack had a good day today.' For the second successive game, Rovers had a man sent off with Wilcox seeing red, making him the first player to receive his marching orders twice in the season, though his crime seemed to have been little more than dropping the ball at a throw-in. 'It's getting beyond a joke,' Dalglish added. 'I'm fed up with having to come out every week to try and explain referees' decisions.'

The official was more to his liking in the next game. A fine Shearer strike gave Blackburn the lead at Sheffield Wednesday and the hosts had a goal disallowed and two penalty shouts turned down. There was some fine play in the second half as Rovers started to find their groove and got into second gear. It was a little overshadowed in the media as Manchester United lost 4-0 in Barcelona on the same evening. There was some mirth in Blackburn at that, though perhaps some relief that it was the Red Devils at the Camp Nou trying to stop Romário and Stoichkov and not the Blues. The Wednesday win was followed by a 2-0 home victory over a Tottenham team that had just fired Ossie Ardiles.

Soon after, during the international break, Dalglish was taking his team to Spain to face Barcelona. The Spanish giants invited Blackburn to Almeria for a friendly and the Rovers got some revenge – albeit served unnoticed – on behalf of their rivals with a 3-1 win.

17

MANCHESTER UNITED: ZERO POINTS, ONE FRENCHMAN AND TWO REFEREES

'They didn't play the beautiful football that the media said they did.
They were a long ball team most of the time, but the media were
not against them like they were against us.'

KEVIN GALLACHER

FOR A COUPLE OF YEARS, MANCHESTER UNITED AND
Blackburn were rivals. It didn't last too long but there was definite needle there.
It was certainly a different feeling for Rovers fans. After years scrapping with
the likes of Swindon, Ipswich and others for promotion, they were grappling
with one of the biggest clubs around.

'When I played at Blackburn, I used to hate Manchester United,' wrote
Sutton is his autobiography, before admitting that the feeling turned to
admiration over the years. Gary Lineker has talked of how players join a new
club and automatically and immediately dislike their rivals and at the time,
there was plenty of rivalry between the two clubs.

There was the history between the two managers from Dalglish's Liverpool days. Then there was United nipping in to take Keane away from Ewood, Shearer choosing East Lancashire over Manchester and the fact that Rovers, for a time, looked like they may just snatch the 1993/94 title away when it had been all done and dusted. On Easter Monday that season, just two days after United had lost 2-0 at Blackburn, Rovers went and won 3-0 at Everton, a fantastic result. On the same day, there was genuine concern and tension at Old Trafford as they fought hard to beat Oldham 3-2. Until midway through the second half it was 1-1, with how Rovers were getting on at Goodison a common topic of conversation. At that point, the title pendulum was still pointing towards United, but there was serious doubt. In the end, an exhausted Blackburn caught the long-time leaders only to fall away. There was respect between the clubs – Rovers knew how talented United were while United couldn't believe that Rovers had closed the gap – if not much affection. The tension heightened when Dalglish outbid Ferguson for Sutton, with Fergie echoing the past complaints of chairman Martin Edwards that Rovers were ruining a transfer market in which Manchester United had long been the major players.

In the first season in the league, it was just exciting to finally face a team like United in the top tier. That changed in the second season as it became clear that Rovers could challenge the champions. Ahead of 1994/95, there was a determination to beat them.

Eric Cantona was always going to play a part. The Frenchman had been sent off twice in the space of four days – against Swindon and Arsenal – in March 1994 and missed the loss at Ewood. The Frenchman was also in the news just ahead of the new season. United's talisman had been sent off in a friendly at Rangers and was due to miss the first three games of the season. A lunge at defender Steven Pressley brought a fourth red card in the space of a year but the volatile Frenchman (as he was described in pretty much every article that mentioned him around this time) told *L'Equipe* that he was not about to change his ways. 'It is my nature to play like I do and to react like I react. It's an instinct and to hell with anybody who is not happy with it.'

Ferguson backed his star. 'If he feels there has been an injustice, he has to prove to the world that he's going to correct it. We are told there will be no tackling from behind, but it happened several times with Pressley. In these situations Eric cannot control his temper. Love him or hate him, we have to live with his faults and we are delighted to have him.'

Ferguson had been accused of being over-protective of Cantona and too soft with the Frenchman over his twin reds from the previous season. 'We all know he has a spark, a temper. There is nothing necessarily wrong with losing your temper providing it is for the right reasons. That has applied to me throughout my own life. Some people are like that. I still have a terrible temper and I'm 52. You do get a little more mellow and the boiling point gets a little higher, but you don't shed it. Eric's problem is that he tries to correct the injustices done to him. If I could take him off the pitch for 10 minutes to calm down, he'd be all right. But there are players around who will commit eight fouls in a game and the referee's attitude has been "Oh that's Tommy. He always does that and nothing happens." Eric's stature is bigger than most players and he plays for United which is bigger than most clubs. So there's a price to pay. People say how great it must be to play here but it comes at a cost. He knows that if he does wrong, I don't let him off, but it is not a manager's job to publicly criticise his employees. That is no good for work relationships. I'm not interested in what people say about me over-protecting my players. Okay, he loses his temper. But what about his extravagant vision of the game? He can thread passes that, if anyone else tried, they couldn't do. I don't know anyone quicker at running with the ball and yet his economy of movement is terrific. People say he can't tackle but who cares?'

The first meeting between the two teams came in October. Rovers were coming off the back of that exciting 3-2 win over Liverpool. After the disaster of Trelleborgs, the Blues were starting to get into their groove and there was confidence going into the Ewood clash. United won 4-2 but there was more to it than that. Cantona or Kanchelskis were not match-winners, at least as far as Rovers fans were concerned. Instead it was Gerald Ashby. The referee is up there with George Courtney in the long memories of Rovers supporters and is perhaps considered even worse after Courtney partially redeemed himself by blowing for two blue penalties in the 1992 play-off final at Wembley. Ashby did not manage to make amends.

It was an afternoon characterised by driving rain and wind and a growing animosity between the two teams. Paul Warhurst had put Rovers ahead with a delightful chip after 15 minutes and the hosts were well on top. As half-time approached, if there was to be another goal, most would have bet on the home team extending their lead. Then there was a penalty given at the Blackburn End that changed the game.

Henning Berg and Lee Sharpe fell over in the area at the end of the first half and not only did Ashby point to the spot to the general disbelief of the home fans, he also sent the Norwegian off. Even Alex Ferguson admitted that it may not have been a penalty. 'After watching a video replay,' the Scot said, 'it looked like Berg took the ball.' Not that Ferguson cared too much. 'The only thing you can do against ten men is win it and we've done that.'

Tim Flowers called it a nightmare decision. Dalglish was furious. 'You prefer to lose because of the ability of the opposition, not the inability of the referee. He saw it differently from everyone else because it was clear that Henning kicked the ball. We will be appealing. The penalty was bad enough but being reduced to ten men made it very difficult for us. It turned the game.' That was the feeling of the fans. Had it just been the penalty, there was still confidence that Rovers would come back and win the game. But being a man down made defeat almost inevitable.

To be fair to Rovers, they bounced back, Hendry restoring the lead early in the second half, but United soon took advantage of the space available, and eventually took the points too with a masterful display of how to play against ten men.

The media was sympathetic to the home team and agreed that the decision probably cost Rovers a game they were controlling. '1-0 up and way ahead on points,' was one verdict. There were few arguments over the two decisions.

The FA said it would certainly examine an appeal, almost ensuring that one would come. Ashby admitted the next day that he may have been wrong according to video evidence. 'When I watch the video, I am prepared to consider that I could have made a harsh decision.' Immediately after the game however, Ashby explained his decision. 'I believed that Berg played the ball having already made contact with the opponent. I sent Berg off because he was denying a clear goalscoring opportunity by committing a professional foul, which demands a sending off in itself. When the incident happened, I had a reasonable view. I made my decision instantly. I gave an honest decision. I hope people respect me for that.'

At the time, it was a wild hope. Rovers were pissed off. Maybe it helped: Dalglish's men won 11 of their next 12 league games. The only draw came against Mark McGhee's Leicester, and much was made of how Ferguson had helped the player he used to manage at Aberdeen come up with a plan to thwart the SAS.

The big clash had been looming – Old Trafford on 22 January. Rovers made the short trip five points clear with a game in hand. A win, said the press, and the title race would be almost over. Blackburn fans were not thinking the same, but the media's predictions were understandable given the form Rovers were in.

Fans were not expecting a win. Ripley was injured and was missed. Gallacher and Batty had yet to step foot on a football pitch all season. The big story in the build-up was that the game would be Andy Cole's debut. The striker had not played in the previous week when Newcastle went to Old Trafford as it was felt his presence could be incendiary. 'Better he sits by the fire for this one,' said Ferguson before Newcastle helped Rovers by taking a point.

In the big game against the leaders Cole was poor, missing a great chance in the opening minutes, and looked to be what he was: an out of form striker playing in a crucial and frantic game. Rovers lost 1-0 thanks to a late Eric Cantona goal. The visitors had been happy to get a draw and had not offered a great deal until the final minute. Then Sherwood headed home to seemingly earn a point and – crucially – deny their closest challengers two. Then Paul Durkin joined Ashby in the halls of Rovers hatred. The referee ruled out the goal for a Shearer push on Roy Keane in the build-up.

Talk to any Rovers fan and the first thing they will say is something like this: 'It was obviously a goal because the United players, even Keane, did not appeal.' The decision was, Dalglish said, 'a disgrace. I can't see any explanation for the goal being chopped off.' When informed that it had been for a Shearer foul, he added, 'That's the referee's opinion. He's got to say that. He's got to defend his actions. I thought we deserved something from the game.'

Ferguson disagreed. 'Shearer was very cute. It was only a little shove, not much but just enough. The referee did well to spot it. It would have been a travesty if we had not won today.' Shearer disagreed. 'I did raise my arms because that's the only way you can get leverage to climb for a high ball, but I barely touched him. The real giveaway is that Roy did not raise a murmur of protest which confirms my opinion that I did not foul him. I kept my feelings to myself because I don't want to get booked or sent off but inside I am seething with anger. It hurts even more when I learn in the player's lounge afterwards from someone who knows Keane that he is admitting that he was not pushed. For the second time this season against United, we feel we have been affected by a refereeing decision.'

Durkin hit back. 'I know I was right. Alan Shearer pushed Roy Keane before the ball was placed into the net. I gave what I saw and I stand by it. We can all do without this sort of fuss from managers, but I suppose it has to be accepted as part and parcel of the game.'

Rovers had not done a great deal in the game but it hardly needs saying that all Blues fans, and even some United supporters that I talked to, felt it was a perfectly good goal. Had those two very controversial decisions in the two meetings gone the way most thought they should have, Rovers could have come away from Old Trafford eleven points ahead with a game in hand, instead of two. The rest of the season could have been very different. Had Rovers continued the form they showed over the next few weeks then the title race would have been won by Easter. Had that title win been a dominant one, then who knows what would have happened? Perhaps the effect would have continued into the following season and beyond. We will never know. Certainly, it would have been a very bitter pill had United actually pipped Rovers to the title on the final day. At the time, there was a slight sense of foreboding that this wasn't to be Blackburn's year.

United fans did not see it that way. 'My memory of that second game was the Cantona goal,' said John Brewin. 'It was a perfect goal. Giggs wins the ball back and the cross is fantastic. Walking away from that game, I felt that we would win the league as we are better than them. I honestly thought that was it and was cock-a-hoop. We felt we were superior to Blackburn but then three days later it all happened.'

The name of Paul Durkin was soon removed from the conversation in a way that nobody would have thought possible. For the second time that month a major football story broke, both involving Manchester United and both affecting Blackburn indirectly. The second was no transfer bombshell but something more surprising and plenty more shocking. On a cold night on 25 January, I was in Blackburn listening to Manchester United take on Crystal Palace at Selhurst Park. The disallowed late goal from Sunday meant that the second-placed team would go top with a win. Rovers would still have two games in hand but being knocked off the top so soon after the team was going so well would have been a blow.

Then Cantona was sent off and there is no reason to go into any detail here as there can be few fans who don't know what happened next. On his way to the dressing-rooms, he attacked a home fan, leading with a flying kung-fu kick and then following up with a series of punches.

Listening to the radio was sensational and unbelievable. There was only one thing for it, to get to the pub. Partly to try and be the first to break the news to others and if that was not possible to be the first to crack the joke that the fences, recently taken down thanks to the Taylor Report, should be put back to protect the fans from the players. Mostly, though, it was because this was one of those moments that you needed to be with others. These days, Twitter would probably suffice – though it may explode – but in 1995 you had to go to the nearest pub and be with people who were as deliciously outraged as you were, though as the game was not live on television nobody had actually seen it yet.

Rarely has an episode of *Sportsnight*, the BBC's midweek sports highlight show, been so eagerly awaited. Des Lynam opened and got right to the point. 'There are two big Premiership games on *Sportsnight* tonight and at one of them, some of the most extraordinary scenes witnessed at a football ground in this country.' Gary Lineker had only just started out as a pundit – and had already upset George Graham, under investigation after accusations that he had taken a bung, by saying that he hoped the Scot's defence was better than Arsenal's – and had to talk about one of the biggest sports stories for years. 'It is one of the most amazing things I have ever seen at a football match. It doesn't matter how you are provoked by the crowd, whatever language they use, you've gotta be above it.'

Reporters were soon digging out his video 'Eric the King' released in 1994, to quote the man's own words. 'I play with passion and fire. I have to accept that sometimes the fire does harm. I know it does harm. I harm myself and I am aware of harming others. But I cannot be what I am without these other sides of my character. I don't have to justify myself. I have no regrets. I have to correct my faults, but I must remain true to myself. That's the big problem. In the past I have tried to correct myself and I have lost my game. What I have to do now is find a solution that works and I think I've found one now.'

Rovers players were as amazed as anyone. 'We knew Cantona was such a wonderful footballer and was such an influence as he showed against us not long before,' said Slater. 'Of course, we couldn't believe what we saw on television. All the players were calling each other and in training, the talk was of nothing else. It was like being at school when something big happens and you talk about it all day. As a player, you never like to see other players get banned but he did something silly and got banned for it.'

There was of course a debate as to how this would benefit Blackburn for the rest of the season and, once the season was over, how it actually did help the club. At the very least, it helped on the night as with United down to ten men, Palace fought back to draw 1-1 and preserved Blackburn's place at the top. There was also no doubt that the Frenchman was missed. His talent and influence were both considerable.

As Slater said, 'There's no doubt that the ban was a massive boost. We all knew it. As a professional, you don't like to see players get banned but it certainly did not harm us.' The stats don't really bear that out as in terms of points per game; United without Cantona were slightly better. Even so, there is little doubt that United were a better team when their French talisman played. Had he not been banned for the rest of the season, it could easily have been a third successive title going to Old Trafford. But then, as mentioned above, had the Reds not had the rub of the green referee wise in the two meetings with Blackburn then Cantona's presence would likely have made little difference. 'Of course, we are aware that it could work to the benefit of Blackburn Rovers, but this is not really a time to gloat,' Shearer gloated.

Wilcox points to the fact that Rovers had plenty of injuries too. Batty, Gallacher, Warhurst and himself all had serious problems. 'I certainly think that it hindered them as he was obviously a big and influential player. I am not sure if it changed anything for us. Hindsight is a great thing and nobody will ever know. At the end of the day, I did my cruciate ligament in March. We had our fair share of troubles. It is part and parcel of football. If it hadn't been Cantona, it could have been someone else. Nobody has a perfect season and you are always going to get injuries over a 42-game season especially in a league that is physical and fast. It is not just about the best team but about who has the best squad. Whoever wins it has the right to win it.'

For Brewin, the highs of the Cantona-inspired 1-0 win were soon forgotten. 'At that point, once that happened, I thought the league had gone. The thing about United, we had won the league for the past two seasons but there was still some fragility, especially without Cantona. He was the catalyst. Like when Robson was injured in the eighties, we felt different. At United, we had that hero complex about certain players, though Ferguson ended that eventually. It really overshadowed the club and it seemed like everything was coming apart.'

Would United have won the league if Cantona had been available? 'Yes, because Cantona's influence was apparent the next season,' said Brewin. 'That iron will to win, that ability to pull things out of the fire, hold his nerve and take other players with him. He just had that ability, more than any other player I've seen, to just pull performances out. In that 92/93 season, we did that coming from behind and putting a run of results together. There were problems in 94/95. Ferguson had fallen out with Ince, United didn't have a great season and were inconsistent and buying Cole midway through showed that Ferguson wasn't satisfied. If we had won the title, it would not have gone down as a great title win like '93, '94, the treble year in '99 or 2007. The team was not functioning at that level. Yet compared to Blackburn we had better players in just about every position except centre-forward. Shearer wasn't likeable if he wasn't on your team, but he was just a machine.'

Lee Sharpe tells the story of what happened from a player's perspective, albeit for comedic effect in an after-dinner speech given in 2017.

'When we saw it, we said "Get in there! There's no way in a million years the manager can bollock us for playing shit after he's just done that. We're scot free…"' After the game the players were keen to get into the dressing room. "This is going to be fucking hilarious."

'The manager comes in and he's absolutely fuming. The door smashes off the back of its hinges. The jacket is off, he's got the short sleeves rolled up; steam coming out of his ears and frothing at the mouth. There's benches in the middle of the room with shirts and balls to be signed. Cups of tea and plates of sandwiches. They're sent fucking flying everywhere.

'We're getting scalded and getting egg sandwiches down the back of our necks. We look at each other, thinking, "Fucking hell, Cantona is getting it here!"

'And then he starts, the manager. "Fucking Pallister, you can't head anything, you can't tackle. Incey, where the fuck have you been? Sharpey, my grandmother runs fucking faster than you! You're all a fucking disgrace. nine o'clock, tomorrow morning, I'm going to run your fucking balls off in training. Fucking shocking. And Eric… [in a softer tone] you can't go round doing things like that son."'

18
LEADING FROM THE FRONT

'People forget that we were top from November all the way until the end.'
JASON WILCOX

AS THE END OF 1994 APPROACHED, ROVERS WERE IN
top gear. Wins at Manchester City on Boxing Day and Crystal Palace on
New Year's Eve (Selhurst Park had rarely been a happy hunting ground) were
achieved despite the absence of Kenny Dalglish. Initially, it was assumed that
the Scot had overindulged over the festive period, but he was recovering from
a Christmas Eve appendix operation. Harford stepped in and called the boss
on the morning of the games to get the team. As Big Ben chimed to herald in
1995, the East Lancs lads were three points clear at the top above Manchester
United, having played a game less.

Harford called Dalglish again on the morning of the game against West

Ham, Blackburn's first of 1995, worried that Shearer would miss out with the flu. In the end he was passed fit and then scored a hat-trick as Rovers came from 2-1 behind to win 4-2. By full-time the lead had gone to six, but Shearer was not getting carried away. Before returning to his sick-bed, he invoked memories of the previous year. 'At one stage last season, Manchester United were 16 points ahead so to say we're pulling away now we are six ahead is ridiculous. I think people are starting to get excited prematurely, but we would rather be here than at the bottom. I think we are safe from the drop now.' Shearer had a point. Later that evening United defeated Coventry at home with the headlines all about how the Reds were keeping the heat on the Blues, a reversal of the year before.

The big story that week, however, was not a link with rising Bolton Wanderers star Jason McAteer, but a much bigger transfer move. On 10 January, Newcastle sold their star striker Andy Cole to Manchester United for a British transfer record fee of £7 million. To say that the move to the Reds came out of the blue was an understatement. 'It was a big shock,' said Cole. 'I didn't think Newcastle would sell me to an English club. It's a brilliant move. I'm excited about the things that will hopefully come from it over the next five years.'

Newcastle fans headed to St James' Park to be greeted by Kevin Keegan, who explained the decision. 'I'm in charge, not you,' he said. 'The deal was too good to turn down. Tough decisions have to be made and if you are scared of making them you shouldn't be in this job. I'm not worried about reactions. I just want to get the right players and spend the money wisely. I accept we're losing a great player but the lad we're getting could be anything.' Keith Gillespie was a makeweight, the 19-year-old heading to Newcastle. 'He's possibly the best youngster I've seen in the game in the three years since I came back.'

Ferguson revealed that Keegan had come calling for the Northern Irish winger. 'We started negotiations because Kevin was interested in Keith Gillespie and very keen to have him. At that point we had to reconsider because he's a good young player but sometimes you have to give something to get something. We never thought we could get Andy. His goalscoring record is unbelievable and hopefully he will get the goals to make us a better team.'

The fact that Cole had not scored in nine games must have made things slightly easier. For the first time, his qualities were being questioned. It was also an acknowledgement from Keegan that his team were out of the title race. Despite some outrage, most backed the boss's judgement and they were soon being linked with Dennis Bergkamp and Les Ferdinand.

It took Ferguson's spending at Old Trafford to £30 million in eight years. Keegan had spent around £27 million since 1992, a similar amount to Dalglish at Blackburn. Arsenal, having a dreadful season and stuck in mid-table, spent up to £4 million two days later in bringing in John Hartson from Luton and Chris Kiwomya from Ipswich. Luton boss David Pleat said that the £2 million, perhaps rising to £2.5 million, could not be refused and there was a 'scramble at the moment, a madness in the transfer market'.

There was little time to discuss the effect of losing to United at Old Trafford towards the end of January and what it may do to Blackburn. There was a home game against struggling Ipswich on the Saturday, the last game of the month, a perfect opportunity to put the Manchester defeat to bed and go four points clear with a game in hand. The game received little coverage with much more attention on the Cantona-less United defeating Wrexham in the FA Cup. Shearer got a hat-trick in a 4-1 win. 'That's my third hat-trick of the season and it gives me as much pleasure as the previous two. There is no greater feeling for me than putting the ball in the net. If I score one I want another. If I am on two goals, I want three; a hat-trick and I'm still going flat out for a fourth. My hunger for goals is never satisfied.'

The rearranged league match with Leeds the following Wednesday was a bigger clash. It came the day after Sutton got married and the striker had to cancel his honeymoon. According to Shearer, teammates had to cancel plans to let their hair down while Flowers did not attend at all due to a desire to prepare for the game that could have seen Rovers go seven clear.

Due to traffic, many fans missed the first 15 minutes and two eye-raising events that occurred in the first 72 seconds. The first was that Shearer missed a one-on-one, with his shot coming back off the legs of John Lukic. There was palpable surprise in Ewood. Such things never happened. From the rebound, Leeds attacked through Brian Deane who was brought down outside the area by Tim Flowers, who was then sent off. The goalie looked as surprised as everyone else and took time to get his towel and little bag from the goal before trotting off to be replaced by an equally surprised Bobby Mimms, who was getting his first action of the season. 'That kind of situation is what you train for, especially as a second-choice goalkeeper,' he said. 'It is a squad game. Of course I wasn't expecting to be on so quickly but when the action starts, the adrenaline starts too and you are back there. It was one of those crazy nights. The fans were very unhappy about the red card and really got behind the players and we almost took all three points. I enjoyed it.'

Five minutes after the red card, Shearer scored from the spot and then gave a performance that can only be described as out of this world. The *Lancashire Evening Telegraph* gave him a rare 10 out of 10. In attack, he did the work of four, running the Leeds defence all over the place. 'I always seemed to do well against Leeds for some reason. I loved a battle and that was a good one that day,' he remembered almost a quarter of a century on. A late Leeds penalty made it 1-1. There was more to the game with Leeds. It took place on what became known as 'Mad Wednesday' by a media still yet to calm down from Cantona. There were three sendings-off and 16 bookings in the two games. The other was Newcastle vs Everton at St James' Park where the Blues finished with nine men. Back at Ewood Park, a 40-year old fan from Accrington was arrested and charged after attempting to confront referee Rodger Gifford. He had to be dragged away by Mimms. The ire was down to the late penalty given to Leeds though there was still the bad feeling from the early red card, with fans pointing out that a week earlier Mark Bosnich had been allowed to stay on the pitch after taking out Klinsmann in a violent-looking incident.

Down to White Hart Lane on 5 February and the German was fine to score the opener through the legs of Mimms in a 3-1 win for the London team. Spurs deserved the win and produced one of their best performances of the season, though Rovers were without luck. The second goal took a major deflection and Stuart Ripley's return from injury lasted an hour. It was not a great sequence of results. It meant four points from the previous 12, with the one win coming against the hapless Ipswich. At the same time Andy Cole scored his first for United in a 1-0 win, a first in 12 games. With Cole ending his dry spell, Sutton's was stretching to eleven league games. Though he had netted home and away against Newcastle in the cup, it was becoming a worry.

He hadn't scored in the league since November. Shearer was banging in the goals, but Sutton had lost his form from the first half of the season with his teammates jokingly, according to Shearer, putting it down to getting married.

And then on 11 February, Rovers were knocked off the top of the table for 24 hours. United had won the Manchester derby 3-0 and moved a point clear, with the previous leaders in action the following day. After being at the summit for over ten weeks, it felt a little strange. With the club's hiccup in form (though the Leeds draw and United loss could easily have been a win and a draw had there been a different referee in charge, and the Spurs loss was just one of those days when the opposition plays out of their skin) there were some nerves heading to the game on a very wet Sunday afternoon. Sherwood scored a belter and Shearer got a classic header in a welcome 3-1 win over Sheffield Wednesday.

The three points meant that Rovers stayed top over the international break, one that fans were looking forward to. England were going to Ireland for a first away game under Terry Venables and the national team had become more interesting. Shearer had obviously become a regular and Le Saux was making the left-back position his own. Flowers had started to become involved, though was out of Ireland game with a broken toe. Batty would probably have made the squad had he been fit though despite all the talk about Sutton, the striker was still waiting for his first call up. For the Ireland game, Sherwood had also been included in the squad.

Yet, and not for the first time that season, football made the front rather than back pages as England fans ran riot at Lansdowne Road, causing the game to be abandoned in the first half. It was the first time an England game had not been completed after kicking off. Sherwood never made it onto the pitch. With England hosting the European Championships the following summer, there was genuine concern.

Shearer's diary entry noted that the squad had learnt of disturbances involving England fans in the city prior to the game, but the real trouble started when David Kelly scored for Ireland. 'A section of English fans seems to be hurling objects at those below them in the lower deck of the stadium, but I still think it is an overreaction when the referee takes the players off the field. Back in the dressing room we are still not fully aware of how serious the trouble is. Terry Venables uses the time to change the way we are playing. Soon, it is clear that the outbreak of violence is serious. I thought we had got rid of this curse from our game years ago. Now it is obvious we have become too complacent about it.'

Venables was furious. 'I haven't got words strong enough to say how I feel. Obviously there could be repercussions. This could have put the game back years.' Bertie Ahern, leader of the Irish opposition, was there: 'The English fans are the greatest scumbags I've ever seen. It's a miracle more people were not hurt.'

It came a week after trouble between Chelsea and Millwall fans in the FA Cup and there were real worries that violence was coming back into football stadiums.

There was something in the air in general that season. Cantona's antics marked the fourth scandal of the season, as many pointed out. Bruce Grobbelaar had been accused of fixing games and letting in goals deliberately. Paul Merson had broken down in a press conference and admitted to cocaine addiction, and then there was George Graham. On 21 February, just a few days after Dublin, Graham was fired by Arsenal for taking a bung from the transfers of John Jensen and Norwegian international defender Pål Lydersen.

The Premier League launched an investigation into transfer deals and the use of bungs and backhanders. Graham was found guilty of receiving £425,000 for the twin transfers. He claimed that it was an unsolicited gift and slammed the kangaroo court that had convicted him and promised to clear his name. 'They had already made their minds up and were demanding my dismissal from Arsenal before the evidence had been presented.' It ended Graham's nine-year tenure.

Soon after Chelsea captain Dennis Wise was sentenced to three months in prison for criminal damage and assault on a taxi driver, while Chris Armstrong, who Crystal Palace had slapped a £6 million price tag on earlier in the season, failed a drugs test, testing positive for cannabis.

To make matters worse, a few hundred of Belgium's worst hooligans were expected at Stamford Bridge for the second leg of the Cup Winners' Cup clash between Chelsea and Club Brugge. On the same day that Chelsea won that quarter-final, police arrested Grobbelaar and Hans Segers and also John

Fashanu in a dawn 'swoop'. With Paul Ince also going before a judge on charges of common assault for his part in the Selhurst Park episode in January and Vinnie Jones in trouble for biting the nose of a journalist, it was noted that there could almost be a team named of disgraced footballers: Merson, Cantona, Armstrong, Wise, Ince, Jones, Fashanu, Segers, Grobbelaar.

The same week, Gordon Taylor, head of the players' union, announced plans to set up an anti-sleaze unit. In March, David Davies, the FA's director of public affairs, warned that the organisation was going to come out fighting, promising a crusade against sleaze as the FA's chief executive Graham Kelly met Home Secretary Michael Howard to discuss the game's issues.

Back on the pitch and the title race was getting closer. United may have lost Cantona but were going well. On 22 February, they won 2-0 at Norwich. The Reds had lost just once in 20 league games. Just like the Rovers the season before, the team in second were in a great run of form and putting pressure on. The difference was that the gap this time had started out a lot smaller.

'We have reached that ticklish stage of the season when we can't make mistakes and have to go on winning,' said Ferguson after the Norwich win. 'The title will be won by the side with the most ability, determination, concentration and luck. I don't mind Blackburn being favourites now but what I am concerned about is who are favourites with four games to go.' Actually, most bookmakers were starting to install the defending champions as the team most likely to be top on the final day of the season.

On the same evening, Blackburn won 2-1 at home to Wimbledon on a pitch that was becoming almost unplayable, thanks, at least in part, to heavy rain and the long-standing drainage issues not helped by the river running directly behind the Riverside stand. The jibe from Joe Kinnear that Wimbledon had passed the ball better with Blackburn being more direct contained some truth, given the state of the playing surface. Unfortunately, three days later, Blackburn couldn't do to Norwich at home what United had done away and were held to a goalless draw. Shearer hit the bar after 12 minutes but despite welcoming back Flowers, Le Saux and Ripley from injury, fans who had sat back and waited for the win were left frustrated. The mud bath had dried out to an extreme degree. In the end, Flowers intervened with a couple of great saves to earn a point. Still, fans that left the ground at the end were feeling disappointed at failing to win a home game against a team doomed to relegation. I vividly remember the cheer that went up as we walked along Bolton Road a few minutes later. United's home game against Everton had kicked off late due to traffic congestion. Once the game finally started, a towering header from Duncan Ferguson gave the Merseysiders a 1-0 win. The gap at the top was now three points, though of course for Rovers fans it felt like it should have been five.

For Rovers fans, this was a real feeling of a title race. It wasn't just about how many points were won but also how the other team performed too. There was also a small victory over United early in March. Blackburn proposed a motion which would mean Premiership clubs had to make more tickets available to away fans, 10 percent of their capacity to a maximum 3,000 seats, and this motion was successfully passed. 'The consensus of opinion between clubs was that football is a game between two teams and that both sets of supporters should have reasonable access to matches,' said Rovers chairman Robert Coar. Arsenal seconded the motion and there was support from most of the smaller clubs in the league as visiting managers were complaining more and more about the decisions made by referees at the biggest stadiums. Manchester United as well as Newcastle were strongly opposed. An Old Trafford spokesperson said: 'We're not happy with this at all. We do not have a single, segregated section capable of hosting 3,000 fans which has the required number of exits and entrances, toilets and refreshment kiosks.'

United got some sort of revenge at the weekend, wiping out Blackburn's goal difference advantage to establish one of their own as Cole scored five in a 9-0 win over the doomed Ipswich. Down in the West Midlands, Rovers had a much tougher test at Aston Villa and came away with a 1-0 win that put the hard into hard-fought. It was quite a contrast as David Lacey, writing in the *Guardian,* pointed out. 'If Saturday was Manchester United's field day, for Blackburn Rovers, it was just another afternoon in the trenches. While Old Trafford witnessed a feeding frenzy, it was more a case of iron rations at Villa Park. United dressed themselves up to the nines; Rovers wore fatigues.'

It wasn't a vintage performance but as Dalglish pointed out after the game, 'You get three points whether you win 1-0 or 9-0.' Peter Withe had been commentating on BBC radio and compared Rovers to the Forest team that won the 1978 league title.

Villa boss Brian Little was complimentary about the victors regardless of the manner of victory. 'There are many ways of winning football matches and we've been shown one today. I thought Blackburn deserved to win. They were in charge for most of the game. Blackburn don't worry too much about losing possession in areas of the pitch that are not dangerous compared to Manchester United.'

The Reds were more workmanlike in their next match, getting a late win in midweek at Wimbledon on 7 March to go back on top but the next day Rovers were impressive in a 3-1 victory over Arsenal, at least in an excellent first half. The games were coming thick and fast with Coventry away at the weekend, a tough test with the Sky Blues improving since appointing Ron Atkinson as boss in mid-February to replace Phil Neal. After a dire first half when Dion Dublin put the hosts ahead, Rovers piled on the pressure in the second, but it took a late header from Shearer, getting ahead of goalkeeper Jonathan Gould to head a hanging Le Saux cross into an empty net, to secure a point. With United defeating QPR in the quarter-final of the FA Cup that weekend, a result that did not go down badly in East Lancs, Rovers were four points ahead but had played a game more. Still, now they had nine games left, down to single figures. United played their game in hand in midweek but were held to a home draw by Spurs. Three points in it with the same games played. Cole missed a number of opportunities and it was clear that he was still to win over those doubting the value of his fee.

The weekend starting 18 March was a big one. Rovers were in action first. Mark Stein gave Chelsea an early lead at Ewood but the hosts came back. Shearer got the first, his 100th league goal and his 30th of the season. He broke the offside trap and then blasted a shot into the roof of the net from just inside the area. Soon after, Sherwood grabbed a well-worked second. The game was also notable for Jeff Kenna's debut. The full-back had been signed from Southampton for £1.5 million. He played left-back with Le Saux playing further up the pitch due to Wilcox's injury. Rovers should have won by considerably more than a single goal and the failure to get a third led to some nerves at the end. But it put pressure on the chasers who had a tough trip to Anfield on Sunday and ended up losing 2-0. There it was – a lead of six points, though it was soon reduced to three as United defeated Arsenal 3-0.

There was still time for another signing as Richard Witschge joined on loan for the rest of the season from Bordeaux. It was quite an exciting addition. Here was a winger who had played for Barcelona and was a Dutch international. Perhaps he could have a similar effect that Cantona had at Leeds when he helped the Yorkshire giants over the line to win the title in 1992.

It didn't seem that he was going to be needed after the first week of April, when the title looked to be heading to Blackburn. Of those two vital away wins, which came within three days of each other, the first in particular was no place for a player who grew up under the purist influence of Johann Cruyff at Ajax. 2 April at Goodison Park was not only a huge game in terms of the title race, it was a performance that has contributed to the reputation of that Blackburn team as one that was far from easy on the eyes.

The reputation may have been unfair but that performance and the win was ugly. Everton had sacked Mike Walker earlier in the season and brought in Joe Royle from Oldham. In order to preserve the Blues' top-flight status, the former striker had called for 'The Dogs of War'. The tag was based on a hard-working midfield and determined defending that hauled them to safety, but by this time of the season safety was looking likely and Everton were to go on to win the FA Cup, defeating Manchester United just a few weeks later. Against Blackburn the home team were missing strikers Duncan Ferguson and Paul Rideout and a number of others, which was encouraging.

What an afternoon it turned out to be. Rovers won 2-1 and while it was a result that showed the team had the resilience to win the title, it perhaps sealed the deal in the public's minds that this was a team that lacked the flair of the defending champions. It was backs to the wall, full-backs to the wall, centre-backs to the wall and the whole team to the wall.

It started so brightly in the early April sunshine. Within 13 seconds, Chris Sutton had silenced the home fans with a well-taken strike from just inside the area, a first league goal since November. It was also his first as a married man. As a supporter, such a goal can be a double-edged sword as it is far too early to score. Success was still new to Rovers fans, who were still getting used to the idea that more games would be won than lost. Scoring in the first few seconds seemed to be tempting fate but then Shearer added a second after five minutes. Surely nothing could go wrong? This was not a team that gave away two-goal leads.

Everton were stunned. Almost 40,000 had come to the ground to see the title pretenders brought down a peg or two, to suffer the same fate as United had a few weeks earlier. Credit to the home team, however – they soon began to gather their wits and push the visitors back. Graham Stuart fired home a fine shot from outside the area midway through the first half. With over an hour left to play, it was going to be a battle, and a tense one. To underline that, Stuart Barlow's shot was pushed onto the post by Flowers. When the half-time whistle sounded, it was not a shell-shocked Everton that were grateful for the chance to regroup and focus, it was Blackburn.

The second half was more of the same. It was an ordeal for Rovers fans to see the team subject to so much pressure, an ordeal for the home supporters to be frustrated in such a way, and also for the neutrals who were watching a game that was far from beautiful. Rovers were becoming increasingly desperate. Nobody will forget Colin Hendry's second half clearance, when he earned his nickname of 'Braveheart'. With the ball on the ground around the six-yard box and a very crowded area with boots flying, the Scot attempted one of the most beautiful and reckless diving headers that you have ever seen.

Robbie Slater was watching from the sidelines. 'I don't think I have ever seen a centre-back put in a performance like that, it was sensational from Colin Hendry and I will never forget it. After we got those early goals, it was like the Alamo. Watching it was tense like you wouldn't believe. We dug in, though, and withstood everything they threw at us, and that was a lot. It was intense and you were just waiting for the ball to go in, but there were goalmouth scrambles and six Blackburn players throwing themselves at the ball. It was just determination not to lose and to protect the three points at any costs. It was just the kind of battling performance that the champions have to do. Everton were desperate to get one over on us and we were desperate too. It wasn't pretty, but we won.'

Points yes, friends and plaudits no. There was some serious time-wasting going on, but when the title is so close for the first time in 81 years, there were no Blackburn fans complaining. This was all about winning, nothing else. When Shearer, the top striker in the league, booted the ball almost to Anfield just to waste a few seconds, the boos rang out around Goodison, but Rovers fans just wanted the points.

The *Independent* said that the sight of Shearer belting the ball away was a gloomy one. 'In that second period, Blackburn could not fashion a chance of note from a performance of ruggedness and resilience but little quality and even less charm.'

'Talk about hanging on for dear life. We got away with the points,' said Sutton. 'It was an ugly performance from us, but it was a huge three points and a massive win. They piled the pressure on and there was almighty scramble in our box that seemed to last for three minutes.'

The final whistle was a relief and greeted once again with jeers and not just for the referee, perceived of being too indulgent of the away team's attempts to run down the clock, but mostly for Blackburn Rovers. 'We defend with great resilience, much to the annoyance of the Goodison fans who boo us off at the finish. We take that as a compliment rather than a criticism because we have survived a very difficult test of character,' wrote Shearer.

It was a horrible game to watch for the Rovers fans too, having to see their team defend for 85 minutes. Dalglish admitted that the result was a lucky one.

'A fortunate three points. It wasn't a purist's game and we certainly didn't perform the way we can. But the players have shown by their actions that they don't want to lose games. We dug in and got the points and now we will look forward to the next game.'

It put pressure on United who were in action the following day against Leeds. The Reds were now six points behind with both teams having seven games to play. The champions were held to a goalless draw at a frustrated Old Trafford. Without Cantona and Kanchelskis, who had been impressive all season but was absent with an undiagnosed stomach problem – perhaps not helped by the fact that that he had eight injections in order to play for Russia in the international break – the hosts struggled.

It was a game notable for two things, as well as its importance to the title race. It marked the Premier League debut for a certain David Beckham, recalled to the club from his Preston loan to cover for the absent Russian. And after it all finished, Ferguson came out with his Devon Loch reference, in regard to the horse that was yards away from the finish line in the Grand

National and well ahead, only to somehow fall over and lose everything.

'Blackburn can only throw the league away now, we must hope they do a Devon Loch.'

Though we did not know it at the time, there were bigger issues afoot. The day when Rovers were due to play Queens Park Rangers, the papers were full of details of the Bosman Case – yet to be known as the Bosman Ruling – which would allow freedom of movement after the expiry of a contract. The ruling was to revolutionise the transfer system and enrich players beyond their wildest dreams.

Blackburn fans cared not a jot about what was going on in the European courts; there was a huge midweek game at Loftus Road to worry about. These days it would have been live on television, but for those who did not make it to West London it was radio or teletext. They didn't miss much in terms of action but the nerves and the tension were just as great, greater for those who could not see what was going on. QPR were having a decent season, finishing eighth, and Ray Wilkins had been talking confidently of taking something off the leaders. It was a tight game with the visitors defending well. The only goal came midway through the second half, another well-taken strike from Sutton. Then it was time to defend. 'Once we have our noses in front there is no way we are going to relinquish our leads. We have become experts at grinding out results like this and it is a satisfying feeling,' said Shearer. The striker noted that the QPR fans did not seem to be too impressed and neither was the *Guardian*, though there was some grudging respect. 'The qualities needed to succeed on opposing grounds are rarely designed to win applause from home supporters, and Blackburn left Loftus Road with the boos of disaffected QPR fans ringing in their ears – a not unfamiliar sound for Dalglish's players. Rovers are not a dirty team but nerves are starting to show and at the moment, with some of their players, a general rattiness is never far below the surface.'

Dalglish agreed that it had not been pretty. 'Points are now more important than performance and you grind out results when you can't play open, attractive football.' Rovers deserved more credit for a fighting performance in a tough away game. It was the kind of win that delivers championships and perhaps had it not come just three days after the Everton display, the praise would have been more forthcoming.

But there it was – eight points clear with six games left to play. There was no action that weekend with the FA Cup semi-finals taking place, but fans had the PFA awards to look forward to. There were no less than six Blues named in the team of the year: Flowers, Le Saux, Hendry, Sherwood, Sutton and Shearer. The latter won the main award, beating off competition from Klinsmann and Le Tissier. The striker's planned speech of referencing the famous 'sardines and trawlers' quote from Cantona was stolen by Dalglish who announced the winner, leaving Shearer to talk about putting some pride back into the image of football. It wasn't easy with a fan dying during trouble at the semi-final between Manchester United and Crystal Palace. Ahead of the replay, both managers appealed for calm. Roy Keane heard nothing and was sent off for a vicious stamp on Gareth Southgate. United won through to the final.

19

THE WOBBLE

'There are always going to be ups and downs in a season but this was a real roller coaster. Later in the season, I think that we lacked experience in this kind of situation and there were nerves at the end. It wasn't said or talked about and we didn't need to talk about it. It was just felt, we could all feel it. It was there all the time. I will always remember the final few games. It was hard to switch off and escape it.'

ROBBIE SLATER

IT STARTED AGAINST LEEDS ON 15 APRIL. WELL, KIND OF.
A 1-1 draw against an in-form Leeds United was, on the face of it, a decent result. The Whites were going well; just three losses in the last 15 games, gunning for Europe and also had a new signing in Tony Yeboah who was rapidly becoming a star.

Yet this was a fine performance from Blackburn. The previous two away wins at Everton and QPR had been real battles, but they controlled the game at Elland Road and they should have taken all three points once more. A towering header from Hendry seemed to have won the game though the lead should have been more than a single goal. In the final seconds, the visitors should have had a penalty. Discussing the incident in his diary, Shearer recalled how Graham Poll had congratulated him on his PFA award. The striker replied that he wouldn't mind a repeat of the penalty that Poll have given against Ipswich in January, but was greeted with an odd response: 'I don't think so. Don't forget you were at home that day.' Shearer notes that it was a strange thing to say, but that it didn't register until the final moments when he was fouled in the area with just John Lukic to beat. As Dalglish said after the game, 'Why would Shearer go down when he is one-on-one with the goalkeeper?' The decision was not given and then Leeds went down the other end and scored. 1-1. It meant seven points from three tough games on the road, a total that would have been happily accepted when the travels started. A good performance and a decent result but with Manchester United winning 4-0 at already relegated Leicester, there were a few nerves. Overall though, there was still confidence with two games at home against struggling teams in the next five days – Manchester City and Crystal Palace. The gap had been cut from eight points to six. If you were a neutral fan, it would have still seemed massive. The mind games continued from Ferguson. 'If Rovers continue to throw points away then we could still do it,' though he conceded that his team needed a miracle. 'If God is a United fan then now is the time to act.'

Rovers had hardly been throwing points away at all. Since the Tottenham loss, the form had been excellent. From the subsequent ten games, seven had been won and three drawn with tough away trips such as Everton, Leeds and Aston Villa.

The Leeds result was actually a good one, just that the last-minute equaliser was a blow. It did mean that a bad result in the next game would be a problem, but there seemed little chance of that happening. There was just 48 hours to wait for the game with struggling Manchester City, who were just three points clear of the relegation zone, at Ewood on Easter Monday. The day started well as United had been held by Chelsea earlier in the early kick-off. Here was a chance to re-establish that eight-point lead with just four games to go. With Palace coming to Ewood three days later, that lead could stretch to 11 by the time United played again. That, surely, would have been that. 'We'll just have to wait and see what happens,' said the Manchester boss.

Everyone in Blackburn expected three points, after all 37 had been taken from the last 39 available at home, but the players were nervous. 'There was a strange atmosphere that night,' Atkins recalled. 'I think it was a feeling of expectation. I don't think anyone thought we could lose.'

'It is the type of game we expect to win,' admitted Shearer in his diary. 'When we arrive at Ewood Park there is an incredible feeling around the place. I do not think I have seen our supporters in such a celebratory mood all season [it was Easter Monday and there had been plenty of time for a few pre-match beers]. When we run out for the warm-up before the kick-off there is a carnival atmosphere waiting for us. You would think that we have already won the Championship. There are two ways this can affect a team. It can either fill you with confidence that you feel it is impossible to lose or it can generate so much confidence that you become complacent.'

On a muddy and wet pitch, it started well. Shearer gave Rovers an early lead, reacting quickly to send Tony Coton's poor clearance back into the only part of the net that the goalkeeper could not reach with a first-time shot. 'That kick, nine times out of ten he would have got away with it but when it is Alan Shearer you present the ball to, you know you are in trouble,' said the commentator. 'That's magnificent, deadly finishing by England's finest.'

Then City suddenly looked more like their neighbours than a team fighting relegation. They equalised through a Keith Curle penalty. It was another mystifying decision to go for a Manchester club against the Rovers. Niall Quinn was not significantly touched by either Ian Pearce or Tim Flowers and nobody in the 28,000 crowd was sure what the offence was. When Hendry restored the lead before half-time – Coton should have saved the low shot – all seemed right, especially as the hosts were still on top and creating chances. But then Uwe Rösler pounced on a Hendry headed clearance to curl home from outside the area. And then with 20 minutes to go, Paul Walsh fired home from close range to give City what was, by that time, a deserved win.

'We couldn't believe it,' said Atkins. 'It was just one of those nights.' In the closing stages, the visitors also had two goals disallowed (one correctly, one probably not) and also hit the bar. Upon the final whistle, it wasn't the Rovers players celebrating on the pitch – they left looking as downhearted as they were soaked – it was the City heroes, high-fiving each other with manager Brian Horton almost doing a David Pleat at Maine Road circa 1983 impression.

'Kenny Dalglish walks very disconsolately away,' said Tony Gubba on the BBC. 'I've never seen Kenny walk away as quickly from a match as that or looking so visibly disappointed.'

Dalglish was keen to downplay the result and focus on the positives. 'It is ironic that they find themselves at the end of the table when they can perform like that,' said Dalglish. 'They deserved the win. We were disappointed, but we are still top and five points in front. You can't have anything more positive than that.' Well, there was an obvious comment to add to that. Five could have, should have, been eight. It could have been ten given what happened at Leeds. Had that happened, then the title would have been clinched at home to Palace on Thursday.

Still five points clear with four left, but now the nerves were there, especially frayed as United had a better goal difference of four. 'We felt the tension,' remembers Atkins. 'The last two months were horrendous. I lost six or seven pounds. I wasn't sleeping at all and it got worse as Manchester United started catching us. At the time, it was hard to know whether to talk about it or not but the nerves were there; we hadn't been in that position before. The only time it was okay was when you were on the pitch and you could let instinct kick in. Everywhere you went, people were talking about it. You felt pressure, it was all around and you couldn't escape it.'

But after life in the fourth tier with Scunthorpe, Atkins also tried to enjoy a situation that he never expected to be in. 'I think I did appreciate it more. I had the experience of playing in the Fourth Division. I learnt very quickly what Division Four football was all about. It was not about winning trophies or anything like that, it was about keeping your head above water. People are trying to make a living and just waiting to be paid. It wasn't nice. I was the young lad and I learnt quickly from the older players to look after myself in games and how to get the best out of myself. I was taught early not to go out after Wednesday night and don't let people see you are hurt and if someone kicked me, they would be sorted out. It put things into perspective, but it didn't make a difference in dealing with the pressure of the title race. It was really hard.'

If the players were starting to feel the tension, so were the fans, including Ian Herbert. 'I think I had forgotten the abject horror of our last five games,' Herbert remembers. 'To win the title having lost seven games and three of those defeats in the last five is quite something in modern day standards – the benchmark has been raised with Manchester City and the rest.

'It tested the spirit of the fans every bit as much as the players. The 3-2 home defeat to Man City was when the seeds of doubt started. When you are playing teams near the bottom then you almost felt you could sit back and enjoy it, especially after we scored early. But then "Hang on a minute, they scored. They've scored again. This wasn't in the script!" There was such a sense of deflation coming out of the ground and then looking at the fixture list then we have two home games and two away: West Ham away won't be easy and then Liverpool is the last game...

'Most of the players had never been exposed to this kind of scrutiny. The season before we finished runners-up and we were the ones doing the chasing, but being out in front... I think we saw the following season how those mind games affected Newcastle. If you have a team that has players not used to that fiery hot cauldron and how to handle it... It probably made it all the more exciting for the neutral but painful for us!'

Palace was a massive game, an unusual Thursday clash. Hendry and Sherwood were out suspended but there were the first starts of the season for Batty and Gallacher. Unlike the City game, there were plenty of nerves on this Thursday night, a game a little overshadowed as Arsenal squeezed past Sampdoria on penalties to move into the final of the Cup Winners' Cup for the second successive year.

The first half was poor with the tension palpable. At half-time Palace were the happier team. The Eagles were improving and ended up unlucky to be relegated, finishing 19th in a season that saw four teams relegated due to the reduction in the number of teams in the Premier League from the start of the 1995/96 campaign. They collected 45 points from their 42 games.

Two goals in five minutes early in the second half ended up winning the game. Kenna scored the first, and his first for the club, before disappearing under a pile of bodies. Shortly after, Gallacher extended the lead. Rarely have

I seen a player so excited to score. Understandably given he had spent 15 months out, the Scot seemed as if he didn't know what to do with himself.

'It was an unbelievable atmosphere. I had been playing reserve football for a while and was maybe 98 percent fit and champing at the bit. The opportunity arose as Jason Wilcox was injured and Kenny asked me to play left wing. He knew it was not my favourite position but said I could do a job. I did [do a job]; scored a goal. I didn't know what to do. It was a lot like the monkey of my injury was off my back and I was telling people I was back.'

Not long after, incredibly, Gallacher was fouled by John Humphrey and broke his leg again. 'I had done a stepover and Humphrey caught me. When you have been through the first, the second one wasn't as bad. It was a hairline fracture, but it allowed me to come back stronger and fitter. I could then play at the Euros and the World Cup.'

However, at the time it was a huge blow for the player and the team. 'I was hoping that it didn't rub off on the dressing room but the atmosphere in there was very nervous and it continued all the way to the end. But I was gutted to be out again.'

With 15 minutes left, Palace pulled one back through Ray Houghton and the tension levels returned and intensified. Towards the end, Flowers pushed an Iain Dowie effort onto the post. Over 28,000 breathed a sigh of relief which must have been felt down in Worcestershire where Herbert was on a course dinner, only able to follow the game through a transistor radio tuned to Radio 5 in the pre-smartphone age. 'I think that the others thought I had a bad stomach complaint as I kept making excuses and leaving,' said Herbert, whose condition can't have been helped by Palace's strong fightback.

After three games from Saturday to Thursday, there was a gap of ten days before the next fixture due to the international break. England had no opponent and for Rovers fans, the one game of note that weekend saw Burnley relegated to the third tier. At one time, that would have been cause for major celebration but there were some who felt, or who argued, that Burnley were no longer a rival. With the tension of the race with Manchester United, it was true that the Clarets dropping through the trapdoor was not the topic of conversation it may otherwise had been – amusing, yes, important, not that much.

Instead the focus was on the upcoming game against West Ham. After the trip to Upton Park, there were only two games left for the Blues. A win would mean that United had to take three points at Coventry or it would all be over. West Ham were fighting for survival and just like City, produced a performance that belied their status and picked up a deserved three points. It was always going to be really tough. The home fans were up for it, as were the players. After the Hammers took the lead Shearer had what seemed to be a good goal disallowed and it wasn't Blackburn's day.

'The one time when we really felt down was after a loss to West Ham,' said Slater. 'We had lost badly and that was one game when we were really down after the game. The trip home was a long one. I remember asking for the first time what was going to happen. Tony Gale told us not to worry. He said that the race would go down to the final game and said that we would lose at Liverpool but that United would lose to West Ham and we would win the title.'

West Ham fans had said the same on the tube out of East London. Even after they won, the atmosphere still felt dicey and one wonders what would have happened had we won, though then the away fans would probably have stayed longer to celebrate than to get to the tube as soon as possible. 'Don't worry,' said one on the District Line, as I looked pointedly at my brother who was wearing a Rovers jumper and ensuring we got plenty of attention, 'there is no way we will let them win here. We will do to them what we just did to you.'

Not all had such confidence. I remember in the concourse on the way out Rovers fans singing 'We are top of the league,' but it sounded less defiant and more a way to comfort each other and remind each other that the team was still in pole position. The lead was eight points but United had two games in hand and would play both before Newcastle came to Ewood on the 50th anniversary of VE Day.

What the West Ham game meant was that a title race that could have been over with plenty of April still to play was probably going to go down to the wire and there was now nothing Rovers could do to stop that. United had four games left and I remember a friend of mine running into Ray Harford at the local bookmakers at that time and the assistant predicting that United would win all four of them – Coventry, Sheffield Wednesday, Southampton and West Ham United. It wasn't the most demanding of run-ins. Rovers still had Newcastle and Liverpool to go.

Andy Cole, who had been under some pressure since his move, had scored the winning goal in a 3-2 victory at Coventry and the gap was down to five with United having a game in hand. That came against a Sheffield Wednesday team that had won just one in the last ten. It ended 1-0, with David May getting the only goal of the game in what was a poor and nervy performance from the hosts.

Ferguson was asked if he was going to go to Ewood Park on the following evening against Newcastle. He said he wasn't and, as he often was unable to do, could not resist a jibe. 'I am as welcome in Blackburn as the black plague. Even when they were nobodies, I wasn't welcome there.'

He missed a thrilling game and perhaps the best atmosphere that has ever been experienced at Ewood, certainly one that beats any I experienced since the stadium became all-seater. Taking place at the end of a three-day weekend, there were more than a few fans who had spent much of the day drinking. Given the events of the past few weeks, who could blame them? This was different to the City game. There was not a celebratory atmosphere for the visit of Newcastle. All knew that if Rovers didn't win, the title would be out of their hands. For a team that had been top since November, give or take a couple of days when United had played first over a weekend, that would have been devastating.

I just remember the nerves and the buzz that had been building all day. David Platt flew into Ewood with Sampdoria teammate Roberto Mancini. The Italian later said that it was one of the best atmospheres he had ever witnessed. Others agreed that it was something special. 'The biggest game for me was Newcastle at home ... in the best atmosphere I'd experienced at Ewood Park,' Le Saux told the *Lancashire Evening Telegraph* 20 years later.

Newcastle arrived in fifth and were obviously a good team, but this was a game that was all about the Rovers. 'Had we not won that night, the title may well have stayed at Old Trafford,' said Sutton.

Talk about tense. It was red hot as Rovers started strongly, pushing Newcastle onto the back foot. Shearer got the goal just before the half-hour. Blocked shots and challenges resulted in the ball flying out to the left side of the area and there was Le Saux. 'They threw everything at us but one time I managed to break down the wing and got to the byline,' said the full-back. 'I knew if I could get the ball over the keeper there was a chance as I didn't have to look – I knew Shearer would be there at the far post steaming in as normal. So I got the sand wedge out and clipped it up, and he just steamrollered in and headed the ball in.'

Never can a goal have been celebrated with such raw delight in Ewood Park. It was primal.

The nerves soon returned, however, and it got worse just before the break as Batty gave the ball away and Peter Beardsley let fly with a screamer from outside the area. The flying save from Flowers, who just managed to get a hand to it, was world-class. There were more to come. The number one, in that classic red shirt, got down well at his near post to keep out a Ruel Fox fizzer. The best was perhaps with 12 minutes remaining. Keith Gillespie sent over a perfect low cross from the right which eluded the entire Rovers backline and reached John Beresford steaming in towards the left side of the six-yard box. The blond defender did everything right, shooting low back across Flowers, but somehow the goalkeeper, who was going the wrong way, got a hand to it. Had Shearer not uncharacteristically missed a one-on-one early in the second half then it might have been a more relaxed evening, or perhaps it was the slender lead that kept the Rovers goalkeeper very much on his toes. Shearer missed three chances in all. 'Maybe the tension has got to me – I know I should have sewn the game up. If we don't win, I'll blame myself, but there is no time to feel any guilt now,' Shearer said. 'When anxiety creeps in, it has a draining effect on a player, both physically and mentally, and stupid mistakes start to occur. We are fortunate to cling on to our lead and the Rovers fans know it. There is a period of about ten to fifteen minutes towards the end when Newcastle seem to be on the attack constantly. Our supporters are stunned into silence, unable to utter a single sound.' After a late penalty shout doesn't go Newcastle's way, the final whistle sounds. 'The eruption of sound is ear-shattering... the relief is incredible.'

Relief is the operative word for Herbert. 'I often wonder if that game had been refereed by modern standards whether Shearer would have been allowed to get away with that header. That was the style of his play, he was physical – "I am going to get to that ball" – but it was such a relief when that went in. Then there were 70 minutes of utter terror, but what a great night that was. There was that release then – "We've given ourselves something to defend." There was always that nervousness about the final Sunday, but at least we had put ourselves in pole position and that is all you can ask. I still think that night against Newcastle is when we clinched the title, we didn't get another point after that.'

That was Flowers' finest hour in a Rovers shirt, and maybe the finest hour enjoyed by any Rovers goalkeeper given what was at stake. Perhaps he had been inspired by Ferguson and his comments the previous evening, questioning the bottle of the leaders. Given the results over the previous weeks, the Scot's words were not exactly out of leftfield. The goalkeeper took it to heart and produced one of the greatest performances ever seen in a Rovers shirt.

'Don't talk to me about bottle,' he told Sky in the famous post-match interview. 'Don't talk to me about bottling it, cos that's bottle out there. That's quality players, giving their all ... we're gonna fight to the death, cos we've got bottle ... all we can say is we'll give exactly what we've given today, exactly what we've given all season, and that's 100 percent bottle.' It's fair to say that the rest of the team gave the goalkeeper a little ribbing. 'We thought it was fantastic,' Sutton said.

Ferguson's mind games may have actually worked against his team. Talking after the infamous Keegan outburst the following season, Stephen Smith, a chartered psychologist, argued this was no stroke of genius on behalf of the Scot. 'Ferguson's tactics could backfire on him. Monday's outburst may act as a catharsis... if Ferguson's comments were a calculated manoeuvre, it has met with only limited success... Newcastle's players now have a vital role. They must have noted the effect this has had on their likeable and honest manager... if they feel Keegan has been unfairly treated by their common foe, their Goliath, it could be the best spur they have for greater motivation and team cohesiveness.'

That seemed to happen for the Rovers on that night. 'It's a thin line between genius and folly,' wrote Scott Murray of the *Guardian* in 2009, 'but somehow Ferguson's reputation as psychological mastermind wins out whatever occurs. Perhaps mindful that his goading appeared to affect the combustible Keegan but had no purchase whatsoever on the more measured Dalglish, Ferguson has, contrary to received wisdom, rarely tried it on since.'

Le Saux remembers the feeling in the dressing room afterwards. 'We got a sense we were really going to win the league, and, in a way, it was a good thing and a bad thing because you didn't want to think, "We've won it", but we knew we were just one step away. We'd had a bit of a bad run but that was by far the toughest fixture we had in that period – apart from the last game at Anfield obviously – and I just felt ecstatic.'

So much so that the Channel Islander recreated the goal after the fans had left with a friend. 'We were walking by the side of the pitch to go back to the cars and it was in the days of Baddiel and Skinner's *Fantasy Football League* show,' Le Saux said. 'She watched it with her husband and I used to watch it. She said, "Phoenix from the Flames, we've got to do it." The stadium was empty but the floodlights were on and I said, "Right, you're me, and I'm Alan Shearer."

'She went running down the wing, crossed this imaginary ball, and I jumped up and headed it into the net. And we did the same celebration that Alan and I had done, running behind the goal, to the fans! We were laughing our heads off as we walked to the corner to get to the cars when all of a sudden I heard this banging and I thought, "What's that?" I looked up to the main stand, where the executive boxes were, and there were about three of them still full of people, and they'd obviously seen us, realised what we were doing, and they were bashing the windows and laughing at us. I was so embarrassed. I was walking off with my head down, hoping maybe they didn't think it was me. But it was all part of a great night.'

While there was relief at the end, there was also a strange feeling. 'What do we do now?' asked Shearer. This was the last home game of an amazing season. There had to be some kind of lap of honour but there was a realisation that any semblance of celebration would be seized upon as premature and would have been thrown back in the Rovers' fans faces for years to come had the title been lost.

United, meanwhile, had to beat an improving Southampton team to stay in the race. It was a strange evening. My dad and I went out to watch the game in the pub to find that not only were the pubs quiet – the three-day weekend that had just gone by may have had something to do with that – the game being shown was the European Cup Winners' Cup final between Arsenal and Real Zaragoza. After checking three or four pubs – in the days when it was easy and quick to do so – the same scene was everywhere. All assumed United would win and didn't really fancy watching them do so. Shearer was the same, watching the final downstairs while his wife was upstairs watching the United-Southampton game, sworn to secrecy.

It can't have been easy when the Saints took the lead in the first half through Simon Charlton. Cole equalised but it wasn't enough and the clock was ticking. Now there was interest. People were coming out to watch. I remember saying to my dad that winning the title was not going to happen this way, it all seemed too easy. It wouldn't have had been exciting, winning it without having to play, and it would not have had the same drama as a final day triumph, but at the time the whole of Blackburn was willing on the south coast team. All were saying that United would score, not because they were playing well, that was not the case, but because they were preparing for the worst and United had a reputation for late goals. Still, the Red Devils were becoming increasingly frantic and desperate.

In the end, it was a soft penalty that did it, after Ken Monkou was adjudged by the referee to have pulled back Cole. Irwin stepped up to calm nerves at Old Trafford. Southampton should have had a penalty of their own and also had chances, but it was United who took the points to close the gap to two and ensure that there were to be no Tuesday night celebrations in Blackburn. From refusing to take any more bets on Rovers lifting the trophy, William Hill reduced the odds from 5/2 to 7/4 for United while the chances of Blackburn went from 1/4 to 9/4. It meant also that all eyes on Sunday were going to be on Upton Park and Anfield and for the first time in the Premier League era, there was going to be a final day denouement. And for the first time ever, fans at home would be able to keep in touch with both games at the same time.

Just four days left and in Blackburn, the talk was of nothing else. Every shop, taxi, pub or bus stop was filled with questions, speculations and predictions. There was no escape, but the tension was delicious.

20

LIVERPOOL

'I've never seen anything like this, this is ridiculous.'

ANDY GRAY, SKY SPORTS 14 MAY 1995

SO ROVERS WENT TO ANFIELD ON 14 MAY 1995 ALREADY
crowned champions of England. The four points taken off Manchester United
had ensured that their lead at the top had become insurmountable by the
beginning of April with the win at QPR putting the team 17 points clear with
six games left. The major celebrations had taken place at home to Newcastle
on 8 May as 30,000 fans hailed the dominant title-winners. All were looking
forward to a final trip to Liverpool and a chance for the home fans to pay
tribute to Kenny Dalglish, but by then the excitement had worn off a little
with thoughts starting to turn to the Champions League.

Had a couple of refereeing decisions been correct then that scenario was not impossible. Had Gerald Ashby not sent off Henning Berg and then given a penalty in October then Rovers, in the lead and in control, were by far the likelier winners, and had Tim Sherwood's perfectly good goal not been ruled out at Old Trafford then Rovers would have had four points more and United five less.

But here we were, down to the final day. It was a little like the promotion season of three years earlier. Promotion had looked to be a done deal weeks before and what should have been a pleasant but almost dull procession to the Premier League ended up being a nail-biting roller coaster that went all the way to an unforgettable day out at Wembley. Looking back, it was the perfect way to go up but at the time, it was a bit painful and very stressful.

It was the same in spring 1995. It could have been a competent coast through the final weeks with the rest of the country focusing on the relegation fight. What happened instead was an afternoon that, looking back, was almost the perfect way to win the title, an almost cinematic experience. At the time, it was traumatic. 'We should never have let the situation get to that point... but we kept frittering points away,' said Sutton.

So, it was down to the Liverpool game at Anfield, a tough place to go when you need a win – usually at least. There were hopes in Blackburn and fears in Manchester that going to Anfield would be easy. After all, even without Dalglish in charge of Blackburn, surely no Liverpool fan wanted their deadly rivals to win three in a row? Not only that but Liverpool had been coasting; their season was well and truly over after winning the League Cup in March and booking a spot in Europe. They took just 13 points from the next nine games following the Wembley win over Bolton. The previous game before Blackburn had been dire: with just one shot on target in a 3-0 loss at, ironically enough, West Ham. That was a bad result for the Rovers though, as surely pride had been stung and coach Roy Evans was demanding an improvement for the final game.

Ferguson was naturally talking Liverpool up. 'After all the championships and European Cups, Liverpool know you have to earn the right to win a title.' Evans was singing from the same hymn sheet. 'There will be no gifts from us for anybody. I wouldn't dream of doing anybody a favour, not in a million years, so Alex Ferguson need have no worries on that score. Kenny Dalglish would be the last person to expect that from us.'

Robbie Slater was on the bench that day and the Ormskirk-born winger knew the score. 'Everyone was saying that the Liverpool players would not try but we knew they would as they are professionals, though of course their fans prefer Blackburn winning the title to Manchester United. Liverpool players may have preferred it too but when you start playing, all thoughts of taking it easy go out of your head. We knew it was going to be difficult and we knew that we would probably have to win. I think most on the team thought United would beat West Ham as that was just what United did.'

But it was an unusual situation. Not only did Blackburn winning deny the chance of Liverpool's greatest rivals winning a hat-trick of titles – something few teams have ever done – but there was the Dalglish factor.

Liverpool fans were unsure what to do. 'It is almost total paranoia,' said Colin Moneypenny, secretary of the Merseyside Football Supporters Association on the weekend of the game. 'Many of the supporters would be quite happy to see Liverpool beaten on this occasion. The only really satisfactory scenario would be for Liverpool to beat Blackburn and West Ham to beat or draw with United.'

Liverpool were not going to roll over and die but Anfield was always going to be a more pleasant destination for Rovers fans than Upton Park for United.

But there was tension in Blackburn. Conversation everywhere was of nothing else. Blue and white shirts were everywhere, the placards selling the local paper outside every newsagent and post office provided the twice-daily update from Ewood Park. Pulling up Teletext and calling Teamtalk have surely never been as popular as they were that week. Getting tickets was harder than finding someone in Blackburn who didn't know what was going on. That week you had to know someone to manage to get a seat. It was the biggest game in the club's history and one of the biggest games in the modern history of English football. Blackburn is not a big town but almost all of the 100,000 residents would have snapped up a ticket that day.

For most then, it was about watching on television (listening to radio can be great but the thought of doing so on that day was surely too much), and many headed to the pubs that were still then required by law to close at 3pm on a Sunday afternoon, an hour before kick-off. I don't think the police were too bothered that they all stayed open. I remember the landlady in the pub that I was in ringing the last orders bell around 2.45 to cries of dismay. She quickly shouted that she was just letting those people who wanted to know that this was usually last orders, and anyhow the police were likely saving their resources for later, when there would either be a massive party or a giant drowning of sorrows.

If there was tension in the town then it was obviously there within the team. 'By the time the Liverpool game came round I was not playing but I was still in the dressing room and I got the sense that everybody was twitchy,' Tony Gale told the *Lancashire Evening Telegraph*. 'Even the manager, Kenny Dalglish, was tense and he had virtually done everything in football.'

Gale was not playing or on the bench, a tough situation. Jason Wilcox was never in the running after being sidelined in March with a cruciate ligament injury. 'In the media, I became a better player as soon as I was not playing,' he remembers. 'Suddenly we weren't getting the results and the media and the fans were all talking about how we had not got the balance on the left. I am not sure that was true, but it is funny how football works. I wasn't playing but I could feel the tension.'

The winger had to sit and watch from the sidelines. 'It was a very difficult time for me. At the time I didn't want the medal. I was like a spoilt brat. Kenny gave me a bollocking on the day, in a nice way, but that was how I was acting. I played 36 games and missed the last six but at the time it was strange.' He was there at Anfield. 'It was emotional. It was an emotional time. My family were there and not being able to play was hard and not being able to play in the build-up is something that I deeply regret. It is not that I did not contribute, I did, but I was limping around and I couldn't even straighten my knee.'

Mark Atkins did expect to be involved, but wasn't. 'It was heart-wrenching. I wanted to play. I did have a slight groin strain, which I had for a couple of months. Kenny knew about it and we managed it and I was doing okay. We played City at home with just a few weeks left and it was a mud bath and that did not help. I was supposed to be on the bench for the Liverpool game, but Ripley woke up with a bit of a problem. Kenny called me and said, "You were going to be substitute and I wanted you to be sub but I need to put Robbie

Slater on the bench as cover." In some ways, it was such a big game that I said "Do what you have to do," as there was nothing else I could say. Kenny told me to have a few drinks. There was me, Kevin Gallacher, Jason Wilcox and Tony Gale. There was a bar around and we went for a drink. It was an L-Shaped bar and around the corner we heard lots of singing, it was karaoke in the sponsor bar and when we looked around it was Razor Ruddock.'

It all added to the surreal atmosphere, with death threats not helping. Sherwood and Dalglish had received letters, from Scandinavia, that they would be killed if Rovers won the title. The hotel that had been used for the Everton win was changed due to the late-night party that kept the players awake. A move to Warrington was met with a stag party. Perhaps there wouldn't have been much sleep anyway. 'I didn't sleep well the night before,' said Sutton. 'I just wasn't in a relaxed frame of mind. I was maybe over-anxious, felt nervous and drained. We played all our games at high intensity and it took its toll on us. We played in a tired manner against Liverpool and I felt I had no energy after the first ten minutes.'

'We are at Liverpool, we hope they will do us a favour and will have a bad performance and West Ham would have their best performance against Manchester United,' said Gallacher. 'Kenny actually told us not to worry as he said we would win at Anfield.

'We were in the dugout in the game, nervous but trying not to be nervous for the players that are playing – gee them up but calm them down. But once it starts, there is nothing you can do about it. SKY TV was in the tunnel and we kept asking them the score from the other game.'

Meanwhile...

The other half of the equation was taking place at Upton Park. I still remembered the promises from the West Ham fans, but their win against Blackburn almost secured survival and after their win over Liverpool, there really wasn't anything for them to play for. There was no doubt that the fans would love it, really love it, if they could stop United and the hated Ince getting another title, but the players may not have felt the same way.

And they didn't. 'We were safe from relegation, we were totally relaxed and there was no tension, really there was nothing at stake for us,' Martin Allen, a substitute that day, told the *Daily Mail*. Tony Gale was doing his utmost to whip his old teammates into shape. 'It was funny because I rung Ian Bishop in midweek and he said, "Listen, mate, we won't let you down,"' said Gale. 'But I said, "Make sure you work your backside off because we might slip up against Liverpool." He told me they wouldn't let me down and that they'd be trying 100 percent. So I was quite happy with that until he said, "But just to let you know, as we're safe now, we're all off to Spain for three days!"'

Not only that but West Ham were leaving for Australia for an end-of-season tour the very next morning after the final game. 'I remember it as clear as night and day,' said Martin Allen in 2011. 'I was sitting in the little gym at the back of the main stand with Ian Bishop and Julian Dicks.' Only goalkeeper Ludo Mikloško was looking busy. 'He was the only one of us who warmed up before kick-off,' he says. 'I remember Julian Dicks pointing to him and saying: "What's he doing?"'

Manchester United were playing well and in good form, going to Upton Park on the back of three straight wins and just three defeats in 32 league games. They also had an FA Cup final the following weekend to look forward to.

At Anfield, it started off fairly low key, though Liverpool were on top and Sherwood had to clear off the line from a close-range Nigel Clough effort while Shearer headed just wide. Suddenly, after 20 minutes, Rovers were ahead after a fine move. Pearce fed Berg at right-back, the Norwegian passed forward to Shearer who, with his back to goal, clipped the ball first-time to his left and the Blackburn right. Ripley had space to run into, took one touch and then sent a low ball into the area. There was Shearer, who had set off for goal as soon as he had freed the winger, about two yards to the right of the penalty spot, checking his stride to shoot into the bottom corner. It was a lovely goal, but the aesthetic aspect was overlooked because it was all too important, intense and nerve-wracking. The celebrations were fairly restrained: it was too early to be going crazy and after events off the past few weeks, nobody was going to be tempting fate.

'When we scored first, I thought we were going to win,' said Herbert, 'I genuinely thought that "Ah Liverpool are really not up for this, we have scored first and it will sort itself out". And then when they equalised, I just had this horrible feeling, that sinking feeling, that there was no way this team is going to score again. The second goal was kind of irrelevant, especially given the time that it was scored. I had it firmly secured in my head that this was a once in a lifetime deal and that if we didn't secure it that day, that was it. I really didn't think that we could ever consider bouncing back the next season. But on that day, it was "This is it and if we don't do it today, that's it and for a generation there will be conversations about how close we had come to winning the league and we never got back there again."

'It was incredibly stressful. I wasn't at Anfield and to be honest, I didn't even try to get a ticket as I didn't think I could cope with it. I lived in Birmingham at the time as well which didn't make it easy. One of my work colleagues said "We have plasma TVs at the gym and we always show the games so why don't you come down and watch it with me?" I went, and the room split into two. I would say that 98 percent of people there didn't want Manchester United to win it, but 50 percent were watching one game and 50 percent the other.'

If the Sky screens were split, then so were the Liverpool fans. Tony Evans was on the Kop that day, and the home support started the game by cheering Blackburn possession and booing Liverpool possession for a short time before it all settled down. 'There were loads of people in Blackburn shirts,' said Evans. 'There were some spats in the Kop with people shouting "Support your team." There were some quite heated arguments and even some fighting. My view was that there were some bigger issues at play. If we win and United win then they will have three in a row and they will match Huddersfield, Arsenal and us. That is more important, and I was desperate for Blackburn to win. I remember when Phil Babb cleared the ball off the line and about a third of the Kop cheered, the idiots who wanted us to win, but two-thirds groaned.'

This day was the one that Sky Sports had been waiting for ever since it had bought the rights to top-flight football, and it broadcast both games live. Not only could you flick between the games, any action of note from the other was shown in a small box.

United fan John Brewin was watching on television. 'That final day, I ended up watching the Liverpool-Blackburn game in a room where everyone was watching and cheering on Liverpool and Blackburn. It was the first time they had the split screens, showing the Hughes goal, then the McClair goal and then the saves. Sky have tried to relive it every season and failed. It was hard to watch.'

After 31 minutes, there was a bigger cheer. Michael Hughes volleyed West Ham into the lead. This was even better. 'Being from Northern Ireland, I know a lot of United supporters and they always tell me I stopped United from winning the league,' Hughes says. 'But I always tell them it wasn't my fault. It was Ludo Mikloško. There was no extra motivation from us to stop United winning the league. What we really wanted was to help Tony Gale win a championship winners' medal.'

The strikes from Shearer and Hughes meant that the half-time situation was healthy for Rovers. I remember thinking that three goals would have to go the wrong way in the second half for it all to go wrong. There were still nerves but a second from the Rovers would surely kill off both games. It never came and shortly after the restart, Brian McClair equalised for Manchester United. Just after the hour, John Barnes did the same for Liverpool and then the torment really started. 'Kenny Dalglish is going to be completely and utterly furious,' said Jon Champion on the BBC in a disapproving tone. 'Blackburn Rovers have really sleepwalked their way through this second half. Liverpool haven't injected much urgency, they have just knocked it about and eventually they are going to create a chance. It's a goal and now the championship race is on again. Would you believe that this late on the final day, we don't know where the championship is going.' Cut to shots of Rovers fans with radios to their ears. 'And now, everyone is back to the transistors [some the size of bricks] again.'

News of that Barnes equaliser had soon reached east London. There was Ferguson standing, turning around, getting and then confirming the news, before signalling to his players. One more United goal would change everything. If the Scot was pleased with Liverpool's efforts then he was less so with West Ham, as the Hammers boss that day, Harry Redknapp remembers.

'What a game,' wrote Redknapp in his autobiography. 'As the news came through that Blackburn were not winning, United absolutely battered us, but we hung on. I think Luděk must have made about 20 saves in as many minutes – he had the game of his life. Alex seemed to throw on every forward that he had at the club. By the end of the game he was playing with Andy Cole, McClair, Mark Hughes and Paul Scholes with Lee Sharpe bombing on and his centre-halves in the mix for every set play. And then he got the hump because with two minutes to go I brought on Simon Webster as an extra defender. He was going bananas on the touchline as if we were doing something tricky.'

The West Ham goalkeeper was busier than Flowers but the Blackburn number one knew what was going on in London. 'Someone from the crowd shouted out that Man United had equalised,' Flowers said. 'I just thought, "Well they're 1-1, they're Man United, they're absolutely bound to get a bastard winner in the 93rd or 94th minute. There's no way they won't nick it".'

As the games progressed, attention started to drift southwards to the capital and it was clear that the traffic at Upton Park was going increasingly one way.

Herbert was still in his local gym, with two sets of fans watching two separate televisions. 'Everyone kept looking over their shoulder, particularly in the last ten minutes, and all you could hear from the other end of the room were these oohs and aahs with save after save. I found myself watching the last two to three minutes of the United game as there was nothing happening at Anfield. This was where the title is going to be won or lost.'

The Rovers bench were doing the same. 'I suppose we got lucky on the day because Luděk Mikloško had a magnificent game for West Ham,' Gale said. 'I was on the bench and I actually watched the last ten minutes of their game on the screen next to me and I kept saying to Kenny, "Oh, he's pulled off another save," and he told me to shut my mouth and get on with watching our game!

'But it was driving me nuts because I knew we weren't winning and that it was all down to West Ham. Luckily for us Luděk pulled through. He was actually one of my room partners in his early days at West Ham, and I helped him with his English. It's fair to say he paid me back and did us a right favour. But I still have to buy him a drink every time I see him!' The Rovers team sent the goalkeeper a crate of champagne.

After the equaliser from Barnes, Rovers roused themselves a little and had opportunities, but it just didn't happen. Sutton had the best chance. A mistake by Babb lead to Shearer challenging goalkeeper David James for a loose ball on the edge of the area, and when he won it he squared it to his strike partner, who had a virtual open goal. There were two defenders sprinting back, but the striker hit it first time when there was time to pick a spot and it was cleared by John Scales.

Even Shearer missed a chance late in the game that he would normally have scored. He rarely put the ball over but did so from close range with a half-volley. Even the goal machine was human. The game was drifting towards a draw when Jamie Redknapp stepped up to take a free-kick that he bent into top corner of the goal beyond the dive of Flowers. 'We just couldn't believe it,' said Atkins. 'It seemed like all the hard work had been for nothing and we had lost it right at the end.'

Even Liverpool fans seemed unsure as to what to do. 'And then we scored at the end and it was unbelievable,' said Evans. 'I have never seen a goal celebrated less – well, perhaps except one of those 11-0 thrashings in the early rounds of European competitions – but certainly a winning goal has never been greeted like that.'

Rovers fans had a great view of the goal but had heads in hands. The thoughts were all the same. The title had been thrown away. Eight points clear with five to play, it was a failure that would never be forgotten.

'We couldn't believe it,' my dad remembers. 'Redknapp scored then we all looked around at each other and then within seconds a guy behind said "It doesn't matter, it doesn't matter, United have drawn." Then the celebrations started.'

Started with the game not finished. 'I've never seen a manager so happy when his team has just conceded a goal,' said Jon Champion. 'Late opportunity for Alan Shearer, he's just missed a chance but he's looking across and he's smiling. This is an unbelievable afternoon.'

Slater was one of the first to hug or be hugged by the boss, he's still not sure. 'We were waiting on the sidelines and while we were dumbstruck by the Redknapp goal, we knew it was all about what was happening at West Ham. People started shouting, I remember Tony Gale was there with his hand in the air and we were all jumping up and down and all hugging each other. It was amazing. Moments like that are special. They are at the time, but you don't really appreciate them until you are older.'

'We very nearly blew it. We had it in the bag with five games to go,' said Ripley. 'The table doesn't lie. We were the best team in that season, but we fell over the line. Just did enough. The game at Anfield was bizarre. Liverpool didn't really want United to win the title and we were getting mixed messages, false information, about their game. We got there in the end. It was great to be at Anfield and the Liverpool fans were very generous.'

If it couldn't be won at Ewood, then Anfield was the perfect place. Liverpool fans were happy to see United miss out and stayed for the presentation, something that probably would not have happened at many other grounds. While at the time I think all fans would have wanted the wins against West Ham and Manchester City to settle it all before the end, what actually happened was more exciting. It meant that something special that you finally felt was within your grasp was almost snatched away at the last second. Just managing to keep hold of it made it more precious. The strong possibility that it could be lost made it all the sweeter when it wasn't. It is like the play-offs. It is much more preferable at the time to finish first and go up automatically. To go through the play-offs and then win at Wembley is emotionally draining but exhilarating. That day in 1992 will never be forgotten. Again, it would have been terrible to lose but that made the win all the more memorable.

And it was a deserved title. Rovers went top on 26 November and, apart from two weekends when United played first, stayed there. Fergie and his men didn't throw it away. They never had it in their possession at all.

Liverpool fans were relieved, at least Tony Evans was. 'It was surreal when Redknapp scored but then the word went round that United had drawn and then all the angst, the divisiveness that had been there just moments before in the Kop disappeared and everyone celebrated as one. We could see the Rovers bench celebrating and I remember standing on my seat and the entire kop was singing "Always look on the bright side of life" and laughing our heads off. Suddenly everyone loved each other. Liverpool won, Blackburn won and United lost. It was a great day. I look back on that as a tremendous day, one that still stands out. The sun was out and everyone was bouncing. I remember talking to a Blackburn fan in the pub afterwards and he was saying that "You'd think youse had won the league by the look on your face." I am smiling now just thinking about it.'

Not so much for John Brewin. 'I remember Redknapp scoring then they cut to Gary Pallister and Denis Irwin rubbing their heads and then Ferguson gathering them together and saying "Let's get out of here." That was the most desolate I've ever felt as a football fan and I am not sure why. United had been so long without winning the title and you wondered if we would have to wait as long again. Will we have Cantona next season? We had problems. That golden team was breaking up. Kanchelskis was on his way out, Parker was never the same again, it was all falling apart.

'My sense was that we had the better players, but you had to accept it. 1994/95 was quite a fractured season for United. I went to many games that season. Giggs was injured and we had problems replacing him. We were more solid in defence but United weren't Barcelona in 2009. We needed Giggs down the left and then Kanchelskis went missing at a certain point. Ferguson was obviously dissatisfied and was soon selling Ince, Hughes and Kanchelskis.'

Rovers winning the title seemed to help United more than themselves even if it was hard to see at the time.

'That was a miserable summer. There was a point where Cantona said he was quitting football and that felt like a deep blow. That sense of winning the title is more fragile than you would think as you can see after Ferguson left. The first time in 1993 would be the best one for fans of a certain age and after that initial flush of success. The next season, we felt that this was fantastic but 94/95 was hard.'

The Rovers danced into the night at a place owned by a Blackburn fan. 'We went straight to a place that Kenny had organised in Preston,' said Slater. 'There was a band there and it was pandemonium as you would expect, with people dancing on the tables. We stayed there all night.'

El vino did flow. 'I can't tell you anything about the next seven days as I can't really remember,' said Kevin Gallacher. 'We had just won the league at Anfield and we asked Kenny what we had organised and he said "Nothing." Myself and Jason Wilcox saw Jack Walker's son Howard and talked to him. He then got a place in Preston booked. We spoke to the owner and he put us in a room and we partied downstairs with everyone including the fans, who couldn't believe they were partying with Blackburn Rovers. Then you get dragged home by the missus and then all the house parties start, with people just loving being champions.'

21

CHAMPIONS BUT...

'It was an amazing achievement from Blackburn Rovers to win the Premier
League but in football, getting to the top is only half of the job.
You have to work harder to stay there.'

SVEN-GÖRAN ERIKSSON

THE FOLLOWING DAY WAS PROBABLY THE HAPPIEST

Monday that Blackburn has ever had. After the final whistle and the trophy
presentation, the fans that had made their way back from Merseyside started
to arrive back home where they were greeted as conquering heroes. As nice
as it was to have a beer or two with Liverpool supporters and let the traffic
die down, there was only one place to be that evening for fans of Blackburn
Rovers and that was Blackburn. People were literally dancing in the street,
there was plenty of singing and a general feeling of delight and disbelief. It
only calmed down when *Match of the Day* started, and we went through it all
again but this time safe in the knowledge that it would all turn out okay in the

end, and stories of the day were swapped.

At least the players did not have to go to work in the morning, they just had to be ready for the public celebrations later that day. 'That week was a great week,' said Kevin Gallacher. 'Colin Hendry was ringing me at seven in the morning and saying "I have just corked open another bottle of champagne." I was like "Colin, I only left you an hour ago."'

The celebrations took place on a warm evening at Ewood as 30,000 fans headed there for a bit of football and the trophy presentation. There were some miffed season ticket holders who were told that their seats had already been taken and they had to hotfoot it to the other side of the ground but it was all worth it once inside. The applause when Jack Walker got on the podium seemed like it would never end, and it only did so as the man started to talk, promising bigger and better things.

'We've got the best and we'll keep the best,' said Jack. 'We probably need just to strengthen the team and bring a couple of players in. But whatever it takes we're prepared to make sure we do it. We want to get it right and we will.'

We didn't though. Jack had done more than enough, more than anyone had ever done, but looking back there is a sense that the club let what it had built slip away so quickly.

There was some good news and that was a new contract for Shearer, who said that he wanted to make Rovers as well known around the world as they were in England. There were rumours of who would come next and everyone sat back and awaited the inevitable big names. But then came the really big news and this was not what anyone expected. 'We all were surprised when Kenny went upstairs,' said Shearer. The sudden announcement that Kenny Dalglish was to become director of football and Ray Harford was to replace him as manager came in June, just weeks after the title had been secured. The club said that it was a natural move to maintain continuity and stability.

Only the man himself knows why he decided to hand control of the champions to his assistant, though there are a few theories.

In his autobiography, Dalglish just said that he had had enough and at the start of the title-winning season refused the offer of a new contract and wanted a week-to-week deal. In the end, he agreed to stay until the campaign finished. 'But even before the end of the season, while the championship was still in the balance, I had decided to stand down.' Days after the triumph, he was there talking to chairman Robert Coar and saying that he wanted to leave. 'It wasn't difficult stepping down, because my mind had been made up some time before. When you have won a trophy the next step is to win it again... but I had no desire to do that. I was leaving anyway, whether we attained our championship goal or not.' He also said that Europe was not an attraction.

Gallacher's theory is that Dalglish went in order to keep Ray Harford, who Dalglish knew was keen to return to management and was in demand, at Ewood. 'Clubs down in London wanted Ray Harford as their manager and with his wife keen, it looked like he would go. Then Kenny thought, "This partnership is fantastic and if I move upstairs then Ray can become manager and he will stay".'

Other players had other explanations. 'Kenny is a smart man and he knew that a club like Blackburn can have their moment, but it is unlikely to last and the big clubs will up their game again,' Ripley said. 'We couldn't recreate that momentum going forward.'

Yet the club should have been in a good position. Now Rovers were champions, they surely would be able to attract almost anyone. I remember watching a documentary of Paul Gascoigne's time in Lazio, which was coming to an end. The player and his agent were talking about his next destination, and they were openly stating they hoped Blackburn entered the market. Rovers were linked with Zinedine Zidane and Christophe Dugarry but they never came. 'We all know that we should have signed players to improve us again as that's what you have to do,' said Shearer.

Gallacher agreed that an opportunity had been missed. 'Kenny and Ray were a great partnership and every single player loved them. We tried to sign players but there was volcanic ash stopping players coming over and it was a nightmare. With hindsight I would have loved to have played with the likes of Zidane and Djorkaeff, who were linked. But I don't know if they would have fitted in. The dressing room was so British it was unbelievable, there was only Henning Berg. It might have made the team stronger, but we will never know.'

That summer, the only signing was Matty Holmes from West Ham, not exactly the kind of star that fans were dreaming of.

'We squandered an opportunity that will not come around again,' Herbert said. 'Whatever it was, and maybe we will never know the real story, that made Dalglish walk away, I think we all knew then, in our heart of hearts. It was an obvious thing to do to get Ray Harford in for continuity but bless him he was never a manager – a great coach but not a manager. The next season, the level of play dropped about 10 percent and the quality of the players we brought in… just Matty Holmes. If it ain't broke don't fix it – that is not what happens at top-class football clubs. You think "Who is the weakest link in the team? We need to improve that position, no matter how good they were last season". Just imagine if we had signed Zidane, just imagine.'

The real problem was the legendary manager moving upstairs. Rovers fans didn't seem angry, it still seemed a bit surreal that such a figure was at Ewood at all and he had been there for almost four intense seasons. 'Dalglish stepping down, that was a major signal and the players who would have considered signing for Dalglish… Harford was never the same draw. We were poor for large parts of the next season, we recovered somewhat but we handed the initiative back at a time when we needed to go on. The symbolism of Dalglish stepping down reduced our appeal instantly and that abysmal Champions League campaign cemented it and people just thought "Nah, they are one-season wonders".'

According to Rovers chairman Robert Coar, the lack of incoming talent was not for want of trying. 'We tried to purchase players last summer because we realised you have to move forward,' he said at a shareholder meeting the following March. 'We were very close to signing a couple of international players.' Rumour had it that Darren Anderton was one. 'But they both eventually signed new contracts with their clubs. We are still on the lookout for international players. But identifying them and then prising them free is another matter.'

At the time, Coar was trying to look on the bright side. 'As far as the club is concerned, the major news of the summer is Alan's decision to sign a new contract. Just look at the transfer fees being paid for the likes of Stan Collymore and Chris Armstrong. We've re-signed for another four years the man in possession of the England centre-forward's shirt.'

That the club recognised, or said they did, that fresh blood was necessary did not make the fans feel any better. Rovers won the opening game against

QPR, then lost three in a row and that was it. Eventually the team limped into seventh and there was the infamous Champions League campaign that almost matched Trelleborgs in the humiliation stakes.

The campaign never really got going. Rovers dominated the opening game against a talented Spartak Moscow but were caught by a sucker punch and lost 1-0. Dismal losses at Rosenborg and Legia Warsaw followed. Yet had Rovers defeated the Poles at home instead of drawing 0-0, as should have happened, then the Blues would have reached the quarter-finals. As it was it was pretty much over before that ill-fated 3-0 loss in Moscow, with Batty and Le Saux making international headlines by exchanging punches. The final 4-1 win over Rosenborg, with a nine-minute Mike Newell hat-trick, was barely even a consolation as the Blues finished bottom of their group.

The team never looked the same as the previous season and Harford found Dalglish's shoes a little too big. 'Kenny leaving was a massive blow and maybe things were never going to be the same after that,' Slater said. 'Ray Harford took over. I don't know if that was the right decision. When you have been an assistant, it is tough. Ray was a terrific coach and a real character, everyone got on very well with him. When you then have to take a step away then to be the boss, it is very difficult and that is what happened. I left for West Ham as, to be honest, I fell out with Ray, so I left immediately. I didn't leave with animosity, but he called me into his office and told me that West Ham were interested. I am not stupid and I know when that happens, then it is time to go. So I went. Next season, when we met he told me that he had made a mistake in letting me go. Maybe not strengthening when you win is a mistake. Blackburn didn't do that.'

Despite some highlights, a 12-1 aggregate win over Forest for example, it was a let-down. Gallacher remembers a team that struggled to get going. 'We wanted an open-top bus through the town but the town hall balcony was deemed unsafe, so we did it inside the stadium. The lads never felt they had really celebrated it and were still celebrating after ten games.'

And then Kenny left his post as manager. 'Everyone thought "What's happening"? It was hard. Some players took it well but others did not.' The likes of Sutton and Batty wrote in their books that Harford struggled to make the step from being a friendly number two to an authoritative head boss.

It seemed fairly clear from the start that things had changed under Harford and not for the best. Sutton gave his take as he went from being one half of the famed SAS to a substitute. 'It was always going to be tough for Ray to make the transition from coach to manager. Being second-in-command is totally different from managing. Relationships and friendships would have been formed with a lot of players in the previous few years Ray had been at Blackburn...'

Sutton was obviously miffed at being left out as his former strike partner continued to score goals. 'He was close to certain players. Alan Shearer was one of them. I felt Ray was definitely influenced by certain players when it came to team selection. I suffered because of this. I had no proof but it's what I felt. Prior to the season starting, Ray had used the phrase, "If it ain't broken then don't try to fix it." We had won the Premiership title and sticking with the same side seemed reasonable. However, from the outside, it may have looked like we should have made a major impact signing or two so we would be able to carry on the momentum. Ray's "if it ain't broken" phrase didn't apply to me. Within a few games I was left out of the starting line-up and I wasn't happy. He reverted back to playing Mike Newell as Alan Shearer's strike partner. We had started the 1995/96 season in the Champions League with a buzz around Ewood Park but it quickly had gone flat.'

Gallacher admitted that there were problems. 'I think that it was a difficult transition for everyone,' added Gallacher. 'Some people can make it but that one wasn't to be. When Kenny went upstairs and Ray Harford took over, everyone thought "Great, Ray is still here". But it didn't work out. The players he brought in were just different and it never worked for us, it never clicked and Ray paid the price.'

As did the Rovers. The club slipped off the summit of English football so smoothly, quickly and quietly and never returned. But did it have to be that way? It is unlikely that Rovers could have consistently matched the big city clubs in terms of support and stature, but they were starting to attract fans from outside the town and could have, with a little more spending, ambition and success, consolidated that position and continued to be a major force. Just because it didn't happen, does not mean that it could not have. The average attendance was 28,000 in 1995/96. There was even talk of renovating the

Riverside/Walkersteel Stand to make the capacity 35,000. A few more years of success and perhaps the fan base could have grown enough.

Herbert believes it would have been difficult. 'Coming up from Birmingham, it wasn't unusual to see coaches going up north and the number of coaches that would park behind the Blackburn End was quite something, but that part of Lancashire is very competitive. But even in that season, it was rare for the games to be sold out because Blackburn is a town and to get 25,000 home fans is a tough ask. For those golden five years, it was as good a time to support Rovers as any and it was great to see kids coming in.'

In an alternative universe, Dalglish stays, signs a couple of genuine world-class players to improve the squad, the team gets into the knockout stages of the Champions League, wins a cup and hangs around the top three. Shearer also stays, and things grow from there. A winning culture takes hold and that is that.

Perhaps Walker was too loyal to the players that had won the league, perhaps he just didn't want to spend money on the kind of players needed, or perhaps success stunted ambition. But Dalglish's decision to step back from the frontline was the beginning of the end.

Fans of rival clubs looked on with interest. 'I think that if things had been different then Rovers could have been rivals for a long time,' said Brewin. 'But the season after, there was a sense that Blackburn were vanquished and seemed to fall apart before our eyes as Kenny wanted to play golf. After that, it seemed that Blackburn retreated into just being another Premier League club. They had achieved what they wanted and fair enough. Had Kenny stayed then maybe Shearer stays. Walker was still spending money years later so the money seemed to be there. Sometimes things happen and you don't know why.'

22

DID ROVERS CHANGE FOOTBALL?

'It was Jack Walker, his dream to win it and we did. He was a very clever and very tough businessman, but he was a winner and one I respected hugely. Immensely proud of what we all achieved. Little old Blackburn took the big boys on and beat them. No one can ever take that away from us.'

ALAN SHEARER

FREE NEWSPAPER *METRO* PROBABLY SHARED THE question of a generation of fans when they asked in 2015 whether Jack Walker's legacy was a negative one for football. '...Would it be wrong to suggest that in doing so he helped to kill off some of the aura and romance which once surrounded English football?' they asked. 'Walker, whilst appearing to be a genial, wise old fella keen on assisting the fortunes of his childhood team ultimately paved the way for further multi-millionaires to join the bandwagon and in the process making some of the most famous, well-loved clubs in the country become playthings for their undoubted massive egos.'

Rovers spent some big money, but no more than the likes of United and Liverpool and were starting from lower down the pyramid. Most of the title team was subsequently sold for serious profit. The problem was that the replacements were not of the same quality. Had Rovers been a top team for a few more years then the success would have seemed more sustained and less of an anomaly.

'Jack Walker was a great man, a great man,' said Sven-Göran Eriksson when I caught up with him in Abu Dhabi. After Harford resigned, Walker went to Italy and in December 1996, signed a deal with the then manager of Sampdoria. Eriksson would finish the season in Serie A and then come to Ewood. The idea of having one of the most sought-after coaches in the world was an exciting one, as was Rovers recruiting from a top club in what was then the best league in the world. But before long, Eriksson changed his mind when Lazio came calling. Walker let him go without making a fuss, something that the former England boss still appreciates.

'I had seen from Italy that Blackburn won the Premier League and Walker was still ambitious and wanted to challenge again,' said Eriksson. 'The problem was that I wanted to bring Roberto Mancini to Blackburn, such a good player. He would have been free, there was no fee, but Jack Walker did not want to pay his wages and so instead we went to Rome together and we won everything.'

'Maybe he did change the transfer market in England but if you are not Manchester United or Liverpool or Arsenal, how can you come from the Second Division to be champions without changing the transfer market?'

The new cash was coming into the game anyway, though Walker did perhaps hurry things along. 'Walker is a fan, not a glory-chaser or political animal,' said the *Independent*. 'He takes no part in the game's politics, he just wants to see Blackburn win. Unlike most fans he is in a position to do something about it. Which of us, in the same position, would not be similarly tempted? But if he has been good for Blackburn, is he good for football? Without him this year could have been a procession for Manchester United and, with due respect to Old Trafford, it is good to have someone else's name on the championship. Less beneficial has been the effect of Walker's money on transfers and, especially, wages. The filter-down effect has damaged clubs at the bottom end and the amount of the Premiership's new wealth being spent on transfers is excessive.'

Rovers were blamed for driving up the price of talent elsewhere. 'Jack Walker has much to answer for,' wrote Steve Curry in the *Daily Express*. 'The Blackburn chairman with his Jersey money tree has allowed Chris Sutton's £5 million transfer to set the benchmark for domestic moves.' That 'ludicrous' amount meant that Liverpool had to pay £3.6 million to Coventry for Phil Babb who was 'no Bobby Moore', added the writer. It seemed harsh to blame the Rovers for Babb.

'Doing a Blackburn' or 'Doing a Jack Walker' became football shorthand for a while to signify the investment of a lot of money over a short space of time. That the amounts in the years to follow dwarfed what was spent by Walker matters little.

'Jack Walker's arrival meant that the big clubs had to sharpen up their acts,' said Brewin. 'Transfers were different then. Agents were involved but not like now. There were meetings at service stations. Most of the players were British or Irish so people knew each other in a different way. Walker came and went but there were others like him who tried to do the same and failed. There were clubs like City in the seventies who spent money and it wasn't until Abramovich and City more recently that changed the way football clubs operate, so Jack Walker feels more innocent.'

Arsenal fan Tom Watt agreed. 'Of course Blackburn were spending money but there wasn't the resentment then that you get now with Chelsea and then Manchester City and that was because of Jack Walker. Everyone knew about what he was trying to do and his relationship with the club and the town. He was an old-fashioned chairman in many ways and that balanced out the millions spent on Shearer and Sutton. How could you knock a fellow for wanting to do that for his hometown? He bought mainly British players and it all seemed quite homespun even if it wasn't quite homegrown. He changed the place entirely. I went there when they were in the Second Division when Frank Stapleton was playing and then returned a few years later with Arsenal and it was very different, and that was down to Walker.'

For Brewin, how you felt about Walker was probably guided by whether your club was a rival of the Rovers or whether it was happy to sell talent for a good price.

'There are two sets of clubs with different views regarding Walker. United were competitors and then had to start paying more, but the clubs that were being paid money would have welcomed him. It seemed that clubs did start spending more money but not ridiculously so. What Jack Walker did in Division Two was much more eye-catching. Has anyone done that since? Coming in and buying the best young prospects in English football? Clubs that come up now don't go and buy the best young English players. It would be like Bournemouth buying Jadon Sancho.'

Rovers were accused at the time of buying the title and also charged with starting the crazy spending that has become the norm in football. Both have elements of truth, though need some context. Rovers did spend plenty of money but did so intelligently. 'It is not Jack Walker, but it goes back to Jimmy Hill who lifted the cap on the maximum wage,' said Gallacher. 'It had nothing to do with Jack. We took it away from the big city boys and they didn't like it. There was some jealousy. We had money and that brought us success. People say that we bought the league, but we didn't spend as much as the big boys. We were always going to get stick for that as a small-town club.'

Most of the money was spent very wisely indeed. There were a few flops who came and went without many noticing, but Dalglish made some shrewd additions. Shearer was the first major signing, the British transfer record. He was, however, a bargain at £3.6 million. Three years earlier, Gary Pallister had joined Manchester United for £2.3 million. Pallister was a fine defender, but the striker Blackburn bought was world-class. Dean Saunders had cost £2.9 million in the previous summer. There was no comparison between the two. If he had cost three times as much, Shearer would not have been overpriced. If other clubs did not see that, it was hardly the fault of Blackburn Rovers. It is possible that the interest of Rovers did help push Sutton's price up but more influential was the fact there were a lot of clubs interested.

Yet Rovers were not one of the big boys and, for a while at least, were going to have to pay more than United, Liverpool and Arsenal. When Alex Ferguson sniped that if he was Sutton he would rather play in front of 45,000 than 15,000, he had a point (even if it was slightly unfair as the Ewood capacity was limited and two years later the average attendance was 28,000). Not even the most rabid of Rovers fans would have claimed that Rovers were a bigger club. While Sutton may well be one of those who genuinely preferred the smaller spotlight and was happy living in a Lancashire village, others would want a little more.

Upon losing out to Rovers for Sutton, the Scot claimed that the club was ruining the transfer market. There were obviously some sour grapes from a manager miffed at losing his pre-eminent place, but Shearer conceded that Ferguson had a point. 'Obviously such moves have an inflationary effect,' Shearer wrote in his diary. 'There is another way of looking at it. Our owner Jack Walker is buying players from his own personal resources which means money is being pumped into the game which otherwise wouldn't have been there. That must be good for football. He is a down to earth type without any airs and graces and loves his football club. How can anyone knock him for wanting the best for Rovers?'

There is no doubt that Blackburn's entry into the top-end of the transfer market did add some extra heat though it should be remembered that the increased television money meant that there were a little more cash swilling around anyway. Other clubs were spending but just not as well – Liverpool being just one. Sutton gave five seasons of fine service to the club before being sold for £10 million, double his original fee. Babb went to Portugal on a free transfer.

Blackburn's title-winning team was not more expensive than their rivals, but the side had been built much more quickly. While the likes of Manchester United, Liverpool and Arsenal had, in the words of Dalglish, had the transfer market to themselves for years, they had also been spending for some time. Rovers went from the middle of the Second Division to title challengers in the space of two years.

The 1994/95 team more than paid for itself. Berg, Le Saux, Hendry and Sherwood were signed for a total of around £2 million. They were sold for almost £20 million. Shearer and Sutton may have cost over £8 million but fetched £25 million upon their departure. Right there is a profit of around £35 million, handy these days but serious cash back then. Batty came in for £2 million and was sold just over two years later for £3.75 million. Rovers made money on their transfer policy, despite the fact they came from the middle of the second tier to the top of the first and almost built two separate teams. There is no doubt that Rovers added cash and impetus to the transfer market but there was no other way for a small club to compete with the big boys and the money was invested soundly. Many others can't say the same. Buying and selling those stars was stunning in business terms, even if the departure of some marked that the good times were over.

'I don't think he started it, he saw where the trend was going,' Herbert said. 'Derby had Lionel Pickering, Wolves had Jack Hayward. We were the first team to be successful doing it and there have been many clubs that have tried since. One of the legacies of Jack Walker's investment is the ground and the training ground and the rest of it. But he actually got his money back on players. Just as Shearer Sutton, Le Saux and Berg alone would probably have covered his investment. it gave a way for the smaller teams to compete.

'I suppose he did distort the market as he signed the players – if he hadn't had distorted the market we would not have signed the players. It made Manchester United sit up and take notice and made fans of Liverpool and others look on enviously, but we were signing good players and good investments. Signing young players and getting four or five good years and then selling them on at a profit, this is a business model that the club needs to get back to.' Even Walker would not be able to compete with some of the owners in the Premier League these days but would surely have seen the money on offer in the top tier as vindication of his credentials as a businessman almost as much as his credentials as a fan.

Both were important. Walker's statue is outside Ewood but more importantly his name is still sung inside Ewood and in stadiums around England. The fans haven't forgotten what he did and will never forget those short but very sweet years when Blackburn Rovers dined at the top table.

EPILOGUE

'Winning the Premier League near the start was amazing and I can't think of a team like Rovers who have done anything similar – except Leicester. I loved the European trips, the players we had and some of the young players who came through the academy like Duff and Dunn who were at a level that we hadn't seen before. I had a great… what was it? Almost 20 years. Whatever happened later, it was all worth it.'

ANTHONY DUERDEN, LIFELONG FAN

'It is about perspective... I started watching the Rovers in the late sixties so lower league football was pretty much the norm. We have been there before and I have seen us flit from the Second Division to the Third. This is normal but if you were born in the late eighties and started watching the Rovers in the glory days then you probably think this is awful.'

IAN HERBERT, LIFELONG FAN

A QUARTER OF A CENTURY BEFORE THE TITLE-WINNING season, Blackburn were in the second tier of English football. A quarter of a century after and the club was back where it had started. It has been a wild ride with plenty of ups and a few steep downs that were worse than anything that happened in the seventies and eighties, but perhaps that is the price a club like Rovers pays for the biggest success of all.

'I would take the low with that high without a second's hesitation,' said Ian Herbert. 'This is the deal with the devil much like Robert Johnson selling his soul (a supposedly mediocre blues guitarist who disappeared for a few months to come back as one of the greatest musicians ever and then died at 27 in 1938). The vast majority of fans would have – especially Rovers fans. The chances of glory for us would have been sneaking into the play-offs and promotion for just one season. That's all we wanted: to play United and Liverpool at home and away but the thought of beating them was something else.

'If you could sweeten the deal to include an FA Cup – not reaching an FA Cup final was my one regret in the Dalglish years – then I would have accepted a drop to the fourth tier.'

While it was frustrating to see the team slip from the mid-nineties summit so meekly, at least the following years were still an exciting time to be a Rovers fan. Four years after the trophy was lifted, the club was relegated at home to Manchester United. It was a bit ironic. United were on their way to the treble and just 48 months after he had watched every Rovers move and tried to get inside the heads of those at Ewood, Alex Ferguson didn't even know (or at least he said he didn't on live television after the final whistle, though it may have been an act to have a little dig at the club and manager Brian Kidd who had left his position as number two at Old Trafford a few months earlier leading to a bit of a fall-out) that the result had sent Rovers down. Money wasn't spent in the summer after the title success, and while that soon changed, too much was spent on players that were never going to take the club back to the top. In the first half of the decade, Rovers bought some of the best talent in British football, beating top clubs to their signatures. The big boys were not exactly lining up to sign the likes of Nathan Blake, Christian Dailly, Ashley Ward, Lee Carsley and Darren Peacock, yet Rovers spent well north of £20 million on these professionals. They were undoubtedly honest and hard-working, but not to be compared with those who had been signed a few years earlier. Kenny was no longer there to help attract the biggest names, but the club was still attractive enough to have recruited better.

Relegation in 1999 was depressing, but at least there were players there good enough to get the club back out of the second tier in the next campaign. However, at the first attempt Rovers were found wanting. The highlight of the campaign – apart from a FA Cup win at Anfield, a bittersweet feeling given that not long before the team went to Liverpool as a respected rival – was the appointment of Graeme Souness in March

2000 to replace the fired Kidd. I was there, on the away terrace at Fulham, for the Scot's first game in charge and expectations weren't high. Souness had struggled at Liverpool and we had passed them on our way up. But at least he had support from Walker and the basis of a good team. There were solid pros such as Garry Flitcroft, Craig Short and Jason McAteer with some fine young talents in Damien Duff, Matt Jansen and David Dunn.

Then in August 2000, Jack Walker died at the age of 71. Jack was a fan and had gone through the same emotions over the years as all the other supporters. There can't have been an owner in history who was as loved. There were emotional tributes in the first game after his death at Crewe and then at home to Norwich. As well as the sorrow and the deep appreciation and affection, there was also some trepidation. With the former steel magnate on board, there was always a feeling that the Rovers would be okay. Perhaps future title challenges would be a big ask but it was surely only a matter of time before the club returned to the Premier League and established itself as a force to be reckoned with once again.

Without him there was uncertainty, though measures had been taken. 'A number of years ago I put in place a family trust structure to own my various business interests, including Blackburn Rovers,' Walker said four months before his death. 'This structure ensures continuity of management and provides the necessary financial support for all my businesses for the foreseeable future. I have made known my wishes to my colleagues, who I am confident will carry forward the policies necessary to promote and enlarge all my business interests.' This 'Walker Trust' was to guide the club forward and provide financial support.

The best tribute to Walker would, of course, have been promotion but that didn't look likely after one point from five games in September and October at the beginning of the 2000/01 season. Then there was a win at Wimbledon, clinched by a Flitcroft special, and the Rovers were on their way. Souness had recruited well in Mark Hughes, Brad Friedel, Stig Inge Bjornebye and Eyal Berkovic, while he also gave plenty of playing time to the likes of Duff, Jansen and Dunn. Rovers duly swept to promotion in thrilling fashion.

Back to the Premier League then. This was an exciting team with skill. The marvellous Turkish midfielder Tugay was an exciting summer edition, and there was plenty of young talent alongside him. There was a relegation fight for a while, though Rovers – helped by new signing Andy Cole – ended up in tenth and won the League Cup for the first time. The year after brought a sixth-place finish and another return to Europe. If Souness had left in that summer of 2003 then he would have been seen as a Rovers manager to rival Dalglish. He had taken a team from the middle of the second tier to the upper reaches of the Premier League without the same spending resources at a time when the likes of Manchester United, Liverpool and Arsenal were as good as any in Europe, which was not the case a decade or so earlier. However, the Scot fell out with players, lost his footing in the transfer market and started to make strange selection and tactical decisions. The 2003/04 season saw the club narrowly avoid relegation and when the next season started poorly, fans were starting to turn against Souness. It was then something of a surprise and a relief when Newcastle United came in to take him to the north-east. It was also fitting that the two teams met in the next game, both yet to make official appointments, with Newcastle winning easily 3-0 and Rovers fans loudly reminding the hosts that their new coach had built the team that looked to be all over the place at St James'. 'Going to Newcastle saved his reputation at the Rovers at least as he would have been sacked within a month,' said Herbert. 'It was starting to go wrong for him, yet despite that last season, overall he did a great job.' In came Mark Hughes, another success who helped the club to continue punching above its weight. Sixth in his first full season, he recruited exciting players like Craig Bellamy, Roque Santa Cruz, Benni McCarthy and David Bentley. The problem was that the transfer market had changed, and the club could not keep hold of such talent for as long. It was the same with the manager. Like Souness, Hughes struggled to replicate his Rovers exploits after leaving Ewood but unlike Souness, it was not a surprise when he left to take over at Manchester City in the summer of 2008 and it was a major blow.

'All through the nineties and up to when Mark Hughes was there, I still felt they had something about them and thought they had a chance of winning cups and a chance of beating anyone on their day. Hughes was a good manager, but he was frustrated by the lack of investment,' said Anthony Duerden. 'After he left [Paul] Ince was the cheap option and that was the point when the decline started.'

Rovers looked for Hughes Mark II and settled on former Manchester United teammate Paul Ince, who had some success two leagues down with Milton Keynes Dons. It is the kind of appointment that deserves some credit as few coaches these days make the jump from the lower leagues to the top flight, and had it been a success then the Rovers board would have received plenty of plaudits. It didn't work. Ince's tenure was as short as relegation odds were becoming. After the title win, Rovers quickly became one of those clubs in the top tier who were a bad decision away from relegation. In this day and age, only the top six, perhaps the top eight, are immune to this. Ince was fired and in came a safe pair of hands in Sam Allardyce. Under Big Sam, the fear of relegation diminished, but there were costs, as Duerden described. 'Allardyce used to throw games at places like Arsenal. You would see the team and know that there was a 4-0 loss coming, and it was the same elsewhere.'

Allardyce was tolerated for a while as he pretty much guaranteed a place in the top tier, but it wasn't pretty. 'I will never forget that [7-1] defeat at United,' said Herbert of the November 2010 loss. 'It was embarrassing as we weren't trying and that was unforgivable and humiliating, but he would look at the fixture list and look at the games we could win and the week after we would be beating Southampton at home with two scrappy goals. 'Under Big Sam, the football was dreadful. I remember my heart sinking when we signed El Hadji Diouf, whose job at free-kicks was just to stop the goalkeeper getting to the ball launched into the area by goalkeeper Paul Robinson. It was like an American football set play. We had some good players then, as under Hughes we could be a swashbuckling team with some great players and we were a good team. Many fans were not sorry to see Sam go.' Big Sam was fired in December 2010 and replaced by the unknown Steve Kean.

Even under Allardyce, the club seemed to be becoming smaller in stature and ambitions. 'They were in decline when Venky's took over and were getting to the point where they were becoming a bottom eight Premier League club,' said Duerden.

'The Walker Trust weren't great and were selling players to fund the club,' he continues. 'It was costing them money and maybe they saw it as a hassle.

Once Hughes left then you knew it was then we were always one bad decision away from going down. I wasn't a big fan of Allardyce. Getting rid of him may not have been wrong but replacing him with Kean and then getting rid of the experienced players was obviously a big mistake.'

Allardyce was fired in December 2010 just weeks after Venky's, an Indian poultry company, bought one of the oldest and most successful clubs in British football. There was cautious optimism at the time, heightened by the relative lack of investment in the playing staff in the preceding years.

Trust chairman Paul Egerton-Vernon said at the time: 'We're very pleased to be passing on the Rovers to the Rao family. We have been impressed with their enthusiasm and their plans and ideas for investment as well as their wish to preserve the legacy of Jack Walker.'

Fans did not – and do not – see it that way. 'There isn't much affection for the Walker Trust,' said Herbert. 'There is a sense that they didn't do what their father would have wanted them to do, but if my parents had died and left this trust that was worth £100 million and I had no interest in football, but every year this club came and asked for 15 million pounds, then you are sure to think that the pot won't last long. Part of it is that if they had sold it to the guys who bought City then it would have been different. If Venky's had been better owners, then the Walker Trust would be better remembered but then I never saw any sense in an Indian poultry firm owning Rovers and I don't think many other people did either.'

Venky's chairman Anuradha J Desai said the company was 'delighted, proud and humbled to be associated with Blackburn Rovers'. She added: 'We will absolutely respect the Jack Walker legacy and will be actively supporting the organisation to ensure that Blackburn Rovers remains one of the best-run clubs within the Premier League. We are particularly pleased that the deal has the full support of the Walker Trust, the chairman and the management team, who will of course remain in place with our full support.'

For a book about the unforgettable events of 1995 and the preceding years, there is no need to go into too much detail on what happened next. Suffice to say that the initial promises of Champions League football, big signings and a huge new fanbase in Asia never materialised. What fans got instead was a novice manager who, to put it kindly, struggled to make the step up and a club that quickly went from being one of the best run in English football to one of the worst.

'It has almost gone full circle with the Venky's,' said Herbert. 'In the beginning they were horribly misguided, perhaps a little arrogant in their actions in that they got rid of the whole management team on and off the field.' Out went people like chairman John Williams, one of the most respected administrators in the business. In came, well, nobody is sure who came in at first. There was an agent Jerome Anderson who seemed to be calling the shots along with Kean, and a client of Anderson's who was promoted above his station to take charge of the team but who also seemed to have plenty of power at the club. At first Rovers fans were often criticised for their protests by much of the mainstream media, who only slowly came round to the opinion that there was something strange happening.

Relegation came in 2012 and was inevitable. It was also terrible timing, as the Premier League was about to receive a huge increase in broadcasting revenue.

'A bit more vision and patience and the Walkers Trust could have brought in other owners,' said Herbert. 'Their timing to sell was spectacularly bad as was the relegation that came. If they had stayed with all the new money and an excellent academy, it could all have been self-sustaining and they could even have handed it to the fans.'

Kean was eventually out in 2012 and there followed a quick succession of managers in Henning Berg, Michael Appleton, Gary Bowyer, Paul Lambert and the hapless Owen Coyle, who left in 2017 with Rovers in danger of the drop to the third tier, a trapdoor that was not avoided.

Worse than the two relegations was the loosening of the connection between club and town that had been in place for not far short of a century and a half. Matters have stabilised, but the distance remains. 'We have owners who don't do communication and though they now do a lot of things right, there is still something missing,' said Duerden. 'Some people think we should act like a big club but we should be a community club and we can still be that. Potentially, the connection can be restored. The promotion season showed that people, to some extent, can forgive. They have put some money in, are keeping hold of the best players and are funding the academy so you can't argue about that. I think fans are not angry anymore and accept that money is being put in, but there is still something missing.'

Promotion back to the second tier in the 2017/18 season under Tony Mowbray was the first enjoyable campaign for fans for at least a decade and stopped the rot. 'In the last three or four seasons when they [the owners] could have bailed and I thought they would, they didn't,' said Herbert. 'When we went to the third division then I thought we would be in liquidation. They stuck with it and we are as well-organised now as we have been at any time in their reign.

'I get whimsical and nostalgic about what happened before their reign, but the promotion year was terrific and did rekindle the enthusiasm in people like me that had been jaded. It was great to go around some of those old small grounds again and stand. But there is a disconnect and it may never be healed. People in Blackburn have long memories and there are still those who don't go because they never got tickets for the 1960 cup final.

'When they took over, they were behaving like children who have got an inheritance and blow the lot and then there is the awful realisation that dawns. Now they are starting to put in place a real structure, but to make money Rovers need to get into the Premier League and need a crop of good young players.'

That is going to be tough. Promotion was followed by a solid performance back in the second tier but in 2020, the future looks uncertain.

'I still don't think Venky's are the right owners but there are no better options at the moment,' Duerden said. 'If the Walkers had kept hold of it, things could have changed and they could have sold it for a lot of money. It was £20 million in the end. Things would have been different a few years later for a club in the Premier League with limited debts, but now the club's just not worth anything.'

He agrees with Herbert that the only way to make money is promotion. 'Burnley is the perfect model but it is not an exciting one. They get away with it because they were rubbish for 30 years before that and it is a club that is close to the community. You can also be like Brentford, who buy and sell players, and if you are lucky it comes together for a year. For the Rovers, they need to be really clever about bringing through young players, get a good scouting network, pick up good young players from abroad or over here and then it can work. It is not an easy model but one they have to follow.

'We probably are where we would have been without Jack Walker.' And the same could perhaps be said about my brother's feelings towards the club and going to games now.

'I enjoyed the [2017/18] promotion season but a lot of that was going to smaller grounds with larger away followings. That didn't happen in the later years in the Premier League. They [away attendances] had become smaller because of the prices and also the feeling that we would lose. I don't get as upset now when we lose. I get more angry at selection decisions or when I see people who are just going through the motions, but I was there at Doncaster when we got promoted [in April 2017] and the kids came and I took my dad. Those moments are still special and still mean something.

'Clubs like Blackburn need people to care about it and need people to feel part of it. The most important thing about supporting the club has never been the quality of the football. It is about sharing something with your friends, family and the community, and connecting. Football brings those moments – both good and bad – and those experiences. That's still there with the Rovers. It may never be as good as it was back in 1995 but it is still there.'

ACKNOWLEDGEMENTS

THERE WERE MANY PEOPLE WHO HELPED TO MAKE THIS book a reality. First and foremost I would like to thank all the people who gave up their time to be interviewed. That so many club legends still talk about the Rovers with such affection after all these years made writing the book such a pleasure.

Ian Herbert of BRFCS.com was a valuable supporter, as was my brother Anthony Duerden. The Lancashire Evening Telegraph has been a mainstay for all Rovers fans over the years, never more so than in the nineties, and it was a valuable resource – at least it was when I stopped trying to find a picture of myself in my old junior school nativity play. Thanks to the staff at the wonderful Blackburn Central Library who helped me out.

And then there are the people at the publishers deCoubertin books. James Corbett is the founder and it was this Everton fan who not only first floated the idea back in 2011 on a bus in Qatar but connected me with Howard Kendall, the first interviewee.

Thanks to Jack Gordon Brown, who helped make the book that much better, and to Megan Pollard, whose enthusiasm is matched by her organisational skills – not bad for a Burnley fan.

And thanks to my family, my wife Myung-joo and daughters Danbi and Yubi, who have put up with me writing this book in Blackburn, Malaysia, Korea, as well as on the Trans-Mongolian Express. A story about my hometown written around the world.

'Lead! serves up a smorgasbord of
wisdom, stories and tools to help your own journey of self-discovery.'

Matt Hyde OBE
Chief Executive, The Scouts

Lead!

Finding Your Voice in a Chaotic World

Barry Dore

Lead!

Finding your Voice in a Chaotic World

Barry Dore

Copyright © 2023 Barry Dore.

Printed by KDP Publishing

First printing, 2023.

www.barrydore.com

ISBN 9798394450273

'Be kind but be fierce, you are needed now more than ever before. Take up the mantle of change for this is your time.'

Winston Churchill

'No-one is too small to make a difference'

Greta Thunberg

Also by Barry Dore

Leadership

'Lead Like Mary'
'Building a Community'

Fiction

'The Lobster Pot Café'
'Choppy Waters' (coming soon)

Contents

The Time is Now:

About the Author

Barry spent the first half of his career in the private sector, running estates of pubs and selling beer, learning lots of leadership lessons along the way (mainly how not to lead!). The autocratic, hierarchical, sometimes bullying culture he experienced and observed, where people kept their heads down, too often operating in an atmosphere of fear, convinced him there was a far better way to lead. One which would unleash the potential and creativity locked inside so many people, delivering amazing results.

Together with a small group of like-minded colleagues he had the opportunity to test his theories in an exhilarating two-year journey running then selling an estate of 1,000 pubs no longer wanted by their former owner. By creating a culture of trust, respect and recognition, alongside focus, holding people accountable and never ducking a difficult conversation, the team were able to galvanise people. Significantly improved results led to a premium in the ultimate sale price of the estate, widely recognised as being attributed to the culture change.

Certain there was now compelling evidence of the need for organisations everywhere to evolve from autocratic, command and control leadership to a model built on authenticity and trust, Barry established his own business in 2002.

Since then Barry has worked with many thousands of people in hundreds of organisations inspiring, challenging and enabling them to change their leadership paradigm and unlock the potential of their people. His involvement encompasses consultancy, facilitation, coaching and mentoring.

In 2014 *'Lead Like Mary'* was published, pulling together Barry's thinking, and enabling him to launch public and corporate programmes based on the book.

As he enters the last years of his professional work, Barry increasingly focuses his efforts on younger leaders, a new generation who, he believes, can and will endorse and drive this leadership evolution. He chairs a conservation leadership charity working with young leaders in the UK and West Africa, has established a cohort of evolving leaders providing networking opportunities as well as a focus on authentic leadership and has established a Lead! Community of like-minded leaders based on this new book. Barry also produces Leadership Reflections, a regular leadership podcast. He continues to mentor young leaders in a voluntary capacity.

Barry lives in Fradswell, a small community in rural Staffordshire, with Jakkie, his wife. They have six children, now scattered far and wide around the world. Together they are involved in their local community, leading a six years project to fund and build a new village hall, which proved to be the spark that ignited a vibrant rural community. The story of this venture is told in Barry's book 'Building a Community.'

In his spare time Barry dabbles in fiction writing, his first novel 'The Lobster Pot Café' was published in 2020. Over several years he also presented two shows on local radio.

Foreword

Matt Hyde OBE
Chief Executive, The Scouts

We live in volatile times. It seems remarkable that my 14 year old son has lived through the 2008 financial crisis, Brexit, 6 UK Prime Ministers (at the time of writing), a global pandemic, Putin's war in Ukraine and Donald Trump as US President.

New challenges present themselves - megatrends that will be long term in nature, with irreversible consequences for the world around us. Notably climate change and resource scarcity mean humanity faces an existential crisis. Demographic shifts are accelerating. Many countries are witnessing ageing populations, whereas, at the same time, nearly 50% of the world's population is under the age of 25. The geopolitical tectonic plates are moving with China in the ascendency. And the pace of change is fuelled by the acceleration of new technologies, where digitisation and transformation reveal both threats and cause for optimism. Artificial intelligence for example is already making our lives easier, but automation will mean jobs are deleted, opening up a whole new set of challenges for working people.

These structural shifts require new thinking, creativity and the adaptability of human ingenuity, particularly if we are to ensure the world we live in tomorrow is fairer and more sustainable. Fundamentally, if the challenges we face are to be confronted, and the opportunities exploited, we need outstanding leaders – leaders who can make sense of the chaos and navigate through the confusion. And that is why Barry Dore's *Lead!* is both timely and much needed.

Lead! picks up the baton from Barry's last leadership book *Lead Like Mary*. Similar themes emerge about what it takes to be a truly great leader, including the importance of authenticity, values, service and selflessness. But *Lead!* pushes us further forward, recognising that if we are to compete and thrive in a chaotic and volatile world we need deeper self-reflection in order to be the best version of ourselves. *Lead!* serves up a smorgasbord of wisdom, stories and tools to help your own journey of self-discovery.

At its core this is a book about hope. It is a rallying call that social justice can be achieved because of exceptional leadership. It's a beacon that shines through the fog and helps us to find our way through. And because self-management is the cornerstone of leading people effectively, this book contains invaluable lessons to support your self-care.

Lead! is for all of us. Inspired by stories of real people, in real communities, it is a reminder that within all of us there is a great leader. As John Quincey Adams said:

'If your actions inspire others to dream more, learn more, do more and become more, you are a leader.'

Once you have read *Lead!* you will certainly have learned more. You will be fired up to help others to do the same. You will want to dream big, to do more and become more. And that is how as leaders we will shape a better world.

Matt Hyde OBE
Chief Executive, The Scouts
February 2023

Matt Hyde is Chief Executive of the Scouts, the UK's largest youth movement. Formerly Chief Executive of the National Union of Students (NUS), he has undertaken a number of leadership roles in the charity sector and as Chief Executive of the Scouts has contributed to a period of record membership growth since he joined in 2013. He has overseen the development and delivery of a rebrand, award-winning campaigns and has spearheaded work to support the growth of Scouting in areas of deprivation.

Matt is also a trustee of Comic Relief, a Patron of UNLOCK (the charity for people with convictions) and was previously Vice-Chair of the National Council for Voluntary Organisations (NCVO). He developed the world's first degree apprenticeship for social change which launched at Queen Mary University of London in 2019.

Matt was awarded an OBE in the 2020 New Years Honours List and an Honorary Fellowship from Queen Mary University of London in 2012. He was named as one of the 25 most influential charity sector leaders by Charity Times in 2019.

Introduction

'Leadership belongs to those who take it'

Sheryl Sandberg.

Skelmersdale, one of the second wave of new towns, was developed in the 1960s to house overspill populations from the north Merseyside conurbation. It's a town with many challenges, poverty levels are well above the national average, impacting 27% of its children. It is the most deprived area in West Lancashire.

If you manage to negotiate the never-ending series of roundabouts unique to new town developments, you will arrive in the suburb of Tanhouse. Follow Eskdale through a large social housing conurbation, past abandoned shopping trolleys, and the local shop with barred windows. At the very end of the cul-de-sac is the entrance to Delph Side Community Primary School.

From the outside the building is non-descript, an example of the 1960s obsession with concrete. It doesn't prepare you for the transformation as you walk through the main doors.

Pass through into the reception area and enter a different world! Pause, close your eyes, and listen. The first thing you hear is the noise, excited chatter of young voices intermingled with laughter. Open your eyes and look around, bright colours, vibrant, welcoming and calming. On the wall directly in front of you, beneath a heading of 'Our Values', just three words, each depicted with a simple graphic, 'Enjoy, Embrace, Evolve.'

Walk along the brightly decorated corridors, adorned with the childrens' artwork, and glance through the windows of the classrooms you pass.

Children in smart uniforms, teachers encouraging them with a smile and a positive word. More laughter. The over-riding impression is of engagement, purposeful endeavour and fun.

To conclude your visit retrace your steps past reception, to the head teacher's office. The door is open, the room welcoming, decorated in pastel shades with fresh flowers and family photos on the desk, a noticeboard full of the childrens work. Two large giraffes dominate one corner of the room. Opposite the desk, a sofa and easy chairs, one of which is occupied by Liz Ormerod, the head teacher, the energy and driving force behind a story of extraordinary transformation.

I'll return to Liz's story later. I wanted to share a taster of it at the very beginning, partly because, being a modest person devoid of ego, she'll hate me for it, and partly because of the amazing person she is, and what she has achieved at Delph Side school. This demonstrates perfectly what the book is about.

Almost a decade ago I published *'Lead Like Mary'*, my first leadership book. I had no pretensions it was destined to be a best seller, rather that it pulled together my leadership beliefs and enabled me to develop *'Lead Like Mary'* programmes where it would act as a workbook and learning journal.

So many leadership books are aimed at CEOs and other senior leaders in organisations, usually in the private sector. *'Lead!'* is different. It is written for anybody, anywhere, at any level in any organisation, and also those in voluntary endeavours, communities, families or friendship groups. In it I seek to articulate and share timeless principles which form the core of my leadership beliefs and teaching. If you've read *'Lead Like Mary'* or participated, like thousands of people have, in my corporate and public programmes, you'll be very familiar with these. If you haven't,

I'll introduce you to them later. The fundamental principle is anyone can be a leader, it's a choice any of us can make.

But what kind of leader? In *'Lead Like Mary'* I introduced the concept of authentic leadership, leaders who are genuine, true to themselves, low in ego and high in humility. Authentic leaders gain their legitimacy to lead not from their job title or size of their office. People choose to follow them because of who they are.

In *'Lead Like Mary'* I describe an evolution to this new way of leading, as a fresh generation of leaders emerge who recognise those who inspire, trust and enable their people will deliver far better results than the 'Command & Control' way of leading that has been around for centuries.

Since then I am so pleased to have witnessed this trend continuing, and to have played my small part in introducing people to the infinite possibilities and opportunities authentic leadership provides.

But here's the thing, the premise of this book. Simply being an authentic leader is no longer enough.

As we will explore in the first chapter we live in troubled times. Deeply troubled times, the worst I have experienced in my sixty odd years on this planet. From a climate emergency to a biodiversity crisis, nuclear threat, abject poverty, war in Europe for the first time since 1945, and a global pandemic. It's a bleak picture whichever way you turn.

It's up to authentic leaders anywhere and everywhere, people like you and me, to stand up, find our voice and play our part in building a better world around us. If your immediate retort is 'what difference can I possibly make?' remember the quote from Greta Thunberg

'No-one is too small to make a difference.'

That's exactly what Liz has done and continues doing every single day at Delph Side Primary School. Every inch an authentic leader she has found her voice, and has built an incredible oasis of calm, endeavour and achievement in a small corner of Lancashire. She has improved and changed so many lives. The ripples are taking effect across her community and beyond. Liz doesn't have superpowers, she's just an ordinary person doing extraordinary things.

 You can be too.

Join me on a journey of enlightenment and discovery. We'll revisit those timeless leadership principles, reacquaint ourselves with Mary, meet other ordinary people doing extraordinary things and then explore together the steps of a framework to inspire and enable you to find your voice.

Use this book as your learning journal, one that can stay by your side and be revisited time and time again. There are exercises to complete and notes pages for your reflections.

Ready? Let's go!

Barry Dore
April 2023

Section I

A Chaotic World

A World Turned Upside Down

'I alone cannot change the world.
But I can cast a stone across the water to create many ripples.'

Mother Teresa

We live in chaotic, challenging, dangerous times. I'm so sorry to begin this book on such a sombre note but I am increasingly scared for the future of our planet. So many other people I speak to feel exactly the same way. I feel I have been lucky to have spent a significant part of my life in a golden age. I was born a decade or so after the end of the Second World War, have lived through primarily peaceful times, in Europe at least, enjoyed free university education, could afford to buy a house in my early twenties, have travelled extensively at affordable prices, lived through a cold war where nuclear weapons were primarily a deterrent not a threat, benefited from a generous pension scheme and never heard of a food bank.

Now I look around me and am genuinely concerned about what the future holds for my grandchildren and their children.

Consider the following.

We are faced with a climate emergency where the very future of our planet hangs in the balance. Opening COP27 in Egypt, United Nations Secretary-General Antonio Guterres warned

'We are on the highway to climate hell with one foot still on the accelerator
...we must co-operate or perish.'

Leaders of the richest nations on earth make grandiose and impassioned speeches at these events, setting targets and committing funds, only to renege on their promises for their own short-term interests as temperatures rise and ice caps melt. Meanwhile much of the world experiences extreme weather causing widespread devastation, from drought in Africa to flooding in Pakistan and wildfires in the USA.

We face a biodiversity crisis with potentially catastrophic consequences. The Living Planet Index, an indicator of the state of global biological diversity, continues to decline. It shows an average 68% decrease in population sizes of mammals, birds, amphibians, reptiles and fish between 1970 and 2016.

Their latest report continues

'It matters because biodiversity is fundamental to human life on Earth, and the evidence is unequivocal – it is being destroyed by us at a rate unprecedented in history. Since the industrial revolution, human activities have increasingly destroyed and degraded forests, grasslands, wetlands and other important ecosystems, threatening human well-being. Seventy-five per cent of the Earth's ice-free land surface has already been significantly altered, most of the oceans are polluted, and more than 85% of the area of wetlands has been lost.'

The first war in mainland Europe since 1945 threatens not only the stability of the region but has also created an energy crisis across much of the continent and famine in parts of Africa. An increasingly beleaguered and isolated Russian leader makes thinly veiled threats about using nuclear weapons.

Meanwhile rogue states armed with their own nuclear arsenal present a constant threat and two of the world's superpowers sabre rattle with a trade war and tensions over Taiwan.

In the world's second biggest democracy political divisions have split the nation right down the middle. In her foreword to a new book on the leadership of Martin Luther King, his daughter Bernice comments

'We the people are experiencing a void of moral leadership. Our nation is fraught with vitriol, divisiveness, racism, white supremacy, hatred, neo-Nazism, misogyny, poverty and unemployment.'

MLK would turn in his grave.

Closer to home we are in the grips of a cost of living crisis driven primarily by energy and food prices. Food banks are struggling to cope and the NHS is overwhelmed as ambulances queue outside A&E departments.

No wonder I fear for my grandchildrens future.

On top of all of this we are just emerging from a global pandemic which has had a profound effect on so many lives, turning our already chaotic world upside down.

The vast majority of us emerged from our 2020 new year celebrations hardly aware of the occasional mention of an emerging virus in some far off random Chinese city. I recall travelling to Leicester in the first week of March to chair a board meeting of the Osprey Leadership Foundation. It was so perfectly normal for people from all over the country to travel to meet in person, words like 'Zoom' and 'hybrid working' were not part of our everyday vocabulary.

As the meeting drew to a close, we fixed the next date and commented on some groups of students we had seen walking around the campus in face masks. It seemed an odd thing to do.

Within a couple of weeks the world changed. On 23 March Boris Johnson announced the first lockdown, ordering people to 'stay at home'; only a few days earlier he had confidently declared that the UK could 'turn the tide of coronavirus' in 12 weeks. Soon he was appearing at daily televised press conferences, flanked by Patrick and Chris, presenting slides of hospital admissions, ventilators and deaths, reminding us all of the strict lockdown rules, before allegedly slipping off to a No 10 drinks party.

We faced the most severe restrictions on our freedom seen in peace time, resulting in tragic circumstances for so many people as loved ones suffered and died alone in closed hospital wards and care homes. So many of us were denied the opportunity to say goodbye at funerals.

My own situation, while far from tragic, was upsetting. Three of our children live in Australia. They all visited the UK in 2019, and we arranged dates for the next visits in the first half of 2020. It was 2022 before we saw them again, getting the first chance to meet our grandson, now two years old.

We learned a new word, 'furlough', as everything we took for granted in the world of work changed overnight. Those furloughed suddenly had time on their hands but nowhere to go. Many lost their self-worth, questioning why they had been selected while colleagues worked on. Some found themselves exposed to abusive relationships.

Many others began working from home. It was the most surreal of experiences and for some a deeply disturbing one. Suddenly they were isolated from work colleagues, stuck in a back bedroom or at the kitchen table for several hours a day. We experienced a cocktail of emotions. For some working from home, it was guilt, upset that other colleagues had been placed on furlough or in some cases laid off. Others were angry, why should they have to work while others were being paid to sit at home?
Many became obsessed with justifying their existence and demonstrating that they were working hard at home. They filled their days with

numerous Zoom and Teams calls, anxious to appear busy. A real opportunity to establish improved work-life balance in this unique situation was lost in a frenzy of activity, time previously spent commuting now consumed by more work.

An additional pressure heaped on many was child-care. With schools closed and home schooling introduced, couples and single parents alike had to attempt to juggle working with keeping their children occupied.

Others had family members fall ill and rushed to hospital, some requiring a ventilator in ICU. There was no visiting, many suffered unbelievable heartbreak as their loved ones never came home. Others were unable to visit elderly relatives in care homes.

We were so scared in that first year, it was only the advent of the vaccination programme that demonstrated we could live with this brutal disease.

However, from these darkest of days something wonderful began to happen. Heroes emerged, normal people who believed they could make a difference. Remember Captain Tom who captured the hearts of the nation? Each week we gathered outside our homes to applaud NHS workers. Many thousands working in social care received less public appreciation but their contribution was as big as their NHS counterparts.

In communities up and down the land volunteers emerged to help others, delivering meals, doing the shopping, collecting medication or just acting as a friend in need to the vulnerable and isolated.

Leaders of organisations were tested to the limit, facing unprecedented challenges. Too many failed the test miserably, communicating poorly at a time when it was never more important. Autocratic, command & control managers found themselves out of their depth, unable to micromanage home workers. Suspicious, and demonstrating appalling lack of trust, some even resorted to covert surveillance systems.

Not Mary and her authentic fellow leaders. Their leadership through those dark days was exemplary. Facing up to the challenge, they created and implemented plans. Many saw an overnight catastrophic drop in revenues and confronted the brutal facts with decisive action. They also demonstrated exemplary communications. Their empathy enabled them to understand the emotional impact on their people, to recognise the additional pressures of child-care and the horrendous personal circumstances many faced. They understood the importance of keeping their people informed, and of verbal communications, spending hours on the phone and recording vlogs.

This was leadership of the highest order. In the Everyday Heroes section later I introduce you to Lesley Dixon, Chief Executive of a social care charity and one such example. There were many others.

That pandemic experience fills me with hope. Do not expect the enormous challenges the world faces to be resolved by political, religious and business leaders. Most are driven by self-interest, an obsession with wealth generation where more is never enough, with outdated beliefs, clinging to power at all costs, drowning in their massive egos. To a very large extent they are the very ones who got us into this mess in the first place.

The answer lies with every one of us. You may well despair and wonder what you can possibly do. How on earth can we make a difference? We are too small to address these challenges which impact every nation and every community.

If we are going to address these issues, change will come from the bottom, not the top. 'Lead Like Mary' sought to demonstrate that anyone, anywhere, can be a leader, it's a choice any of us can make. It set out the case for authentic leadership, where people choose to follow you because of who you are, not the position you hold.

However simply being an authentic leader is not enough. There is now a demand like never before for authentic leaders everywhere to find their voice, to stand up, take action, inspire and enable others to build a better world around them.

That's the key. No-one on their own can change the world, but all of us can do things to build a better world for those people around us. We need authentic leaders everywhere to come to the fore, in families, schools, communities, voluntary endeavours, politics, charities and corporations. To deliver changes that make a difference.

There's a further compelling reason why this is just so important. The young leaders of today will build their careers in whatever chosen field. Some of those young leaders one day will find themselves at the very top of governments, the civil service, the media, international corporations, charities and NGOs. Out there somewhere today are young leaders who will tomorrow be Prime Ministers, Presidents, Environment Ministers, top industrialists, philanthropists, Nobel prize winning scientists. People who really can change the world.

Incidentally there is a distinct possibility that I've already worked with a future UK Prime Minister. I'll keep my powder dry for now but watch this space!

Imagine if we managed to shape their thinking in these early years, to inspire and enable them to be authentic, values-led leaders, committed to serving others, finding their voice to build a kinder, safer, fairer, happier world on the biggest stages. Imagine!
We can't afford to wait until then, though. If we want to build a better world starting today, it will be by millions of small actions by millions of people, delivering change that at first is a trickle but becomes a tsunami.

Together we can build a better world, one that is kinder, fairer, safer and happier. Where people thrive, flourish and collaborate.

It's already happening. Across the world individuals, communities and social enterprises are tackling local problems- plastic waste, flooding, food poverty, declining biodiversity- and implementing pragmatic local solutions.

You can, indeed you must, be part of that mission.

A world pulled back from the very brink.

We cannot wait, the clock is ticking, we need to start now!

Reflections

Timeless Leadership Principles

'There are three constants in life- change, choice and principles'

Stephen R Covey

Let's start at the beginning. Before we move on I'd like us to revisit the timeless leadership principles which underpin all that I do.

Whenever I work with any new group of people I ask one question. 'Are you a leader?'

Sounds simple, but my experience over the years is that it's anything but. I watch the furrowed brows as participants consider their answers. Hesitatingly, out come a combination of replies, split between 'yes' 'no' and 'not sure.'

Why do people find that question so hard? I guess because it's not one we ask ourselves regularly. Why are there so many 'no' and 'don't know' responses? It's because we grow up believing leadership is the sole domain of those sat the top of organisations or public bodies- Managing Directors, CEOs, Prime Ministers, Council Chiefs. Leadership exhibited through grand job titles, large offices, lots of staff and the like.

I disagree completely. It's crucial that we explode this myth.

I base all my teaching of leadership on a small number of deep rooted, timeless principles. They've served me well since I was first taught them many years ago. Understanding them is a crucial prerequisite to finding your voice. Over time I've refined my early thinking and have focused on just six principles, they're the DNA of leadership, fundamental building blocks for our journey ahead.

Anyone can be a leader. It's a choice every one of us can make. I have no doubt you are already a leader, even if you don't realise it. Let me bring this proposition to life. On my *'Lead Like Mary'* programmes I run an exercise where I ask participants to choose someone who, now or at some point in their life, has been a role model for them. It could be anyone, it's that person who has played a significant part in their lives. People make a myriad of choices, from a family member, to a friend, a teacher, a work boss or colleague, even someone famous who they've never met but who has inspired them from afar. I ask people to introduce their role model and explain what it was about them that they really valued and admired.

The feedback from these discussions is always so meaningful. These role models have, invariably, had a significant and invaluable impact. So often, that impact has been so simple. It might be that they believed in the person, helped them, listened, inspired, found time for them. Whoever the person was, whether a parent, relative, friend, work colleague, the words used are much the same. I then asked if this role model would have considered themselves to be a leader. The answer is usually 'no.' My proposition in return is they might not have identified with the term 'leader' but they absolutely were one. Believing in someone, helping, listening, inspiring, giving time are all examples of what leaders do. These people, from all walks of life, are as much leaders as the boss of a large corporation. Anyone can be a leader.

Leaders are needed at every level of organisations. It goes without saying that we want those people at the top of organisations to be leaders, we need them to set the direction, inspire their people, deliver (the right) results. However, for any organisation to flourish, to be truly successful, it needs leaders at every level. Forget the link to hierarchy, it's not even necessary to line manage a single other person in order to be a leader. People on the front line, interacting daily with customers, for example, can be a leader as much as the CEO or departmental manager. At this very moment as you read this, many of those people are leading. Maybe they work for you and you've never thought of it this way before. They are leading not by telling others what to do (that's rarely the best way to lead at any level) but by helping them, dealing with queries and resolving issues.

Leadership is a whole life activity. We are mistaken if we believe leadership is something that only happens at work. Effective leadership is crucial outside work, in our personal life as well as our professional one. We don't take our leadership hat off as we commute home from the office. We need leaders in families, friendship groups, communities, voluntary activities, in every element of society. Leaders who are there to listen, care, nurture, develop, grow and hold to account. To listen to a child, help a friend, build a community, develop a voluntary endeavour, shape a society.

Leadership is an inside-out activity. On the next page, take a look at a simple model, re-produced from *'Lead Like Mary.'*

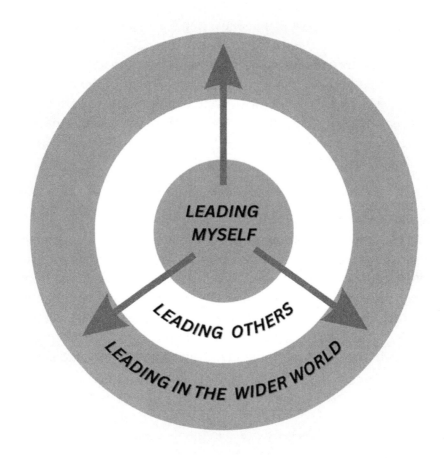

Leadership must begin in the inner of these three circles, for that is where we **lead ourselves.** It's the only place the leadership journey can begin, because it's not until we are leading ourselves effectively that we gain the ability and legitimacy to lead in the other circles. When we lead ourselves, we have taken control and reached an acceptable level of personal effectiveness. Guided by our values, we are focused on modelling the behaviours we want to see in others. We are taking care physically, mentally and emotionally, striving to be the best version of ourselves.

Now, and only now, can we move to the middle circle. This is where we **lead others,** getting the very best out of those around us. These are the people we have regular contact with, people who, metaphorically, we can touch daily. At work this would include your team, boss, colleagues, people in partner organisations, and maybe customers, depending on your role. Equally the principle applies outside work with our family, friends, community, volunteering activities and so on. If we want to have a positive impact on their lives, to lead them effectively, we do so because of who we are in the inner circle.

Now, and only now, we push outwards, to the outer circle, where we **lead in the wider world.** This is where we have the opportunity to exercise change on a far wider level, to truly make a difference to the world around us. However, in virtually every example, we cannot make that change happen on our own, it happens through people in the middle circle.

For example, suppose you want to tackle the issue of food poverty in your community. It's an outer circle challenge. From the inner circle you are committed to doing it. It's consistent with your values, you want to make a difference. You can try and do it on your own, but it will be far more effective if you can inspire others in the middle circle- your local councillors, representatives of the media, your immediate friends and neighbours, people from local charities. Your passion shines through, you inspire these people with your clarity of vision and determination, you drive collaboration. People are motivated to act and slowly, change in the wider community begins to occur- a food bank, grants, publicity, drop-in centre, advice clinics, a community gardening club. The possibilities are endless.

Or, at work you have a senior role. You want to introduce a new way of working, one customers will benefit from, and will lead to increased loyalty and profitability. You have the ideas, the inspiration, the belief it will work. But there are thousands of customers! What do you do? You inspire your sales managers, marketing people, finance team. They create the delivery plans, inspire and enable their teams, and in turn your whole sales force engages with their customers to promote the benefits of the changes.

Never underestimate the power of inside-out leadership!

Great leaders are authentic.

The more I study leadership, and observe leaders in action, the more convinced I become that great leaders are authentic. They lead because of who they are, not the position they hold. People choose to follow them, they are not coerced into doing so.

Authentic leaders are genuine people, low in ego, high in humility. They have a deep commitment to serving others and promote an environment of trust. They are empathic and steeped in Emotional Intelligence. They possess an inner steel, have a determination to succeed, are relentless and resilient but always fair. They constantly strive to do the right thing in the right way and possess a deep-rooted desire and commitment to improve the lives of others.

It's through leadership that things get done

Leadership is the catalyst by which any change occurs. Without leadership- in organisations, at home, in friendship groups, in communities, in society, things stagnate. They don't move forward, results flat line, there is no progress. I believe leaders do two things-they cope with today and they build a better tomorrow. Coping with today is a necessity, we need to keep the wheels turning, but to make progress we must do more. We also need to focus on building that better tomorrow, creating a better world for others.

It is through authentic, effective and brave leadership that this happens. Leaders always need to be focused on the future, and passionate about improving it for others. Remember, so much of building that better tomorrow is not about delivering transformational change. It's about inspiring, helping others to realise their potential, equipping them with the knowledge, skills and desire to do so, opening their minds to opportunities, pushing them to succeed, being there for them.

In 2019 the Harvard Business Review published an interview with the Dalai Lama, seeking advice for leaders today. His views resonate so strongly with the concept of authentic leadership.

His message was short and simple. Leaders must be mindful, selfless and compassionate, and be part of creating organisations, communities and societies where people thrive, flourish and collaborate.

Leaders who are mindful focus on the task in hand and on their people while at the same time being aware of the bigger picture. Mindfulness is being present with a calm, focused and clear mind.

Selfless leaders combine a strong will and self-confidence with humility. Leaders who curb their ego serve the interests of their team or organisation and create better results.

Compassionate leaders take in the perspective of others. Don't mistake compassion for softness, compassion takes courage and strength.

Central to the Dali Lama's teaching is that leadership is less about what we do and more about who we are. Leadership in the 21st century is about unlearning management and re-learning being human. He observed:

'We should remember that we are visitors on this planet. During this time, we should work to leave the world a better place. What might a better world look like? I believe the answer is straightforward. A better world is one where people are happier. Our desire for happiness is something we all have in common.'

Compare this to recent data on the state of leadership in organisations. 77% of managers evaluate themselves as being motivational and good at engaging their people. However, 82% of employees find their managers uninspiring!

I do believe things are slowly changing. Increasingly organisations are placing greater emphasis on developing positive values and behaviours rather than just focusing on skills. This is completely consistent with the principle of inside-out leadership. Leadership starts in the mind. Only when we understand and master ourselves can we understand and lead others. Only when we lead others can we impact on the wider world.

There you have it! Six leadership principles, the fundamental building blocks for our journey ahead together.

Reflections

A Call to Arms

'If we did all the things we are capable of doing we would astound ourselves'

Thomas Edison

Sometime around the middle of November 2022, somewhere on our planet, the eight billionth person was born. We can't know for certain who they are, and we know nothing of the life they will lead, this United Nations estimate is the best we can do.

What we can say with certainty is that number eight billion, whoever they are, is a unique individual. There is no-one exactly like them. You are a unique individual as well. What you have in common with our 8 billion friends is that you were both born with so much potential inside you. Both of you are capable of making such a difference. Of building a better world around you.

So many factors will determine how much potential is realised. Where you are born, socio-economic background, ethnicity, gender, access to education and upbringing are all highly relevant, it really is a roll of the dice, but that potential is still there. If you are one of the lucky ones, and the chances are if you have purchased and are reading this book you are, it's time to unlock your potential.

Just for a moment, imagine what could be achieved if all eight billion people who share our planet worked together, united in a single purpose for the common good, collaborating, building a safer, fairer, kinder and happier world.

We know that's not going to happen, for many reasons, including those I referred to earlier. Self-survival, unfettered ego, ruthless ambition and money rule the roost. Don't get me started on religion...

Our world is a chaotic place, turned upside-down by the global pandemic. There are a multitude of issues to address, and so many of us feel overwhelmed by the sheer scale of them. We want to have an impact, to make a difference, but where on earth (literally) do we begin?

The first answer is easy- begin with you. Back to the simple but all-powerful concept of inside-out leadership. If you want to build that better world for others you must first be the best version of you. That means taking care of yourself, focusing on your mental and physical well-being, developing your personal effectiveness and impact.

It also means understanding, just like Mary, you can be and are a leader. You can choose to lead in all parts of your life. Just like Mary, you can become an authentic leader committed to serving others, led by your deep-rooted values, both trusting and trustworthy.

But simply being an authentic leader is not enough. Now is the time to begin a life-long journey improving the lives of others and building a better tomorrow.

It is time to find your voice.

Finding your voice means being willing to put your head above the parapet, standing up for what you believe in, being courageous, overcoming resistance, focusing on a prize and inspiring and enabling others to work with you to deliver change.

It means building relationships, collaborating, challenging others when necessary, building alliances and networks, focusing on possibilities, not problems. Never, ever giving up.

If you want a quiet life, stop reading now. Pass this book to a friend or stick it on Ebay. However, if you consider that you just might be able to make a small difference, keep reading.

If you are daunted, don't worry. It's important to take a step back here and understand all the various levels where change can occur. No individual on Earth can solve the biggest challenges we face single handed. No one person can alter the course of global warming, restore biodiversity, stop wars, bring rogue nations into line, eradicate poverty.

No one person can change the whole world.

However, there is nothing that can stop you changing things in **your** world, the world around you. If you can inspire, enable and galvanise other people to work with you, or join a group already engaged in change, some progress may be possible.

We don't need to start big, we can start small. There is so much we can do, a positive difference we can make to the world around us, and for others in that world. Start small, join with others, and watch your influence and impact grow.

I love this quote:

'Maybe your life purpose isn't supposed to be a thrill seeking narrative. What if you're meant to be the sunshine to someone's stormy day. Or the voice of clarity in a frantic mind. You don't have to be a superhero to save the day.'

Tiny Buddha

Authentic leaders don't stand on a soap box making grandiose speeches, they get on with building a better tomorrow quietly, with little fuss. They never stop believing they can make a difference.

Take a few moments out to read (hopefully re-read) the starfish story which begins on page 40 of *'Lead Like Mary'*. It perfectly illustrates what I mean by small changes.

To quote Jane Goodall, a role model to many:

'What you do makes a difference,
you need to decide what difference you want to make.'

It's time to find your voice.

Of course, so many of you already have. You are already committed to building a better world and engaged in positive action. That's wonderful, you are ahead of the game. But here's the challenge, do more, aim higher! Not only can you have an even bigger impact, but you can also inspire and enable others to do more.

Here's just a few ways people like you and me, ordinary people, can build a better tomorrow around us.

As a positive influence, a caring but determined role model, for your family and friends. Encouraging a child, caring for a loved one, helping your partner realise their ambitions, having a difficult conversation with a friend because you know it's the right thing to do. I'm thinking now of two younger leaders I mentor. One is seeking to resolve a deep-rooted family dispute, the other is facing up to helping tackle a parent's addiction issues. Action that won't change the world but may just change someone's world.

By making a difference in your local community. Starting a gardening club, helping with a foodbank, organising a litter pick, running a play scheme.

By volunteering. There are so many opportunities. Becoming a scout leader, spending time with an elderly person, helping out at a care home, joining the trustee board of a local charity, getting involved with your local conservation charity.

If you lead a team at work, resolving to lead authentically, focusing on Mary's traits. Developing people in the team, building a values-based culture, creating a compelling vision, engaging your people.

If you line manage nobody, and work on the front line, become the best version of you. Care for your customers, be a positive influence on colleagues, choose your attitude, find better ways to do things, be proud of your work.

If you are head of, or a senior leader in an organisation, whatever its size, resolve to build something amazing. Create an environment where your people are inspired and enabled to give their best every single day. Be a positive role model. Align mission, strategy, processes and culture. Engage with and understand your audience. Set a clear and compelling vision, encourage others to grow, unlock potential, deliver the right results in the right way, be relentless, be the best version of you.

If it's community change you want to focus on, do so across your wider neighbourhood. Inspire people with what you have done more locally, push the boundaries, engage people, secure funding, improve lives.

Set up your own charity focused on something close to your heart. Whatever you choose - young people, wildlife, the environment, elderly people, health related issues, education, do it with maximum effort, passion, resolve and belief.

If it's your bag get involved in politics. Start local. Focus on what you want to change, and never, ever stop being authentic.

Believe in yourself.

'What lies behind us and what lies before us are tiny matters compared to what
lies within us'.

Ralph Waldo Emerson.

This is your call to arms. It doesn't matter if you want to build a better world for one person or a thousand people. Be authentic, be the best version of you, find your voice and deliver the change.

'Walk with the dreamers. The believers. The courageous. The cheerful.
The planners. The Doers. The successful people with their heads in the
clouds and their feet on the ground. Let their spirit ignite a fire within you
to leave this world better than when you found it.'

Wilferd Arian Peterson

You have the potential to do so much. Ignite that fire inside you, be the spark that lights other fires. Together on the pages ahead we will meet ordinary people, everyday heroes, who have changed lives, and explore together a framework that will equip you for a lifetime building a safer, fairer, kinder, happier world.

Together, we'll find your voice.

Reflections

Section II

Mary Re-Visited

Pre-amble

Mary first popped into my head over Christmas 2012. As much as I enjoy the main days of the festive season (I live in a Christmas obsessed home!) I've always loved those quieter few days between Christmas and New Year. I find they give me time to catchup with myself and to think.

I'd been running leadership programmes, and facilitating, coaching and consulting, for a decade already but had been aware for a while an opportunity existed to pull my views, teaching and material into one place. I could build a more focused and coherent set of leadership programmes. I wanted to put it all together into a book of some sort. I had no pretensions of it becoming a best seller, my own version of imposter syndrome saw to that, but I was anxious to develop a workbook, which could double as a learning journal and reference tool post programmes.

I've no idea where the name Mary came from. I wanted to build the book around a central character, and somehow the Mary emerged and stuck. I was aware it was an old-fashioned name (but then so is Barry!) and also that it was of the female gender. There was no particular relevance to this, plenty of men I know lead like Mary, and plenty of women don't, it just felt right.

When I mentioned the working title to friends some raised the issue of religious connotations with the chosen name. I guess that should have occurred to me but it had passed me by. A quick Google search revealed a possible issue, but by now my mind was made up, Mary it was and Mary it would be. For the sake of clarity the name has no religious relevance in this case.

The structure of the book was clear to me from the beginning. I wanted to share the deep-rooted principles which shape and influence all my beliefs and teaching, It was essential to position Mary as an authentic leader who could exist anywhere. I was determined to outline my views of the traits that truly effective authentic leaders consistently demonstrated.

My research and reference points came partly through reading. Two books in particular inspired me and helped shape my understanding of leadership.

Firstly, 'The 7 Habits of Highly Effective People' by Stephen Covey. I had been lucky enough to attend a '7 Habits' leadership workshop a few years before and the powerful descriptions of principle-centred leadership truly inspired me. It was this material which introduced me to inside-out leadership and enabled my understanding that leadership is a whole-life activity. I will refer to this material on a number of occasions in this book.

The second was 'Good to Great' by Jim Collins. I loved that Collins and his research team amassed a strong evidence base to support the six common factors they identified which are demonstrated by highly effective and sustainably great companies. I was introduced for the first time to 'Right People on the Bus', 'Freedom within a Framework' and 'Zoom Out' meetings, concepts that are now embedded at the heart of my teaching and have become a common language for so many when discussing great leadership.

However, although these books were important, it was my observation and experience of so many different types of leaders I had worked with over more than thirty years that provided me with the perfect opportunity to develop my thinking on what makes a great leader.

Unfortunately, much of the leadership I experienced in my corporate days was at best poor and at worst frankly appalling. The approach was top down, autocratic, often threatening, too often bullying. Not surprisingly that created a toxic culture based on low trust and high blame. As a result people kept their heads down and so much potential was never unleashed. There was no encouragement to think for yourself, the 'grown ups' would tell you what to do.

Here's the thing, you can learn as much from observing and experiencing how not to lead as you can from inspiring leaders.

Conversely, since launching my own business in 2002, I have been privileged to support and observe some great leaders. The chasm between those and the corporate leaders above is vast. Although all individuals, there are common themes. I see high humility, low egos, genuine people determined to do the right thing in the right way. I see passion. People choose to follow them because of who they are not the position they hold. Above all they are authentic. They are also focused, determined to succeed, but always through their people. Authenticity and determination, it's a powerful cocktail. Mary is a fictional character, but she is based on the very best of these leaders.

Slowly, one by one, I compiled the traits I most commonly and consistently saw these leaders demonstrate. As they emerged, they dovetailed neatly with the principle of inside-out leadership. Mary's first four traits are her character traits, they define who Mary is, and lie deep within the inner circle, where we lead ourselves. The remaining six traits are about what Mary does, how she gets the best out of those people around her, unlocking potential in the middle circle.

From that thinking the very simple *'Lead Like Mary'* model emerged...

Although in my head I had an emerging picture of what each trait was about, I needed to articulate them. At that time I was publishing a weekly blog and so, for the following few weeks, I focused on one trait each time, explaining and developing my thinking. As much for my benefit as anyone else.

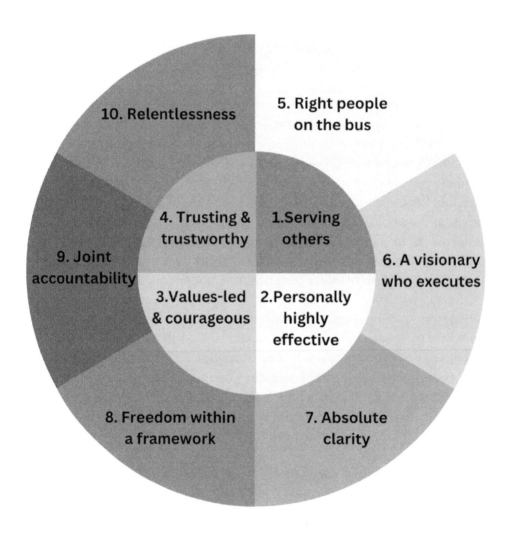

As winter turned into spring I needed to test the traits with a live audience. An opportunity presented itself in an already iconic venue, a training room overlooking the Olympic Stadium, less than a year after the vibrant spectacle of London 2012 which had showcased all that is great about our country.

I presented *'Lead Like Mary'* for the first time to a room full of charity leaders and was happy enough with the reception to move forward with increased confidence. The next few months were spent drafting and redrafting the chapters, seeking feedback from a small group of people I trusted to be honest and objective - the right people on the bus.

By early 2014, a year after the project commenced, the final draft was submitted and *'Lead Like Mary'* was published, soon followed by a launch event, a proud moment indeed!

Over the years that followed I developed my *'Lead Like Mary'* programmes, public and corporate, and have presented them on numerous occasions, first face to face before, like so much else, then moving them online as the pandemic emerged.

I've reviewed the traits many times since, questioning their continued relevance, but, with one exception, I have remained happy with them. The only change I have made is a small but very significant redraft of the second trait. Rather than *'Mary is personally highly effective'* I now go with *'Mary strives to be personally highly effective'*, recognising the self-evident fact that being truly highly effective is a life-long goal we can pursue but cannot achieve. However, we can constantly strive to be.

Let us revisit Mary's ten traits. My intention is not to repeat everything in *'Lead Like Mary'* (I am hoping you have read it, if not I hope you will order your copy today!) Rather it is to add any observations and thoughts almost a decade on, based on the numerous conversations I have had on leadership, that most fascinating of subjects, with many, many people on my programmes, coaching and mentoring assignments, through on-line forums and my own on-line leadership community.

Reflections

Serving Others

'I stand here before you not as a prophet,
but as a humble servant of you, the people.'

Nelson Mandela

The trait in 20 words.

Mary cares about people, seeks to unleash their potential but also holds them accountable and never ducks a difficult conversation.

Over the years since *'Lead Like Mary'* was published, I have explained to countless numbers of people that Mary's first trait - she truly believes her first role as a leader is to serve others - was the hardest to decide to include. To this day it remains the most nebulous.

It's easy to reach out and touch the other nine traits, absolute clarity and joint accountability are much more objective, serving others is not.

I thought long and hard about originally including it, but every time I wavered, I kept coming back to the understanding that every great leader I had encountered seemed to share this belief. It was buried deep inside them and defined every aspect of the way they led themselves and others.

Indeed, I would now go further. In my honest opinion, backed by many years of evidence, I contest it is simply not possible to be a truly authentic leader without this belief. I also am certain this first trait is the essential point of entry from which every other trait flows. If you were not committed to serving others why would you focus on giving them clarity, encouraging freedom with support, practicing joint accountability?

It completely dovetails with the point about ego. A genuine commitment to serving others cannot co-exist with someone who has an inflated ego. Those who have this belief are high in humility and low in ego.

What do I mean by serving others? What is this first trait all about? It means that deep inside us we are committed to the idea of service. We want others to grow, to flourish, to realise their potential. We care deeply about them, we are determined to guide and assist their development. We believe in being kind to others, we take pride in their achievements.

It is crucial to understand that serving others does not mean being subservient. You are not there to be at their beck and call, to take on all their problems, to do their job for them. Far from it.

The problem with the very term 'serving others' is that it can have negative connotations. We associate it with the word 'servant.' Let me repeat the crucial point, there is nothing subservient about serving others. It's about caring for your people, helping them develop, being there for them, but when we serve others we also hold them to account, challenge them, push them to grow, take them out of their comfort zone, have difficult conversations, address uncomfortable realities, get them to face unpalatable truths. Only when we do these things as well when they are necessary, are we truly serving others.

If one of our friends is in an abusive relationship, but is in denial, we may decide we need to intervene for their sake. That intervention, initially at least, might not be welcomed, but if we believe it is the right thing to do we cannot ignore it.

If a team member lacks the confidence to take on a new challenge and we are convinced it is the right thing to do for their growth and personal development, we should take the right steps to overcome that lack of confidence, even if initially at least it is an uncomfortable experience for them.

If another team member is exhibiting poor behaviours, we are not serving them (or others) if we ignore it. We must intervene, seek to find the reasons, and hold them to account if appropriate.

When we start to understand the concept of leading by serving others, and look around us, we can begin to recognise those leaders who have this belief and demonstrate it through their actions every single day.

It's the leader who knows their friend is unhappy in their job and makes the time to listen to them, in an empathetic and non-judgmental way, and when they understand why they are unhappy helps them find the solutions, whatever they may be.

It's the leader in a community who every week or month, organises a lunch club for senior citizens, providing a hot meal in warm, convivial surroundings and much needed company.

It's the leader in the workplace who notices one of their colleagues is struggling with their workload and takes the time to assist, enabling them to resolve the issues themselves

It's the team leader who gives one of their people responsibility for an important project, knowing their capability while recognising their lack of self-belief, who offers just the right balance of support and encouragement that enables the team member to successfully deliver and to grow.

One more thought- you can't fake this belief. You either have it deep inside you or you don't.

Leaders who believe their first role is to serve others are everywhere. They can even be found leading nations (and how I wish there were more of them). Over the past few years much attention and praise has been focused on Jacinda Ardern, Prime Minister of New Zealand.

Here's her own quote:

> *'Everything I have ever thought about doing*
> *has been in some sense about helping people.'*

The thing with that quote is I reckon most world leaders would say the same thing, but how many really mean it? How many would demonstrate it with their actions every single day?

Jacinda Ardern does.

Outside New Zealand she particularly came to the fore with her leadership through the global pandemic. From the very beginning of the outbreak, in early 2020, as other world leaders dithered, she moved swiftly and acted decisively, while effectively communicating the thinking behind those actions to her nation's five million citizens. She took a 20% pay cut in solidarity with those who lost their jobs and were struggling. She displayed a different kind of leadership, one which put kindness at the top of the agenda. She communicated directly with her people, thanking her 'team of five million' for their great efforts and sacrifices. Throughout she was concise and direct about her strategy while being honest about her concerns.

I understand there are others who argue that Ardern took the wrong route in her approach by addressing the pandemic head on. Let history be the judge, my point is around her commitment to serving others, her clarity and determination, her compassion and communication skills.

It wasn't the first time she had demonstrated her authenticity during a national crisis. In March 2019 a dreadful terrorist attack on the Muslim community in Christchurch left 51 dead. Once again Ardern combined strength and courage with compassion. At a news conference she said of the victims

'They chose New Zealand because it was safe, because it was no place for hatred or racism. Because we represent diversity, kindness, compassion, home for those who share our values.'

Addressing the perpetrator directly she said

'You might have chosen us- we utterly reject and condemn you.'

Her next action? She immediately implemented tighter gun laws across the nation.

Her authentic leadership is not just demonstrated in moments of national crisis, it's implicit in her approach to motherhood and multi-tasking, (she was the first head of government to give birth in office since Benazir Bhutto). Jacinda has a passion to address climate change *('I see ourselves as having a responsibility to demonstrate that we can and will lead the change'),* works to improve women's rights and listens to children.

Jacinda Ardern again.

'To me leadership is not about necessarily being the loudest in the room, but instead being the bridge, or at least the thing that is missing in the discussion and trying to build a consensus from there.'

Postscript: On 19 January 2023 Jacinda announced she was standing down as New Zealand's Prime Minister citing burnout and that she no longer had 'enough in the tank' to lead. When I heard the news three thoughts emerged.

Firstly, what an amazingly brave decision. As we will explore later in the book, looking after ourselves, our mental and physical well-being, is more important than anything. It's too easy to try to soldier on. Knowing the right time to step back and having the courage to do so is typical of the woman.

Secondly, the world is definitely a poorer place following Jacinda's decision. She is a wonderful example of an authentic leader, if there were more world leaders like her the world would be on the way to being that safer, fairer, kinder, happier place.

Finally, I predict we have not heard the last of her. She is still just 42. Whatever she chooses to do next, wherever she decides to focus her efforts, she will have a positive impact. Indeed, as I write, I hear she has joined the Board of Prince William's Earthshot charity.

Jacinda concluded her announcement by saying she hoped her legacy would be 'as someone who always tried to be kind.'

She continued

'I hope I leave New Zealanders with a belief that you can be kind, but strong, empathetic but decisive, optimistic but focused. And that you can be your own kind of leader - one who knows when it's time to go.'

As I wrote *'Lead Like Mary'* I became more and more convinced that every truly great leader I came across demonstrated their deep-rooted belief that their first role as a leader is to serve others. The new thinking in this book moves my belief to another level. Why would anyone commit to building a better tomorrow for others unless the belief in serving others was deeply ingrained within them?

Reflections

Personally Highly Effective

*'It's your determination to take control of your life
that drives how fulfilled your life will be.'*

James Grebey

The trait in 20 words

**Mary strives to be the best version of herself focusing on her well-
being, work/life balance and time management.**

When teaching Mary's traits, I go out of my way to consistently make the
point they are all equally important. Each is important in its own right
but they are also highly interdependent, together they become the force
they are, in building effectiveness and delivering results.

However, the more I witness people everywhere struggling to be
effective, inside and outside work, because of the stuff life throws at us,
the more I believe this one may just be (with apologies to Jeffrey Archer)
first among equals.

We already confirmed in the pre-amble today I would re-title this trait
'Mary strives to be personally highly effective', reflecting the fact no-one
is perfect, we all make mistakes, we just need to learn from them.

Time and time again these days I come across people who are
overwhelmed with everything on their plate. This may be happening at
work, with so much to do, conflicting priorities, limited resources and
support, others gate crashing our schedules with stuff important to them,

email inboxes rammed with irrelevances. They may well be working excessive hours to try and cope, creating more stress and guilt as they compromise on family time.

If you recognise this person, stick with this book, I'll share a framework later which can bring all of this back under control.

Or the issues may be outside work. Conflict in relationships, money worries, health concerns, anxiety and stress, all of these will impact on our effectiveness.

Remember the inside-out leadership model, if we don't take care of ourselves first, how can we be effective with others?

In *'Lead Like Mary'*, leaning heavily on Stephen Covey's 'The 7 Habits of Highly Effective People', I set out six principles which define personal effectiveness.

They were:

Mary models the behaviours she wants to see in others.

Mary tries to keep an open mind and to challenge beliefs

Mary understands she can always make choices and strives to make the right choices

Mary sets clear goals at every level

Mary manages her time as effectively as she can, focusing on what is truly important

Mary constantly acts to re-energise herself.

As I read them again, I remain happy these statements represent a good summary of personal effectiveness.

Let's revisit just a few of them.

We must model the **behaviours** we want to see in others. If we are the boss and want to establish a work-life balance within our team, how can we expect to if they see us working until 10pm at night and answering emails on a Sunday? How can we expect our friends to keep confidences if we can't ourselves? Why should our children be diligent in completing their homework if we show no interest in what they are doing or boast about cutting corners at work? Other people watch us constantly, we must model the right behaviours.

Keeping an open mind and challenging both ours and other people's **beliefs** is just so important. How often do you come across people with closed minds, who refuse to countenance alternative views to their own, who are convinced they are right all the time? The beliefs they hold within those closed minds determine the way they act and behave, which in turn determine the results they are getting. All too often those results only serve to re-enforce the beliefs they had to start with. They are stuck in a beliefs-behaviours-results-beliefs cycle.

When we come across someone with a closed mind, we may well find their beliefs are stalling any progress. For example, if they are in an unhappy relationship, they might feel they have no alternative, *'it's just the way life is'* you will hear them say (incidentally there's a wonderful link to the principle of choice there, coming up next). Their behaviours and actions, driven by that belief, might include arguments, resignation, a feeling of despair. Nothing changes as a result, re-enforcing their view that they have no alternative.

Likewise, if someone feels they can't challenge the behaviour of their boss at work because it's unsafe to do so how will they act and behave?

Obvious really, they won't raise issues, they'll tolerate the behaviour, they might just look for another job. What results do they get? None different. They are stuck in that beliefs-behaviours-results-beliefs cycle.

If we see either of these scenarios playing out I think we have a responsibility, a duty, to intervene, to challenge the beliefs of our friend or colleague or whoever, to help them see a situation differently. For any significant change leading to transformational results is only possible when there is a change of beliefs.

What about you? What beliefs do you have that might be holding you back? It takes a high dose of self-awareness and courage to even begin to examine your own beliefs. It doesn't mean all the beliefs you have, about yourself, other people, situations, are wrong, of course they're not. Many are the right beliefs, and are driving the right behaviours, actions and results, but which are the ones which are preventing you from making progress?

What about **choice**? I never find this principle easy to teach, it takes some getting, but when we understand we always have choices it can be extraordinarily liberating. Have you ever heard someone say *'I have no choice'*? Do you ever hear yourself saying it? It's simply not true. We always have choices. If we are unhappy at work and we think we don't have a choice what do we do? We gripe, we complain, we apportion blame, we spread negative energy. When we understand we have choices the situation changes dramatically. We may well be unhappy but there are so many choices we can make. We can examine why we are unhappy, chat to a friend, speak to our boss, approach the HR team.

We can also choose to leave our job. There may well be consequences if we do, mouths to feed, next month's rent or mortgage to pay, but don't let's mask an understanding of the principle. You have that choice, we always have choices. As ever, it's about making the right choice.

One more. If someone is in an unhappy relationship, even an abusive one, do they have a choice? Yes they do, they can choose to leave that relationship. The consequences, which may be around children, money, guilt, even violence, may well make that course of action very difficult, but doesn't mean choice doesn't exist.

Final thought, from this moment onwards you can make a choice. You can choose to be a positive influence on those around you, to be happy, to be a role model, to make a difference.

We always have choices.

Reflections

Values-Led and Courageous

'Live so that when your children think of fairness and integrity they think of you.'

H Jackson Brown Jr.

The trait in 20 words

Mary has a deeply rooted set of personal values which guide her decision making, enabling her to act with courage.

Living by our values, being values-led, is such a powerful concept. Every piece of evidence I have amassed over many years of observing and studying leaders of every shape and size has led to the same conclusion. Great leaders, wherever they are found, heading up or deep inside organisations, at home, in the community, base their decision making on deep-rooted principles, their values.

I believe it's the primary factor that makes great leaders stand out from not only the poor and mediocre ones but even the good ones.

'The most important thing about leadership is your behaviour and the values that guide your life.'

Brenda Barnes

The more I've thought about this since *'Lead Like Mary'* was published, the more I've realised that so many other of her traits emanate from being values-led. It's her value of service that leads her to serve others, her value of striving to be effective that focuses her on time management, goal setting and being the best version of herself, her values of trust, clarity, growth and never giving up, make her the person she is.

A similar picture emerges on *'Lead Like Mary'* programmes when I ask participants to share the story of someone who has had a positive impact on their lives. I've already mentioned this exercise earlier. Whether they choose a parent, friend, teacher, teammate, fellow volunteer, boss, colleague or famous person, and I've had multiple examples of each of these, their description of why that particular person was so important to them commonly covers areas like:

'They always found time for me'

'They were there for me when I needed them.'

'They listened to me.'

'They trusted me.'

'They believed in me.'

'They encouraged me to grow.'

It's not difficult to make the link to values like service, listening, growth and trust.

A grounding built upon a strong values framework can also help us to be ourselves. How many people do you come across who put on an act at work, pretending to be someone they're not? They often display the need to maintain control of themselves, not to let their guard down, not to display any emotions. All of which is designed to not show any weakness. At work they are a very different person to who they are at home.

Notice all the 'not-to's' in that last paragraph. Values-led people are just so different. They bring their true selves to work. They let their guard down and are not scared to show emotions. When they don't know the answer they're not afraid to admit it. That sounds like an authentic leader to me.

Never was this better demonstrated than during the early stages of the pandemic. I worked with authentic leaders who came to the fore. They cared for their people, showed compassion, listened, understood that everyone's circumstance were different, while at the same time facing up to the current reality, making the tough decisions, determined to do the right thing in the right way.

Those weeks and months took many of us into unchartered waters, it was a scary time, leaders were not immune from their own challenges at home. Sometimes it was just overwhelming, and I watched leaders cry, overwhelmed by the challenges they faced. Be yourself, be genuine, never put on an act.

'Leadership simply begins with the courage to be yourself
so that everyone else can be too.'

Umair Haque

Don't lose sight of the second part of this trait. It's being values-led that enables us to be courageous, to take the hard decisions, to stand up and be counted, to put ourselves out there, to be brave.

When our decision making is rooted in our values we know what the right thing to do is, and that gives us the courage to do that right thing.

Living your values, being courageous, finding your voice is the very essence of what this book is about. We shall return to it many times.

Reflections

Trusting and Trustworthy

'I prefer to give my trust a hundred times and risk being disappointed two or three times, than to live perpetually in an atmosphere of mistrust.'

Kamel A.

The trait in 20 words

Mary's first inclination is always to trust others. Extending trust is the way to enable people to grow and flourish.

Exploration of this trait has led to some fascinating conversations over the past few years. Part of it, of course, is easy to grasp. Mary is highly trustworthy - authentic and genuine leaders always are. It's an integral part of her values system.

It's my proposition that she is trusting which stimulates the debate. That her first inclination is always to trust.

Trust is such a simple word but, in my view, one of the most powerful words in the world. It's defined by the Oxford English Dictionary as:

'Firm belief in the reliability, truth or ability of someone or something.'

Trust lies at the heart of everything. Picture in your mind your most truly important, valuable, productive, special and effective relationships, the ones you cherish the most, the ones that produce the best outcomes, that are the most rewarding. It could be with your life partner, a child, a friend, a colleague, a team member. What is at the heart of those relationships? I would lay a sizable wager that the word trust comes up pretty quickly. Now think of the opposite. This may be painful. Think of a relationship that has severed, fallen apart. I'm guessing a lack of trust, a breakdown of trust, was a root cause.

This quote is so true.

'When people feel trusted, they'll do almost anything under the sun not to disappoint the person who gave them the gift of trust'

Rob Lebow

Every great team I have ever been part of at work has trust at its core. Where there is high trust people just get on with things, micro-management is unnecessary, people are willing to stick their necks out, to take (calculated) risks. They support each other, look out for each other, there is a feeling of mutual pride, respect and achievement. They rely less and less on the traditional role of a boss, each member can step up and lead as necessary. They deliver the right results in the right way and they do so at pace- there is a direct link between the speed things move forward at in a high trust environment and economic or stakeholder benefit.

Let me give you an opposite example from my corporate past. Early in my career I took over the regional management of twenty pub businesses. Each pub had a manager and I was their boss. Wanting to make an impact and grow each business I arranged a date and time for a meeting with each manager, to get to know them, understand each business and draw up some plans. Reflecting back I should have picked up how surprised they were that I actually wanted to make appointments.

Back at the office were a team of stock takers. Nice chaps when you got to know them, but long in the tooth, had seen it all and were somewhat scary to a young guy like me. I'm trying not to be unkind here but 'dyed in the wool cynics' wouldn't be an unfair description. When they heard of my plan they were appalled. I was summoned to their office. 'What do you think you are doing?' they demanded. I tried to explain but they were having none of it. 'You can't go letting these managers know when you are visiting. How will you catch them out? Thieves every one of them.'

I kid you not, they were serious. It was a sign of the times. Most people doing my job played the role of policemen, making unannounced visits, suspicious. It's a pretty obvious statement that trust was non-existent. And it wasn't just that the stock takers and regional managers didn't trust their pub managers. Inevitably there was no trust in return.

It's no surprise the business was flatlining and getting anything done took so much time.

That example was of its time, the mid 1980s, and things will have changed significantly over the years, but it doesn't take a genius to work out that planning for business growth was non-existent.

Let me refer to another example, far more serious. In 1999 the Post Office began installation of its Horizon computer accounting system. Almost immediately sub-postmasters began reporting unexplained discrepancies and losses. The Post Office maintained that the system was robust and began prosecution for theft, false accounting and fraud. Between 1991 and 2015 there were 918 successful prosecutions. According to press reports these actions caused bankruptcy, divorce, unwarranted prison sentences and, tragically, one suicide.

In 2019 the High Court found that software issues and defects did exist that undermined the reliability of the system. By 2022, 555 convictions have been declared unsafe, and multi compensation claims are underway. The case constitutes the most widespread miscarriage of justice in British legal history.

One word lies at the heart of this scandal. Trust, or rather a complete lack of it. Alongside appalling leadership and no doubt a toxic culture.

In both those instances there was a failure to trust employees. The result when this happens may not be as traumatic as the Post Office, but will still lead to suspicion, resentment and stagnation.

When discussing this trait I think the conclusion people sometimes jump to is I am suggesting that people should always be given unlimited trust. This is simply not the case. There's a world of difference between a first inclination being to trust and a blank cheque.

Every situation is different and every person unique. The amount of trust Mary extends is based on an array of factors. What is the task that needs completing? How high is the risk if trust is misplaced? How much confidence does she have that the desired result will be delivered? What she will always have, however, is an inclination and desire to trust, a willingness to go just that bit further than can feel safe, and the belief and knowledge in the vast majority of circumstances, if she extends trust it will prove justified and reward handsomely.

If her trust is abused she will shut down firmly, but she knows it's the only route to people growing, potential being unleashed, things moving forward, results improving.

It's not just about trusting her team. She applies exactly the same principle at work with colleagues, her boss, partner organisations. Outside work it's with family, friends, fellow volunteers and so on.

When we talk about leading a team, there's a very important point to remember.

> *'A team is not a group of people who work together.*
> *A team is a group of people who trust each other.'*
>
> *Simon Sinek*

Trust really does lie at the heart of everything.

Reflections

Right People on the Bus

'People are not your greatest asset. The right people are your greatest asset.'

Jim Collins

The trait in 20 words

Getting the right people - a continuous journey based on nurturing and enabling growth, inspiring high performance and timely issue resolution.

I wonder when Jim Collins published his excellent *'Good to Great'* at the dawn of the new Millennium, whether he envisaged what a widely used term 'right people on the bus' would become?

It sure has and I throw my hands up as one of the more guilty perpetrators. It just works so well visually. People can picture a bus, they can see people (their team, their colleagues, whoever) on the bus and can picture where various people are sat. If they are the team leader they almost always agree with me that they need to be up front driving the bus. I have to say occasionally that's not the case, but it's usually for the right reasons - they want one of their team to be there taking over the driving. I do try to steer them (get it?) away from this perfectly laudable notion- I just think leaders of teams need to be visible, setting the direction, 'in the driving seat'.

The bus analogy has brought much creativity to my workshops. Asking the group to teach back their understanding of the principle is great fun. I've had entire training rooms rearranged into a life-sized bus, with participants moving from seat to seat to illustrate the issues and opportunities, beautiful drawings, cut outs and models of buses which must have taken hours to make at home, and many a toy bus in the room, appropriated from some poor child. We chat about people towards the front of the bus, good and great performers with the right attitudes and behaviours, those in the middle, some with feet on the seats in front gazing at the passing countryside, literally passengers on the bus, and those at the back, at worst making every effort to disrupt the journey.

It's not just me. Search online for 'Right People on the Bus' and peruse the images. Every shape and size imaginable!

All in all it's not hard to relate to the analogy. The challenge is doing something about it. How do we nurture the front seat passengers, engage and encourage the middle seat dreamers and deal with the disruptors? How do we ensure we have the right people on the bus to undertake our journey?

Often people on my programmes begin by telling me in no uncertain terms it's impossible. You can never get to a situation where everyone's up there in the front seats. They cite perfectly legitimate examples of inheriting a team. They weren't responsible for hiring them, in many cases have been landed with a crock of smelly stuff. I get that, but here's the thing. You cannot achieve all you want to deliver as the leader of the team unless you have the right people around you with the right attitudes. It's just not possible. So, whatever situation you inherit, you must give it your best shot. To settle for anything else is at best to accept mediocrity. Who wants to be known as the leader of mediocrity? Certainly not Mary, and if you're reading this book my best guess is not you.

I do believe that leading people is right up there with the hardest thing a leader does. It involves constant effort, sleepless nights, challenging conversations, difficult decisions. Stick at it and the rewards are amazing.

What have I learned since Mary was published? Loads, and it starts with the incredible opportunity recruiting to the team offers. One that is too often missed. Every time we recruit to fill a vacancy we should be raising the bar, bringing in talent and the right behaviours that improve the quality, performance and in due course, results of the team. Recruitment is strewn with potential pitfalls and trip wires.

Arising from literally hundreds of debates I've had with people over the last decade here's just a few thoughts which might at least reduce the problem of poor recruitment.

What is the actual role you need to recruit for?

This one's easy surely? Someone is moving on, advertise their job, get someone in to replace them. No, stop! Are you absolutely certain the departing person's role is really what you want the new person to do? Were they even doing the role in their job description, or had they been side-tracked over time, or made the job fit their particular interests? Step back, take some time, think, carve the right role first. Time spent thinking and planning up front will save lots of missed opportunity down the line.

How well do we sell ourselves?

You want to recruit great people. So does everyone else. There's a host of organisations out there competing for the best talent. Great people have so much choice, and they will carefully choose who they want to work for. We have to sell ourselves as much as we expect applicants to do the same. Why should a great person choose to join you? A competitive salary and benefits package is obviously important, but may I suggest often less important now than an engaging culture, inspirational leadership, a meaningful purpose and connected values.

How clunky are your recruitment processes? Do they make applying to join you easy, a streamlined process? Review your recruitment material through the eyes of an applicant. It can be an eye-opening experience!

Never rely on interview alone

Too often when people recruit it's done at speed, based on an interview only, which nowadays may even be by Teams or Zoom. Stop! That's not good enough. Interviews alone present potential pitfalls. Some people can bull s*** their way through, while others freeze and don't do themselves justice, even though they might be just what you're looking for. In both cases the candidates have not been exposed to a range of recruitment options.

By all means have interviews (plural preferably) as the centrepiece of your recruitment process, but wrap around that a menu of options including a presentation, tests, practical demonstration (if relevant), group exercises etc.

I understand all of this takes time and resource, but you owe it to yourself and the candidates to be thorough. It can only increase your chance of finding that right candidate.

Involve a wide range of people in the process (and listen to them)

I'm a great believer in involving a significant number of people in the recruitment process. Mix and match options could include peers the successful applicant will work with, or a colleague of yours not directly involved but who's judgement you trust. Why not even let the team 'interview' their prospective new boss? Don't forget your receptionist. They are a goldmine of information. How do the candidates act and behave in an informal setting? It can often be very different to their interview.

Ensure you take feedback from all involved. That doesn't necessarily mean you'll act on what you hear, but it will be invaluable in informing your decision.

Focus on cultural fit above capability

You want someone who will hit the ground running, delivering results from day one. Or do you? More and more now organisations are prioritising the right cultural fit above performance expectations, at least in the short term. They seek to appoint the person with the right behaviours, knowing they can develop skills and performance. Of course, if you can get both that's wonderful, seems like win-win to me.

It can be hard when recruiting to gain insight into how the candidates will prove to have the right behaviours. Focus on asking for evidence and giving examples of situations they have found themselves in. You might also organise an exercise of some sort (group or individual) where behaviours will be demonstrated. Or, and here's my favourite, so many organisations recruit people from others they are already familiar with (maybe through previous employment, competitors or partner organisations). So many of you operate in incestuous worlds. Lean on that, call someone you know and trust, and get the inside track.

'If in doubt don't recruit'

The big one. We've all been there. We need to recruit for a role, it needs filling quickly. We are down to the final two candidates. They're both 'ok', in fact one is maybe slightly more 'ok' than the other. We appoint.

It may well work out, but all too often it doesn't. At best we've settled for mediocrity. The middle of the bus. We need to remember the old adage, 'recruit in haste, repent at leisure.'

We may reach the end of a recruitment process, down to the last candidate. It's looking good, nearly every box ticked. Take that breath, step back. There is still a niggling doubt. It could be something fed back to you from their prospective colleagues or team, a chance remark to the receptionist, a couple of years missing from the CV, concerns about them performing under pressure (although they do a neat Bohemian Rhapsody- old joke...).

Don't confirm the appointment until you've settled the niggle. Call them back one more time, drill deep, and only then make your decision.

'If in doubt don't recruit'. Make it your watch word. Hang it on your wall, give the HR team mugs with it printed on (they love a good cup of tea.)

Make arrival and induction a meaningful experience

I have heard this so many times. Someone goes through the recruitment process, is offered and accepts the job. They walk in purposefully, on Day 1, bright and early, bubbling with enthusiasm to be greeted by...no-one. Their computer and phone are not there, no induction has been organised, they don't even know where the bathroom is or where to hang their coat. Sounds familiar? Regrettably it is. What message are they being sent? It's so easy- warm welcome, basic needs, equipment and a well-planned induction.

Recruitment tips that just might help you get those right people on the bus.

There is a further thought on recruitment. When I say you should go out of your way to recruit people who will be a cultural fit, I am not advocating we build teams of identical automatons. Far from it. We need to seek a complementary multitude of talent and skills if we are to build a truly effective team.

It's important to employ people who are going to challenge you, not always be 'yes' people. We need rebels. But there's a world of difference between a good rebel and a bad rebel. Bad rebels break rules, obsess about problems, lecture, alienate, point fingers and are 'me' focussed. Good rebels, conversely, change rules, pursue opportunities, listen, attract, pinpoint causes and are mission focused. They are the ones you want!

There's a great graphic available on-line which explores what these good rebels want from their boss. It goes like this.

'We are not troublemakers. We are motivated to make our organisation better.'

'We care about work more than anyone else. That's why we are willing to engage in conflict.'

'We need an environment where it is safe to disagree and challenge the status quo.'

'Love our differences and quirks. We may not be like you and that's a good thing.'

'Challenge us. Give us the thorniest problems. We want to be stretched. Let us prove our ideas work.'

'Don't give us lip service, tell us like it is.'

'Coach us how to navigate organisational politics so we avoid making mistakes.'

'Rebelliousness is a positive behaviour, it's an act of courage and risk taking.'

'Appreciate us and we'll move mountains for you.'

As an authentic leader why would you not want a rebel or two like that in your team?

Let's move on. Think now about your good and great people, your real talent. The ones at the front of the bus. If you've got your copy handy, remind yourself of the Capability and Attitude Matrix featured in *'Lead Like Mary.'* These are your top right hand corner people, high scoring in capability/performance and behaviours/attitude. The glowing stars.

I continue to encourage use of this matrix as a desk-based tool and as a base point for team talent management discussions. It's a simple, robust and highly effective way of identifying and then addressing issues. Used with care it's also an incredibly powerful tool to open a difficult discussion with a team member.

How easy is it to ignore that top right talent? Why do we do that? Because we are so busy trying to sort issues and resolve problems elsewhere. We just don't have time to spend on them!

While struggling to find time is understandable, we ignore our best people at our peril. We run a real risk of losing them, by their very nature they are attractive to other potential employers. If we ignore them, we fail to get their best and may well end up losing them.

There is so much we can and must do. Here's just a few thoughts...

Spend time with them, in 1-1s and in more informal settings. Really get to know the whole person. What are their hopes, dreams and ambitions, their career expectations, what difference do they want to make? While I'm on the subject, cancel 1-1s at your peril. Think of the message it sends. For a whole lot more stuff on effective 1-1s, the bed rock of a successful boss and team member relationship, refer back to *'Lead Like Mary.'*

Focus with each individual on creating a development plan. However good they are there's room to be even more effective. I often complete the Capability and Attitude matrix with a leadership team and discover they have a whole number of people who have scores of 6, 7 or 8. Top right hand quadrant people. I ask them what they think and they seem satisfied. Beware, to quote Jim Collins

'Good is the enemy of the great.'

If things are good we become complacent. If you want to build something sustainably great you need great people. People who score 9-9 and above on the matrix. How do you get them there?

The most important thing is to devote time to them.

Create a development plan. Coaching, mentoring, education, training, secondments, shadowing may all have a role to play, remember every person is a unique individual.

Build a career plan. I realise this is far more difficult in smaller organisations where internal routes will inevitably be more limited. Here's the challenging message, their career plan may well involve a move out of your team, even your organisation. Why would you be willing to lose a good person? Because (if you are Mary) you are an authentic leader who has the courage to let people fly if it's the right thing to do. It may well be the case that your paths cross again. Very often what goes around comes around.

Give them more freedom (within a wider framework), set them challenging assignments, immerse them more in what you are doing, encourage, enable and celebrate their growth. Be careful, these are already busy people, don't overload them, but the more you push, the more they will flourish.

Most of all, inspire and engage them. Many people, particularly the younger ones, more and more want to work somewhere where the organisation's mission engages their spirit. Where they feel part of a noble purpose. This is especially true of, but not exclusive to, Millennials and Generation X. More on this later.

The other issue that is invariably discussed when I am working with groups on Right People on the Bus is what to do with the thorny issue of the wrong people, how to act when someone needs to leave the bus.

I appreciate this is a challenge, I would even go as far as to say it's the hardest thing a leader has to do. Bill enjoys throwing people off the bus, Sidney would never tackle the issues. Mary does not enjoy having a difficult conversation, she may well have a sleepless night before, but she never ducks that conversation. Her oft repeated mantra is to do the right thing in the right way.

The moment I find particularly frustrating is when I am working with some (not all by any means) voluntary sector organisations. People say something along the lines of 'we're a charity, we don't sack people.'

If that's true, it's an absolute nonsense! Dismissal should also be a last resort, and over many years I have learned it very rarely comes down to that, but to declare it would never happen is crazy. At the very least it's condemning the organisation to long term mediocrity. A failure to resolve issues of behaviour and performance will result in great people choosing to work elsewhere.

So how should you deal with this most difficult of challenges? First by never forgetting two mantras:

'if you want to achieve sustainable greatness, as a team or organisation, you cannot do so with the wrong people on the bus.'

'When you know you have a people issue, act.'

Some thoughts to consider:

Your first commitment should be to do all you can (to a point) to make the wrong person the right person. This means tackling under performance, poor behaviours, or both. Do so by engaging with the individual, being positive and caring, but also assertive and determined. Provide evidence in support of your concerns. This is easier when poor performance is the issue, more difficult when it's about behaviours, but evidence is essential. Dig deep and listen effectively. What are the real reasons for the issues, it may be nothing to do with work, it could be outside work factors affecting performance or behaviours. Fix an action plan and demonstrate joint accountability. Set clear targets, time scales, support available and consequences. If you do so and ensure absolute clarity of expectations you can now hold the person accountable for delivering the plan.

If this doesn't work, you cannot let things drift. Involve your HR support. At the risk of upsetting my many HR friends and clients, can I just focus on that word 'support.' HR people are rightly there to ensure you follow due process, and to protect the organisation, but if you are doing the right thing in the right way they should work with you. The good ones do.

If someone does need to leave your bus there are many ways of achieving this. As I said before, in my experience dismissals are rare, there is often a more pragmatic resolution which works for both parties. Often this starts with a 'protected conversation', an off-the-record meeting with the individual. Talk with HR before taking this step but I find time and time again it can pave a way forward to a resolution satisfactory to both parties.

Too often people are simply on the wrong bus. They may not realise it at the time but stepping off at a bus stop and boarding the right bus is the right thing, and they will recognise and acknowledge that further down the line.

Mary is no advocate of a 'sack them' approach to managing people. She always tries to help and encourage people to move forward on the bus. But neither does she procrastinate and avoid difficult conversations and issues. She is caring but decisive. It's her hallmark.

When you know you have a people issue, act. Do so with dignity and determination. Always do the right thing in the right way and you won't go far wrong.

Recruitment, retention and resolution. The three challenges leaders of teams face every day. Remember where we started - getting the right people on the bus is never-ending. It can and should also be the most rewarding thing you do.

Reflections

A Visionary Who Executes

'The visionary starts with a clean sheet of paper and reimagines the world.'

Malcolm Gladwell

The trait in 20 words

Mary creates an inspirational and engaging picture of the future and a clear route to making that vision a reality.

I was concerned when I first began to articulate this trait people might struggle with the use of the word 'visionary'. It can bring forward images of Martin Luther King, Steve Jobs, Thomas Edison and Bill Gates, people who really have changed the world.

Balance that against my assertion anyone can be a leader, and any leader needs to be visionary. Whatever position or role we have, inside and outside work, we need to be visionary if we are to change and improve things.

It's one of the 34 strengths of leaders identified by Tom Rath in his excellent 'Strengths Finder 2.0' material. He calls it 'Futuristic.' Here's an extract of his description of the trait.

'You are the kind of person who loves to peer over the horizon. The future fascinates you. You are a dreamer who sees visions of what could be. People look to you to describe your visions of the future. They want a

picture that can raise their sights and therefore their spirits. You can paint it for them. Choose your words carefully. Make the picture as vivid as possible.'

My concern was valid, I do find myself frequently having to explain my use of the word. It occurs to me that I could have called the trait 'Sets a Clear Goal and Delivers It,' but that really doesn't light my fire.

This trait is an important one for me from a personal perspective as well. A few years ago I completed the Strengths Finder material, which identifies your five biggest strengths from that list of 34. I'd second guessed some of the ones I expected to make my top 5, including positivity, empathy and developer. They did indeed make the list but my number one strength was futuristic. Reflecting on this I realised I am passionate when working with clients to persuade them to focus on the future, whether it's facilitating the creation and development of an organisation's strategic plan, putting together a project vision or helping someone create a personal life plan.

I really do believe leadership is not complicated. Remember it's about 'coping with today and building a better tomorrow'. To build a better tomorrow we must be able to paint a picture of what we want it to look like. That's all that I mean by visionary.

Building a better tomorrow is not the sole responsibility of those people at the top of organisations. Whatever level leaders are at the need to be visionary is just as important. The extent of the vision will be different- at the top it might be a vision for the whole organisation, further down it could be a project contributing to the bigger picture, the principle is the same.

As ever the same applies in our lives outside work. Now the picture of the future could be about a gap year, travel plans, house move, family celebration, community projects and so on.

Most importantly it needs to be inspirational, something worthwhile, needed, taking you somewhere better, that engages and excites others so much they want to climb onto your bus, fasten their seatbelt and come on the journey with you.

Being visionary is only part of this trait. Remember Bill Gates and his wise words *'vision without execution is daydreaming.'* Effective execution is crucial to make dreams become a reality. I've lost count of how many times I've witnessed great ideas fail because of imperfect execution.

Dip back into *'Lead Like Mary'* and take a look at John Kotter's eight step framework for delivering successful change. It's still the best I know and is a great guide for effective execution. Also look at how Mary's traits provide their own execution model- 'Absolute Clarity', 'Freedom Within a Framework', 'Joint Accountability' and being 'Relentless' are interdependent and essential facets.

Don't be put off if you still think the title of this trait is too grand. Focus on that picture of the future, whatever you want to call it. Painting a compelling future and making it happen is up there with the most exciting and important things leaders do.

Reflections

Absolute Clarity

'Life is really simple, but we insist on making it complicated.'

Confucius

The trait in 20 words

People only give their best when they have absolute clarity of what is expected of them and how to deliver.

One issue I commonly encounter when working with clients is the obsession people have of making things far more complicated than they need to be. I'm still no nearer to discovering the reason for this because most things in life are really simple and straightforward.

Nowhere is this better demonstrated at work than in our roles. Maybe it's to do with self- importance, or justifying our existence, whatever the reason I believe it's possibly the biggest barrier to people being truly effective.

To quote Bruce Lee

'Simplicity is the key to brilliance.'

I can already hear you sighing because I obviously don't understand your job. Stick with this, the Absolute Clarity trait is built around the following premise- whatever your role it can be broken down into one clear job purpose and a small number of focused objectives.

The purpose of any role should be crystal clear. We need to be able to articulate it in one simple sentence, a maximum of 20-25 words following on from the opening of 'my job exists to…'. Imagine your job was being advertised today. It should be the top line of the advert.

'We require a (job title) to… (job purpose)'.

On *'Lead Like Mary'* programmes I get participants to have a go at their own job purpose. They start off confidently, often followed by some pencil chewing and head scratching, before emerging with a fairly clear picture.

The problem comes when they reflect on what they've written and realise that, in reality, the job they are doing is somewhat removed from the intended purpose. That's because all too often we are given additional responsibilities, become unfocussed or have shaped the job to what we enjoy doing.

It's a harsh thing to say but too many organisations are full of people doing great jobs that don't need doing.

Which brings us to objectives (or goals) and a myriad, or maybe a minefield, of different approaches and levels of complexity. No two organisations seem to approach it in the same way, and few, in my opinion, manage to get to the point where the objectives are completely clear, relevant, timely and drive the right behaviours, actions and results.

In *'Lead Like Mary'* I introduced the concept of the 'Power of 3', arguing the optimum number of objectives (or goals) that we should focus on at any one time is 3, and we should be delivering on them for 70-75% of an effective week. Over the years since, this level of discipline has been a hard act to sell. Too often there is a belief that this is all very well in theory, but unrealistic in the real world where people have to juggle a myriad of competing priorities and a wide range of responsibilities. I get the impression that there's an underlying narrative of 'it's all very well you teaching this stuff Barry, but you're out of touch with the real world!'

I understand that argument, but I also know that, where teams and organisations have really gone for the 'Power of 3' and have stuck with it, breakthrough has been achieved and a step change in effectiveness and results has followed.

I'm a bit less concerned now there can only be three objectives, I'll stretch to four, even five at a push, but I still whole heartedly endorse an approach driven by simplicity and clarity.

I still come across people who have no objectives set for them. Just as bad is, when objectives are set at the beginning of the year (or halfway through too often!) as part of an appraisal or performance management process and never see the light of day again until the end of year review. In the meantime, people are left with little or no guidance on what they are supposed to be doing.

To understand the impact of this lack of clarity I reference later research originated by Stephen Covey. An extensive study revealed in typical organisations people spend on average 60% of their time engaged in activities that are simply not important to them. That's three days a week, time when they may well be helping other people be effective but are not being so themselves!

My proposition to you is that can be mostly resolved by focus on a limited number of clear, relevant, timely objectives.

The flow really is straightforward.

A crystal clear role purpose statement, which has line of sight to the organisation's overall mission.

3, 4, an absolute maximum of 5 crystal clear objectives which encompass the truly important elements of the job.

Let's try a fictional example. The General Manager of a hospitality business.

Purpose:

To inspire and enable the unit team to deliver excellent customer service, and to lead a safe and secure business.

Objectives:

Inspire and enable the unit team to deliver excellent customer service that delights customers and achieves a customer NPS score >+20

Ensure all relevant legislative and safety requirements, and financial controls and processes are strictly adhered to, delivering a >95% audit score.

Develop a three year strategic plan for the unit, to include market positioning, capital investment, a people and culture plan and financial targets. First draft complete by 1 November.

Lead a cross functional project team on behalf of the region to devise a new recruitment and retention strategy focused on talent, cultural fit and development opportunities. First draft prepared by 1 February.

Have another read of these. How simple are they, how clear are the expectations of the role? I am confident that in an effective week a disciplined GM will be able to achieve that target of 70-75% of their time focused on these four objectives.

Crucially, when they are so clear, it makes it far easier to challenge anything not directly linked to these four objectives. For example, the HQ Marketing team send an e-mail requesting information be collected on soft drink prices in ten competitor venues. They need the answer within 48 hours. This may well be important stuff for someone in Marketing (yes, really) but it's simply not a priority when viewed in the light of the four clear objectives. It may well be something the unit GM is willing to complete, very likely because they want to help and build a good relationship. In that case it's a good example of an activity that fits into the 25% remaining time.

I also maintain these four objectives, as well as being simple and clear, are relevant, timely and measurable, and at least three of them are forward looking and focused on building a better tomorrow.

A further observation, which to Command & Control managers is an anathema, is the objectives do not include specific performance numbers (sales, gross profit, costs). This is all too common, but I maintain they are an outcome of delivering the first two objectives above. Inspire and enable your people to deliver excellent customer service which delights customers, together with ensuring controls and are in place, and you will deliver the numbers.

To the final element of Absolute Clarity in *'Lead Like Mary'* - the assertion effective, regular 1-1s between line managers and team members are essential.

Far too frequently there is a disconnect between what senior teams believe happen and the reality on the ground. Senior teams tell me 1-1s are consistently happening, but a dive into their organisations quickly reveals this is simply not the case. They are sporadic, inconsistent and prone to regular late cancellations.

This is a crying shame and represents a massive missed opportunity. Effective 1-1s: forward looking, an opportunity to step back and zoom out, with a personal element and where the line manager sees their role as a coach are invaluable.

Whatever your role in an organisation, you will have a boss. I believe the opportunity to have a 1-1 with them on a regular basis is your right. If they are not happening make sure they do! If you manage a team please ensure they are at the heart of your relationships.

Final point- if you have objectives as clear as the unit GM example above, how easy does it make a significant portion of your 1-1s? These sessions are not task reviews and updates, hold those separately as needed. These objectives are the correct level to review at a monthly 1-1.   What progress since the last 1-1? What are the barriers to progress before the next 1-1 and how can you ensure joint accountability in overcoming them?

'Clarity is power. The more clear we are about what we want the more likely we are to achieve it.'

Billy Cox

Whatever you do focus on building absolute clarity. The principle is so simple and the rewards enormous.

Reflections

Freedom Within a Framework

*'All that is valuable in human society depends on the opportunity for development
accorded the individual.'*

Albert Einstein

The trait in 20 words

People grow and flourish when they have freedom within a framework of clarity, support and feel truly inspired and engaged.

It only took a short while after publishing *'Lead Like Mary'* to realise the title didn't do the contents of the chapter justice. 'Freedom Within a Framework' was an important element but the chapter also focused on the connected areas of engagement and culture.

Having said that, in my numerous client interactions 'Freedom Within a Framework' has become as much a quoted term as 'Right People on the Bus.'

I love it, I searched for many years for a description of empowerment and this one is perfect. Thank you so much to Jim Collins for introducing me to it.

Let's strip it back to basics. Great leadership is all about encouraging people to grow, to achieve more, to be more. Authentic leaders absolutely understand this simple principle. People have so much potential inside them, are capable of so much. Your job as a leader is to tap into that potential, nurture it, unleash it. It's the catalyst to building a better tomorrow. Provide the spark and watch people catch fire.

Contrast that with the Command & Control leader. They have little interest in, or intention to enable growth. They see their role as to tell people what to do, keep them on a short leash, micromanage them.

If your people don't grow how can you? Command & Control leaders constantly look down, not up. People can only grow when they are given as much freedom as possible, but only ever within a framework. If the framework didn't exist, if they were given unlimited freedom, you would be abandoning them, and I truly believe that is as dangerous as no freedom. There are two imperatives. The first is to get the level of freedom right, and that will always vary according to the individual and the task. The second is always to be committed to pushing the envelope- to give as much freedom as you possibly can.

Let's look at the difference and the impact in practice by returning to the four objectives for the hospitality unit GM introduced in the last chapter.

Inspire and enable the unit team to deliver excellent customer service that delights customers and achieves a customer NPS score >+20

Ensure all relevant legislative and safety requirements, and financial controls and processes are strictly adhered to delivering a >95% audit score.

Develop a three years strategic plan for the unit, to include market positioning, capital investment, people and culture plan and financial targets. First draft complete by 1 November.

Lead a cross functional project team on behalf of the region to devise a new recruitment and retention strategy focused on talent, cultural fit and development opportunities. First draft prepared by 1 February.

Let's assume our GM is a competent individual, and that their line manager, the Regional Manager, is an authentic leader who understands and believes in the principle of Freedom Within a Framework. The Regional Manager will set a clear framework with the GM. Clarity of end in mind, targets, 1-1 review dates, scope of decision making. The fourth objective illustrates the confidence the boss has. The GM will be encouraged to make the most of this example of peer leadership, a great development opportunity.

They will review progress against all four objectives at monthly 1-1s, the GM also knows they can make contact with their boss at any time if additional support is needed.

In this instance there is a wonderful opportunity for both the GM and Regional Manager to grow.

Consider an alternative. The GM is newer to the role, having recently been promoted. They are inexperienced but show great potential. In this instance it's highly unlikely the final objective would exist in that form. They may be a member of the regional project team, not lead it. The other three objectives remain completely valid but this time there might be weekly review meetings, reducing the level of autonomy. See what is happening here, Freedom Within a Framework is absolutely still being practiced, with a narrower framework.

Contrast this with our friend the Command & Control Regional Manager. With objectives 1&2 even an experienced GM will have little or no autonomy, will be subject to additional targets and controls, will expect weekly checking up meetings and daily phone calls. The Regional

Manager will almost certainly create the plan themselves with little or no involvement from the GM and they will similarly control any regional project team if one is established as well.

It's not difficult to speculate which approach will reap the best rewards!

It's also not difficult here to see the link between Mary's trait of Freedom Within a Framework and Trusting and Trustworthy. Giving any level of freedom requires trust. The higher the trust the greater the freedom.

When people are extended trust they respond so positively. Consider this quote from Rob Lebow:

'When people feel trusted, they'll do almost anything under the sun not to disappoint the person who gave them the gift of trust.'

A further quote to close.

'The growth and development of people is the highest calling of leadership.'

Harvey S Firestone.

Reflections

Joint Accountability

*'Feedback is a gift. Ideas are the currency of our next success.
Let people see you value both feedback and ideas.'*

Jim Trinka and Les Wallace.

The trait in 20 words

**Mary holds people accountable for delivering results but only if she has
provided the clarity, resources and support they need.**

At the risk of repeating my opening to Freedom Within a Framework, the
title Joint Accountability does not fully cover all included in this chapter.
A significant part of it focuses on the importance of feedback.

Mary places a massive emphasis on feedback. The reason is simple, she
is determined to improve. Whatever her role (at work and in her life
outside work) she knows she is far from the finished article. Her absence
of ego enables her to receive feedback with an open mind. She knows it
is crucial not to be defensive, the vast majority of feedback is given
honestly and constructively, it's the life blood that enables her to
improve.

There's an important point here. If you don't want or value feedback,
you will have a closed mind, you will not seek it, therefore you will get
little. The bit you get, if it is remotely critical, will not be believed.
Imagine Bill or Sidney receiving a 360 degree appraisal. Bill will storm

around blaming everyone else, seeking to find out who said what, while Sidney will withdraw to behind the filing cabinet!

Now see how different Mary's approach is. She will ensure she opens up numerous feedback routes. At work consider the following opportunities.

Internal, formal: 360 degree appraisal, feedback session with team, staff satisfaction survey, 1-1 with boss, interviews with or survey to internal customers

Internal, informal: ad hoc chats with team members, boss, peers and internal customers.

External, formal: NPS customer satisfaction survey (for a full explanation of NPS refer to *'Lead Like Mary'*), customer focus groups, interviews with customers and partner organisations.

External, informal: customer visits, phone calls.

Time for reflection is a very important part of Mary's week. Having received feedback she needs time to consider it and devise actions. She schedules this time, often choosing to take a stroll while reflecting,

I've not a lot to add on Joint Accountability. People don't find it a difficult concept to grasp. The link with Freedom Within a Framework is important. When you give someone freedom, accountability goes hand in hand with it.

'I recommend that the Statue of Liberty on the East Coast should be supplemented by a Statue of Responsibility on the West Coast.'

Viktor E Frankl.

Equally you can't hold someone accountable unless you demonstrate joint accountability. This is the framework, and includes providing clarity of what is required, necessary resources, 1-1 formal reviews and informal support.

My final thought concerns responsibility when things go wrong. It's inevitable from time to time that they will. In these circumstances Mary and Bill demonstrate diametrically opposed approaches. To borrow from Jim Collins and 'Good to Great', when things go well Bill looks in the mirror while Mary looks out of the window. When things go wrong the opposite occurs.

To quote General Bruce Clarke:

'When things go wrong in your command start searching for the reason in increasingly large circles around your own desk.'

Reflections

Relentless

'Leadership requires belief in the mission and an unyielding perseverance to achieve victory.'

Jocko Willink

The trait in 20 words

Building a better tomorrow is almost always a journey strewn with obstacles. Mary has the determination to find the path.

As I approach the end of each *'Lead Like Mary'* programme I'm very conscious of how little time I've left to explore Mary's final trait, that she is relentless.

The reason is partly because of how long I've spent on earlier material (especially time management, life planning, Absolute Clarity and Freedom Within a Framework), and partly because the trait is so straightforward and easily understood.

Which also means I'm not going to take up much of your time revisiting it here.

When I included Relentlessness as a final trait back when writing *'Lead Like Mary'* it was, to a certain extent, an afterthought. In the years that have followed I have significantly altered my view. I now believe it to be a crucially important part of Mary's make up. I would go as far as to say you cannot be a truly effective leader without being relentless.

Why? Those who aspire to be great leaders want to make a difference. They want to build a better world. This involves delivering what can often be complex, controversial change. That takes time and there will be many pitfalls along the way. This will be the case wherever the change takes place, whether it be at work, in your community, in a voluntary role or within a family. In so many instances you will need to be relentless, to refuse to give up, if you are to prevail.

> *'Many of life's failures are people who did not know*
> *how close they were to success when they gave up.'*
>
> *Thomas Edison*

Alongside being relentless, leaders need to be resilient. It is so easy to become downhearted; especially if the changes are taking a long time, or if there is significant opposition. Intransigence can often be even more frustrating than outright opposition. Resilience enables us to regroup, take stock and resume the battle.

Another very similar word is perseverance. There's growing evidence to support the view that this may be one of the very most important leadership characteristics.

There's a fascinating TED talk by Angela Lee Duckworth exploring this subject. In her late twenties she quit management consulting to become a maths (or math) teacher. As she attempted to teach ratios, fractions and geometry to her students she became aware that there was no connection between IQ level and success in this subject. The key was perseverance. Those students with lower IQs who made the effort and didn't give up out-performed those with higher IQs who didn't apply themselves and make the effort.

She went on to train as a psychologist and to study the proposition that determination and application would out-perform intelligence not just in school but in life.

She and her team visited West Point Military Academy to try to predict which cadets would stay in training and which would drop out. They studied teachers in challenging areas to see which ones would still be there at the end of the academic year, and who would be the most effective in their roles. In both cases the answer wasn't to do with IQ, social intelligence or good health. It was what Angela calls grit. She defines grit as being passion and perseverance in delivering long-term goals, sticking with the future over years, having stamina and working hard. Living life as a marathon not a sprint.

Which is exactly what it takes to build that better world around you.

Whether we call it being relentless, resilient, persevering or grit, the principle is the same, great leaders are in it for the long haul, and as we shall revisit later - they never, ever give up.

Reflections

The Mary Paradox

'One of the criticisms I've faced over the years is that I'm not aggressive enough or assertive enough, or maybe somehow, because I'm empathetic, I'm weak. I totally rebel against that. I refuse to believe that you cannot be both compassionate and strong.'

Jacinda Ardern

Back in my corporate days I was just about surrounded by Bills. They were everywhere, controlling the company from the top down. This was old school leadership at its most blatant, a domineering macho culture. Directors and senior managers found their authority in their job title, their pay grade, how grand their office was and the size of their company car (yes, there was many a 'mine is bigger than yours' conversation going on!).

There was no room for dissension, it was their way or the highway. I have ample evidence that good young leaders, stars of the future, were lost along the way, while others kept their heads down, played by the rules, avoiding putting their heads above the parapet, so much wasted potential inside them.

Intuitively I realised there was another way. I didn't have the benefit of management theories or training (this was never encouraged) but as I inherited each new team I knew that there was a much better way to get the very best from them- by encouraging them, listening, developing, nurturing, protecting them from the worst excesses of my bosses and others.

I developed a reputation amongst my bosses and peers. In their eyes I was too *soft* to be an effective manager. Nurture your people, develop them, ridiculous! I was regarded as weak and not really 'one of the boys.'

What I now realise I had plenty of (although I would have no idea it was called this) was EI, or Emotional Intelligence. I do not believe the collective senior team of the company had ever heard the term, let alone possessed it. For me EI simply means that you care about others, want to understand them, demonstrate empathy. As the years have gone by I have become more and more convinced that truly authentic, effective leaders are stacked in Emotional Intelligence.

That approach would never have fitted the company culture back then though. Shouting and bullying was all too often 'the way things got done round here'.

Thing was, I wasn't soft or weak, I just believed you got the best out of people if you treat them well. I found that if people were trusted and encouraged they would repay you many times over. However, and this is crucial, I was also clear that if that trust was abused I needed to take firm, decisive action to resolve the issue.

Let me give you a real example. My first director level role in the company was back at the end of the 1980s. I inherited an estate of 140 pubs and bars from an archetypal Bill. He spent the entire handover period telling me how none of the managers of these pubs could be trusted; they were dishonest, crooks even. The only way to handle them was to show them who was boss.

To prove his point he showed me the stock results for the pubs, overall large deficits, the business appeared to be haemorrhaging money through the back door. I asked what action he had taken. Now here's the thing, he had first addressed the issue like a bull in a china shop, dismissing people, demanding improvement. But little had changed. The stick on its own was not enough. Then his eye had drifted off the ball, other priorities had taken over.

I knew that the stick on its own would not work effectively. You could get rid of people but that didn't address the root causes of the problem. Many of these pub managers were completely honest, but stock loss was taking place somewhere in their business, they were simply not motivated enough to resolve it.

I wasn't naïve. I knew the carrot on its own wasn't enough either, it needed a dose of both carrot and stick. Honest conversations, a clear spotlight on the issue, close monitoring of performance, a level of trust, encouragement, support and training, along with regular and consistent reporting of progress.

I set myself and my area team three months to solve the issue. I made it clear the bottom line was that it would be resolved. I visited the pubs, giving a simple, unequivocal message. We had an issue, it needed resolving, we would work together to do so. I stressed I trusted them to deliver the change and would support them. It absolutely must be resolved, there was no room for dishonesty in the business, and there would be consequences if it was not resolved.

An early example of Joint Accountability in action!

My boss was sceptical to say the least, my peers derisory, but I was convinced this approach would work. Most of the time anyway - I did have some sleepless nights! I brought the Trade Union Representative into the fold, taking him into my confidence, ensuring he was involved. He strongly supported the approach, it was fair and open, and the last thing he was willing to tolerate were dishonest members.

Things stalled at first, but I kept up the pressure, monitoring progress daily, combining carrot and stick, encouragement and support where deserved, disciplinary warnings where equally deserved.

Quicker than I had hoped or anticipated, the tide turned. Overall results improved, slowly at first, then faster. You could see managers running their businesses more tightly. There were casualties, that was inevitable, I think we dismissed four or five people for clear evidence of theft. The Trade Union Representative supported our actions, he was satisfied these were transparent and appropriate decisions.

We kept the focus for a number of months it didn't slip back, saving the business many tens of thousands of pounds.

Have another look at Jacinda Ardern's quote at the beginning of this chapter. I am convinced great leaders, authentic leaders, can, must be and are both compassionate and strong.

Fast forward over a quarter of a century to Mary. Since *'Lead Like Mary'* was first published readers and programme participants have frequently told me working for Mary would be wonderful because she is so nice. They are partly right, Mary is fun to work for, kind, caring, loyal, trustworthy and trusting, but it would also be far from an easy ride.

That's the Mary paradox.

If you are lucky enough to work for Mary, she wants you to flourish. She will inspire, nurture and develop you, and watch your back. She also wants you to grow, to broaden your experience, be visible and to have a positive impact. She will push you hard, taking you out your comfort zone, giving you additional responsibilities, arranging for you to make presentations that expose you to senior managers, asking you to attend meetings in her absence, challenging you, giving you bigger and more complex assignments. You will find many aspects of working for Mary challenging, you will be given more responsibility than you might be comfortable with. But however much freedom she gives you and encourages you to take there will always be a framework in place.

Remember, she is doing this because she wants you to grow, to prepare you for bigger roles. Why would she not do this, it's integral to serving others.

Mary takes exactly the same approach to her dealings with all others around her- peers, colleagues, boss, customers, her contacts in partner organisations. She is positive, friendly, open and trusting. She wants to and strives to build long-term, highly effective, mutually beneficial relationships. Yet she is never soft. She never ducks an issue that needs resolving, a difficult conversation, negativity, a breach of trust. In all those instances she will seek to do the right thing, always in the right way.

Remember that Mary leads this way in her whole life, not just at work. She tries to bring up her children in exactly the same way. She loves them unconditionally, she cares for, nurtures and protects them, but she is also strict when she needs to be. She wants them to understand right from wrong, and that 'no means no.' She pushes them out of their comfort zone, encouraging them to flourish. She wants them to develop academically but also to grow their confidence, to become good citizens.

There are many similarities between bringing up children and leading a work team!

Let's finish with a quote which delightfully demonstrates the Mary Paradox.

'It is entirely possible to be a kind, loving person who refuses to tolerate bullshit. In fact, it's not only possible, it's absolutely necessary.'
Nanea Hoffman

Reflections

The Command and Control Death Knell

'You say to yourself if only I could unleash the power of everybody in the organisation what would we accomplish?'

Andy Pearson, Yum Brands

In *'Lead Like Mary'* I described an evolution underway to a new kind of leadership, one based around authenticity, trust, a belief in serving others and unleashing potential. I was already witnessing the change beginning to happen.

Although I may not have articulated it well at the time, I was observing the beginning of the end for the traditional role of a leader - best described as Command & Control.

Leadership had always been about Command & Control. For centuries the role of a boss had been to tell people what to do, ensure they did it, and punish them if they didn't.

Think of the 19th Century mill owner, factory managers, business owners, corporate executives, line managers, supervisors, generations of people who only knew one way to lead.

I thought back over my own corporate career, growing up in an environment where power resided with those with the biggest offices, watching my boss and their boss be the epitome of Command & Control. Inevitably, early in my career, I did the same. I told people what to do. Surely that's what leaders did?

Colleagues back then, in the macho, tough world we operated in, were actually proud of their oft repeated leadership mantra 'when you've got them by the balls their hearts and minds will follow.' Yes, really! Horrific!

The thing is it works - to a point. Command & Control gets results, if you shout at someone loud enough they'll get on and do stuff. Not willingly, not with a happy heart, not engaged, keeping their head down, but they will deliver. Whole industries were built around this philosophy, training courses taught new generations of managers to do the same, management books endorsed the approach, bosses bossed and workers did what they were told.

In *'Lead Like Mary'* I describe the worst example of a Command & Control leader. Bill, my fictional character recognised by so many, is an autocratic bully. He shouts, humiliates, terrorises, rules by fear. On my programmes most people can relate to Bill, having experienced one for themselves, many still carrying the scars.

Command & Control is a broad church. Bill the bully lies at the extreme end of a continuum.

Move along it and you'll find plenty of other examples, less threatening and unpleasant than working for Bill, but still stuck in a time warp. Towards the opposite end of the continuum, you'll find really pleasant managers, kind hearted, wanting people to develop, but unable to cast off the leadership paradigm they've been part of all their working lives. They cannot break away from telling people what to do, they have never grasped or been shown there is a far better way.

All too commonly they resort to micro-managing, often with the best of intentions, believing they are helping while strangling creativity and individuality at birth.

Consider these dictionary definitions:

Manager- a person responsible for controlling or administering an organisation or group of staff.

Micromanage- control every part, however small.

Sounds familiar?

Command & Control is no longer a viable option in the new world of work. It has no future. Its time is up. The world of work is undergoing dramatic change and a new leadership paradigm is essential, a pre-requisite for anyone wanting to survive, let alone prosper, in this new world. It's so exciting, the potential is limitless!

'Trust & Inspire' is a recently published book by Stephen M. R. Covey, the son of the 7 Habits man. In it Covey Jnr. identifies five emerging forces that are sweeping through our world. They were happening anyway, but the global pandemic has accelerated the trend. It really is a world turned upside down.

A technological revolution is bringing extraordinary changes. Technological innovation is happening in all areas, impacting on every society, industry, organisation and person. Until 1900 experts estimated that human knowledge doubled every century. Now experts suggest that human knowledge doubles every 12 hours.

The nature of work has changed. Work is now much more collaborative, innovative and creative that ever before. We need more and more people to work with their heads, not their hands. People need to work in flexible, interdependent teams- to create and innovate together.

The nature of the workplace has changed. Working from home or another location has been growing even before the pandemic massively accelerated this trend. People are working virtually in flexible inter-connected teams. We increasingly don't have the need for conventional offices. Hybrid working is here to stay.

The nature of the workforce has changed. Our workforce is far more diverse than ever before. As Millennials and Gen Z form an increasing proportion of the workforce they bring with them different experiences, perspectives and ideas. They do not want to be micromanaged. They want to be listened to, given freedom, and to know that their contribution really matters. They want to connect to a noble purpose.

The nature of choice has changed. Technology and changes to the workplace have given people far more choice, flexibility and opportunities. It is imperative that organisations create the kind of culture that attracts, retains and inspires people. People have more choices of what they do with their life than ever before.

A pretty persuasive list! If you would like further evidence here's some facts:

Millennials are 22 times more likely to stay in a high trust culture
Generation X are 16 times more likely
Even Baby Boomers (that's me!) are 14 times more likely

One in five workers will change jobs in the next twelve months. People increasingly want to work somewhere they can make a difference. They will vote with their feet if their expectations on company culture, reward, flexibility and learning are not being largely met.

60% of people would prefer to work mostly or fully from home. You can't micromanage people working from home.

68% of people give the primary reason for moving jobs as wanting a more fulfilling job where they can 'truly be themselves at work.'

89% of people choosing to move away from the private sector cite 'wanting a career with a strong sense of purpose' as the primary motivator.

The death knell is sounding for Command & Control leadership. It's time to move from evolution to seismic change.

Why is that important in finding your voice? To deliver the changes you want to make, to build that better tomorrow, will require highly effective leadership. It can't be achieved through command and control.

There's a new leadership paradigm in town, one I call 'Inspire & Enable.' At its heart is authenticity, trust, serving others and unleashing potential. We'll explore it together later.

Reflections

Section III

Everyday Heroes

Preamble

I wanted to share with you just a few examples of leaders who have found their voice, building a better world around them every single day. I call them Everyday Heroes, although the latter word would not be something they would recognise. Each of them is an authentic leader, low in ego and high in humility, who wouldn't believe they are doing anything out of the ordinary.

They are, and in doing what they do, they have inspired and enabled countless people around them to take up the mantle and find their voice.

I've had the privilege of working with each of them over the last few years, indeed they have become friends.

I hope you enjoy their stories.

Lesley Dixon

A tale of organisational transformation

I've worked with Lesley for the best part of two decades and have had the privilege of witnessing first-hand her transformation of two organisations from mediocrity to sustainable greatness.

She is a truly authentic leader who combines (to quote Jim Collins) personal humility and professional will, consistently demonstrating Mary's dual characteristics of being kind and caring, and at the same time being strong and determined.

Lesley is the CEO of PSS, a social enterprise that supports people to live happy, healthy and hopeful lives whether they're adults who have learning or physical disabilities, people in or around the criminal justice system or families who've been through unsteady times.

To what extent did your early life shape the person you are today?

What drives me is a sense of fairness and social justice. I get that from my Grandad and my Mum. Grandad was a Prisoner of War of the Japanese in WWII, and was not treated well, he had his appendix removed without anaesthetic. Like so many others he rarely talked about his experiences, but I remember him teaching us to count from 1-10 in Japanese.

He talked a lot about the importance of fairness. He was a milkman in the days the floats were pulled by horses, and active in a trade union. If he dealt with an issue which would leave him personally worse off, but less fortunate people better off, he would always support it.

My Mum was a massive influence on me, and my Dad was a gentle and kind man. My values of fairness, social justice and kindness have always been there and still are today.

Tell us about your early career.

After I graduated with a Business Studies degree I had no idea of what I wanted to do, I just knew I didn't want to work in the private sector. During my time at university, I'd been a student activist and a Students' Union sabbatical officer so maybe it was no surprise that I went to work at a Students' Union. The surprise is that it was as a Commercial Manager!

I had no experience of managing people or of commercial operations apart from running student entertainments, but I had the confidence of youth. Bill Rammell (later an MP, Minister of State, and University Vice-Chancellor), had just joined Kings SU as General Manager, and observed the interview. I fear if he had been longer in post I wouldn't have got the job!

Bill was a brilliant manager to have, very supportive. I stayed there seven years, the final two as General Manager, succeeding Bill. Then I was head-hunted for a job at what is now London Metropolitan University. The University had shut down its Students' Union. As manager of the Student Centre my job was to recreate it. I lasted eleven months, the final three of which were my notice period. It was a toxic environment, where organisational politics dominated, and it was very difficult to get things done. It taught me so much about how not to run an organisation, that can be a very powerful, if painful, learning experience.

In 1997 I moved on to become General Manager of the University of London Union, following Bill Rammell once more who had just been elected as an MP. I experienced prejudice after being appointed, there were few women in senior roles in the sector, I was regarded as being too young and inexperienced.

Your next move gave you your first opportunity to build something special.

Yes, after three years in the role I was appointed CEO of Leeds University Union (LUU), a big move north for someone who had spent much of her working life in London! I decided it would be my last job in the sector.

LUU was a dinosaur. I definitely saw the potential, it thought it was the best, but it wasn't. It was an iconic entertainments venue, but had a misguided view of itself. I knew it could be fantastic.

To help them to recognise the reality I took the student officers on a tour of other Students' Unions. I remember arriving at Sheffield, which was already really great. The officers were in despair, not believing Leeds could ever be like Sheffield. My reply was it will take time but if we set the foundations now it can be.

One of my first challenges was dealing with staff arrogance. As people left the organisation I focused on bringing in the right people, who were up for the changes I envisaged and shared with them.

Under your leadership you transformed LUU into a great organisation. What were your main learnings from the experience?

Getting the right people is essential, you can't do it without the right people. The key is building the right culture and great relationships everywhere. You also must be honest with people, they have to understand the reality, or people work in a false world.

You decided you were ready for a new challenge?

I was at LUU for nine years, I decided it was time to move a year before I left. This was a great organisation, making a difference for countless students. I wasn't going to give that up for any job, it had to be the right one. An example is a job that came up close to where I live, it looked great on paper, paid well, but their work, which was to do with science, was not something I felt passionate about.

I saw an advert for the Chief Executive of a social care organisation in Liverpool called PSS. I was fascinated and applied. I understood my weakness was having no real social care background, but in fact PSS were looking for a candidate with wider experience.

I believe above all that in a recruitment process you must be at your most authentic self at interview. In preparing I found three separate versions of a PSS vision on- line. This did not suggest great clarity. I made sure I pointed that out at the interview.

Being a trustee of a small local charity helped. That charity merged with MIND in York and I went on to become national MIND Vice-Chair. This

142

gave me some relevant insights and experience of social care challenges. Volunteering gives so many opportunities to build your experience. Mental health is a very important area for me, when my Grandad returned from the Far East he spent time in a mental hospital, and my other Grandad had dementia at a young age. My Dad remembers a padded cell and straitjackets.

You got the job. What were your first impressions and early challenges?

There was a real difference between PSS and my job at Leeds. Students are, on the whole, a privileged group and as much as I loved Leeds I wanted a role where I could make a difference for people who hadn't been dealt a fair hand in life.

My predecessor, Robin, had been in the job over twenty-five years and had great social care experience, he was much more knowledgeable than me. He was also kind, on the day he retired he left a card on my desk which said simply 'do it your own way.'

PSS had a very special history stretching back almost 100 years. On the day I arrived I felt its warmth immediately; the receptionist, a lovely lady called Rhonna, came out from behind her desk and gave me a big hug of welcome! People seemed really excited to have me there, which I thought was amazing.

I spent the first three months or so meeting people to listen and learn about PSS. I devised seven questions which I consistently asked people, whether they were Board members, my direct reports, their direct reports, front-line staff or commissioners. Thinking back, I can't believe I didn't include the people we were supporting, that would be unthinkable now.

What were your conclusions and what did you do with them?

It was a great listening experience and enabled me to build up a clear understanding of what I had inherited and to begin to formulate an action plan. PSS was very like Leeds in that in truth it thought of itself as being far better than it actually was. There was an air of complacency, people wanted changes to happen, but not if it required them personally to change.

I fed back to staff at a series of roadshows, a method of communication I still use today. I presented to the Board, setting out the changes I believed were needed to the structure and culture of PSS. Board members nodded and asked me to go back and do more work here and there, they kept kicking the changes I was proposing into the long grass. They were reluctant or unwilling to commit to changes.

I soon faced my first big challenge A senior staff member put in a formal grievance, accusing me of bullying. I remember the Chair called me, was supportive up to a point, but then added 'I have to say Lesley, there's no smoke without fire.' At that moment I felt highly exposed, if the Chair hasn't got your back it's a very difficult place to be.

One of the Trustees was asked to carry out an investigation. I owe him a lot. He came back to the Board, and told them that we have to back Lesley, unless we let her take the actions she has recommended nothing is going to change. This was a defining moment, with this support behind me I was able to re-structure the organisation, bringing in the right people to help lead the change.

What were the main challenges you identified?

I discovered PSS was built around its Central Services team, with operational staff existing to support them. That was clearly the wrong way round. The organisation did not have a clear sense of itself, its purpose, or a clear vision. It was also focused on the wrong priorities.

A good example of this was at an early meeting of the senior leadership team I had inherited. We were reviewing the results of a staff satisfaction survey. I asked if we were going to agree to make changes having received the results. They looked at me, 'whatever for?' They had no intention of feeding the results and actions back to staff. I explained that there was no point in asking for views if we don't feed back, what is going to change as a result, and involve them in the creation and application of solutions.

The first priority was change to the senior leadership team. It was inevitable that a number of them had to leave the bus. My challenge was to find the right people to replace them.

Once a new team was in place, we began to formulate plans to create and build a new vision, strategy and culture. First, though, I put together a 'fix-it plan', focusing on things that needed to change now before we could even begin the journey to greatness.

This was a major change project. How did you take it forward?

An early focus was on governance. Members of the Board had been there a very long time and there was no-one with a social care background, they were primarily accountants and lawyers. There were no role descriptions for Trustees, no expectations of them, we changed a raft of things with regards to governance.
There was also no over-arching plan for PSS people, nothing that linked their objectives to the bigger picture, no values framework.

I inherited an organisation that was self-satisfied and complacent. in too many areas it was not even good, there was certainly no effort to get feedback from the people we supported, it was not even on the radar. There were also far too many examples of silo working. Central Services regarded themselves as core staff, and in a safe job, while the front line was operational, dispensable if a contract was lost. What Central Services hadn't grasped was that a lost contract would have a commensurate impact on the size of the Central Services team.

We had to shift that thinking. We needed Central Services to understand our purpose. We weren't there to produce management accounts, we were there to make a positive difference to people's lives. To do so we had to be financially robust, which included providing information to Central Services to enable them to produce the accounts. It sounded like a pedantic difference, but it required a significant mind shift.

How important was it to make changes early to ensure you had the right people on the bus before commencing the journey?

It was massively important. You can't make changes on your own, you need the right people. It also sends clear messages through the organisation, change must begin at the top. An example was a manager who was a creative thinker but she was also a bully. I was told I couldn't get rid of her, she was too valuable. But if we say we don't accept that kind of behaviour we either mean it or we don't. If we say poor behaviour is unacceptable unless you are good at your job we are saying it's okay. It's not okay, if we kept the wrong people on the bus the changes wouldn't have happened.

It was so important to get the Board right as well. The Chair had announced he was standing down and the Board had agreed a successor. When I met with him it was clear he wanted to be too involved in day-to-day operational matters. I discussed these concerns with the outgoing Chair, explaining I would try to make the relationship work, if necessary, but the changes I was driving were my priority. The Board agreed to change the Chair-designate. My mentor at the time observed that this was a big card to play so early, but it was the right thing to do. The card also had to be played in the right way- properly, respectfully, and sensibly.

How did you set about delivering a change of culture?

It starts with you modelling the behaviours you want to see in others. It has to start there. Then you must challenge where things are wrong, as with the bully above. Bring on board people who share your views, you must have allies, people who are positive about the journey and can help lead the change. Slowly people begin to buy in, to become enthusiasts, these people, the early adopters, become your champions, when they do it becomes very powerful.

We developed our first Big Plan, set out our strategy, but as Drucker famously said, 'culture eats strategy for breakfast.' We couldn't hope to successfully execute the plan unless we made the cultural changes first. Without people with you delivering the strategy is impossible.

It's difficult to measure progress on cultural change, but you sense it, you feel it in your gut, you get a sense of progress from the way people talk to each other.

How would you articulate the culture you wanted to create?

It's words like collaboration, ambition (for the people we support), positivity, kindness, curiosity, creativity (coming up with new ideas of how things could be better), drive and determination.

Your values embody the culture and provide your behavioural framework. I wanted as many people in PSS as possible to be involved in the creation of our values. We first brought together eight people from across PSS, none from the senior team, chosen on the basis of positivity and willingness to change. We got them to talk about what was really important to them. They then went out and chatted to people across PSS. After time the values emerged. When I hear of senior teams going away to decide on the values I think how can you do that?'

The values that emerged- big hearted, genuine, open-minded, determined and professional, are now used throughout PSS and have been embedded into recruitment and performance management processes. Our annual Big Awards are directly linked to the values.

How did you improve communications?

There was no focus on internal communications when I joined. It's just so crucial. When the time was right I brought in a Head of Communications, Rachael, who would play a big part in shaping the PSS we have today.

We now have regular staff surveys, incorporating the Net Promoter Score, which enable us to measure how we are doing and take action when needed, together with ongoing roadshows. I wrote a weekly blog for several years, now supplanted by a live stream we first introduced in the pandemic, enabling me to speak directly to staff across PSS.

How big a challenge was leading through the pandemic?

It was the biggest leadership challenge I'd ever faced. I wasn't able to visit our services. These were circumstances I never expected to come across. We had colleagues out there on the front line when me and many others were working from home. We kept in touch by introducing a fortnightly live stream, I really worked hard to stay connected with our people. I would randomly call team members to see how they were, *which I know freaked some people out, although once they realised I was only calling for a chat they were positive about the experience. We sent a gift box out based on our values, it was just so important to let everyone know they were valued.*

Early on in the pandemic I was called and told that Paula, who we looked after, had died. This was our first death, it made it so real and unbelievably tough. I made sure we reached out and cared for our people who had supported her.

I was aware of how important relationships were at this time. A sub-group of the Board met weekly, and I spoke regularly to other CEOs. Staff satisfaction scores hardly dipped through the pandemic, this does not happen by luck, I am certain the culture we created, based around the values and excellent communication, was the biggest factor.

You've led PSS for 13 years, how difficult it is to keep going, to re-energise yourself?

In part it's about who you surround yourself with. You need people who are enthusiastic and energetic. The Board provide high support and also high challenge, there's recently been a change of Chair, and we already have a positive relationship. Maybe most of all it's about seeing the difference we make to peoples' lives.

What message would you give to the younger version of yourself arriving at PSS?

I would tell me that this will take longer than you think, but that's okay because it will be better for it so don't get frustrated.

My Mum used to make a Christmas cake each year, a tradition my sister and I have continued. She would make holes all the way down with a knitting needle and add brandy. She then left the cake to let the alcohol seep in, topping it up with more brandy from time to time. It's the same with building a new culture, you have to give it time to properly sink in and embed. You can't rush it, but you can do things to help it on its way. Have confidence in yourself that you can and will do it.

Liz Ormerod

Transforming lives with values-based leadership

Liz Ormerod is the Head Teacher of Delph Side Primary School in Skelmersdale. 58% of children at the school are classed as disadvantaged.

 Hers is a remarkable story of transformation and the impact it has had on so many children, their families and their community.

Tell me about your early life and how it shaped the person you are today.

I've grown up in Lancashire, however my father was in the RAF, so prior to settling up north, we travelled around the world, and I attended several RAF and village schools.

The teacher who had the greatest impact on me, was Mr Goodwin. I remember he had time for everybody, he understood what made us tick. I grew up wanting to be a teacher, like Mr. Goodwin, or a social worker like my Grandpa who worked as a social worker in Manchester, I never met him but I've heard all about him and he's still a role model.

My mum would say I was 'determined' from an early age! At six years old I decided to become vegetarian. I was passionate about it. It led to a five-hour stand-off in the kitchen with her because I wouldn't eat my dinner! Over thirty-four years later I'm still vegetarian (although I never forced it on my own children).

How did you first get into teaching?

I had always planned on becoming a teacher (although my Dad suggested I'd make a good lawyer!), and chose to take the post-graduate training route, studying a Geography degree first at the University of Birmingham.

I took a bit of a tangential route though, taking a year out as an elected student representative at the University of Birmingham Guild of Students – an experience which has continued to offer much life value. My year-long teacher training course was taken at the Marches Consortium in Herefordshire. This was a predominantly school-centred course, with the bulk of the learning done in-school, which really suited me, and I took inspiration from a brilliant Deputy Headteacher, Julie Henry, who took me under her wing and inspired me long after.

I remember how nervous I was before my first teaching experience; a trainee placement at a school in Shropshire. I was so panicky - I didn't even know how I was going to be able to stand in front of a class and take the register, huge imposter syndrome (that never goes away!). It's ridiculous looking back, but it has enabled me to this day to empathise with new teachers; I really feel for them.

Share some of your early experiences

My first teaching job was at a school in Blackpool and in one of the most deprived boroughs in the UK. It was a difficult setting with challenges I'd not experienced before. It made me realise the job was more than just a teaching role, and that through teaching I could help to instill ambition and remove barriers for kids who otherwise have limited chance in life. I found a real sense of purpose and motivation there which has lived with me ever since.

It turned out I was pretty good, and no one was more surprised than me when the local authority asked me to become a "leading Maths teacher" for the area, sharing technique and feedback with other schools.

It wasn't all good though. I was super-keen and ambitious, but I was also naïve and keen not to upset the apple cart. I encountered some behaviours which I would now recognise without much thought to be sexist, harassment, and even bullying. I look back on that experience as character building, but also with some frustration with myself – I never raised the issues formally and put up with the situation for too long.

I loved my job, but it felt like I had to find a way out, so I applied for another job. I'd got some decent experience and successes on my CV by now, so I chanced it and applied for an Assistant Head role, this time in a small Lancashire village school, partly because it was in a different local authority area.

My new school was very different to the one in Blackpool; more affluent, with capable children but expectant and very demanding parents. In fact, I remember one parent saying to me early on "I don't know where you've come from, or who you think you are, but we have high standards here!". I was at this school for about 3 years and learned a lot; most of all that my heart lay with those less privileged. But I strongly believe that any child, from any background, deserves the very best from their school teaching team – all schools face very different challenges, but children are simply children.

How did the move to Delph Side come about and what were your early experiences?

I had started looking and applying for Deputy Headteacher roles. I applied for a few, without success and started to get frustrated. I was told on a few occasions that I was the brilliant second best, but they had offered it to the internal candidate. I'd started to see, and get to know, quite a few of the same faces from these interviews; local authority school advisors who support Headteachers with these things. I approached one informally and asked for a conversation about how I might do better at interview. They invited me to their offices, and I was a bit concerned that I was going to be put back in my place. Instead, they offered me a secondment, as Deputy Headteacher at Delph Side Primary in Skelmersdale. Now I was the internal candidate...

The Headteacher at Delph Side had been brought in to turn the school around from an Ofsted "Requires Improvement" judgement. It has always been a community-focused school with much love for the local children, but it had started to lose its way on educational standards.

The new Headteacher adopted an assertive, directive approach, which was incredibly effective in establishing new standards and direction. I found my place at his side, sharing his vision for the school, and acting as the linkage, and sometimes buffer, between him and the wider staff. The secondment was initially intended to be for 6 months, but happily it *became a permanent appointment.*

The area the school is in is hugely disadvantaged - something like three times the national average ratio of kids officially classed as 'disadvantaged'. With that comes various challenges, and I felt back in the right sort of place to 'make a difference'. There is high crime and anxiety in the community, many of the parents had bad experiences at school themselves, and some are embarrassed by their own inability to support their children's learning. But they're also very proud in Skelmersdale, and they have ambition for their families. They want to break the cycles of disadvantage they've found themselves in and want better for their children.

Initially, things were quite lacklustre. I would hear things like 'this is a disadvantaged community, and this is as good as it gets.' But that was used as an excuse for poor performance. It's no excuse, the children deserved better. I just knew that if they were given a chance they would perform and that we had some great people on the team to help move us into the next chapter.

Having established a foundation of quality and rigour, and with it a 'Good Ofsted rating, we had earned the freedom and flexibility to innovate beyond the baseline framework. Job done, the Headteacher took the opportunity to take his next career step and joined a larger school elsewhere in the county.

Which was when you stepped into his shoes?

I really wanted the job. I knew it had come early for me; one person told me it was too early, but I'm very ambitious and competitive and that just gave me even more motivation. I was told the acting role would be for two terms while they went through the recruitment process. This frightened me; if another person was recruited, I'd likely have to move on, but I'd grown to love the children and their families as well as the team. Likewise, I worried parents wouldn't be happy with me in the role - I guess I had imposter syndrome (again!). One Governor, who was also a parent, took me to one side to tell me they didn't think I should have been appointed to the 'acting' role, and I needed to do something to prove the school was mine.

I decided to give it my best crack, but also, and most importantly, I decided to just be 'me'. I wanted to create an atmosphere of kindness and warmth, so I posted a lot on the school's Facebook page, something my predecessor had never really done, introducing my family and even my chocolate Labrador...Poppy, who is now very much our Delph Side doggy, helping so many everyday as our official 'school dog'. I posted photos of my own children, shared a Christmas Day video, I wanted to instil a sense of family as that was important to me, and to the school community.

Eventually, I was interviewed for the permanent role. Along with the external candidates I was asked to present my vision for Delph Side.

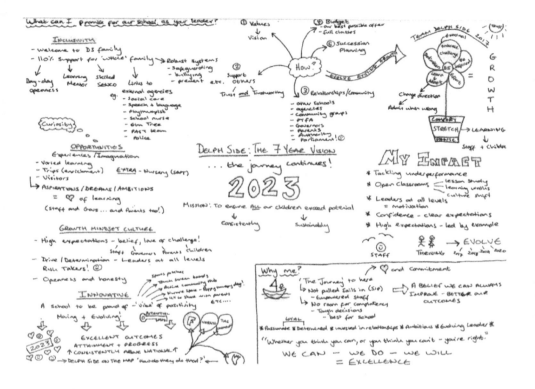

I decided to do something different and present a picture – a sort of map of my thoughts, ideas and standards, like a proper teacher! I took that approach because I didn't want to do PowerPoint slides, I knew what I wanted to say and I wanted the panel to focus on me, not the slides. It must have worked because they offered me the job!

So now you're the Head Teacher. Did you have a plan?

My only plan was my interview picture map, but I knew it was about putting warmth back into the team and building trust. I wanted to be my own person and to show the team how much I cared about them. I knew there was a lot more about each person than the bit that came into school, and I wanted to know who they all were, so I talked with each of them about what they wanted to do and what interested them and why.

I wanted work to feel safe, to give permission for people to try things where it wouldn't matter if they failed, providing we learned from it, to create a new culture, to support each other.

So your first focus was your teaching and support staff?

It was. I wanted to enthuse them and show I cared, but it wasn't all woolly and fluffy. All the time that was balanced with high expectations. We were striving to do something brilliant, not just provide a nice place to work, but somewhere with a shared purpose and end goal, where we could have an impact.

You don't deliver that through command and control, you don't need an overly hierarchical organisation, you do it by enthusing people, creating an atmosphere of positivity, giving that freedom within a clear framework. What I had learned over the years is that nothing is unachievable, if you have an idea just go out and make it happen.

We wanted to grow, to become better every single day. I knew we had to invest in our people, to empower them, to build the right culture. But you can only do that with the right people. I inherited some people who didn't want to come to work to 'make the difference'. That's not sustainable, and while that existed, we couldn't thrive.

Some people were naturally negative, but if you surround them with positive people, it's harder for them to carry on being negative. So, some people did change, but there were still islands of negativity and those who wouldn't or couldn't change had to leave. There were also people who realised this wasn't the right place for them and took their own decision to move on. Our mission was not for them, they chose something else, and I really respected them for that.

I learned here that it's entirely possible to be both caring and ambitious, empathic and strong.

158

I needed to build a senior team around me who would help drive the transformation. I knew I couldn't do it on my own. A key person was another Liz, Liz Burton, a long-standing team member, who became our Assistant Head.

Liz is my rock, she's patient and funny, and everyone loves her. She manages relationships so well. She's been here a long time, and she's become one of my best friends. But of course, the team is wider than that, and together with Jonathan Fyne, our other Assistant Headteacher who has such a huge heart for our school, and the rest of the senior leadership team, we've developed such a brilliant leadership dynamic, based on care, trust and friendship. And you can't underestimate the power of a supportive and invested governing body – magic!

Every time we recruited a new person I was nervous, I still am! We were so scared of making mistakes, it was so important to get the right people and we went to great lengths to ensure that candidates understood what we were about, and in choosing people who fitted in with our values, culture and ambition.

What were you looking for when you recruited?

It's very hard to describe what a 'Delph Sider' is. I wanted people with low ego, who were easy to get on with, wouldn't talk about others behind their backs, positive, decent humans who were ambitious for themselves, the school, and the children, and who were also loads of fun! I looked for people with the right character and behaviours rather than just their technical ability to do the job.

What about the local community?

We used social media extensively to communicate with the community. Many people carried bad memories from their school days; they hadn't liked their teachers, and we had to show them we were different. It was about being present, we invited people to come into the school, we made it warm and welcoming, tiny things like offering brews, knowing the parents by their first names, wanting them to feel they were part of something. If there were niggles, we'd invite the parents in proactively, make them feel part of it, be open and honest. We knew that we needed to understand the community we were working for, to be one big 'family'. I often see our role at Delph Side as a real honour; it's our little piece of the world where each of those who work there can have actual, direct and powerful influence. A gift.

You put a lot of emphasis on your values of Enjoy, Embrace, Evolve. Why are they so important?

They proved to be absolutely integral to building and sustaining the right culture. They were created by the whole staff team. There were values before, but far too many of them, you see this in too many primary schools, a long list of well-meaning words on the wall which end up meaning nothing. Developing our values was just so important, they define our culture and everything we do and we refer to them all the time.

They are incredibly powerful, it's difficult to describe how or why, but they are fundamental to everything we do. #Enjoy, #Embrace, #Evolve - if we're not being led by at least one of them at any one time, what are we doing and why? It differentiates our 'offer' from other schools in the area, we all have the same purpose but we deliver it, for our own communities, in different ways.

How important is safeguarding?

It's a huge part of the job, particularly in our setting. We have to work incredibly hard on it in a school like Delph Side, you are not just a teacher, you are so much more. But that's why I choose to work here. Everyone has social care responsibilities, and as a professional you have a voice, often in lieu of the children.

Every single day there are real issues to deal with, you can still be at school at 6 or 7pm waiting for a social worker or a police visit, or have to engage during the school 'holidays' - we take it in our stride and have developed very productive relationships with the local authorities and within our own senior team, supporting each other, being there for one another.

Why did you go to the trouble and expense of introducing a new uniform?

I wanted our kids to have the best, that's not what they've always had, I wanted them to stand out from the crowd, to be valued, to feel like they belong, to be proud of their school and of themselves. The comments from the local community were amazing!

We subsidise the cost and run a second-hand uniform swap shop to help people out as much as possible. When anyone comes to our school I want the first impressions to be so powerful, for the children to believe they can be the best and to flourish in life.

Walking into the school I got such a feeling of tranquillity

That's 100% what I wanted to create for everyone; the children, staff, parents, visiting professionals, it gets commented on all the time. It's the little things, for example the radio playing in the communal areas, and the branding we have created, it's more than a school, it's a culture.

You said you're ambitious, have you been tempted to apply for bigger roles?

No, I love this job and everything about it. When I was appointed, I knew *it was for the long-term. I'm still ambitious, but it's focused on the success of Delph Side. There's always so much more to do - we were successful in securing funding to develop a Special Educational Needs unit and, more recently, we have just opened an Art and Design Studio – the jewel of our crown. Not only do all children access exceptional creative lessons in here, our community are also invited in to participate in adult led sessions- - breaking down social barriers and building a stronger community.*

I became a judge for the Pearson Teaching Awards (more of that to follow) and now get to visit other high-performing schools. One school had a brilliant Art studio and I thought why can't our kids have that? The next morning, I outlined the idea to my team, and by lunchtime a plan was in place and a funding bid prepared! Everyone was buzzing. By the following week, mood boards had been prepared and one colleague admitted she had hardly slept she was so excited!

To what extent has the development of the culture impacted on academic results?

We are consistently above average with our results, which is incredible seeing we have three times the national average of disadvantaged children. The focus is now on sustaining those results, which has been particularly challenging because of Covid. But this whole journey has been about far more than just academic results.

During 2019 you decided to submit an entry for Delph Side in the Pearson National Teaching Awards. Why?

Because I wanted to articulate to the team how proud I was. I wanted them to feel proud, valued and appreciated. I believed what we had achieved at Delph Side was very special and I wanted to test it against a national standard.

Amazingly we were shortlisted for the prestigious award of 'Primary School of the Year – Making a Difference', and in May 2019 a panel of judges paid us a visit. They were due to be with us for just one afternoon. We wanted to make it as special as possible, to showcase what we are about. Various performances by the children took place, they put so much humour into it, really living our value of #Enjoy. People from the community joined us for afternoon tea, and we had so much going on all over the school, in every classroom. There were activities in the hall for residents of the local care home, with children dancing with residents who had become so known to us. They met parents, toured classes and heard from the wider community. The judges loved it, they didn't want to leave, more than one of them were close to tears!

Months later, we were invited to London for the grand final ceremony in Camden, which was to be televised on BBC 2 and where the 'Gold' winner of each category would be announced. We recognised this was a special moment, so a whole, super proud, group of us attended the event.

'Primary School of the Year' was the first award of the evening. Amazingly our school name was read out; we had won, and we gathered on the stage in shock!

I was determined that we celebrated this extraordinary news, I wanted the whole school, the whole community, the whole town of Skelmersdale, to celebrate our achievement. The next day we toured London with the trophy, already christened "Goldie". We photographed it at all the landmarks! For our children London is so far away, I wanted them to share the moment and we made a big presentation for them back at school.

The Delph Side team organised a week-long celebration for our children and community. There was even extra TV coverage, it was a big story in Skelmersdale, and beyond.

Looking back at all you and your team created, how do you sustain the new culture?

Keep going, it never stops. It can't stop, it's relentless, never think the job's done. You have to retain the positivity, you don't stand still, that's what makes it so exciting, it's what keeps people engaged.

We still have milestones, we measure progress and impact, we hold each other to account, we're constantly evolving, that's what makes us fresh and different, it's never the finished article, we always keep changing and adapting.

What advice would you give the younger version of yourself just starting the journey?

I'd say believe in yourself, be more confident, break up the negativity earlier, understand that some people can't change, and act sooner.

My favourite feeling is walking round the school, seeing the environment we have created, how beautiful it is, how smart the children are in their uniforms, heads down, getting on with their learning but also having fun. I look at them so happy and engaged, and safe in their school, and I think 'we've done this together.'

Here's what the Pearson Teaching Awards judges said about their visit to Delph Side, and on their website.

'Delph Side Primary School lives its school values of enjoy, embrace and evolve, and all staff are clearly committed to making a difference for each and every child. The school is a big community player.

This was a truly joyous, wonderful visit and we left feeling uplifted, inspired and full of admiration for this awesome school.

Delph Side strives to be a shining beacon for its Lancashire community: a hub of aspiration and determination mixed with a haven of sanctuary, support, kindness, and simple consistency. Various community projects build collaboration within Skelmersdale, which is often referred to locally as the 'forgotten' town.

The school's attainment and progress measures have been on a positive trajectory over recent years, having moved from 'Requires Improvement' to 'Good.' Staff consider themselves as one extended family and work closely with the school's many and varied stakeholders to ensure that support is available for the 'whole' family.'

I've included a copy of the entry Liz submitted for the Pearson Teaching Awards at the end of the book.

Sarah Parry

Building a better tomorrow with on the ground action

Sarah Is one of those people who have been put on this Earth to better the lives of others. She is a positive force with a can-do attitude that demolishes obstacles in her way. Whether it's trekking in the Himalayas, renovating a school in Brazil, supporting an orphanage in Sri Lanka or running one of her legendary gin raffles to raise funds for her local Women's Aid, she throws herself into every endeavour with energy, humour and determination.

Tell us about your early life and how it shaped you.

I grew up on a council estate in Bloxwich, my two brothers are fourteen years older than me.

I was the only girl on my street, that shaped my confidence around people, I had to fight my own corner.

I went to an all-girls high school, I wouldn't say it was the happiest time of my life. There was a real class divide, the girls from south Walsall had professional parents- doctors and teachers, while we were the children of manual workers. Looking back, it created prejudice, we kept ourselves to ourselves and it stopped me making friends with girls across the divide. Now I'm friends with former classmates from both sides of town, I wish I'd let them in back then, school would have been so much better.

Our council estate had a real sense of community, my Mum was one of the organisers, if someone died she would organise a collection and she arranged street parties to celebrate events like the royal wedding. My Mum was a real influence on me, and still is, I see myself in her all the time.

I spent most of my time at school avoiding lessons and bunking off. I didn't know what I wanted to do career-wise, so I enrolled at Art College. Unfortunately, it didn't last long, it was 1983 and the whole country was deep in recession. As a builder, my Dad had no work, so I thought if I left college I could get a job and pay my way. I was gutted to leave Art College, although I never told my parents. I loved art and design and wanted to be a textile designer.

What were your early experiences of the world of work?

The mother of my *boyfriend at the time told me about a vacancy with the local council on their Manpower Services Scheme and I was lucky enough to get the job as an Admin Assistant.*

I worked in this office for about 6 months, but I knew if I was to earn more money I needed qualifications, so I enrolled at college and completed various courses over the next few years - HNC, office management, a diploma in HR. I loved being at college but always saw it as a means to an end, giving me the opportunity to apply for better paid jobs.

I tried HR, but it wasn't for me, I hated being the HR Police, I think that was the socialist coming out in me. Instead, I got a job in the council's housing department which gave me the chance to see some of the realities of life. I was visiting people who were having a really hard time. I realised each person had an individual story to tell, and you need to understand that story. If you're living at the top of a block of flats, as a single parent with young children, and not many prospects, don't judge, there's always a story.

How did your career develop?

An opening to manage part of the council's cleaning service became vacant. I looked at the job description and it was the first time I'd ever thought 'I can do all of that.' The courses I'd done at college together with the opportunities taken with internal training meant that I was in a really good position to apply. When I got the job it was a big promotion and put me in a role where I was managing people and finances and I was also part of the Senior Management team.

I saw a chance to make a wider impact when the council asked for women volunteers to become trainers on their Springboard programme.

The purpose of Springboard was to develop women from admin backgrounds, by opening their eyes to the wider possibilities. It was another opportunity to hear peoples' stories. I realised there was major talent here which wasn't being used. The downside was that when we did open eyes, a significant number of the women on the course left to pursue new opportunities. The Council responded by stopping the programme!

I understood the importance of women's rights and opportunities from my mum, she was very vocal, a really strong and steadfast person. Like so many others she had difficult times, she got married in 1950 and shortly after was diagnosed with tuberculosis while pregnant with my younger brother. She was told she wouldn't live, but then was offered a chance to be a guinea pig for a new medicine trial. I'm glad to say it saved her life and she went on to have me and passed away in 2016, aged 90.
She didn't see my younger brother until he was nearly three because of how contagious the disease was and, he had been sent away to a care home miles away while she was ill. Looking back I don't know how she got through that time, but she did. She once told me 'life is never so precious as when you think it's slipping away'. I understand fully what she meant and it's a mantra I often repeat to myself. She is the person who shaped me the most.

Even back then was it all about making a difference?

I was brought up to believe that life is a gift but not all lives are blessed. And that if you can make something better for someone then you should. And that sometimes it's about seeking out those opportunities.

I got a job working on a community re-generation project in one of Walsall's most deprived areas. My role was to set up community groups and encourage and enable people to identify and find solutions for their local issues. We focused on key needs - housing, community facilities, employment, facilities for young people etc. . It involved me working with different faith organisations which I hadn't done before and was a great learning experience.

The project had some government funding but the time scales for achieving any tangible results were far too short. We were able to kick start some initiatives around anti-social behaviour, training and employment but the social problems were deep seated and needed a more long-term approach, which I found very frustrating. But this role gave me an invaluable insight into economic and community regeneration. Something I would pick up later in my career.

This was when you had a first life-changing experience

I slipped on some ice on the way to work and ended up in A&E. As I lay there my mind was full of fear that I might never walk again. I'd fractured 3 vertebrae and was off work for four months, making a full recovery. But the result was that I could no longer take being able to walk for granted.

This coincided with a time at work when a significant number of the women I worked with were diagnosed with breast cancer. I wanted to do something tangible, so I combined fund raising for a cancer charity by signing up for a challenge to trek the Himalayas. That experience took me completely out of my comfort zone but also gave me so much confidence and sparked my determination to get out there and make a difference wherever I could.

My next charity challenge took me to Vietnam, walking through the central highlands, followed by the Great Wall of China and after that it was off to Brazil with the Bobby Moore Foundation, renovating a school in the rain forest where we got to do practical tasks; I was in charge of renovating the windows!

How did things move on from there?

The community development work I'd been involved with really sparked my interest so I enrolled with Coventry University and completed a Masters' Degree in Community Re-
generation and Sustainable Communities in 2010. I was working at Staffordshire County Council by then and my degree allowed me to move into a community development role.

At the time, partnership working in Staffordshire needed to be improved and this was the challenge for the team in which I now worked. My role was to work closely with local councillors, businesses, community and voluntary groups and other public sector organisations like police, fire service, public health, NHS etc and work together to achieve better results for local residents. I loved every minute of this job. It was challenging and rewarding and involved trying to improve things for people.

Then another life-changing challenge.

In 2018 I was diagnosed with stage 2 breast cancer. Like everyone else who gets a similar diagnosis I went through various emotions; being scared, thinking I'm going to die soon, becoming more resigned, then getting scared again. Like others before me, a diagnosis like this focuses your mind on to what is really important and forces you to prioritise. Life will never be the same. It's a different life. A new normal. But it's still a life.

But sometimes opportunities can appear from bad situations. So when I was offered voluntary redundancy I knew I now had an opportunity to shape the rest of my life.

Where did you focus your efforts?

I knew I wanted to do things that would make a difference and as luck would have it an opportunity arose to do some work with Staffordshire Women's Aid, one of the organisations I'd worked with in my partnership role.

Back in 2005 I had travelled to Kenya on holiday and was able to visit a local orphanage and get to know the Dutch woman who managed the organisation. On my return to the UK I set up a charity called the Free Town Trust Fund to support this orphanage. This involved organizing many fundraising events over the years. I returned to Kenya twice more to work alongside the staff and the outreach team which gave me a better understanding of their needs.

Most of the children were orphans, others were there because their parents couldn't look after them. The orphanage also did outreach work, supporting desperately poor people with food parcels, medication, and small loans to help them start small businesses, such as selling food at the local market.

It seems to me that what you were now doing is a perfect example of inside-out leadership.

I know that in the whole scheme of things my work is very small. But I can see that it does make a difference. If I just impact one person, if their life becomes better through being educated or they get the medication they need, then one person's life has been changed

I remember my dad saying to me that whatever I did the situation in Africa would still be the same in the next 100 years. I could see where he was coming from but although many of the problems are long standing, I absolutely see the difference my charity has been able to make to many children who now have qualifications, a job, a safe place to live and a future they would not have had otherwise.

How has your work developed since?

By 2016 both my parents had passed away and I wanted to expand the charity in their memory. I decided on Sri Lanka as my Dad had spent time there in WW11 and had spoken to me about the poverty. I found an orphanage just outside Gallecalled Yasodara, which was being supported by a guy in Australia called Justin. The orphanage was for girls, which was important factor to me. I got in touch with Justin to offer my help. One thing led to another and through the power of the internet we combined forces; I now sit on the Committee of his Australian charity, Karuna Sri Lanka, I've been recently appointed as secretary and Justin and I have even met face to face in Tasmania where he now lives with his family.

Unfortunately, the Yasodara orphanage closed in 2018, because the building was no longer fit for purpose, and the girls were dispersed to other facilities.

We have managed to employ a social worker, paid for by the charity, who keeps in touch with all the girls and distributes food, other essential items and ensures their transition from school into work and independent living. We also provide on-line English lessons, swimming and IT lessons.

Why is supporting girls and women so important to you?

I'm a feminist, I've always understood the importance of female education, particularly in countries like Kenya and Sri Lanka where cultures are very different and who are decades behind us in terms of women's equality. It costs us a small amount of money to provide education and training to these girls but is the only way they can be independent and self-sufficient.

'The charity has also received endorsement and financial support from the actor James Krishna Floyd, who was in Sri Lanka filming 'Good Karma Hospital'.

I am still working with Staffordshire Women's Aid, mainly doing their social media, fundraising and developing partnership working. They are an amazing charity, literally saving lives of women affected by domestic and sexual violence. I continue to learn about this incredibly important work on a daily basis and find it very rewarding playing a very small part in the work they do.

What continues to drive you?

I know it's a cliché, but when your life is turned upside down it makes you think so much more about the contribution you are making and what your legacy is going to be. I only told a select group of people about my cancer diagnosis and the way those people responded blew me away.

We all have an expiry date. My hope is that when mine comes I can look back and feel that I did my best and made a positive contribution and changed a few lives for the better along the way.

I'm not from a rich family, we lived in a council house, didn't have holidays abroad but I just always felt I was luckier than a lot of people. My mum was always the person who got things done. I've definitely got that from her. And my dad always taught me to be kind to people less fortunate. I don't think you could have a more important life lesson than that.

Tim Mackrill

Unleashing the potential that can build a better world.

You do not need to spend long in Tim's company to be inspired by his two passions - his love of the natural world and his deeply held belief that young people hold the key to nature's recovery.

He has combined these passions by founding the Osprey Leadership Foundation, a charity whose purpose is to 'inspire and enable tomorrow's conservation leaders to find their voice and deliver sustainable environmental change to the world around them.'

Where did your love of the natural world begin?

I have a sense I was born with it. I grew up in a small market town in Lincolnshire and I can remember going into the garden to look for butterflies and bugs. Family holidays often involved hill walking. We lived close to Rutland Water which really helped.

I didn't like school very much, I've always hated institutions of any kind, I'm too much of a free spirit.

I had a geography teacher, Mike Davies, he was always really supportive, I found secondary school very difficult and he helped me through that. More than anything he was encouraging, he knew my interest in nature and would ask what I'd been doing. When I started volunteering with the Rutland Water Osprey Project he took a real interest in that. Looking back he had enormous empathy.

Tell us about those early years at Rutland Water.

I visited Rutland Water a lot, I was a keen bird watcher. I was 15 when my interest really sparked, I became involved with the Osprey Project, which was seeking to re-introduce osprey to England after a gap of 150 years.

I saw an advert asking for volunteers, applied, was interviewed, and got the job! One of the first people I volunteered with was a guy called Paul Stammers, who today is a trustee of my charity. Paul became a significant person in my life, right from my first shift he took me under his wing (no pun intended). Watching these magnificent birds flying around was amazing, I felt so privileged to be involved.

After my A-Levels I was offered a summer job caring for the birds, releasing and monitoring them, for the princely sum of £30 a week. It was great, I liked that I was being trusted at so young an age. It's why even now I think it's important to trust people and give them responsibility.

Your involvement with Rutland Water and the Osprey project blossomed from there?

I went to the University of East Anglia to study Ecology, coming back to work at Rutland Water every summer. I think one of the reasons I have got to where I have in my life now is because of volunteering. I say to young people that qualifications are important but volunteering and vocational experience are essential, so get out there and do things if you can!

I also began to gain an understanding of wider environmental challenges. Rutland Water played host to an annual Bird Fair, a global event, where people came together to discuss conservation issues.

The Osprey Project was also developing its scope. We got permission to satellite-tag osprey, which gave us so much data as they flew off to west Africa for winter. You can't help but see the world in a different way when you watch these birds fly thousands of miles, it gives you a different perspective.

After graduating I enjoyed another summer at Rutland Water, the highlight of which was monitoring the first breeding pairs of osprey. I knew that I needed to broaden my horizons, and spent some time travelling to south-east Asia, Australia, Fiji, Hawaii and New York.

Then you returned to Rutland Water to run the osprey project?

This was a wonderful opportunity, I was still young and it felt so good to be given this level of responsibility. The Reserves Manager was a guy called Tim Appleton, who would become another huge influence on my career. He wasn't like other conservationists I had met, he was a maverick, an entrepreneur, his whole ethos was built around being pro-active, Roy Dennis was also involved in the project, and became another big influence, he was never afraid to try things.

I learned quickly that if you are not pro-active nothing changes. You have to be positive, for example we can't afford to simply conserve what we have got, we have to restore the species we have lost.

Over the next couple of years I focused on building a team of volunteers, ensuring I got the right people on the bus. What I really enjoyed was leading around 150 volunteers, who were just so engaged. We built up a team with real positivity, enthusiastic about what they did.

Although I was enjoying my role at Rutland I was increasingly thinking that we could do more. Could we make more of our link to West Africa? Tim Appleton was of the same mind and encouraged me to explore possibilities. I decided to lead a trip to West Africa and in January 2011 I took thirty people there. We had been recommended to use the services of a local bird guide, Junkung Jadama (known to everyone as JJ). I invested an enormous amount of trust in JJ to organise the details of our trip.

How was the experience?

Interesting! JJ met us at the airport and we boarded a bus to take us to our accommodation. I was aware the hotel was called Paradise Inn, which had caused me some anxiety in advance of the trip. When we arrived my worst fears came to reality, paradise it was not! But our group were up for an adventure and nobody seemed that bothered. After

180

The Gambia we visited Senegal and stayed in a far more luxurious hotel, but the group wanted to get back to the Paradise Inn!

While I was out there I wanted to visit some schools, we were already working with schools in Rutland. I was now beginning to see how the osprey could link people three thousand miles apart. People in west Africa were living in real poverty and there was me with my telescope and binoculars. I realised we had an obligation, not to go around in a patronising way telling people what to do, but to use our relative prosperity and privileged position to help out in the right way. That's how our schools work came about.

That was when your work in West Africa took off?

Yes, over the next few years I made regular return visits to west Africa hosting more bird enthusiasts, continuing to build up links.

In our world we are defined by where we live but the osprey allowed us to link up with people from very different backgrounds who we have so much in common with. There are so many divisions in society and issues around immigration and xenophobia. Experiencing West Africa made me realise even more that we are all born on the same planet, and it's an accident of birth whether it's in the UK or a fishing village in The Gambia.

We got schools in Rutland to write to schools in The Gambia leding to an exchange of letters, and a Skype link up of assemblies. The Rutland kids are from privileged backgrounds and it was so important for them to talk to and learn from their counterparts in The Gambia.

There was so much potential to build connections along the osprey flyway, we linked up with conservation organisations in Spain, Italy and America, leading to the launch of an inaugural World Osprey Week, including on-line lesson plans for schools.

Was this the moment you decided to set up your charity?

I thought about it but there was too much happening. I was trying to combine working at Rutland Water alongside finishing my PhD and completing a book on osprey I had been commissioned to write. It was overwhelming, something had to give.

You [Barry] were kind enough to help me step back, take control and think. I decided to take a year out from Rutland Water to focus on my PhD. Perhaps inevitably, I didn't go back.

Stepping back was so important to me. That was when I decided to set up the Osprey Leadership Foundation (OLF) and also to focus on other conservation work I believed could make a difference. I knew I could do so much more. I took the big decision to leave Rutland Water and, having completed my PhD, to work for myself.

We were running Osprey Clubs in The Gambia and were already working with young people who really stood out, but there were so few opportunities for them to fulfil their potential. I realised that maybe I could help people in the early stages of a conservation career to really make a difference. That's what OLF was all about. I remembered back to the time I attended your Leadership Development Programme when I began to understand the importance of engaging people in the early stages of their careers. Maybe OLF could help young people in the UK and West Africa to grasp the vital importance of effective leadership.

As I began to set up my charity I commenced working with the Roy Dennis Foundation leading a project to reintroduce white tailed eagles to England. The last pair had been recorded in the Isle of Wight in 1780. Where better to plan their return?

We had a wonderful response from the public but others, particularly sheep farmers, were understandably concerned. All our evidence, though, showed that the extensive availability of prey in southern England meant farmers would have little to fear.

We worked hard to grow our relationships with the farmers, we knew this couldn't be based around conflict, we had to focus on building empathy and understanding. It took time, patience, and leadership, but we eventually secured the necessary agreements and these beautiful birds have been successfully re-introduced.

Tell us about the Osprey Leadership Foundation.

Like so many other people in the sector I was distressed at the biodiversity loss we were experiencing. I saw so many young conservationists, early in their careers, who cared deeply about the crisis we were facing but felt helpless to do anything about it. The challenges were so enormous they just couldn't see how they could make a difference.

There's this great quote from Greta Thunberg, who perhaps more than anyone else has shown what can be done to draw attention to the climate emergency we face:

'no-one is too small to make a difference.'

That really resonated with me, I realised that young conservationists could make a difference locally, and if enough people did that what could be achieved. Effective, on the ground, local action could spur national, even international action. There were plenty of experts in the sector focused on conservation, the crucial issue here was about leadership. I knew to achieve anything you need to demonstrate leadership. Young conservationists were unlikely to spend any time developing their leadership capability. It just wasn't happening.

I had this idea I could help build a community of like-minded young conservationists in the early stages of their careers, which could inspire, enable and support them, and provide networking opportunities, but most of all could teach them about effective leadership. I was convinced this was the key to enable local progress, and that this could be done in both the UK and West Africa. I asked Barry to chair the charity because he has had such a key influence on my career and is such an inspiration to so many people. I was thrilled when he agreed.

How is the Osprey Leadership Foundation doing?

It's early days yet, but it's thriving. We created an entry programme called 'Becoming a Conservation Leader', a six weeks long on-line leadership experience. It's really taken off since then, we are running regular programmes and getting great feedback.

So many young conservationists did not regard themselves as leaders, they thought that was restricted to those at the top of organisations. We set out to challenge and change that belief, to demonstrate anyone, anywhere can be a leader, and leadership begins with ourselves. We have focused our work around OLF's three values - authentic, effective and brave, seeking to help them find their voice and go out and make local change happen.

Once people have completed this first programme they can apply to join our Evolving Leaders community. We offer each member mentoring support and encourage them to network with like-minded colleagues.

One thing that makes our offering unique is that both the first programme and membership of the community are free of charge. That puts additional pressure on us finding funding elsewhere but that's a really important principle for me.

What are your plans for OLF going forward?

We're at the beginning of the journey, there is so much potential for this to grow. I can see many hundreds of young conservationists joining an increasingly wide community and the focus on local action leading to some real breakthroughs on a wide scale. These young people have the potential to make that happen as their careers develop. Our job is to inspire and enable them to unleash that potential.

Reflections

Section IV

Find Your Voice

Preamble

'Your voice is your superpower'

Lisa Congdon

Liz, Sarah, Lesley and Tim. Amazing stories from four extraordinary people. Would they consider themselves to be special? Absolutely not, primarily because each of them is an authentic leader, low in ego, high in humility who already leads like Mary.

They also are far from unique. They just happen to be four people I have had the privilege to know and to work with. I could have featured many others instead. They are only four examples of what millions of people are doing across the UK and the world.

Ordinary people doing extraordinary things. Authentic leaders who have found their voice and are building a better world for others.

Authentic leaders who do it every single day. Everywhere. In so many ways.

Authentic leaders in families, nurturing, loving and supporting those closest to them, protecting them while encouraging them to grow.

Authentic leaders in friendship groups, loving, encouraging but also having those difficult conversations, challenging beliefs.

Authentic leaders in communities, building support networks, helping the vulnerable, creating cohesion, bringing people together.

Authentic leaders in voluntary endeavours, like Sarah, fighting injustice.

Authentic leaders in charities, totally committed to their cause, dedicating every single day to making a positive difference for others.

Authentic leaders in schools, like Liz, inspiring, educating and growing young people, setting them on the road to becoming tomorrow's authentic leaders.

Authentic leaders in conservation and the environment, like Tim, championing the natural world, leading nature's recovery, arguing the case for addressing climate change and the loss of biodiversity before it's too late.

Authentic leaders at the top of organisations, like Lesley, driving sustainable change, creating a vision, inspiring their people, leading by example, unlocking potential.

Authentic leaders at every level of organisations, leading teams, delighting customers, a force spreading positive energy, communicating brilliantly, building mutually beneficial relationships, delivering the right results in the right way.

Authentic leaders in society, driven by the determination to do the right thing and to improve lives.

Authentic leaders who serve others, are selfless and caring, while also being determined, brave, challenging and relentless.

Authentic leaders following their own dreams, yearning for a big adventure, alive with possibilities.

Authentic leaders like you.

It's time to stand up and find your voice.

I'd like to help you do that if I can. I have created a 'Lead! Framework,' consisting of steps you can choose to take to inspire and enable you to focus, plan and deliver.
See the next page for the framework -

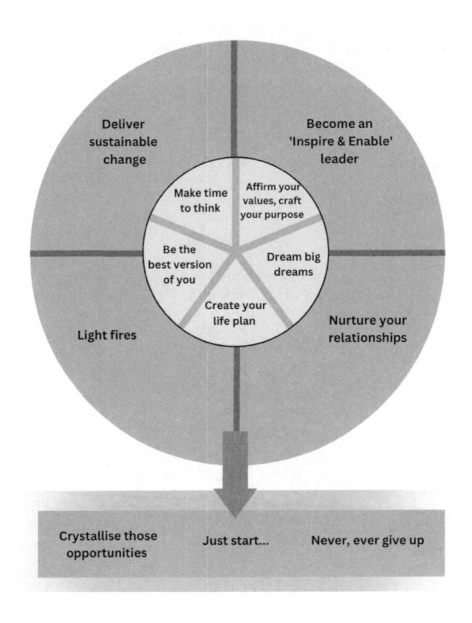

As with the *'Lead Like Mary'* model I've tried to keep this as simple as possible. You might remember the quote from the Absolute Clarity trait.

'If you can't explain it to a six year old, then you don't understand it yourself'

Albert Einstein

It splits into 3 levels with steps grouped under each one.

The levels follow the principles of inside-out leadership.

Begin by finding the voice within you. That's the first five steps.

The Voice Within

Affirm your Values, Craft your Purpose
A clear purpose, based on your deep-rooted values will set you off in the right direction.

Dream Big Dreams
Imagine just what could be possible if you were to truly unleash your potential.

Create a 'Life Plan'
Build a flexible framework that provides a road map for your future.

Be the Best Version of You
Focus on every element of your well-being on the journey ahead.

Make Time to Think
Ensure you have time for reflective and creative thinking by taking control of your time.

Then amplify your voice, so it is heard by others. That's the next four steps.

The Voice Amplified

Become an Inspire & Enable Leader
Command and control is dead. Embrace the new leadership paradigm

Nurture your Relationships
Build relationships based on mutual respect and benefit

Light Fires
Inspire those around you to build a better world together

Deliver Sustainable Change
Whatever you do make it stick, create that better world.

Now, having found and amplified your voice, you are ready to build a better tomorrow for others. That's the final three steps.

The Time is Now

Crystallize your Opportunities
Create a clear picture of the difference you are going to make to the world around you.

Just Start...
We need to begin at once, before it is too late.

Never, Ever Give Up
Be resolute and relentless in building that better tomorrow

Each step has exercises at the end to enable you to get started.

Together we'll explore each step in turn.

'It only takes one voice, at the right pitch, to start an avalanche.'

Dianna Hardy

Let's go find your voice!

Reflections

The Voice Within

Affirm your Values, Craft your Purpose

'The two most important days in life are the day you are born and the day you find out why.'

Mark Twain

Let's leap straight in at the deep end. Why do you want to make a difference, to build a better world around you, to improve the lives of others? 'Why' happens to be my favourite word in the English language, and it's the starting point to finding your voice.

Your journey begins with understanding what's most important to you, what's your burning passion, what do you want to change, what difference do you want to make? It's about developing a clear understanding of why **you** exist.

It's time to affirm your values and craft your purpose.

We begin with your values. It's such a nebulous word, what do we mean by values? As we explored *in 'Lead Like Mary'* these are the beliefs we have that lie deep within us, they are what makes us the person we are, shapes our lives, and act as a beacon when faced with a difficult decision.

 It's rare for us to think about them, let alone attempt to articulate them, but that's where our journey begins and that's exactly what I'm going to ask you to do. In a short while I'm going to invite you to turn to the end of this chapter and to spend some time working through the values exercises. Our aim is to affirm them, because, of course, they are already there, even if we have never thought deeply about them.

Authentic leaders are values-led. Mary certainly is. Authentic leaders live their lives based on their values. When they need to make a difficult decision or face a challenging situation, these values come to the fore. They don't need to articulate them, they are just there, at the forefront, enabling us to understand what the right thing to do is. Where we are values-led it is far easier to make those difficult decisions, far easier to be courageous.

Values are a completely personal thing, everyone is different, there is no list of 'right' values. Words like integrity, fairness and trust often spring to mind when describing what a value is, but they could be anything. You might regard those examples as being 'soft' values, equally we could have values based around creativity, accountability or courage.

Let me share mine. I'll start with **kindness**- I genuinely believe people should be kind to each other (and to themselves). Imagine a world where 8 billion humans were kind to each other.

Next, **caring.** You can relate it to kindness but I think it goes further. I care about people, about the world around me, about making a difference. From that value comes my belief that I am here to serve others.

Third, **enabling**. This links for me into serving others (as I guess kindness and caring do as well.). I want to help others, unlock potential, inspire and motivate them to do amazing things. It's the motivation that drives me every day.

Next, **learning.** We should never stop learning. I'm in my sixties and I still do - every single day! Imagine having a closed mind or thinking you have nothing left to learn.

Finally, **fun.** Whatever we are doing have fun doing it!

How many values should we have? That is, of course, entirely up to you but it feels to me the optimum number may be between 3 and 6.

Take some time out to complete exercise 1 at the end of the chapter. See if you can articulate and affirm your values, adding a brief explanation of each one, as I have done above.

Let's turn now to what you are deeply passionate about. It's unlikely to be one thing, there may be several. Consider just a few examples.

Is it your passion to tackle the climate emergency and persuade others to do the same?

Is it about tackling local issues such as food poverty?

Standing up for the vulnerable?

Creating a better life for your family?

Becoming the best you can be at your chosen sport?

Reinvigorating the PTFA at your child's school?

Unlocking potential in your workplace?

Or any one of hundreds, if not thousands, of issues and causes.

In short, what are you passionate about?

Much of the work I do is supporting people to help them answer this question for themselves. I primarily focus my efforts on those in the early stages of their career. Why? Because so many of these younger people inspire me. They are passionate, energetic and anxious to learn. They are ready to tackle the world but have no route map.

Each of these people is a unique individual and as I have got to know them I am in awe of what they have done already in their short lives. Many have travelled and worked abroad, exploring the wider world; they are intelligent and articulate, passionate about changing the world around them, making a difference, improving lives.

Their problem is they don't know how to make that difference, where to focus their efforts, how to get started.

I help them to untangle the web, build clarity, understand what's possible, to begin to develop their life plan. To focus on their passion and why they exist.

For me the journey begins with exploring what we are deeply passionate about, what do we care about, what sends our heart singing or makes our blood boil, what gets us up in the morning, what excites us? It could be anything, at this point it's crucial not to condition or direct your thinking. It could be about the love of your family, wanting to care for them, the community in which you live, exploring new opportunities, the environment, social change, injustice in the world.

I love these two quotes:

'The mystery of human existence lies not in just staying alive, but in finding something to live for.'

Fyodor Dostoyevsky

'If you can't figure out your purpose figure out your passion. For your passion will lead you right into your purpose.'

Bishop T D Jakes

Identifying what you are deeply passionate about will enable you to craft your purpose.

Skip to the end of the chapter again and have a go at Exercise 2. articulating what you are deeply passionate about.

Now we come to the third element- discovering and crafting your purpose. Why do you exist? What drives you? What do you want to do with your life? What difference do you want to make? What do you want your legacy to be?

Goodness, what deep questions!

Discovering and crafting their purpose is probably the deepest thing I do with people and there's no easy route to articulating it. It comes from deep inside. It's driven from our passion and shaped by our values.

Search on the internet and you'll find a host of suggested structures for compiling a purpose or mission statement. Have a look, and use them if they work for you, I don't tend to myself. I like to challenge people to try and keep their purpose statement to no more than 20-25 words (be succinct) and to begin with 'I exist to...' I think this focuses the mind.

Here's some examples of purpose statements crafted by people I work with.

'I exist to bring positivity to those around me, humans and non-humans alike, while harmonising with nature for personal contentment.'

'I exist to care for the vulnerable, the voiceless, love and protect, magnify beauty, to realise my true potential.'

'I exist to give my family a safe, nurturing environment, so they can grow into who they want to be, to be happy, to be the best they can be. Whatever I'm doing I want to be the best I can be.'

'I exist to positively contribute to my communities, to remain curious through constantly learning and challenging myself. To appreciate my life and find joy in family and adventure. My legacy is to leave the world a better place.'

'I exist to be part of the environmental solution, not to be perfect but to always be learning and improving- at work, in relationships and life.'

'My purpose is to live authentically, continuously striving to grow personally and professionally to become the truest, happiest and wisest version of myself and to inspire others to do the same.'

Real people with a deep-rooted passion to build a better world around them. I think these are amazing.

There are other ways of shaping your statements, here's some examples from some well-known people using a variety of approaches.

Maya Angelou, American poet and civil rights activist

'My mission in life is not merely to survive, but to thrive; and to do so with some passion, some compassion, some humour, and some style.'

Oprah Winfrey, American talk show host

'To be a teacher. And to be known for inspiring my students to be more than they thought they could be.'

Richard Branson, British entrepreneur

'To have fun in my journey through life and learn from my mistakes.'

Mahatma Gandhi, Indian lawyer and anti-colonial nationalist

'I shall not fear anyone on Earth. I shall fear only God. I shall not bear ill will toward anyone. I shall not submit to injustice from anyone. I shall conquer untruth by truth. And in resisting untruth, I shall put up with all suffering.'

Ralph Waldo Emerson, American essayist, philosopher and abolitionist

'To laugh often and much. To win the respect of intelligent people and the affection of children. To earn the appreciation of honest critics and endure the betrayal of false friends. To appreciate beauty, to find the best in others. To leave the world a bit better, whether by a healthy child, a garden patch, or a redeemed social condition. To know even one life has breathed easier because you have lived. This is to have succeeded.'

Amanda Steinberg, Founder of Daily Worth

'To use my gifts of intelligence, charisma, and serial optimism to cultivate the self-worth and net-worth of women around the world.'

Denise Morrison, American businesswoman

'To serve as a leader, live a balanced life, and apply ethical principles to make a significant difference.'

Go to exercise 3 to craft your purpose. Good luck!

Our journey to find your voice is underway. You have now affirmed your values, explored your passion and crafted your purpose. Now it's time to consider what's possible.

Exercise 1: Affirming my Values

List your values below with a brief explanation of what each one means to you. Aim for between 3 & 6 values.

Exercise 2: What am I deeply passionate about?

Whether you choose to use words or pictures, explore what you are truly passionate about.

Exercise 3: Crafting my Purpose

Craft a 20-25 word statement below that articulates your purpose. Why do you exist?

I exist to...

Reflections

Dream Big Dreams

'Be fearless in the pursuit of what sets your soul on fire'

Jennifer Lee

Go have a look at yourself in the mirror. A proper look. What do you see? I see an amazing person. You are unique, there's no-one else exactly like you in the world. Celebrate your uniqueness. You are one in 8 billion.

Inside you are bursting with potential, even if you don't realise it yet. There's so much you are capable of achieving in your life, such a difference you can make for others, such a legacy you can leave. We are only on this planet for a short period, do not waste a single moment of it.

Back in the distant past (BC- Before Covid), when I delivered *'Lead Like Mary'* and other leadership programmes face to face, I would set a challenge by asking participants to identify one great achievement still inside them. I explained that this could be anything in their professional lives or their personal lives and it was up to them to interpret the word 'great'. At first there was silence, this was a fast ball, it's not something we would normally talk about, but when they shared their achievements there was such a variety of amazing thoughts.

It's impossible to remember them all from over the years but there were definitely some common themes. A number of people chose writing a novel or a non-fiction book. They say everyone has a book inside them and for some that was certainly the case. Others included climbing mountains, travel to exotic, far-off places, running a marathon, completing a PhD. One person wanted to sell their home so their family could sail round the world. Wow! Several people over the years wanted to live more simply in the future, maybe a small holding, growing and rearing their own food. 'Living lightly on the Earth' was a common description.

Having listened to these, others shared that their achievements were with their family, a desire for their children to grow up as well rounded, confident young people. They were apologetic, concerned that their achievements paled into insignificance compared to climbing mountains and sailing seas. Nothing could be further from the truth, what could be more important than the role of a parent in preparing their children for the future?

Other people had the burning desire to really make a difference in the world, to leave their footprint, founding charities, leading global conservation projects, making medical breakthroughs, delivering change through elected office.

I loved these sessions, the dreams people had never failed to inspire me.

I would then ask a further question. What can possibly stop you realising these dreams?

The early answers would include factors like insufficient money, too many barriers to overcome, the views of other people, responsibilities, ill-health. Then we always arrived at the biggest barrier of all- themselves. They recognised they held the key. There were other real barriers to overcome, but the biggest one of all would be around their own lack of belief, lack of motivation, lack of focus, listening too much to the views of others, lack of confidence. Overcoming the barriers we create ourselves is probably the most important element that will determine whether you achieve your dreams.

What difference do you want to make and where? What does the better tomorrow look like that you want to create?

Your dreams are the stepping-stone between your purpose, which I invited you to discover and articulate in the previous chapter, and the picture of a future birthday party we will visualise in the next one.

'The size of your dreams must always exceed your current capacity to achieve them. If your dreams don't scare you, they are not big enough'

Ellen Johnson Sirleaf

Dream big. Return to your purpose. If you haven't managed to articulate it yet, work on that first. That should provide you with the direction of travel you want to make. That's your compass, heading due north. Your values form your moral compass, keeping you on the straight and narrow, guiding you through turbulent waters.

I invite you to imagine something. At some point in the future a book has been written about you. Your contribution, your achievements, your life. This book could take many forms:

It may simply be a labour of love, produced by your partner, your children or another family member, never intended for publication, describing all you have done for those close to you, full of memories, photos and anecdotes.

Maybe, also unpublished, it has been produced by your friends, describing the deep relationship you all share.

Or local people have self-published a book about your contribution to the community, championing those most vulnerable, leading positive local change.

Perhaps a voluntary body is indebted to you for your efforts and achievements, and the changes you have led. They've published a book full of contributions from recipients and colleagues.

Your organisation may have decided to record how, through your unstinting leadership, you have built an amazing place to work, and excellent, sustainable results.

Maybe the book celebrates your contribution on a wider basis, making a difference further afield, perhaps abroad, building a better world, tackling environmental challenges, fighting injustice, championing diversity, a voice for the vulnerable.

Or just possibly this is a best-selling book, the story of an amazing breakthrough, discovery or invention, or of a life given to political leadership. Maybe you have changed the world.

Or it could be any combination of the above.

Picture the book in your mind. Have a look at the front cover. Let your imagination soar. What do you see? What is the title of the book? Describe the cover. Use the pages at the end of this chapter to note your thinking.

Now it's time to really dream big. Find somewhere quiet, a special place that works for you.

Open your book, the one celebrating a life well lived. Begin to flick through the pages, look at the photos, check out the chapter headings, read the quotes, dive in, read some of the words. What's the book about? Have a look back at the possibilities above. Close the book, close your eyes and dream big.

To quote John Keating from the wonderful Dead Poets Society,

'The powerful play goes on and you may contribute a verse.'

What will your verse be?

It's time to create your 'life plan.'

Exercise 1

What will be the title of your book?

Design the cover. What do you see? Do a rough drawing.

Exercise 2

What are your dreams? Write down what you see as you turn the pages of the book.

Reflections

Create Your Life Plan

'There are dreamers and there are planners;
the planners make their dreams come true.'

Edwin Louis Cole

We have explored what you are passionate about, affirmed your values, crafted your purpose and dared to dream. Now it's time to create your life plan.

Let me say this right at the beginning. Although I am going to strongly encourage you to create a plan, it is not an essential element to finding your voice, unlike some other parts of the framework.

I say this because there are a handful of people I work with who really struggle with the whole concept of having a life plan, either because they like to live life as it comes along and regard having any kind of plan for the future as the anathema of being a free spirit, or because, for whatever reason, they find it difficult, if not terrifying to think about the future.

How do you feel about creating your life plan? Would you regard it as too restrictive to have a plan? Maybe you might miss new opportunities, perhaps you worry that if you don't achieve your plan you could be branded a failure? Or can you see the sense in it, giving you a structure and direction to move forward?

The most important thing to say up front is that this is a broad plan, a framework and nothing more. It is essential it's not restrictive, if it's too firm be prepared to be disappointed and to miss opportunities along the way.

I was first introduced to the concept of producing a life plan when I attended the Stephen Covey 'The 7 Habits of Highly Effective People' programme some twenty-five years ago. If you've read *'Lead Like Mary'* you'll already know how impactful and influential those 7 Habits have been to me over the years. It formed part of the second habit, 'Begin with the End in Mind.' Covey called it a Personal Mission Statement and summed up his view of its importance with this quote.

'A mission statement is not something you write overnight, but fundamentally your mission statement becomes your constitution, the solid expression of our vision and values. It becomes the criterion by which you measure everything else in your life.'

The purpose of your life plan is to create a broad picture of what your future could look like (remember those dreams) and then to put together a plan that can take you from today to that future point. If this whole book is about challenging and imploring you to find your voice, to realise your potential and to build a better tomorrow, this will be your blueprint.

Why is it important to plan? That's probably an obvious question but worth considering. Planning is the link between vision and execution.

No less than Pablo Picasso said,

'Our goals can only be reached through the medium of a plan in which we must fervently believe, and upon which we must vigorously act. There is no other route to success.'

You can have the clearest possible vision and/or goals but it is a waste of time without a clear plan which you then execute. One more quote, this time Bill Gates,

'Vision without execution is daydreaming.'

Let's get to work and begin to construct your life plan. This is not a five-minute job. It is so important it needs time to do it justice and do it properly. Begin it now but allocate time to work on it over the next few days and weeks. It's an iterative process, the investment of your time will be repaid many times. There's a template for your plan in Exercise 2 at the end of this chapter.

Your Purpose and Values

The first two elements of the plan are straightforward. They are your purpose and values which you have already been introduced to and worked on. To remind you, your purpose is why you exist, and your values are what's important to you. Take some time to put them into the template, but do so with an open mind, consider them again, are they right, do you need to work on them further?

Your Vision

Now it's time to create your vision, your picture of the future, in Covey's language your End in Mind. In his 7 Habits book Covey takes an approach to this that I find uncomfortable. He invites the reader to observe their own funeral, and to listen to what the various mourners say about your life. Sorry, but that doesn't work for me!

Instead, I use the medium of a future birthday. Not just any birthday. How important to you are those 'big birthdays' that occur every ten years, your decade birthdays, or as I call them 'Big Zero' birthdays? The day you become 20, 30, 40, 50 etc. Look ahead to a forthcoming Big Zero Birthday of yours, but (and you may hate this!) not the next one but the one after that. If you are in your twenties that will be your 40th, in your thirties that will be your 50th etc. When I teach this people often look aghast. That future Big Zero Birthday makes them feel so old. I remind them that age is a relative thing, for me it will be my 80th!

Why a decade birthday and why not the next one? It's because our Big Zero birthdays are, for a lot of people, significant. We tend to plan the phases of our life in decades (it's no coincidence that the most common time people change jobs or get divorced is in a 'Big Zero' birthday year), and also because we need enough time to deliver the amazing things you dreamed of. Depending on where you are in your current decade, that birthday will be between 11 and 19 years away. Not so long that it's impossible to envisage life that far ahead, but enough time to deliver your vision.

It's time to populate that future vision. Step on to my magic carpet and take a journey with me into the future. Look down and watch the years slip by, then fasten your seatbelt as we come into land on the day of that big birthday.

The problem we may well have at this point is the picture is hazy. So it should be, remember we agreed earlier that it needs to be a broad picture, but we do need to give it some structure. If you've read 'Lead Like Mary' you'll be familiar with this, we are going to divide our thinking into three areas - have, do and be.

First **have**. When you reach this future birthday what do you want to have in your life? The problem with this is it could sound too materialistic. Let's divide it into tangible and intangible. Look around you. Tangible could include things like property (where you are living and in what), possessions and wealth. Children may be in the picture as well, and here it may become a little emotional. Maybe you have no children now but yearn to start a family. How old would those children be on this future birthday? Close your eyes, can you see them? Powerful stuff.

Health may be there as well. Very few of us would say we want to be in poor health when we reach this future birthday. We know we can't guarantee that's going to be the case, what we can guarantee is all of us could do more, from today onwards, to give ourselves the best chance of being in robust health on that future birthday.

Now intangible. What about words like happiness, contentment, fulfilment and love? None of us envisaging that future birthday would want no happiness or love in our lives. Nothing can be guaranteed, what you can do is to resolve today to work even harder to make those words a reality in the future.

Next, we come to **do**. What are you doing in your life on this future birthday, and as you look back along the journey, what have you done? There is so much to consider here. This may well include your job (what kind of work are you doing at the time of this future birthday, what have you done, remember broad ideas don't try to be too specific). It will include a whole plethora of other things- volunteering, your family time, friends, holidays, travel, adventures, hobbies, education, community involvement and so much more. There's a lot to consider here.

Now is the time to think about your contribution, the difference you have made to the world around you, everything we have focused on in this book. What have you been doing over the last decade or two leading up to this birthday? Have you found your voice, what have you done to build a better tomorrow? What is your legacy? Take time to deeply think about this, your contribution may have been with your family, with friends, in your community, in voluntary endeavours, in your professional life. It may be in a myriad of different ways. Stretch yourself, return to those dreams, imagine what could be possible.

Finally **be**. Here it becomes even deeper. Find yourself somewhere quiet and peaceful to contemplate and come with me on a journey. It is the day of that future Big Zero birthday, and others have planned an event to celebrate this milestone day in your life. Or, more accurately, to celebrate you and your life to date. For you have led a special life.

You are at the event. Look around you, who can you see? Family, friends, people from your community and your voluntary activities, current and past work colleagues, all the people you hope would be there.

This is a poignant moment in this exercise, when I teach this tears are common. Often people are thinking of elderly family members, maybe their parents, who may have passed away before then, or a hoped-for child, as yet unborn, who will be in their teens on that day. Maybe this will resolve you to spend more time with those special people who might not be there on that day. Don't leave it until it's too late.

Now you need to listen carefully. One after another a number of those present are going to stand up and talk about you. They want to share with those assembled the kind of person you are, why you are so special, the rich and rewarding life you have lived, the difference you have made for them and others, your legacy. Listen to what each of them says, you can if you try hard enough, and once they have spoken write down what you heard.

Time to reflect. Would those people say those things about you now, or do you have to focus even more on being the person you want to be, making the difference you want to make?

Now it's time to get that vision down onto paper. You are going to create the picture of your life on that future birthday, capturing all your thinking from the Have, Do, Be exercise. You'll articulate it soon, and draft your vision, but first you're going to literally create that future birthday picture- by drawing it.

Your immediate reaction might be that this sounds like nonsense, that you can't draw. Of course you can! The reason this approach is important is because of the creativity it unlocks, I guarantee it allows you to be more imaginative than writing would be at this point. You can use Exercise 1 at the end of this chapter if you choose to.

Once you have finished drawing it's time to write. You are about to create your vision statement. Take your time, based on your picture construct a few paragraphs describing your life on your Big Zero birthday, including things you have done as you look backwards.

Good luck!

Your Themes

It's now time to turn your vision into tangible goals which you can focus on delivering, real things you are going to do to realise your vision.

Where to begin? To build the bridge between vision and goals we should first identify around four, maximum five, themes. These are not tangible goals but are the subject areas which fall out of the vision and will allow coherent, clear goals to follow. It's your vision and it's up to you to select the appropriate themes, but typically these might be areas like Family and Friends, Well-Being, Professional Life, Hobbies, Contribution. There's no one right answer and they do emerge when you re-read your vision. There's one person who is so important they deserve a theme of their own. It's you!

Your Goals

We come to the final element of your life plan, which is to create goals under each theme. These are the things, if you make them happen, which will enable you to achieve your vision. They are the bridge between vision and execution.

Because your vision is still between 11 and 19 years away it's important to break the goals down into more manageable chunks, I think setting one, five and ten year goals works pretty well.

An example could, under a Family and Friends theme, be about a house move. In one year your goal might be to have made a decision on the area you want to move to, the five year goal could be about completing the move in the 1-5 year time period and the ten year goal about extending your new property.

Let's come to the theme about you. You might have an ambition to run a marathon. At this stage it might be no more than a dream. Do nothing about it and it will remain a dream. When you commit to goals you take the first very significant step towards realising that dream. The one-year goal may be around weight loss and exercise, five years a half marathon and within ten years achieving your goal.

What about finding your voice? Committing yourself to building that better tomorrow? Because there are so many ways in which you could be making that difference it's difficult to focus on one area, but let's

224

assume your driving ambition is to found your own charity helping to address poverty and inequality in your community (or anywhere else in the world, the principle is the same). Your year one goal might be to research your ideas further and to do relevant voluntary work, within five years, having developed your plan, you might found and launch the charity; within ten years your goal would be around growth, funding and impact.

I hope there's enough there to convince you to have a go at creating your own life plan. If you're willing to have a go I promise your efforts will be rewarded. It will also provide you with the platform and the focus to plan how you are going to make that difference in the world.

Ensuring part of your life plan is about you is just so important. Let's focus next on being the very best version of you.

Exercise 1

My future birthday

Use this page to draw your future birthday...let your imagination run away with you!

Exercise 2

My Life Plan

My Purpose

I exist to...

My Values

Future Birthday Vision

The Big Themes

Theme 1

10 Year Goals

5 Year Goals

1 Year Goals

Theme 2

10 Year Goals

5 Year Goals

1 Year Goals

Theme 3

10 Year Goals

5 Year Goals

1 Year Goals

Theme 4

10 Year Goals

5 Year Goals

1 Year Goals

Theme 5

10 Year Goals

5 Year Goals

1 Year Goals

Reflections

Be the Best Version of You

'Self-care means giving the world the best of you, not what's left of you'.

Katie Reed

It's a joy the principles underpinning the premise of this book are so simple. I want you to stand up, find your voice and build a better world around you in all parts of your life. You cannot do so effectively if you are not in a good place, you must be the best version of you.

Being the best version of you goes right to the heart of the principle of inside-out leadership. It all begins with you. If you are not leading yourself effectively, not at your best, not in control, personally effective and modelling the behaviours you want to see in others, how can you expect to lead others?

Being the best version of you is about your well-being, and also a lot more - how you project yourself, choose your attitude, live your values and give your best every day.

Let's begin with well-being, a term that has become so popular over the last few years. It's defined as 'the state of being comfortable, healthy or happy.' We all understand the importance of looking after ourselves, it's only common sense, but, as they say, common sense isn't always common practice. In the chaotic world in which we live it's so easy to forget that caring for ourselves should and must be our number one priority.

If we want to care for others, serve them and build that better tomorrow, we must look after ourselves first. The most crucial word in that sentence is 'first.' You cannot drink from an empty cup.

Covey's final one of the 7 Habits is 'Sharpen the Saw.' He argues if we are to be at our best in all aspects of our life we must constantly renew ourselves. A consistent message here! He proposes renewal should focus on four dimension- our body, heart, mind and spirit.

In what ways could we renew ourselves in each of these areas? Here's a non-exhaustive list to get you started.

Body: exercise, walk in the countryside, go to the gym, review what you eat, reduce your alcohol intake, dance, sleep more, go to bed earlier, get up earlier, walk or cycle instead of driving, join a sports team, run a marathon, go on holiday, take up yoga, Pilates or tai chi, book a massage.

Heart: smile, laugh, pay someone a compliment, deposit in others relationship bank accounts (we'll cover this later in the book), spend quality time with your family and friends, call the friends you've lost contact with, help someone, serve others, perform random acts of kindness, volunteer, find someone who needs listening to, do things you enjoy, go on holiday, garden, buy flowers.

Mind: read, study, learn a new language, take up a new hobby, keep abreast of professional journals, sign up for development courses, book a place at a conference or seminar, review your professional development with your boss, start a degree, take on new work responsibilities, stretch yourself, create a career development plan, learn to play a musical instrument.

Spirit: review your purpose and values, live your values, walk in the countryside, look around you, create or revisit your life plan, listen to music, walk and think, renew your commitment to your religion, go to

236

church, go to the pub, celebrate your life with your family, re-commit your marriage vows.

It's time to make some commitments. What will you do, in the next couple of weeks, to renew in each of these four dimensions? If you already have things planned, include them (and well done!) but stretch yourself, what else could you do? Use Exercise 1 at the end of this chapter to record your commitments.

There's no point in compiling your list if you are not going to keep to it. In the next chapter we'll explore the principles and practices of effective time management. There are just four of them, and the final one is 'execute daily with discipline.'

Covey further believes renewal should be a daily activity, scheduled into our weekly plan. At first that seems strange. Can you really schedule a walk, quality time with your children or starting a new hobby alongside the normal meetings? The answer is you must. It's the only way we can ensure that time is not stolen from us by yet another meeting, or wasted drifting through life, watching random television, surfing the net. We should schedule our non-work time with the same discipline as we do our office hours. It's the secret to ensuring we live a productive life.

We can do none of this unless we have balance in our lives, particularly between our work and personal time. You can't be the best version of yourself if you are working excessive hours, always in the office or your home workstation, sending or answering e-mails in the late evening or at the weekend, anxious, stressed and exhausted. More to come in a few moments.

When I work with people in 1-1 mentoring or coaching sessions they are much more likely now to raise the issue of their mental health. Not so long ago it was a taboo subject, back in my corporate days anyone who admitted to problems would have been ridiculed. The issues were there back then too, they were just brushed under the carpet. A colleague of mine from maybe twenty years ago, a senior guy, early fifties, softly spoken, took his own life by jumping off a boat in the Lake District. It emerged that he was a tormented soul, with financial issues, who just couldn't see a way forward. We never knew, and if we had I fear it would have made no difference. Looking back the signs were there, we just never looked for them.

Mental health at work is now a massive issue. Take a look at these statistics:

Up to 300,000 people with mental health problems lose their job every year. (One example; one worker, after telling her boss about her depression, became the subject of office gossip.   After several anxious months, she left.)

89% of workers with mental health problems report an impact on their working lives.

91,000 NHS staff have taken at least a month off work with stress since 2014.

Just 13% of employees would be comfortable talking about mental illness at work.

Mental health issues cost UK businesses £42 billion per year.

95% of employees calling in sick with stress give a different reason.

(source: mypossibleself.com)

I came across a delightful graphic on-line which set out five ways of well-being:

Connect with family, friends and colleagues. Invest time in building relationships.

Be active, discover activity you enjoy.

Take notice, catch sight of the beautiful. Be aware of the world around you.

Keep learning. Try something new. It builds confidence. Rediscover an old interest.

Give. Do something nice for a friend. Smile. Volunteer your time. Say thanks often.

There's a lovely book by Charlie Mackesy called 'The Boy, The Mole, The Fox and The Horse.' Beautifully illustrated, it was published in 2019 and became a best seller.

It follows the developing friendship between the four protagonists in the title, and is a story of love, hope, friendship and courage. It really resonates at a time when a focus on mental health is so important.

Here's a few quotes from the book.

'I'm so small' said the mole. 'Yes', said the boy, 'but you make a huge difference.'

'What do you want to be when you grow up?' 'Kind' said the boy.'

'What do you think is the biggest waste of time?' 'Comparing yourself to others' said the mole.'

'Imagine how we would be if we were less afraid.'

'Being kind to yourself is one of the greatest kindnesses.'

'What is the bravest thing you've ever said?' asked the boy. 'Help' said the horse.'

'The greatest illusion is that life should be perfect.'

'When the dark clouds come...keep going...'

'Always remember you matter, you are important and you are loved, and you bring to this world things no-one else can.'

Looking after yourself, mentally and physically, is crucial, but being the best version of you is about a lot more than that. It's also about how you project yourself, and the way you role model the behaviours you want to see in others. It's about getting up in the morning and resolving that each day you will be the best version of you. It's about living your values. It's about being authentic, effective and brave - leading like Mary.

Ever woken up, felt lousy, dragged yourself off to work and known that you've been in a bad mood all day, spreading negative energy? I'm sure you have, we all have. Every single day, when you wake up, you can choose your attitude.

I first came across this simple truth in a training video called Fish! featuring a group of employees from the Pike Place fish market in Seattle. It's an uplifting video focused on providing excellent customer service, based on four simple messages:

Enjoy: whatever your job, make sure that you generate and have fun at work. Happy teams are far more productive and that enjoyment will rub off on your customers.

Be There: whenever you are with a customer (or indeed anyone else) be there. Give them your complete, undivided attention. Make them, during this interaction, the most important person in the world.

Make Their Day: delight them, leave them with a warm and lasting memory of their interaction with you. Remember the quote from Maya Angelou:

'People will forget what you said, people will forget what you did, but people will never forget how you made them feel.'

Choose Your Attitude: when you wake up in the morning you can choose your attitude for the day. Choose to be happy and positive.

Not every job is glamorous, selling fish certainly isn't. Whatever your job, determine you will do it to the best of your ability. My son Chris taught me this lesson. He had part time hospitality roles when younger, including waiting on and bartender in busy venues. He resolved to be the best waiter or bartender he could possibly be. Whatever you do, be proud.

There's a lovely quote from Roald Dahl.

'I began to realize how important it was to be an enthusiast in life. If you are interested in something, no matter what it is, go at it full speed. Embrace it with both arms, hug it, love it and above all become passionate about it. Lukewarm is no good.'

One more thought. The mark of a person is how they treat serving staff, in shops, restaurants or bars. If someone is rude or off hand with serving staff, drop that person from your life.

I once came across this mantra for living a purposeful, fulfilling life.

'Live, love, learn, laugh and leave a legacy.'

Seems like a pretty good recipe to me!

Let's finish with a quote I shared recently, which for me sums up what being the best version of you is about.

'Wake up early. Drink coffee. Be ambitious. Keep your priorities straight, your mind right, and your head up. Do well, live well and dress really well. Do what you love, love what you do. It's time to start living.'

Being the best version of you is just so important if you are to find your voice. Equally essential is finding the time to think.

Exercise 1

What are you going to do, in the next couple of weeks, to renew in each of these four dimensions?

Body

Heart

Mind

Spirit

Reflections

Make Time to Think

'Sometimes I just need my alone time. This world is so crazy and unpredictable.
I just need some time to think, relax and breathe.'

Anon

The premise of this book, the challenge I am setting you, is simple. I'm asking you not just to be an authentic leader, but to find your voice, to build a better world around you, to be at the vanguard of building a better tomorrow, whether it's for your family, friends, community, team, organisation or society. To make that a life-long challenge.

It's a tough challenge, and one which will require vast amounts of your belief, energy, resilience and determination.

There's also one other thing it will require, and maybe it's the hardest of all to find. It will need you to make time to think.

Time to think? What a luxury! I can already hear your howls of protest. But unless you make time to think you simply cannot deliver that better tomorrow.

What do you need to find time to think about? Well, try these for starters.

Self-reflection. Taking the time to step back and look in that mirror. How am I doing? How do I know? What feedback have I sought and received? What am I going to do more of, or differently, or what am I going to stop doing as a result of that feedback? How did I do this week? How can I do a little bit better next week?

'Time spent in reflection is never wasted. It's an intimate date with yourself.'

Paul Wong.

How is the work project going? Are we on course? Have we got the right team in place? What further resources do we need? What are the next deadlines? What barriers do I need to remove? How shall we celebrate the next quick win?

How do I address the people issue in my team? What will happen if I don't act now? What are the potential pitfalls of intervening? What are the implications for the rest of the team? What help do I need?

What do I truly want from this relationship? How do I feel about my trust being abused? How can we move forward? Do I want to?

What impact do I want to have on the world? Where do I want to make a difference? Do I have the courage to make it happen? Can I find my voice?

Big issues indeed, which need and deserve deep thought.

'You can't hurry creativity so take time to ponder your ideas. Make time to sit back and think things over. That's usually how the best ideas bloom.'

Harvey MacKay

We can think this in a variety of settings but I strongly recommend you include being outside, thinking whilst you walk, in a simulating environment. My best thinking takes place walking in a park, the countryside or especially by the sea.

'Sometimes you need to step outside, take some air and remind yourself of who you want to be.'

Anon.

Time on our own to think is important, and so is time with others. Thinking in these situations is about 1-1 or group exploration, exchange of ideas, and planning. It's about creativity. It could take a variety of forms depending on which opportunities you are progressing. It might be with a colleague, a friend, your boss, the team you line manage, a project team you have assembled, a customer, supplier, funder or partner organisation. Truly effective thinking in these instances requires an open mind, empathic listening, creativity, mutual respect and a mutually beneficial mentality.

Hold these sessions regularly, both to review progress and plan ahead. The best teams I work with do just that, they schedule regular 'away days' to step back, zoom out, take stock, re-group, and plan. They are also great opportunities for team building.

Of course it's not just about thinking, it's about doing as well and great teams need a combination of thinkers and doers. Never underestimate the value of the thinkers though and how effective they can be. Many years ago I was a participant on a training programme. We were divided into two groups, the 'thinkers' and the 'doers', presumably based on test results or observation. I was placed with the doers, which delighted me, I loved to think of myself as a man of action.

Our task appeared on a slide.

'10 miles down the road, in the local town, is a police station. Above the entrance is a date brick. Find out the year on it.'

Us doers leapt to our collective feet and ran from the room. We piled into cars and headed for the local town, no doubt committing multiple traffic offences along the way (I'm not sure the exercise had been risk assessed!). We were determined to win.

The thinkers? They did just that for five minutes then telephoned the police station...

Never forget the importance of thinking time. Schedule it into your calendar. I guarantee you will deliver your opportunities more effectively.

However, there is a problem.

Over the last few years or so I have watched a disease spread at disturbing speed across organisations large and small. On this occasion I'm not talking about Covid, but one I call the 'Busy Busy Disease.'

It goes like this. Whenever I meet people and ask how work is going the response is always the same. They sigh deeply and say 'I'm busy, so busy, there's just so much to do.' They share stories of a never-ending set of demands on their time, unclear or conflicting priorities, constant interruptions, excessive hours, e-mails arriving in the evenings and at weekends, and back-to-back Teams or Zoom calls.

They look at me with glazed eyes when I ask what they have done about it. They are caught in a maelstrom from which there seems to be no escape.

Does this sound familiar? I'm concerned I have exaggerated, surely it can't be so widespread and consistent a story, but when I reflect I know I haven't, I hear the same conversation all the time.

Ironically, changing working practices during the past two or three years, driven by the pandemic and forged during lockdown, have made the situation worse. For so many people this meant an overnight transformation from working in offices to working from home. I say ironically because this should have brought so many improvements. Free of the burden of commuting, which can often involve a two or three hours round trip daily, people should have enjoyed a welcome boost to their leisure time able to start later and finish earlier than was possible before. Now people would be able to focus on the important stuff, free of colleagues' interruptions, coffee machine chat, wasteful meetings, and office politics.

The experience of far too many has been the polar opposite. As people began to figure out how to work in this strange new world some kind of collective guilt and desperate need to justify one's existence took hold. If they weren't seen to be working all hours then the assumption was made that others would believe they must be skiving. How to do that? Be seen on video calls. Choose your background carefully, artificial or not, so others couldn't see your unmade bed or messy kitchen. Don't waste time with small talk. Start early, finish late, be seen to be busy - send a load of emails and answer them at weekends would be a good way to do that.

As the course of the pandemic has moved on, teams and organisations have been thinking through future working patterns - 'hybrid working' has entered the glossary of new terms, often a combination of working from home some days of the week while returning to the workplace on others. It is now understood that informal time with colleagues is essential (people spark off each other). But the core of the problem is still there. It existed long before the pandemic. People in so many roles in far too many organisations are just too busy. That should be okay, surely preferable to being at a loose end, but the problem here is simple. People are busy, but not busy on their most important things.

My over-riding point is it can't continue. If organisations allow their people to carry on working excessive hours unaddressed, with the inevitable resultant stress it creates, we will reach a tipping point. Absence through stress, burn out and mental illness will increase exponentially, I honestly believe we are standing on the edge of a precipice.

It's a dark picture I paint, but even if it's exaggerated, we cannot escape the fact that people who work excessive hours, who feel overwhelmed and burned out are not, cannot, be effective. Fundamentally there is no link between increased hours and increased effectiveness. Indeed, I am convinced the contra rule applies, the more hours someone works the less effective they become. To validate my point, I would urge you to look at people who work part time. Someone who works three days a week must be efficient; they have to fit their work into those three days. They have no time to drift. Time and time again I find them more effective than their full-time colleagues.

Excessive hours are only part of the issue. Clarity and focus are essential. Time is a finite resource, and we cannot waste a single moment of it at work doing something which is not important. The vast majority of what we do must link directly to one of our goals, to the purpose of our role, ultimately to the big picture of our organisation's vision and strategy. We shall return to this later.

As people outline to me their busy working lives I can only reply with one question. What can you do about it? Far too often their answer is they can do nothing. Meetings are added to their schedule by others, the flow of work is constant and never-ending, the demands on them don't go away, their boss allows it to happen unchecked etc.

It must stop but only one person is going to stop it. I'm sorry to break this to you but it's not going to be your boss. Or their boss. It's you. It's time to take control. No-one else can but you and no-one else will.

Let's go back to the first section of this book, and indeed to the beginning of *'Lead Like Mary'* where we explored the principle of inside-out leadership. Remember the inner circle, the only place your leadership journey can begin, where you are leading yourself? One of the elements of leading yourself is being in control.

If any of this chapter so far resonates, if you feel you are working too many hours, are overwhelmed, are not as effective as you could be, you must take control.

Let's do it! The first question for you is what are the biggest barriers to effectively managing your time? Common answers from people I work with are:

-Other people
-Interruptions
-Too many priorities
-Unclear priorities
-Conflicting priorities
-Changing priorities
-Too many meetings
-Irrelevant meetings
-Too many e-mails
-Crises and firefighting
-My boss

And finally...me! It takes a while but we always get there. That moment of self-awareness, that sudden realisation that often the biggest barrier to effectively managing your time is you! The above may be contributory factors but ultimately you are both the problem and the solution.

You'll remember that we looked at the power of our beliefs early in this book. Our beliefs govern our actions which govern our results, which in turn re-enforce our beliefs. If we believe there is nothing we can do about how busy we are, how will we act and behave? Almost certainly negatively, angry, complaining about our lot, blaming everyone else, resigned to our fate. What results will we get? Nothing will change, re-enforcing our beliefs.

But if our belief changes to 'it's me and only me who can solve this, I can take control', watch what happens. Now we act and behave differently. We find the solutions, we experience improved results. Remember this maxim,

'we can only achieve quantum leap improvements when we change our beliefs.'

Let's address the problem together, it's time to take control.

In 'The 7 Habits of Highly Effective People' Covey introduces us to a simple time management matrix. Many of you will be familiar with it, I've seen it used subsequently as the bedrock of countless time management articles and training. It's in the public domain, google 'time management matrix' and there you are.

The matrix consists of a large square divided into four quadrants as follows:

Quadrant I consists of things we do which are **urgent and important**
Quadrant II consists of things we do which are **important but not urgent**

252

Quadrant III consists of things we do which are **urgent but not important**
Quadrant IV consists of things we do which are **neither urgent nor important**

Everything we do at work (which is where we will focus even though the principle applies in our whole life) can be placed into one of the four quadrants, depending on its relative importance and urgency. With a crucial caveat. For something to be important it must be important to you, not merely to someone else. This is a critical distinction, and only you know whether it is important to you.

Have a think about the things you do at work that fall into each quadrant. Jot them down, trying to get a couple of examples for each quadrant.

Quadrant I (urgent and important) typically consists of items that have a deadline or involve firefighting. Examples could be a report required by the end of the week, a people issue, a deadline for circulating a project brief, a systems malfunction, a customer complaint. If this was the fire brigade in Quadrant I they'd be fighting fires. It's the quadrant that copes with today.

Quadrant II (important, not urgent) is mainly longer-term stuff, typically linked to planning and people. Planning and executing a project, developing a strategy, continual improvement, building relationships, a performance management review, recruiting a new team member, a 1-1 session with your boss, visiting customers. The fire brigade's fire prevention and education efforts. It's the quadrant that builds a better tomorrow.

Quadrant III (urgent, not important) typically includes other people's emergencies and crises, such as a request for help which is not about something important for you, or urgent demands from colleagues to enable them to deliver their important priorities. The point here is you are very likely to provide that help or give in to those demands. Why? Because you are a nice person who wants to help! But beware, it's the quadrant that eats away at our time.

Quadrant IV (neither urgent nor important) is a random list which could include surfing the net, some filing or coffee machine gossip. It's nice to escape here if we're feeling a bit overwhelmed with everything we have to do in the other quadrants. It's the quadrant we escape to, though we know it's unproductive.

Now have a think, in a typical week of work what percentage of your time do you spend in each of the four quadrants? All I'm looking for is your best guess, using your intuition. You may well resolve, next week, to record more carefully all that you do, and decide, as objectively as possible, which quadrants everything fits into.

When I do this exercise with groups, the vast majority of people tend to estimate the percentage of their time spent in quadrants I & II combined (in other words on important stuff) at around 70-80% or even higher. They will therefore have a corresponding much lower percentage for quadrants III & IV. A couple of people will have a different picture, estimating their quadrant III figure to be nearer to 50% or even higher.

How do your estimates compare with the numbers above? If they are high for quadrants I & II that must, at this point, be reassuring, surely this is a sign of effectiveness? Or is your quadrant III figure higher, around 50%? If so, you may just be demonstrating your self-awareness.

Why? Because of the following statistics. The results of a comprehensive survey, analytically conducted across a whole number of people in many different organisations, examining closely the split of their time across the quadrants. Now came the crunch, those organisations were divided into two groups. The first, significantly larger group, were typical organisations, not poor, not failing, doing ok. The much smaller group were highly effective organisations, evidenced by a range of criteria, both quantitative and qualitative.

The results? Take a look at this.

In those **typical** organisations people's time was split as follows:

Quadrant I: 25%
Quadrant II: 15%
Quadrant III: 55%
Quadrant IV: 5%

However, in the **highly effective** organisations, people were spending their precious, finite time very differently:

Quadrant I: 20%
Quadrant II: 65%
Quadrant III: 15%
Quadrant IV: <1%

The difference is stark. In typical organisations just 15% of time, on average, is being spent on people and planning, building that better tomorrow. 60% of their time (a combination of quadrants 3&4) is taken up with things that are simply not important to them. 60% of a typical working week, that's three whole days!

There's a vastly different picture in the highly effective organisations- now 65% of time is spent on important, value-adding work and only 15% in quadrant III. A massive change.

Look again at your numbers. If your quadrants I & II percentage is high (above 70%) I am certainly not saying you are wrong. You may already be highly effective, especially if your quadrant II number is higher than your quadrant I. All I'm asking at this stage is you keep an open mind. My evidence, based on years of observations and analysis, is nearly all of us spend far more time in quadrant III than we realise or admit to. Keep remembering it is quadrant II (important but not urgent) that gives us the greatest longer-term benefit. It's here we build that better tomorrow. If we are spending a significant amount of time in quadrant III we will either be trying to cope by working excessive hours or it will be at the detriment of quadrant II. Either way that is not a formula for effectiveness.

Covey called quadrant III the 'quadrant of deception'. Why? Because it is so easy to kid ourselves we are not in it. Surely all the work we do is important? That's the point, it is important, but to somebody else, not us. This is not about becoming unhelpful overnight, but it's about recognising the impact quadrant III has on our overall effectiveness, and taking the steps to reduce, not eradicate, its existence.

My challenge to you is to take up my earlier suggestion and to spend the next week recording what you are doing at work hour by hour. Which quadrants are you in for particular tasks and activities? Can you identify those quadrant III activities? I promise you they are there.

You have now taken the first big step to taking control of your time. Let's move on to the next steps. The proposition to you is breakthrough requires absolute adherence to just four principles of effective time management, which are:

Be in control
Focus on the truly important
Plan weekly
Execute daily with discipline

Be in control

This is critical. If you don't take control external factors will control you. We've already addressed a major part of the battle- recognising and reducing quadrant III activity. But that's not all.

Here are some other actions to focus on to take control:

Stop working excessive hours. I'm not suggesting you slavishly follow your contracted hours, many people are happy to put in the extra time when it is needed, but when it becomes the norm we have surrendered control.

Take breaks. Go for a stretch, make coffee, chat to colleagues, get away from that screen.

Do not let others seize control of your calendar by booking your time out. I realise it's difficult to stop if it's 'what is done round here' but recognise the detrimental impact on your effectiveness. Make a habit of booking out your own time when you need to be in quadrant II. Arrange meetings with yourself and get them into your calendar!

Deal with your emails then switch them off. Yes, really! Do not check your emails at times you are not working.

Do not fall into the trap of back-to-back meetings. You need breaks between them to reflect and plan.

Let people know when you need to focus, particularly on quadrant II activity.

Learn that there are many ways to say 'no.' Do not develop a reputation for being unhelpful, say when it's not a convenient time and why, then arrange an alternative time. People will quickly learn to respect your need for focus.

If working at home, at the end of the day switch off your computer and go for a walk. Make this the equivalent of a commute, and far more pleasant.

Understand how you act and behave influences others. Particularly if you are in a management role. Role model the behaviours you want to see in others.

Focus on the truly important

 Adherence to this principle provides the breakthrough for reducing quadrant III activity. The starting point is you can't focus on the truly important if you don't know what it is. In *'Lead Like Mary'* the trait of Absolute Clarity provides the framework.

The proposition is simple. When you develop absolute clarity you:

-have line of sight into how what you do helps to deliver your organisation's overall vision and strategy. Your work has purpose.

-are crystal clear on the purpose of your role, why it exists (and can articulate it in 20-25 words at most.)

-have clear, unambiguous goals or objectives (no more than 5, ideally 3). They should focus on the most important things you are there to deliver.

Only once you are clear on what is truly important can you work to ensure you focus the majority of your time on those most important things. I reckon in a typical week it's where you should spend 70-75% of your time. Any less and you're not being truly effective, any more is unrealistic, there will always be other things to do.

Plan weekly

Hands up if you use a 'to do' list. Lots of hands, most of us do. Where it works the to-do list is a useful tool to remind us of things we need to do, but used wrongly, as it is so often, it inevitably increases ineffectiveness.

Picture the scene. The beginning of the working day. Computer on, coffee poured, to-do list, full of items, in front of us. Off we go. Which items on the list do we do first? Typically the quick ones, the easy ones, the most urgent, the ones colleagues are shouting loudest for, the ones we enjoy. Look at the list, all those ticks, we must be making so much progress.

Incidentally, sometimes people tell me they are so driven by lots of ticks on their to-do list that they complete a task then they write it on the list and tick it. Fancy that!

Lunch time, a sandwich, then off again. New items have been added to the list but we focus on the quick and easy ones again. End of the day. List reduced, feels good.

Next morning, write a list. First thing we do is to copy across the things we didn't do yesterday. Here's the issue. The things we didn't do yesterday are almost certainly those longer, bigger jobs, which invariably are quadrant II activities. Why didn't we do them? Firstly by their definition they may be important but they are not urgent. Doing them takes far more time than the quick ones, and if we tackle one or two of them we'll have very little ticked off our to-do list by the end of the day. They're also hard to do, we'll need to think, we may well need information from others. So the quick, easy and merely urgent ones get done at the expense of these important ones.

Problem is, these quadrant II activities - to do with people and planning- are the things that will take us forward, they're not merely about coping with today, they're about building that better tomorrow.

The breakthrough occurs when you restrict your to-do list to quadrant I (and where necessary quadrant III) tasks only and schedule into your calendar those quadrant II activities, ensuring we allow sufficient time to complete them. Plan on a weekly basis, schedule the week ahead, be determined to make it as effective as possible. Also schedule in time to complete the remaining to-do list items, to deal with emails, to take a break, to chat with colleagues. Take control and plan weekly.

Execute daily with discipline.

You can have the most elegant of weekly plans, perfectly crafted with time carefully allocated to focus on those quadrant II activities, but it's not worth the effort if you then fail to execute with discipline.

It's essential to review progress weekly. Take time out at the end of the week to reflect. How did you do? How well did you stick to your schedule? For example, if on Tuesday morning you had scheduled two hours to write a project brief, did you do it? If you did, well done. If not, what stopped you? Was it a genuine crisis you had to deal with? If so, no issue, that's sometimes unavoidable. If the fire brigade has a training session scheduled on Tuesday morning and the alarm sounds they're not going to refuse to attend the emergency. Or was it your lack of discipline, failing to start something you weren't looking forward to and creating excuses to avoid doing it?

Once you have reviewed the previous week, plan the new one, resolving to do all you can to keep to your schedule. It's all about continual improvement, just trying to make every week a little bit better than the last. We can never achieve perfection, in the chaotic world we live in it's unrealistic.

There you go, an examination of the issues and exploration of the steps to help you take control of your time. Resolve today to take up the challenge, it's an essential element to enable you to find your voice.

Managing your time effectively is not easy, it's a real challenge, but the upside is enormous so stick at it. Take it a day at a time, a week at a time, keep a daily log, reflect regularly. Celebrate small wins. Find a buddy to hold you to account. If you are persistent things will improve, and you and others will notice a step change in your effectiveness.

As you make progress it becomes self-perpetuating. People will know when there are times you are not to be disturbed. They will respect that. Equally they will relish the additional time you now have to build relationships with them. You will play your part in making those meetings you choose to attend more effective. Your team will benefit from deeper, more effective 1-1s.

If you are focused on your most important goals improved results will follow.

What to do with the additional time you have?

If it's an issue resolve your work/life balance. No more late nights in the office, taking work home, and answering emails 24 hours a day.

Take time to repair, nurture and grow your most important relationships inside and outside work.

Focus on the things at work that add the most long-term value. 1-1s, planning, continual improvement, project reviews, strategy. The link should be obvious, these are all Quadrant II activities.

Never forget the importance of building relationships, wandering around is time well spent.

Use the time to think!

The exercises at the end of this chapter may help to focus your mind on the opportunity here.

This has been a lengthy chapter, for which I offer no apology. Finding time to think is essential if you are to build that better tomorrow. You will never find time until you take control. Do it effectively and the difference will be enormous.

That's the last of our five steps finding your voice within. It's time to amplify your voice!

Exercise 1

The Time Management Matrix

Draw the Matrix below (find it by searching for Covey Time Management Matrix if you need to.)

In each quadrant list 2 or 3 things you do at work on a regular basis

Exercise 2

Focus on the Truly Important

What is the purpose of your role?

My role exists to...(max 20-25 words)

My Line of Sight

How does my role contribute to achieving my organisation's vision and strategy?

My Most Important Goals (3-5)

Reflections

The Voice Amplified

Become an Inspire & Enable Leader

'I've learned that people will forget what you said, people will forget what you did, but people will never forget how you made them feel.'

Mary Angelou

Earlier on I set out for you the proposition that the death knell has sounded for Command & Control leadership. The paradigm that has existed for years, even centuries, is no longer an option in our new world. The notion that as a boss at work we get the best out of people by controlling them, stunting their growth, keeping them in the dark, telling them what to do, leaning over their shoulder, micro-managing, suffocating them, not trusting them, is outdated.

I referenced earlier that Stephen M R Covey, in his new book, described five emerging forces which demand a new kind of leadership at work. To remind you, they were:

A technological revolution which is bringing extraordinary changes

The changing nature of work. It is now far more collaborative and creative than ever before.

The changing nature of the workplace. Hybrid working is here to stay.

The changing nature of the workforce. Millennials and Gen Z demand a different type of leadership

The changing nature of choice. People have far more choices about what they do with their life than ever before.

The proposition to you is simple. We need to make the move to a new leadership paradigm, where Command & Control is replaced with Inspire & Enable.

I guarantee it will make building that better tomorrow much more achievable, whatever your leadership role inside or outside work.

What do we mean by Inspire & Enable leadership? It's about unleashing the potential for greatness people have inside them, igniting fires, creating an environment, a culture, where that is possible and welcomed.

Inspire & Enable leaders move from managing things and people to managing things and leading people. They move from boss to coach. Nothing creates dependency better than Command & Control, nothing lights fires within better than Inspire & Enable.

In a world where people can live and work anywhere it's about leaders creating a culture which attracts, retains, engages and inspires the best people. A culture based on trust.

Remember these facts

Millennials are 22 times more likely to stay in a high trust culture
Gen X are 16 times more likely
Even Baby Boomers are 14 times more likely

Many people I work with may well believe they are already Inspire & Enable leaders. The truth is many of those want to be Inspire & Enable leaders, but in reality have not made the leap. They may well be trying, but when the going gets tough, when they are under pressure, they revert to Command & Control.

Imagine a continuum. At one end our old friend Bill. A bully, undermining, manipulative, shouting and balling, the most extreme examples of Command & Control.

Move along to the other end of the continuum, here you find my example from above, people who mean well, are kind people, in many cases authentic leaders who want to lead like Mary, but they haven't made the leap.

What a leap it is! I believe there is a significant gap between the two. Successfully making the leap to Inspire & Enable requires self-awareness, belief, determination and courage. Those who do so have an amazing opportunity to unleash potential in others, to enable growth and lead a step change in engagement, performance and results.

What does an Inspire & Enable leader do? As the title suggests let's break it into two parts.

They inspire those around them. They do so because of who they are (authentic, a role model, trustworthy, humble, determined, high in integrity, open, genuine, caring). They also do so by setting out a compelling picture of the future in a way that others want to join them on the journey.

They enable those around them. They create absolute clarity, give as much freedom as possible, but always within a framework, encourage growth, allow mistakes, support, trust, encourage but also hold others accountable (practicing joint accountability) and have difficult conversations when needed. They treat everyone as a unique individual, getting to understand what makes them tick.

Some people will be uncomfortable with Inspire & Enable leadership. They like being told what to do, to have their work closely monitored, it makes them feels safe. An Inspire & Enable leader understands that, but never reverts to the old paradigm, they more gently encourage growth, giving some freedom within a smaller framework. Over time many of these people respond positively to the approach and begin to blossom. Those that don't are likely to look for another role somewhere more suited to them., and that's fine.

If we revert to Covey's five emerging forces it is not difficult to understand how Inspire & Enable leadership at work is not only desirable, it's also essential.

As technology develops at speed, leaders have to understand they can no longer exercise the control they traditionally had. People work far more independently.

As the nature of work changes it is Inspire & Enable leaders who welcome creativity and collaboration. Command & Control leaders cannot deal with the loss of control.

As the nature of the workplace changes, Command & Control leaders realise their approach is incompatible with home and hybrid working. They attempt to regain control by insisting a return to the traditional workplace, but soon understand there is an unstoppable change in working practices.

As the nature of the workforce changes, Millennials and Gen Z will increasingly need and demand a leadership approach which encourages growth.

As the nature of choice changes good people will leave if their expectations at work are not met.

Inspire & Enable leaders are building a new world of work, a world of freedom, disciplined but creative working, choice, growth, trust and meaningful work. The resulting unleashing of potential will deliver extraordinary results for those people, teams and organisations.

Why is all this important in the context of the premise of this book? In encouraging you to find your voice, why am I making the case for this new approach to leadership so strongly? Simply because I regard it as essential if you are to be able to build that better world.

Let's start with your boss and the prevailing organisational culture where you work. If it's based around Command & Control you simply will not have the flexibility, encouragement, permission and resources to make the changes you desire. Command & Control dislikes change, the status quo is fine.

If you line manage a team, however large or small, becoming an Inspire & Enable leader yourself is essential to unleash their potential, allow them to flourish, and to work with you to build that better tomorrow.

Whether you manage a team or not there will be many other people you need to work effectively with - colleagues, other teams, project teams, volunteers, partner organisations, customers, suppliers etc. As an Inspire & Enable leader you have as much opportunity to influence them as you do your own team. You need them on the journey with you.

Can you be an Inspire & Enable leader in your life outside work? Absolutely you can! In your voluntary endeavours or in your community, inspiring and enabling others to deliver the changes you all desire.

What about in your family? Take a step back and imagine for a moment the difference between the two in the way you raise your children. Command & Control means always telling them what they can and can't do, restricting horizons, shattering dreams, denying opportunity. Inspire & Enabling means being a role model for them, encouraging growth, giving them the freedom to explore things for themselves. Freedom but always within a framework, in this case one which loves and protects but does not stifle.

I have no doubt which children will grow into rounded, confident adults ready to make their own mark in the world.

I love the description of parenting as giving your children roots and wings. Give them security and safety, teach them to know right from wrong, encourage them, let them grow, then watch them fly.

Consider the other big influence on your children, their teachers. Remember back to your own school days. Which teachers had the greatest positive influence on you? Those who inspired you, believed in you, encouraged you to explore and grow? They were few and far between. What kind of leaders are your child's teachers?

If that is what an Inspire & Enable leader is, it's also important to spell out what it is not. As I outlined in the earlier chapter 'The Mary Paradox' an Inspire & Enable leader is not soft. They hold others accountable (practicing joint accountability), have difficult conversations, and take decisive and firm action where it is needed. Yes, of course they occasionally need to tell people what to do, but they always do so within an Inspire & Enable paradigm.

Inspire & Enable leadership inverts the traditional hierarchical pyramid. Now the most senior person (typically the CEO) is at the base of the pyramid. Their primary role is to inspire and enable those above them (the Directors/Heads of). They in turn do so to the managers, who inspire and enable the supervisors and on to the front-line team. Their job is to delight their customers.

Nurture Your Relationships

'Communication and Trust are the two main ingredients
for a successful relationship.'

Phil Urwin.

Finding your voice in our chaotic world is not easy. Whatever changes you want to make there will be many barriers to overcome, whether it's people resistant to change, the intransigence of those in authority, or your own lack of self-belief and confidence.

The key to making progress lies back with our old friend, the Inside-Out Leadership Model. In the inner circle you know the change you wish to bring about. It could be big, or small, but either way it will contribute to building that better world. The challenge is how to make it a reality, and the answer invariably lies in the middle circle.

Any change we wish to bring about is almost certainly dependent on others. We need people to work with us, to help, to provide resources, to be champions of the change, to give legitimacy and permission. Equally if there is resistance from people in the middle circle, we need to be able to understand and break down the barriers in order to make progress.

The good news is that in that middle circle are people from all different parts of our life, people we know, are in contact with and who can help. They might be colleagues, decision makers, peers, your team members, people in partner organisations, people in positions of influence, family members, friends, community leaders; the list is endless.

The important point is they are real people, and you can communicate with them, work together, collaborate. Most of all you can build long-term relationships with them. There is no doubt the stronger those relationships are, the more beneficial they will be. The strength of those relationships is the breakthrough point to deliver your better world.

Great leaders in all walks of life understand the importance of building and nurturing relationships. They devote a considerable amount of their time to ensuring they are robust. They understand that long-term, highly effective relationships require mutual respect and mutual benefit.

Consider some of the changes you want to make. I guarantee you success is far more likely if you are able to use the strength of those relationships you have nurtured over a period of time. For change to happen we need to inspire people in that middle circle to come on that journey with us. In sales terms, we need them to buy from us, to buy into the change. Who are we most likely to buy from in any part of our lives? I would suggest we most readily buy from people we like, from people with whom we have established a relationship.

In the Trusting and Trustworthy chapter of *Lead Like Mary* we examined the importance of relationships, and I introduced the concept of the Relationship Bank Account. It's a relevant and powerful tool and worthy of revisiting. Imagine a bank account exists with every person with whom you have a relationship. Indeed, there are two bank accounts at play, you have one with them and they with you. If you choose to you can put deposits into their bank account and take withdrawals. Just like in a real bank account, only this time is doesn't usually involve depositing or withdrawing cash (most of the time!). Instead deposits could include giving them time, being there for them, listening, helping, caring, teaching, developing. It could also involve being honest with them, having important conversations, challenging them, helping them develop. Withdrawals would often be the contra actions, not listening, unreasonable demands etc.

On occasions it is inevitable we have to take withdrawals. For example, your boss might need to ask you to work late one evening. May I suggest if your relationship with your boss is strong, if there are lots of deposits in your bank account, you will be more likely to accept this withdrawal without it having a detrimental effect on your relationship.

Take a few minutes to think of your various relationships, across all parts of your life. Which ones are robust, high in credit? Which ones are around nil balance? Which ones have fallen into overdraft, or might even be close to bankruptcy? Armed with this understanding, resolve to work even harder at your relationships, to make more regular deposits, to get even more benefit from those already high in credit and to salvage and rebuild others. You never know when you will need them to enable you to build that better world.

Also be honest and clear. If there is an overdrawn relationship do you wish to salvage it? If not maybe it's time to terminate it.

Take time to identify your most important relationships in the context of the changes you want to make. Those are the ones we need to nurture. Be authentic, always let others see the real you, not an act, and show your passion.

Let's return to the concept of mutual benefit. For relationships to flourish they must deliver mutual benefit. In other words both parties must be able to feel they have got something out of the relationship, there must be win-win outcomes. This is the secret to delivering effective results in partnership with others and is the catalyst that enables breakthrough in so many situations. Think about the changes you want to deliver, the better tomorrow you want to build. Successful delivery will involve working with others, leveraging your relationships. Now think about how much easier making the breakthrough will be if you can demonstrate mutual benefit to the other party.

An example, you head up the finance function in a large organisation. You want to introduce a new sales reporting system. The key people involved are the sales force, who will be required to operate the new system and convince customers of its benefits. Sales managers are your primary stakeholders, their role will be crucial in bringing the sales force on board. But you have no established relationship with these sales managers. Indeed the sales force believe implementing the new system will be time consuming and deliver no benefits. In fact the sales managers told them just that. The chances of a successful systems implementation? I'd suggest pretty close to zero.

Now consider this. Over the last couple of years you have worked hard at your relationships with sales managers. You have attended meetings, delivered reports on time, built friendships and alliances. Now you engage them in the benefits of the new system. Reduced order times, better stock control, faster, more accurate, information. You invest time in selling the benefits to them. Chances of success? I'd say pretty high.

How about this one? The conservation group you volunteer with want to persuade a local landowner to allow part of their land to return to nature. You have met the landowner twice, both times in acrimonious circumstances. You ask for a meeting so you can tell the landowner why the change will be good for nature. Not a promising scenario.

Or, over the years you have worked hard at your relationship with the landowner. You have visited them, got to know them, taken an interest in their work, kept them up to date with local and national developments. You may not agree on everything but you have built mutual respect. You arrange to take the landowner to a similar project a few miles away. You walk and talk, explaining the benefits in terms of the environment, but also practical elements such as grants available as compensation. You devote time, build trust and confidence. Will it work? I can't guarantee it, but I reckon you've increased your chances many fold.

You cannot guarantee you will deliver mutual benefit in every interaction. Even though you have worked hard to build a relationship, some people just don't believe in win-win outcomes. They're far more likely to have a win-lose mentality, they want everything for themselves. Although you can't be sure of positive outcomes you can always demonstrate a win-win mentality. As an authentic leader you can always choose to strive for and search for mutual benefit.

What does it take to think win-win and to deliver mutually beneficial outcomes? A whole host of things. Humility, a low ego, belief it's the right thing to search for, courage, patience, understanding, empathy, time, imagination, creativity, new thinking, an open mind.

A crucial ingredient in building great relationships is the ability, and willingness, of all parties to listen to each other. It sounds obvious, doesn't it? Problem is, I so rarely come across someone who is a genuinely good listener. So many people think they are, but they are only listening for the right to respond, to reply, to put their views across. As soon as there is a lull in the conversation, they will be in there, like a rat up a drainpipe! Effective listening takes us to a new level, for now we are listening not for the right to reply, but for the right to understand. We are now listening empathically, we want to truly understand what the other person is saying, and even to share how they are feeling.

When we reach this level of listening we can have a transformational impact on the other party. Now they feel genuinely understood. A number of factors need to be in place to enable this level of listening.

The environment we are listening in must be right. It sounds obvious, but don't try and listen in a noisy room, or somewhere interruptions or distractions are likely. I've sat in a crowded hotel lounge and eaves dropped on an annual performance review taking place at the next table. No matter how rich the entertainment it doesn't work! A great alternative environment for listening is to go for a walk, ideally somewhere peaceful. It creates a very different mindset, it's a great place to explore and resolve issues. Bill Gates and Steve Jobs are two examples of leaders who were great fans of this approach. Incidentally walking also works really well on your own if you need to clear your head, sort a problem, think clearly or give yourself a damn good listening to!

You must allocate sufficient time to listen properly to someone. It doesn't work if you're trying to squeeze it into five minutes between meetings. Take steps to ensure you're not going to be interrupted- go somewhere you can't be found or shut your door.

Clear your head of everything else. During this time the person you are listening to is the most important person in the world. It doesn't work if your head is full of other issues, or you are planning how to approach your next meeting. Returning to that Fish! training video, this is the message of 'Be There.' If you want to listen effectively be absolutely present, in mind as well as body.

Perhaps most importantly to listen empathically you must listen with an open mind. It's essential you avoid analysing what they are saying based on your own experiences, views and prejudices.

Try to listen without interrupting, or initially asking questions. That might sound strange, surely asking questions is essential to building your understanding? The danger, however, when you do so is that you stop the other party in mid flow, disrupting their thoughts.

You aren't going to listen for ever, at some point the other person will have told all they have to tell. How can you both be sure you understand? One way is to play back a summary, it's a powerful re-enforcer to the other party that you do understand, or it allows clarification where needed.

Now, and only now, can you move to solutions, working with the other person to find a way forward. But remember, a solution is not always necessary. They might just have needed to be properly listened to, and you have enabled them to get something off their chest by doing just that.

Empathic listening is a leadership skill you can learn and perfect like any other. It takes time, effort and commitment but it's so worth the effort. Practice it whenever you can, it's a very powerful tool.

Building long-term, productive relationships based on mutual respect and mutual benefit, a commitment to empathic listening, it all sounds so obvious, but consider for a moment how often it doesn't happen. Far too frequently the alternative is entrenched positions, lack of respect, closed minds, a win at all costs mentality.

Consider this all too familiar scenario. A contract dispute between two companies. Teams from each company agree to meet to resolve the issue. Both teams know they're in the right, the other company must be forced to understand that, and to admit they are wrong.

They meet in the board room of one of the companies. Where do they sit? Either side of the table, facing each other, the boss in the middle. Look at the body language, folded arms, stern expressions, an absence of friendly chat.

The boss of the host company starts proceedings. 'Let me tell you why you are in the wrong.'

Before he has even finished the sentence the boss from across the table interjects. 'No, we're not wrong, you are, let me tell you...'

Next moment everyone is talking at once, accusing fingers pointing across the table. Threats of legal action, writs, lawyer's letters. Where does it end? At worse stalemate, antagonism, court cases. Or at best, maybe compromise, because both parties know a resolution must be found eventually. More on compromise later.

Now imagine a very different scenario. The two companies still have their contract dispute, from time to time that is inevitable. But they have always had a good relationship in the past and both parties want to resolve the issue amicably. Both believe, at this point, they are right, but they maintain open minds. This time they agree to meet in a neutral venue, a meeting room of a local hotel. There's a round table they gather around or better still they do away with tables altogether, pulling chairs into a circle.

They first chat over coffee, about anything other than the dispute. Then, with the permission of all, one person starts the discussion. They outline their position, and everyone listens without interruption, focusing on keeping an open mind and building understanding. When the person has finished there are questions of clarification to ensure understanding.

Then the other party outlines their position and the process is repeated. Once there is mutual understanding the two parties work together in an atmosphere of mutual respect and trust to resolve the issue.

I cannot guarantee a successful outcome every time. These are real issues and are not simple. What I can guarantee is this later example increases the chances of a positive outcome multiple times.

We return to compromise, one of my least favourite words. I know compromise has helped the world go round, it has resolved industrial disputes, papered over cracks in personal relationships, enabled parliament to function. I can't help feeling when we compromise we are giving something away. We will always end up getting less than we originally wanted. I'm not suggesting it will work every time, but I absolutely believe if we are willing to search for it there is, in many cases, a better resolution available than compromise. It will often take more time, commitment, belief and effort, but it truly is worth it.

If you'll permit me, may I share a personal example of the importance of relationships. Many readers will be familiar with our campaign to build a new village hall in my home village of Fradswell. I made reference to it at the start of the book. Way back in 2008, the project got underway. Our small team soon became all too aware of the challenges ahead and obstacles in our way. Not least of these was the need to complete a land deal with an individual who owned the freehold of our existing village hall, and a local endowment charity who owned the land behind the hall which we wished to designate as a village green.

The way forward seemed clear cut to me, we needed to build a relationship with both the landowner and charity, demonstrate mutual benefit in our proposals and move things forward. We had reckoned without the long memories and entrenched positions of longer serving fellow Trustees of our village hall charity and a number of local residents. We were told in no uncertain terms that these were not people to be trusted, not the people to do deals with. This animosity stretched back into the mists of time, it was certainly deeply entrenched.

We knew we had to move things forward if we were to ever get our new village hall and the starting point had to be building relationships. Eventually our colleagues agreed and a small group of us made initial contact. It was not easy at first, the fissures ran deep but we were consistent and persistent. Over the next few weeks and months we met regularly with the landowner and the charity, demonstrating our genuine intentions and trustworthiness at every opportunity.
Slowly things moved forward and we realised we shared common aims over wanting the best for our community. We developed a plan together and reached agreement in principle which enabled our fundraiser to

draft our funding bid for the rebuild, and for our lawyer to prepare the necessary documentation for the land swap.

Our wonderful new village hall, opened in 2016, is now the hub of a vibrant rural community. It is living testimony to the absolute necessity to build and nurture relationships if we are to make progress and build that better tomorrow.

Three thoughts to finish with.

There is nothing weak or soft about nurturing relationships. The 'Bills' of this world would have you believe strong leadership means demanding, threatening, cajoling, winning at all costs, and wanting to build relationships is a sign of weakness. Nothing could be further from the truth. The secret to making progress anywhere, to achieving breakthrough, to creating that better world lies in the strength of our relationships, mutual benefit, trust and collaboration.

Not all relationships are worthy of nurturing. Sometimes you get nothing back in return, your Relationship Bank Account slips quickly into overdraft. In those instances do not prolong the agony. Terminate the relationship and move on. Devote your time instead to your far more productive relationships.

Remember you cannot please everyone and should not try to. Delivering the changes you wish to make to the world will ruffle some feathers. You can't make an omelette without breaking eggs, as they say. To quote the immortal words of Steve Jobs

'If you want to make everybody happy, don't be a leader, go sell ice cream.'

Finding your voice in our chaotic world and building that better tomorrow is a tough gig. There is no doubt the strength of our relationships is a crucial ingredient of success.

Now it's time to light some fires.

Exercise 1

The Relationship Bank Account

Below are two lines, one for your professional life and one for your life outside work.

Plot your important relationships on the relevant lines, from very high credit through nil balance to heavily overdrawn.

PROFESSIONAL LIFE

HIGH CREDIT   **NIL BALANCE**   **HEAVILY OVERDRAWN**

MY LIFE OUTSIDE WORK

HIGH CREDIT   **NIL BALANCE**   **HEAVILY OVERDRAWN**

Exercise 2:

Look back at exercise 1 and select four relationships.

Take time to think how you are going to place deposits into those relationships to either increase or maintain a high credit rating.

Relationship 1

Relationship 2

Relationship 3

Relationship 4

Reflections

Light Fires

'You can't start a fire without a spark'

Bruce Springsteen

As we explored in the previous chapter, developing and nurturing mutually beneficial relationships is so important in helping us to build that better tomorrow. Breakthrough occurs when we excite people in those relationships with our passion, our energy, our belief that together we can build that better world. When we light fires in their souls.

We cannot achieve all we yearn to do by ourselves. We need to surround ourselves with the right people, on the front seats of the bus who want to be an integral part of the journey. People who are equally passionate, share our belief that anything is possible and are ready to fight alongside us to achieve it.

We need positive people around us. Think of a time in the past when you have been surrounded by negativity. Maybe it was at work, or amongst friends. Do you remember how soul destroying it was? Many people face negativity in the office. As soon as they arrive at work a dark cloud descends. People moaning, criticising, talking behind other peoples' backs. Never willing to try anything new *'because we tried it in 1992 and it didn't work then so it won't now.'* Sound familiar? People counting down the years to retirement. The problem is negativity breeds negativity, and a downward spiral quickly sets in.

If this is all too familiar and you are facing this situation now, you need to act! You can focus on being a positive force, counteracting the negativity. Sometimes it works but it takes time and effort. It may be time to change you job, or your friends!

To light fires in others we must light our own fire first. We return to the principle of inside-out leadership. It can only begin with us. In an earlier chapter (on your purpose and values) you described what you are passionate about. You may have already been thinking of the opportunities you have to build a better world around you. We will crystallize those opportunities soon, but I am already certain the passion is burning within you! Let it burn, use the sparks to ignite fires in others.

As Gandhi said

'Be the change you wish to see in the world'.

Demonstrate your passion, commitment and belief at every opportunity.

Now it's time to engage others, to light their fires. Remember Mary's trait that she is a Visionary who Executes? Let's bring that to life. If you want to take people with you in any endeavour, they need to know where they are going. They have to want to be on the journey with you. They need to share your passion, to contribute, to truly be part of the journey. This is where vision comes in. Your vision is your picture of a given point in the future. Your End in Mind, it's where we bring to life and share what the future will be like when your shared passion, your shared burning desire, becomes reality.

What should a vision be? Let me throw in the following words; inspirational, engaging, audacious, stretching, achievable (at a push), needed, clear, simple to understand, measurable. It should make the world around you a better place.

Consider these from a range of not-for-profit organisations

'Bringing clean and safe drinking water to people in developing nations.'

'Working with communities we will increase income, improve child nutrition, care for the Earth and ultimately end world hunger and poverty'

'To bring forward the day when all cancers are cured.'

'A world where people can live their lives free of cancer as a life-threatening disease.'

'People close to nature, with land and seas rich in wildlife.'

I don't know how you feel as you read these but writing them sent shivers up my spine.

Your vision may not be as far reaching as these (or it might be!). If it isn't, that doesn't matter. Whatever you aim to achieve, create, articulate and communicate your vision with similar passion, clarity and belief. Light those fires!

Focusing on your vision is one way to light those fires in others, but it's about a whole lot more. It's about getting the most out of people around you, whether it's the team who work for you, colleagues, people in partner organisations or on project teams. It's about you as a leader exciting, inspiring and energising your people, supporting them, developing them, encouraging them to grow, giving freedom within that framework, unlocking their potential. Lighting the fire within them to be the best they possibly can be.

One way we can do so is to engage our peoples' spirit. I'm hoping you remember this from Mary's 'Freedom Within a Framework' trait. It describes engaging people at four levels - their body, heart, mind and spirit. Spirit is the highest level of engagement, it's when people feel they are doing worthwhile work that is truly making a difference. They have line of sight, they can see how their work contributes to the overall mission of their organisation. Ultimately, they feel they are engaged in a noble purpose.

The other three levels of engagement (body, heart and mind) are important too, you cannot engage the spirit alone and ignore the other three. But a reasonable wage, a safe working environment, recognition, respect, having fun at work, being listened to, being given challenging assignments, while they are important, are about preparing the fire. Engaging the spirit is where the sparks catch hold, the fire bursts into life and may even become a raging inferno.

Fundamental to engaging the spirit is when people understand not what the organisation does, or how they do it, but why they do it. This is the premise of Simon Sinek's excellent book 'Start with Why.' He argues that it's those leaders and organisations who articulate why they do what they do (their purpose and vision) who truly inspire and engage their people to want to contribute fully to the mission.

'Happiness comes from WHAT we do. Fulfilment comes from WHY we do it.'

Simon Sinek

When I ask participants on my programmes to name a leader from the world of work who inspires them, two names crop up most. They are Steve Jobs and Richard Branson. Note the question here, a leader from the world of work, if I'd asked a more general question, I'd be more likely to get Gandhi, Nelson Mandela, Barak Obama and the like. These latter names are all examples, I believe, of authentic leaders, inspirational because they are selfless, visionary and committed to serving others.

This is primarily my perception, but I don't believe Jobs and Branson are (or were) necessarily authentic leaders. In Walter Issacson's excellent

294

biography of Steve Jobs, a picture of a flawed genius emerges. He was the creative genius behind an extraordinary brand which took the world by storm, he understood how a focus on design was as likely to engage people as the technology. When he combined the two, the results were stunning. However, he had a short temper, and treated people extremely badly, with 'Bill-like' bullying. Branson is more difficult to read, authenticity may well be there but it's cloaked by a rampant self-publicist who, rightly or wrongly, seems much more committed to a space race than addressing the global challenges his contemporary Bill Gates has done.

What they are, (or in Jobs' case, was) without a shadow of a doubt is entrepreneurs. When pressed this is what my participants found most inspiring. The word is French in origin, from *'entreprendre'* which means to undertake a project.

Incidentally I still enjoy the story that George W Bush, in conversation with Tony Blair, uttered the immortal line 'the trouble with the French is they've got no word for entrepreneur.' An urban myth it might be but it's still delightful!

Branson and Jobs seem miles away as leaders from Gandhi, Mandela and Obama. But here's a thought. Why can't authentic leaders at every level in organisations be entrepreneurial leaders? Why can't it happen in the voluntary sector? Why does an entrepreneur create a picture in your mind, not of someone striving to build a better world, but of an inventor, a creative genius, a maverick.

My argument is that leaders can be both authentic and entrepreneurial. Indeed, I'll go further. I believe it's essential to be both. Back on my programmes I ask people to describe the characteristics of a successful entrepreneur. Note the specific reference to 'successful' here. The following words most commonly appear: creative, innovative, imaginative, inspiring, passionate, clear, able to sell their ideas, visionary, persuasive, driven, determined, relentless, resilient.

Look at that list again. How many of these words would we also use when describing Mary and other authentic, effective and brave leaders? I reckon all of them. How can Mary build that better tomorrow in an organisation without being creative, innovative and imaginative? How can she bring others with her on the journey without being inspiring, passionate, clear, able to sell her ideas, visionary and persuasive? How can she overcome all those obstacles along the way without being driven, determined, relentless and resilient?

If we want to be that leader who finds their voice and builds a better tomorrow, we need to light our own fires and then light fires in others. We need to be passionate, willing to take risks, creative in our thinking, driven in our approach. Each and every one of us needs to be an entrepreneur.

Perhaps most importantly we need to persevere. Delivering long-term, sustainable change is never a quick fix. Let's give the last words on this subject to Steve Jobs:

> '*I'm convinced that about half of what separates a successful entrepreneur from a non-successful one is pure perseverance.*'

Now let's focus on the team you lead. If you want to deliver consistent and sustainably great results, you will only do so if your team are firing on all cylinders. As a truly authentic leader you want your team to be absolutely the best they can be. You understand your job is to unleash their potential and encourage their growth. You want their fires to burn brightly, inspired and ignited by the fire within you.

Each member of your team is a unique individual. Every one of them is wired in a different way. To get the most from them you must understand them. It is essential you take the time to listen to them, discover their motivations, their issues and challenges.

Remember, each of your people has a life outside work as well. You need to gain an insight into and understanding of their background, relationships and challenges. So much of their performance at work will be driven from what's happening outside. I'm conscious there's a thin line of divide here, there's a point where it would be seen as intrusive and prying, and that point is different for each individual, but as a principle push towards that line.

There are two ideal environments for you getting to know your people better. Firstly, your formal 1-1 reviews. Always devote part of that 1-1 (at the start is ideal) to chat informally. As trust grows you will find out more and more. Secondly, I'm a great advocate of teams enjoying social time. Get out of the workplace, organise a walk, meal, bowling evening, BBQ, whatever works best for you all. It's a great way to build relationships.

This very morning I was chatting to a Chief Executive I coach who told me how she engages with a new direct report who works remotely. At 9am every Monday they walk and talk (by phone) for half an hour and choose a subject to chat about each time, such as childhood memories, their families and the like. What a wonderful and relaxed way to get to get to know your people!

The change you want to deliver may be nothing to do with your working life. But the same principles will apply. Take this example. You want to lead a community project to create a meeting space, social centre and support hub in a deprived neighbourhood. Return to the Inside-Out Leadership model. It begins with you. Lighting your own fire comes first. You really want to do this, the community needs it and it will make a real difference. Let your fire burn bright. You have identified a building, currently unused, which will be perfect. You have created a vision, at least in your own mind. You can see the finished project, the building, its users. In your imagination you can even feel the warm, positive engagement of volunteers and users.

That wonderful vision cannot remain inside you. Your fire is burning bright, we need to light others' fires.

We can only proceed inside-out. In the middle circle are people you know who you now need to engage and inspire. They may include some residents, community leaders, local councillors, a reporter from the local paper or radio station and other people who have already expressed an interest in volunteering for the project.

Your success depends on you lighting fires amongst as many of these people as possible. They are the gateway to your vision becoming a reality. There's no substitute for hard work now. Hone the vision, go meet these people, build those relationships, understand what makes them tick, inspire and excite them with your vision - light their fires!

The brighter their fires burn the more actively and enthusiastically they will help. They can introduce you to the property owner, facilitate a possible purchase, recommend funding routes, organise public meetings, write feature articles for the local paper, drum up local support, publicise and engage with their social media followers. The brighter their fires burn the more they will do.

They are now the sparks lighting fires in the outer circle of Inside-Out leadership.

Just a word on how we light those middle circle fires. There are two interdependent ways we inspire. It's about the vision itself, how clear, exciting, meaningful and engaging it is. It's also about you, your positivity, energy and passion, your belief, conviction and confidence it can be delivered and make a difference.

Don't think there is only one way to sell the vision. Maybe a picture of an extravert comes to mind, waxing lyrical on a soap box. Not at all. Many authentic leaders are introverts, quiet, unassuming people who prefer to be out of the limelight. But these people are so often charismatic, and equally passionate and committed. They are hugely effective firelighters.

We finish with a quote

'Light yourself on fire with passion,
and people will come from miles to watch you burn'

John Wesley

The ability to make changes, to build that better world, may now be in your hands. But how do we sustain and embed those changes?

Exercise 1

Think of a vision you want to deliver at work or in your life outside work. Use the space below to articulate the vision. What is your End in Mind?

Exercise 2

Who can help you deliver the vision? Whose fires do you need to light?

Write the names of some people below and make some notes of how you will light their fires

300

Reflections

Deliver Sustainable Change

'The secret of change is to focus all your energy not on fighting the old but on building the new.'

Socrates

What a clever chap Socrates was. Not the Brazilian playmaker from the 1982 World Cup but the Greek guy. I love that quote. Almost 2,500 years after he allegedly uttered those words, it still makes perfect sense and I can relate it to so much change I have witnessed or experienced. Changing anything is tough, so many people are naturally resistant. If we focus our efforts solely on these naysayers, with their heads in the sand, stuck in the past with closed minds and entrenched positions, we will become exhausted and disillusioned. So often much needed change fails for this very reason.

Incidentally, there is much doubt as to whether those wise words should be attributed to Socrates the philosopher. Somewhat disappointedly they first appeared in a 1980 memoir by gymnast Dan Millman called 'Way of the Peaceful Warrior' and are spoken by Millman's mentor, an all-night petrol station attendant no less.

Every day's a school day.

Finding your voice is about delivering change. Building a better tomorrow is invariably about changing something. A leader is always engaged in change. As much as people may feel comfortable with the way things are, the status quo, things can only improve when change occurs.

If you want to build a highly effective team or organisation, to improve results, there will have to be changes- to strategy, processes, culture and people.

If you want to start a re-cycling scheme in your local community you will need to change attitudes, secure funding and demonstrate its importance.

If you want to set up a scout group in a disadvantaged community you will have to convince sceptics, recruit volunteers, build enthusiasm.

If you want to change a local council's policy you will need to lobby, build alliances, demonstrate benefit.

The challenge is two-fold. Firstly, where do you begin? How can you create a clear picture of what needs to be done to deliver the change? Secondly, how can you ensure the change is sustainable, and prevent a quick slide back to the status quo?

It was a challenge I consistently came up against in my corporate days. As is so common in large organisations, every year or two I would find myself promoted or moved into a new role, inheriting a new team to lead. As I made each move, a succession of different bosses would say the same thing.

'You are going there to improve results, things need to change.'

Although I may have hidden it well, I often felt like a rabbit in headlights. What needed to change, and how could I make that change happen?

Then, maybe 25 years ago, on a leadership training programme, I was introduced to a change model and the lights came on. I now had a framework which could be used everywhere, a holistic model which demonstrated the connectivity and interdependency between each element of change. It laid out a logical path for diagnosing and delivering that better tomorrow.

I do mean it can be used anywhere. Over the years I've used it hundreds of times. It has proved to be relevant, robust and effective with FTSE 250 companies, large and small charities, my own business, a local radio station, a school and building a new village hall.

Over time I have developed and refined the model. I call it the Sustainable Change Framework.

As we work through the model, focus on a real change you want to deliver, an opportunity you have to build a better tomorrow, and see if you can apply it to this framework. I'll make a small side bet with you that you can.

We first need to use it as a diagnostic tool. If we want to change anything we need to understand why the status quo is broken, or at least needs to change. Imagine going to the doctor's and being handed pills immediately with no examination or discussion. Or visiting the optician and being given new glasses as soon as you enter the premises. It's pretty obvious we want those professionals to diagnose symptoms and cause before they prescribe solutions. It's exactly the same with any change proposal.

Start with **results**. Explore what is currently being delivered. Whatever those results are (and there's a myriad of different ones depending on what you wish to change) why are they not good enough? What are the root causes?

Now we explore your various **audiences**. These consist of any people, or other organisations, that are or may be involved in whatever it is you wish to change. For example, if you wanted to set up a neighbourhood recycling scheme your audience would include residents, community leaders, the local Council, maybe a national support body who could advise you, potential funders etc. If you want to make changes within a team you have inherited, the audience would be the team members, but also other colleagues in the organisation, senior leaders, HR, internal or external customers, maybe partner organisations and suppliers.

The principle here is any change you make should improve results because it meets the wants and needs of your audiences. Any change will be much more likely to be effective and sustainable if it does that. When that happens, the gap on the model between Results and Audience will narrow.

The problem is, these audiences are many and varied, and each group may well have diverse wants and needs. Even within one audience there may well be differing wants and needs. The whole of a neighbourhood may be in favour of a recycling scheme, while the local council, for whatever reason, may be opposed. Even more likely, there will be differing views within the community, some residents will welcome the scheme, others may be opposed to it.

What you can and must always do before seeking to implement change is to engage with your various audiences to ensure you understand their wants and needs. You will never be able to meet them all, but that understanding will inform your next steps. It will be gained in a variety of ways (maybe surveys, interviews, doorstep chats, social media, focus groups) but most importantly, it comes from listening effectively.

I've seen too many unsuccessful change initiatives because there was a failure to engage with and understand the audience. It's an essential element of successful and sustainable change.

Now consider the four elements remaining around the circle, first from a diagnostic perspective. This part will not apply in all instances, where something does not currently exist, like the recycling project, but will be absolutely relevant for the inherited team.

Mission is the big picture, the overall direction of travel. It splits into three areas-

Purpose- why something exists

Values- what are the most important, deep-rooted principles?

Vision- what is the picture at some point in the future, what does success look like?

In the example of inheriting a new team, at this point of the diagnosis we are examining what already exists. Is there a purpose statement? Do the team have a values framework? If so, is there evidence it is practiced through behaviours? Is there a vision in place?

If the vision is where we want to get to, next we have **the plan**, which is how we get from here to there. At the grave risk of mixing analogies, forget Jim Collins and his bus. This time picture an ocean-going liner, a grand old ship.

Its purpose may be something like 'delight our customers through giving them loads of food while making a packet for the owners.' (I only half jest, I've done cruising.)

Its vision is its port of destination, far away across the ocean. Fort Lauderdale possibly, gateway to a Caribbean cruise (I'm getting a bit carried away here).

The plan is how it gets there, a series of charts that will guide it safely across the ocean, avoiding rocks (like the Azores).

But however attractive the destination is and however detailed the charts, it cannot undertake the journey successfully if its **engine room** is not fit for purpose. The engine room consists of a host of things that enable effective operation, including people, systems, processes, policies, resources and infrastructure.

The final element of our circle is **culture,** defined as 'what's it like round here?' This encompasses elements of engagement, freedom to perform, behaviour, recognition and reward.

There should be little surprise that we finish in the centre of the model with the word **leadership.** It lies at the heart of everything. If the diagnostics identify failure, poor performance, you can lay a safe bet on what's missing. Delivering change through the application of the model will require significantly changed mindsets supported by effective leadership.

Once the diagnostic is complete, you will have built up a clear picture of where things are at the moment. If you inherited the team, you have essential insight into how things have been and where the issues lie. Your engagement with the various audiences will have given you much greater clarity on the challenges ahead and barriers to change. You will know whether a vision and plan are currently in place and you will have tinkered in the engine room. If you're setting up the community recycling team you will much better understand likely resistance, support available and where the opportunity lies.

Now is the time to turn it on its head and use the framework to plan, communicate and execute the changes.

Begin by analysing all you have heard from your various audience interactions. Armed with a clearer picture of what each group, even individuals, want and need, you can use that learning to inform your mission. Involve members of your audiences in creating the purpose, a values framework and your vision- an inspirational picture of what success would look like at a point in the future.

The purpose should be restricted to a maximum of 20 words, describing with absolute clarity what the proposed change is about. Returning to our two examples maybe something like this.

'To build an inspired and highly effective team, clear on their goals, working together to deliver outstanding results.'

'To establish a community recycling scheme, funded by the Council, to inspire local people to take action to reduce waste.'

Just a word on the vision. It is essential it inspires other people to come on the journey with you. It's also essential you are able to articulate your vision clearly, succinctly and with passion. You've heard of the 'elevator speech'. As you enter a lift someone who can help you steps in as well. They ask you about your project. You have a minute to explain it in a way that, as they leave the lift, they will want to meet you to see how they can help.

The next step is to build the plan that will deliver the vision. What needs to happen, what do you and others need to do? Make sure the plan is as simple as possible, can be easily communicated, that all involved will be clear on their part, and clear targets and timescales will allow progress to be measured and celebrated.

On to the engine room. What needs to be put in place to enable delivery of the plan? Do you have the right people, resources, funding, systems, processes, equipment, information, infrastructure etc? No matter how engaging the vision and clear the plan, you cannot undertake the voyage without a fully functioning engine room.

So to culture. What kind of culture needs to be in place to give your project the best chance of success? How do you want people to feel and behave? How can you inspire and enable others to want to and feel equipped to play their part? How can you make this a positive experience where people feel included, fairly treated, praised for a job well done, recognised for their contributions, and fairly held accountable? How can you build a high level of trust?

As your work on each area unfolds, you will increasingly be aware that if you want to deliver sustainable change, every element of the circle must be addressed, and aligned to every other part. If you don't understand your various audiences how can you create your mission? You can have a compelling mission but if you can't break it down into a clear and workable plan you cannot deliver. You can have a watertight plan, but if there aren't the people or resources in the engine room to deliver it, your ship is likely to flounder on the rocks. All this can be in place but if this isn't somewhere people want to give their best, you cannot deliver effectively.

The joy of the Sustainable Change Framework is that it is dynamic and can be used over a long period of time, providing a holistic view of progress while enabling you to dive deeply to fix any part of it as the need arises.

Use the framework in exercises 1&2 to work through an example of change you want to bring about. It could be anything - the model is very flexible.

Over the many years I have been using it as a holistic change framework, with every kind of team and organisation, it has proved to be invaluable in providing clarity, stimulating thinking, understanding interdependencies and driving action. It's the bedrock which enables the delivery of successful and sustainable change.

I commend it to you.

Okay, that's enough talking. Now is the time for action. Let's crystallize your opportunities.

Exercise 1

The Diagnostics

What is it you want to change, and why?

What results are currently being delivered?

Who are the various audiences?   How well do we currently understand their wants and needs?

What issues in the Engine Room can slow down or prevent successful change?

Exercise 2

Building the Solution

What have you learned from your various audiences?

How will you go about creating your Mission (Purpose, Values & Vision)?

How will you turn that into a plan?

How will you address engine room issues?

How will you address cultural issues?

Reflections

The Time is Now

Crystallize Those Opportunities

'The difference between what we're doing, and are capable of doing, would solve most of the world's problems'

Gandhi

The nine steps we've progressed so far through the *'Lead! Framework'* are designed to inspire and enable you to think deeply about yourself, the potential inside you, what you are capable of and the difference you can make.

They also prompt you to consider where you have already found your voice, and how you could make even more of a contribution.

We cannot wait a moment longer. We need to act. This chaotic world turned upside down is desperate for your contribution, large or small. The time is now!

It's time to crystallize your opportunities. You are capable of so much. Let's unleash your potential on a waiting world!

'You can achieve anything you want in life if you have the courage to dream it, the intelligence to make a realistic plan, and the will to see that plan through to the end.'

Sidney Friedman

When we crystallize something we make it definite and clear. We ensure we can articulate and communicate it in a way that inspires and engages others.

Use the format at the end of this chapter to set out the opportunities you are going to progress, as follows:

Restate your Purpose and Values (step 1 of Finding Your Voice). That will enable you to ensure that each commitment is consistent with your purpose and in line with your values.

Next state clearly each opportunity you will focus on and progress. I propose at this stage you restrict it to an absolute maximum of three.

Under each opportunity take the time to compose a few lines on why it is needed.

Here's a fictional example, focusing on 3 opportunities.

My Purpose:

To live a purposeful life, becoming even more of a role model for my family and friends. To make a difference in my community. To fulfil my ambition to write a book.

My Values:

Caring
Serving others
Fairness
Always give 100%
Never give up

Opportunity 1:

To become an even more caring, and when needed, challenging role model for my family and friends

Why is this important to me?

I already feel I make a contribution in this area but I know I could do much more. I love my family and friends and I know sometimes difficult conversations are necessary to help them make the right choices. I want my children to grow into well-rounded, confident adults.

What difference will it make for others?

My partner to feel more supported, my friends to feel they can come to me for advice and our children will flourish.

Opportunity 2:

To lead the project to open a new community centre in my neighbourhood

Why is this important to me?

A new community centre is badly needed in our neighbourhood. I have stood back and watched the project falter. It's too important, and I believe that in taking over leadership of the project I could successfully deliver.

What difference will it make for others?

A new community centre providing space to meet, a range of activities and an advice centre, would greatly benefit the neighbourhood. People who volunteer to help deliver the project will learn new skills, teamwork, and be part of a worthwhile and important endeavour.

Opportunity 3:

To write and publish a fiction novel.

Why is this important to me?

I have always wanted to write a novel but never managed to get started. I have blamed other things - too busy at work, too many other commitments, but I know my lack of confidence and determination is the real reason. I would take great personal pride and satisfaction in achieving this goal.

What difference will it make for others?

It may stimulate others to unlock their own creativity in their chosen field.

It's time to crystallize your opportunities. Aim high, stretch yourself, unleash that potential.

As Thomas Edison said

'If we did all the things we are capable of we would literally astound ourselves.'

The clock is ticking, we can't wait, we need to start building that better world now!

Exercise 1

Crystallize your Opportunities

My Purpose:

My Values:

Opportunity 1:

Why is this important to me?

What difference will it make for others?

Opportunity 2:

Why is this important to me?

What difference will it make for others?

Opportunity 3:

Why is this important to me?

What difference will it make for others?

Reflections

Just Start...

'Whatever you do, or dream you can, begin it.
Boldness has genius, power and magic in it.'

Goethe

We've come this far on our journey together. Thank you for sticking with me. If you've engaged at each stage you'll have reflected and thought deeply about yourself, and the contribution you want to make. You'll have crafted your purpose, affirmed your values, dreamed big, created a 'life plan', explored ways to be the best version of yourself and found space to think by taking control of your time. The steps to finding the voice within.

By becoming an Inspire & Enable leader you'll be working effectively with those around you. By nurturing relationships, lighting fires and understanding how to deliver sustainable change, you'll have amplified your voice.

You'll have crystallized your opportunities. You're ready to build that better tomorrow.

What can possibly stop you?

Just one thing.

You.

We shouldn't be surprised. Stepping forward from today, crossing the line, embarking on a lifelong leadership journey focused on building a better world, improving lives, being a role model for positive change, is daunting. But as Christopher Columbus, no less, said:

'You can never cross the ocean unless you have the courage to lose sight of the shore.'

Casting off the lines and setting sail into unknown waters is never easy. On countless occasions over the years I have coached and mentored people who are at a point of decision and are wavering. It could be anything- taking a new role, moving jobs, beginning or ending relationships, a health issue, moving abroad, starting their own business. These are tough, life-changing decisions.

In those sessions I don't see it as my role to give them the answer, they need to work it out for themselves, but I do try to share a few principles, set out below, to help their decision.

You can't put off the decision. It has to be made. Set yourself a timescale to act, but you cannot and must not prevaricate.

In many instances there is not a right or wrong answer. Whichever route is chosen, life will work out. It's a sliding doors moment.

Imagine one year from today. Create a picture of your life on that day. What do you see?

(You may find this one controversial) If your heart and your head are telling you different things go with the heart.

'Always go with your passions'

Deepak Chopra

Explore your personal values.   What is the right thing to do here?

On just about every occasion the subsequent feedback I get is positive. Whatever they decided to do has worked out, not without challenges and pitfalls of course, and most importantly they were glad they made the decision.

Why am I urging you to take the leap forward and to progress those opportunities now? Because you cannot wait. The need is too great. It's the whole premise of this book. Our chaotic world, turned upside down, is desperate for people everywhere, ordinary people, to stand up, take the leap and make a difference. It needs you to play your part, however big or small, in building a better world around you.

Millions of people already are, delivering change, bottom up, to the world around them. Small, individual actions which together can become colossal.

Whether your stage is your family, friends, community, voluntary endeavours, your work or politics, you need to step forward into the spotlight now. The play is about to begin and in your world you are the leading actor.

'It's a terrible thing, I think, in life to wait until you're ready. I have this feeling now that actually no one is ever ready to do anything. There is only now. And you may as well do it now. Generally speaking, now is as good a time as any.'

Hugh Laurie.

I ask previous participants on my face to face leadership programmes what they remember most. Apart from Jakkie's excellent lunches they invariably mention the ribbon exercise.

You will recall that in the Dream Big Dreams chapter I spoke of the exercise I ran on 'Lead Like Mary' programmes asking participants to share one great achievement still inside them. Invariably they shared wide ranging examples.

I then produce a length of ribbon and ask a couple of participants to hold an end each. I explain that this ribbon represents their life, one end being birth and the other end death. We then establish the average age people live to in the UK and an estimate of the average age of people in the room. I cut the ribbon at the average age, typically around halfway. I ask what the early part represents and we agree it is our past. Our lives up to today. We chat about what we can do about it and agree we can celebrate it and learn from it.

We turn our attention to the remaining ribbon, representing the rest of our lives. The time we have left to realise so many achievements. The scissors go to work. A third disappears for the time we are asleep, and soon the carpet looks like a cutting room floor as we discard parts of the ribbon for time wasted in pointless meetings (usually a lot), unnecessary e-mails, traffic jams, supermarket queues, rubbish television and times we are ill.

I hold up the remaining ribbon and ask what it is. I've only been disappointed once when a group of senior medics (surgeons and consultants) decided it was a ribbon...

We agree that it's the productive time we have left, and it's a very short piece of ribbon.

What are you going to do with yours?

'Twenty years from now you'll be more disappointed by the things you didn't do than by the ones you did do.'

Mark Twain

Which brings me neatly to a closing thought on your potential. Locked inside you is a special box. Inside it lies your potential, and it's bursting to get out. Only you have the key. Once it's out of the box it's enormous, limitless, there is virtually nothing you cannot do. Others can help you with the escape plan, but only you can turn the key.

I'll let Mel Robbins, author of the '5 Second Rule' have the last word.

'Start now. Start where you are. Start with fear. Start with pain. Start with doubt. Start with your hands shaking. Just start.'

Exercise 1

What are the barriers to beginning this journey today?

How can you overcome those barriers?

Reflections

Never, Ever Give Up

'Never give up on something that you can't go a day without thinking about.'

Winston Churchill

The premise of this book, as if you need reminding, is that you are already (almost certainly) an authentic leader. You already strive to lead like Mary. You understand that leaders can exist, and are needed, everywhere. But that is not enough. In the chaotic world in which we live, we need those authentic leaders to find their voice, deliver the changes that improve lives and build a better tomorrow. To join countless others across the world delivering change, bottom up.

Whatever and wherever the changes are that you want to make, it is inevitable you will face obstacles. These could be anything- resistance to change, insufficient resources, your own lack of belief that the goal, vision or dream can be delivered. However, and this is the toughest message of all, no matter how daunting, how hard, even impossible it seems you cannot, must not, ever give up. The ultimate test for you as a leader is how you overcome the obstacles and prevail in the end.

This will take an enormous dose of perseverance. You'll recall earlier in the book I mentioned the recruits entering a prestigious US Marines officer training programme at West Point Academy. The ones who made it through were not the ones with the highest IQs, but the most determined and relentless, the ones who persevered.

Perseverance is defined as 'persistence in doing something despite difficulty or delay in achieving success.' The best authentic leaders I know demonstrate this constantly. It shone through in Lesley, Liz, Sarah and Tim's stories earlier. It links straight back to Mary's tenth and final trait, she is relentless, and without it we cannot build that better tomorrow.

As Denzel Washington said

'You can have anything good you want so claim it. Work hard to get it. When you get it reach back and pull someone else up. Don't just aspire to make a living, aspire to make a difference.'

If you are as big a fan of 'Good to Great' by Jim Collins, as I am, you are no doubt already familiar with Vice-Admiral James Stockdale and the Stockdale Paradox. If you're not here's a synopsis.

Stockdale was the most senior naval officer held captive in North Vietnam during the Vietnam war. He was a prisoner of war for over seven years after his A-4 Skyhawk jet was shot down, held in Hoa Lo prison, the infamous Hanoi Hilton. He was routinely tortured and denied medical attention. Despite this he remained one of the primary organisers of prisoner resistance.

Jim Collins talked with Stockdale regarding his coping strategy during his time as a prisoner. When Collins asked him which prisoners didn't make it out of Vietnam Stockdale replied:

'Oh that's easy, the optimists. They're the ones who said 'we're going to be out by Christmas.' And Christmas would come and Christmas would go. Then they'd say 'we're going to be out by Easter. And Easter would come and Easter would go. And then Thanksgiving, then it would be Christmas again. And they died of a broken heart. This is a very

important lesson. You must never confuse faith that you will prevail in the end - which you can never afford to lose - with the discipline to confront the brutal facts of your current reality.'

Collins called this the Stockdale Paradox. To me, it's absolutely at the heart of what Never, Ever Give Up is about. Always maintain the faith that in the end you will prevail, you will realise your goal, your vision, your dream, while at the same time dealing with the current reality, facing up to those roadblocks and obstacles, dealing with them, overcoming them. A powerful and essential combination.

History is littered with examples of leaders who achieved extraordinary things because they didn't give up. Churchill in the darkest days of WWII springs to mind immediately.

One of the most compelling is the story of Sir Ernest Shackleton. It is a tale of incredible courage, determination and fortitude.

It is also a story born out of failure. In 1914 the Endurance, under Shackleton's command, set sail for Antarctica. It was his third attempt to reach the south pole, having previously failed in 1902 and 1908. This time was no more successful, the Endurance became trapped in pack ice and was slowly crushed. Shackleton and his men were stranded on Elephant Island in the Antarctic ice twelve hundred miles from civilisation with no means of communication and no hope of rescue. The temperatures were so low the men could hear water freeze. They survived on a diet of penguins and seals. When the ice began to break up Shackleton set out to save them all, a heroic eight hundred mile trip in little more than a rowing boat. Leading a team of five they somehow survived fifteen days at sea to reach South Georgia. He then made the return journey to Elephant Island to rescue his men. His first three attempts were foiled by sea ice, but eventually he got there rescuing all

22 men. Think about the number of times Shackleton could have given up.

Margot Morrell and Stephanie Capparell published a book called 'Shackleton's Way', exploring the leadership lessons we can learn. Their summary was as follows:

-Hire an outstanding crew
-Create a spirit of camaraderie
-Get the best from each individual
-Lead effectively in a crisis
-Form the right teams for tough assignments
-Overcome obstacles to reach a goal

I reckon there's a pretty close correlation to Mary there!

Permit me to share a couple of my own examples.

For many years I dreamed of being a published fiction author. Back in 2001 I tentatively began a novel based in Aberdovey, the beautiful seaside village on the mid Wales coast where Jakkie and I spend as much of our time as we can. I loved planning the book, I still have the dog-eared notebook with the mind maps of the early chapters, spider diagrams of characters and plot, together with research into everything from lobster fishing to seafood cooking.

Inevitably, after that early burst of enthusiasm, my planning and writing slowed before grinding to a halt. Over the next few years it remained on the back burner as I made the excuse of work and too little time preventing any progress. While this was partly true, I was very busy building up my business, but ultimately they were just excuses.

I never gave up my dream. I would wander into Waterstones just to see where I would be on the shelves! Eventually, with Jakkie's encouragement, I signed up for a creative writing on-line programme where I met other want-to-be authors. The group we formed, even more than the course content, proved to be the catalyst that got me writing again.

It wasn't easy, there was still so much to do, including rewriting the opening chapter several times, but I was determined to complete it and slowly the finishing line got closer. Authors talk about that wonderful moment when they type the words 'the end.' It's all true, it feels great, even though I discovered that in reality that's far from the end. Now came the proof reading, editing, re-writing sections and editing again. Even in these later moments it takes an enormous amount of resolve to keep going.

It was worth it. The moment the first author's copies arrived through the post was wonderful! *'The Lobster Pot Café'* was published in the summer of 2020, almost twenty years after the journey began. Sometimes things can take a little longer than you expect!

My other example is a personal battle I continue to face and fight every day. In the autumn of 2015 I was diagnosed with the early stages of Parkinson's Disease (PD). PD is a degenerative disease of the central nervous system which affects the body leading to involuntary shaking, slow movement, balance problems and stiff and inflexible muscles.

Following diagnosis I went through a classic denial phase. This was partly because even though I had been diagnosed with the early stages of PD (and had been aware for some time of exhibiting some of the symptoms), I still felt fine, and partly because I was embarrassed that there was something wrong with me. This led to me trying to hide the fact I had PD from all but my closest family and friends.

After a while though, with Jakkie's support and encouragement, I realised how stupid I was being. I had PD, it was nothing to be ashamed of, why should I try to hide it? That change of mindset made so much difference.

The thing with PD, for which at the moment there is no cure despite extensive research going on, is that everyone is affected in a slightly different way. There is also ample evidence that if you look after yourself, and exercise extensively, you can keep progression at bay over a sustained period of time. This requires physical effort, but it requires even more mental determination. You come across so many people with a physical condition who just seem to have given up. You can't! Every day you have to get up, face the world, and live the best life you are capable of. You can never, ever give up.

A postscript - my daughter Charlotte is in the early stages of a career in neurology. She has completed her Masters and commenced a PhD. She has chosen to focus her professional career into researching PD. I am humbled.

As with so many challenges it's tough to keep going on your own. It's that little bit easier if someone is on the side-lines, or stood next to you, cheering you on. Jakkie's unwavering support has been so important for me. If you haven't got that person there is always help out there be it support groups, community organisations or online support and advice.

Here's my final tip to enable you to find your voice. Ahead of you are two paths. One is an easy stroll along which you can drift through the rest of your life. The other path is narrow, winding and rocky, littered with obstacles. But beyond those barriers, ahead in the distance, is a life with a myriad of opportunities to make a difference, to contribute, to leave a legacy. Choosing to take this path requires enormous resoluteness, resolve and courage. It's easy to drift through life letting other people take the lead while you sit on the side-lines.

If you are determined enough you will prevail.

As Anita Roddick said -

> *'To succeed you have to believe in something with such a passion it becomes a reality.'*

Never, ever give up.

Exercise 1

What is the dream, vision or goal that you are pursuing?

What are the brutal facts and obstacles that are hampering progress?

How can you overcome those obstacles?

Reflections

A Final Thought

My friend told me recently that I am both an optimist and a realist. They were right.

We cannot run away or hide from the enormous challenges our planet faces. Denying the existence of climate change does not make it go away. We have no magic wand to end wars, eradicate poverty and replace ego driven, vacuous leaders with kind but strong authentic leaders.

Our chaotic world is full of enormous challenges. In my worst nightmares we are sleep walking towards oblivion. Don't wait for the rich and powerful to solve them. They are the cause and the problem.

As Jim Collins tells us, we must confront these brutal facts. That's being a realist.

However, I'm also an optimist. I truly believe local actions can make a difference. I see so many examples where it's already happening.

As Matt Hyde said in his foreword, at its core this is a book about hope.

Together we can build that better tomorrow, a world that is kinder, safer, fairer and happier. We owe it to our grandchildren and their grandchildren.

I have no doubt you are already building a better world around you. My plea to you is to do even more. Become a beacon for change. Join with others and build that better tomorrow. Be a leader at the vanguard of change. Use the *Lead!* framework to plan your way forward.

As Nelson Mandela said:

> *'What counts in life is not the mere fact that we have lived,*
> *it is what difference we have made to the lives of others*
> *that will determine the significance of the life we lead.'*

You are amazing. Your potential is limitless. Unleash it.

Go find your voice.

Go *Lead!*

Section V

Signposting and Resources

Recommended reading and links.

Here's a list of the leadership books that have most inspired me over the last 25 years and taught me the most about authentic leadership.

'The 7 Habits of Highly Effective People'. Stephen R Covey
'Good to Great'. Jim Collins
'Leaders Eat Last'. Simon Sinek
'Start with Why'. Simon Sinek
'Trust & Inspire'. Stephen M R Covey
'Our Iceberg is Melting'. John Kotter
'Management in Ten Words'. Terry Leahy
'The Ultimate Question'. Fred Reichheld
'Liberating the Corporate Soul'. Richard Barrett
'And Dignity for All'. James Despain

You can explore further via the links below.

www.franklincovey.com
www.jimcollins.com
www.simonsinek.com
www.kotterinc.com
www.netpromotersytem.com

Lead! Community

I facilitate Lead! Community, a Facebook group created as a forum to allow like-minded leaders to network, share leadership material, seek advice and explore leadership challenges.

I'd like to develop and grow the group into a powerful force connecting, enabling and supporting authentic leaders to find their voice and be at the vanguard of change, striving to build a kinder, fairer, safer and happier world.

If you'd like to be part of this network here's the link..

https://www.facebook.com/groups/2661468793900453/?ref=share

Alternatively search 'Lead! Community' on Facebook.

Leadership Reflections podcasts

Leadership Reflections is my collection of leadership podcasts.

Posted regularly, the podcasts cover an extensive range of leadership issues, challenges and thinking,

To view the full collection, listen and subscribe, follow this link

https://anchor.fm/barry-dore

Also available via Spotify, Apple podcasts, Facebook and Twitter by searching for Barry Dore

Get in Touch!

If you'd like to chat to me about any aspect of finding your voice, seek advice on any leadership issue or challenge, or visit my website, here are my contact details.

Website: www.barrydore.com

E Mail: Barry@barrydore.com

Facebook: www.facebook.com/barrydore

Twitter: www.twitter.com/barrydore

If you are interested in details of my leadership programme based on this book, contact me via any of the above.

Here is the entry Head Teacher Liz Ormerod submitted to the Pearson Teaching Awards.

"Our school is incredible... one in a million!

This school has been on a journey. We represent and support some of the most deprived families in the country, in a town called Skelmersdale, not far out of Liverpool. Some say we are the 'forgotten' town, with services being pulled, employment at an all-time high, crime rife, a shadow of anxiety cast across the estates and optimism within the community being, understandably, low. Our school acts as a shining beacon for our community, a hub of aspiration and determination, mixed with a haven of sanctuary, support, kindness and simple consistency. We are a constant. We, as our vision states, 'Make the Difference'.

With over 50% of children identified as 'disadvantaged', our team work relentlessly, passionately and with a smile to ensure we give our little people (and their families) the very best of opportunities day in and day out. We do go above and beyond. We do live and breathe this community, their barriers, their challenges, their successes, their pride - the lot. Our team are the most dedicated I have had the privilege to work with. We really are a 'synergy'. Pushing each other to strive for the best, living our values, day in day out, in all we do - #enjoy, #embrace, #evolve. We make the difference.

From organising community event weeks, inviting along local care homes and Special Needs schools and colleges, to Christmas recitals in the town centre, to winning the local public speaking competition two years in a row (as underdogs!), to leading the fight to save a local 3G pitch, to welcoming our Syrian families the day after they stepped off the plane, to smashing our Y6 SAT results this year - top 1% in the country for

Math's......we genuinely give our sparky, dynamic and amazing children everything we can to inspire them to be the best they can truly be.

We challenge, we fight, we represent, we support, we teach, we inspire, we guide, we encourage, we collaborate, we evolve, we are relentless, we enrich, we strive, we laugh, we empower, we celebrate, we reflect, we open doors, we believe... we 'make the difference'.

I couldn't be more proud of our team, our school, and our community. I feel unbelievably lucky this is my job to lead this school, but I'm not alone - every teacher at the school is a leader, and that's why we are so utterly (happy!) successful.

Our school was RI. 3 years ago we were finally graded as 'Good' - this has involved tireless leadership at all levels, getting the right people in the right seats and ensuring we are a truly values-led school. We are located in one of the most deprived wards in the UK, facing significant challenges, yet, we have turned the tables. Scoring exceptionally above the national figures with our Y6 SAT results, commended by the DFE for being in the top 1% in the country for Maths. We are truly bucking the trend, changing perceptions. Daily. It now has the most driven team you will find in a school, exceptional quality, but also commitment. Thinking out of the box, trialling new approaches and initiatives, including in and with the wider community, working collaboratively and openly, pushing one another - the place is simply inspirational. We don't, we can't, stand still.

We face challenges beyond the classroom – domestic violence, high crime, huge community anxiety, gang presence, knife crime, limited aspirations, children in care, numerous families on Child Protection orders, strained resources, parents in prison, high drug usage, reliability on the foodbank, poor engagement with education, vicious cycles, disguised compliance, depletion of services to support etc. etc. A locally described, if not nationally, 'forgotten town'. We support, drive change, challenge inequality and encourage cohesion and pride within our community. It is an exceptional place, worthy of accolade.

We inspire! We challenge! We innovate! We believe.

Standards have been improved, smashing national figures, through dedicated teachers who are prepared to reflect on practice, hold each other to account, help one another and who strive to give their very best. Our staff think, constantly, of methods, ideas, initiatives to 'hook' our learners - they inspire one another to be better, the incentive to improve is genuinely from the heart. The team go above and beyond the normal classroom practices, ensuring our children get ultimate enrichment - from an annual calendar of trips and visitors for each year group, to inspired and topically themed weeks. Key groups are meticulously tracked and monitored, not only by SLT, but by all leaders. School improvement is transparent and is disseminated to all. We all play a part, be it in our free breakfast club, through our free offer of music lessons for Y4 and Y5, free Nursery swimming or the relentless free offer of additional and targeted clubs from our teaching team. We know just exactly who receives additional offers through school, track the progress and evaluate the impact, tweaking and changing, constantly. All our children are unique and quirky, we ensure we find what works for them. We are open-door to the core. With a very active Facebook page, online platforms, and a human front, we put our families first in learning - we love nothing more than taking work out into the community, or inviting parents in, in person or through cyber space.

We want to learn! We want to be better, always! We have a wealth of CPD logs, with noted impact, everyone is open minded and eager to improve. If we improve and trial approaches, we can be certain our children are getting the best possible offer. Nothing stands still. We work within a very strong cluster of 22 schools, sharing good practice and expertise. In addition, we have forged further links with other schools to moderate and challenge practice, we are never the finished article, that's *the beauty of education! Most recently we have worked with the local Maths Hub to introduce and embed a Mastery Approach - the impact is immense. 80% of Y6 pupil achieved Age Related Expectations! We welcome anyone to learn from and with us.*

Parents are hugely valued, welcomed at every opportunity, involved via apps throughout the day, invited in for sharing/stay and play etc. We have assemblies, performances, key messages on education delivered from and by the children. But more than anything, we know our families. We know how to support them when they need us, we know how to be their 'rock'. We know how to help them feel at ease to access support. We know their names, their family tree, how they take their brews! It's the small stuff, but really it's the big stuff.

We have wonderful links with Kingsbury Special Needs School, Aaron Crest Care Home, Midstream Special Needs (adults) and West Lanc's College We love being inclusive and have a reputation within the local community and authority for just this. How could we be any other way? We love our embedded place in the community, it is incredibly rewarding. We share celebration weeks, most notably our summer community week with afternoon teas, talent shows and parties - involving all our local partners, led by our children. We celebrate these collaborations, on our social media, websites and in the press, we want to lead by example. In addition we have amazing links with Oaks Church and Devine Days - both of which bring their mission of faith and tolerance in to our school, through clubs and weekend services. We aren't simply a school, we are a hub for our community. All we want to do is learn from others and share our experiences of successes (and failures!). We do this through forums, moderation and by being known as a school who have an open door to others. In all these additional commitments, we ensure our children truly understand their place in the world, but particularly in their community - they are the future of the community. We also install big picture thinking - the world is their oyster, and we will do all we can to show them before they leave us.

The team care. They deliver consistently inspiring learning opportunities, evolving to meet the needs of current cohorts. Most recently, we had a 'Bee week' - it encompassed World Book Day events with Eco priorities and expressive arts. It was absolutely amazing! Both children and parents were 'buzzing'! Initiatives such as this show our children just how valued they are. Attendance isn't an issue in these peaks of awesomeness, parents don't want them to miss out - here we have huge peaks! Otherwise, attendance is a constant battle, but through a dedicated lead, and timely and varied initiatives, we do our very best. Most mornings we are knocking on doors, collecting children and challenging parental behaviours... just part of the job.

We couldn't be more proud of the achievement of our children. 80% in Y6 achieved ARE, with us being identified as the top 1% in the country for Math's. With our challenges, we can't help but be proud. Our progress measures over the last 3 years have also been brilliant, children exceed the expectations at Delph Side - from Y6, to attainment in Y2, these children make wonderful progress. We believe in them.

There is certainly a real sense of pride in school, amongst the community. We do stand out; we do genuinely go above and beyond for our families. A big commitment has been trying to save the local 3G pitch for the town - a fight the school has led, for the benefit of all. It still rumbles on...

Please - come and visit us!

Delph Side is unique. We hadn't quite realised that, but we are. We are blessed with a team of heroes. I would absolutely love to be able to recognise the contribution of the team with a nomination for 'Primary School of the Year'. It would mean the world to this humble bunch of human beings. They don't ask for credit, ever, but it would be truly fitting if we could celebrate our little island of positivity within the world of education. They are pioneers, in the most humble and unassuming way.

I am the proudest Headteacher, the Delph Side team make every day a joy, a journey, an adventure. A success.

We make the difference - #enjoy #embrace #evolve"

Acknowledgements

Thank you to:

Lesley, Liz, Sarah and Tim for allowing me to share your stories. Each of you is an inspiration to me.

Matt for finding time in a hectic schedule to read the draft and write such a generous foreword. The most effective leaders always seem to find the time.

Victoria for managing the project, proof reading, cover design and somehow turning a word document into a book.

And to Jakkie, who helped and encouraged me to find my voice many years ago and to keep using it.